Gender and Succession in Medieval and Early Modern Islam

The Early and Medieval Islamic World

Published in collaboration with the Society for the Medieval Mediterranean

Society for the Medieval Mediterranean

As recent scholarship resoundingly attests, the medieval Mediterranean and Middle East bore witness to a prolonged period of flourishing intellectual and cultural diversity. Seeking to contribute to this ever-more nuanced and contextual picture, The Early and Medieval Islamic World book series promotes innovative research on the period 500–1500 AD with the Islamic world, as it ebbed and flowed from Marrakesh to Palermo and Cairo to Kabul, as the central pivot. Thematic focus within this remit is broad, from the cultural and social to the political and economic, with preference given to studies of societies and cultures from a socio-historical perspective. It will foster a community of unique voices on the medieval Islamic world, shining light into its lesser-studied corners.

Series editor
Professor Roy Mottahedeh, Harvard University

Advisors
Professor Amira Bennison, University of Cambridge
Professor Farhad Daftary, Institute of Ismaili Studies
Professor Simon Doubleday, Hofstra University
Professor Frank Griffel, Yale University
Professor Remke Kruk, Leiden University
Professor Beatrice Manz, Tufts University
Dr Bernard O'Kane, American University in Cairo
Professor Andrew Peacock, University of St Andrews
Dr Yossef Rapoport, Queen Mary University of London

New and forthcoming titles

Cross Veneration in the Medieval Islamic World: Christian Identity and Practice under Muslim Rule, Charles Tieszen (Fuller Theological Seminary/Simpson University)

Power and Knowledge in Medieval Islam: Shi'i and Sunni Encounters in Baghdad, Tariq al-Jamil (Swathmore College)

The Eastern Frontier: Limits of Empire in Late Antique and Early Medieval Central Asia, Robert Haug (University of Cincinnati)

Writing History in the Medieval Islamic World: The Value of Chronicles as Archives, Fozia Bora (University of Leeds)

Gypsies in the Medieval Islamic World: The History of a People, Kristina Richardson (City University, New York)

Narrating Muslim Sicily: War and Peace in the Medieval Mediterranean World, William Granara (Harvard University)

Gender and Succession in Medieval and Early Modern Islam: Bilateral Descent and the Legacy of Fatima, Alyssa Gabbay (The University of North Carolina at Greensboro)

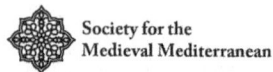

Gender and Succession in Medieval and Early Modern Islam

Bilateral Descent and the Legacy of Fatima

Alyssa Gabbay

I.B.TAURIS
LONDON • NEW YORK • OXFORD • NEW DELHI • SYDNEY

Bloomsbury Publishing Plc
50 Bedford Square, London, WC1B 3DP, UK
1385 Broadway, New York, NY 10018, USA
29 Earlsfort Terrace, Dublin 2, Ireland

BLOOMSBURY, I.B. TAURIS and the I.B. Tauris logo are trademarks of
Bloomsbury Publishing Plc

First published in Great Britain 2020
This paperback edition published in 2021

Series design by www.paulsmithdesign.com
Cover image: From the *Siyer-i Nebī*, CBL T 419, fol. 40v. (© The Trustees of the Chester
Beatty Library, Dublin)

A catalogue record for this book is available from the British Library.

A catalog record for this book is available from the Library of Congress.

ISBN: HB: 978-1-8386-0231-4
PB: 978-0-7556-4621-0
ePDF: 978-1-8386-0234-5
eBook: 978-1-8386-0233-8

Typeset by Deanta Global Publishing Services, Chennai, India

For my mother
And in memory of my father and grandparents

Contents

List of illustrations viii
Preface and acknowledgements ix
Transliteration, periodization and dates xii

Introduction: Redrawing family trees 1

Part One Mothers

1 *Umms* and wombs: How and (maybe) why Shiʿis reckoned descent through Fatima 17
2 Other mothers, other sons 49

Part Two Heiresses

3 Heiress to the Prophet: Fatima, Fadak and female inheritance 79
4 Endowing agency: Daughters, waqfs and semi-matrilineal inheritance 102

Part Three Successors

5 Speaking in her father's name: Fatima as successor to the Prophet Muhammad 123
6 Fatima's royal shadow: Muslim female rulers' quest for legitimacy and sovereignty 153
Epilogue: Whither Fatima? 185

Notes 189
Bibliography 243
Index 263

Illustrations

Figures

2.1 Genealogy chart showing lines of descent among early Shiʿi and Shiʿi-affiliated groups 55
5.1 The Prophet Muhammad presiding over the marriage of Fatima and ʿAli, from the *Siyer-i Nebī* 124
5.2 Twentieth-century poster by Iranian artist Mohammad Khazāʾī depicting Fatima as a soldier 140

Tables

3.1 Inheritance Divisions for Deceased Who Leaves Behind a Paternal Grandfather, a Wife and a Daughter 88
3.2 Inheritance Divisions for Deceased Who Leaves Behind a Paternal Uncle, a Uterine Brother and a Daughter's Son 88

Preface and acknowledgements

One dusty afternoon while leafing through manuscripts in the Maulana Azad Library of Aligarh University in India, I came across a short poem in Persian whose contents interested me so deeply I read it several times.[1] Of only five lines, it plainly stated that daughters were better than sons – and gave among its justifications the fact that the Prophet Muhammad's lineage had continued through his daughter, Fatima. Written by the medieval Indian poet Amīr Khusraw, the poem echoed sentiments I had encountered in other Khusraw works, in which he referred to his young daughter as his 'mother' and wrote that he expected to be reborn through her eventual progeny. But it clarified and emphasized those statements in a way that ran forcefully and surprisingly counter to the stereotypical view in Muslim societies of daughters as, at best, burdens to be patiently borne.

Why did Amīr Khusraw say these things? What did he mean by them, and how common among medieval Muslims were his sentiments? The chance encounter made my head buzz with questions. My efforts to answer them produced the book that you now hold in your hands (or that glows upon your screen). The story of bilateral descent in medieval and early modern Islam – that is, the recognition that lineage can be traced through daughters as well as sons – is a story that encompasses many daughters and mothers, and many sons and fathers. Ultimately, however, as Khusraw himself indicated, it is the story of Fatima, the primordial *umm abīhā*, or mother of her father, whose sons, Hasan and Husayn, renewed the illustrious qualities of their maternal grandfather.

It is a story that, at least in this incarnation, has had a very long gestation and has depended upon the aid of many midwives, to all of whom I owe a deep debt of gratitude. My first conversations about the concept of Fatima as *umm abīhā* occurred with Karen Ruffle and Firoozeh Papan-Matin during a conference at the University of Washington in Seattle in 2007, where I was then a visiting scholar. Ruffle and I subsequently organized a panel for the Middle East Studies Association annual meeting featuring different cases of bilateral descent in Islamic history – a panel that culminated in the 2011 publication of a special issue of the *Journal of Persianate Studies* (volume 4, no. 1). I benefited greatly from my conversations with Ruffle and my co-editor of the special issue, Julia Clancy-Smith, as well as from the work of my other fellow panellists, Afshan Bokhari, Christine Isom-Verhaaren and Paul E. Walker, much of whose research informs this volume. In their various capacities at the *Journal*, Said Arjomand, Habib Borjian and, especially, Sunil Sharma were instrumental in encouraging the project. I am also grateful to Koninklijke Brill NV for permission to reprint portions of my contributions to the *Journal* here.

At a subsequent panel at a meeting of the Association for Iranian Studies, Firuza Abdullaeva and Charles Melville offered helpful remarks on a paper addressing female agency and succession which was later published in *Shahnama Studies III: The Reception of the Shahnama*, edited by Melville and Gabrielle van den Berg (2018). I thank each of them and again Brill for the right to reprint here.

I appreciate the comments of everyone who participated in a 2014 Princeton University workshop on female religious authority in Shiʿi Islam, especially Karen Bauer, Robert Gleave, Mirjam Künkler, Raffaele Mauriello, Keiko Sakurai and Devin Stewart. Künkler and Stewart later wielded expert skills in editing my contribution to a publication emerging from the workshop, 'Female Religious Authority in Shiʿi Islam: Past and Present' (2019). I thank them, as well as Edinburgh University Press for permission to reproduce portions of my contribution here.

At this project's first home, at the University of Washington, Jack Brown, Felicia Hecker, Scott Noegel, Joel Walker and, most especially, Selim Kuru provided valuable encouragement and advice regarding what was at the time a pretty vague idea. Members of the Department of Religious Studies at the University of North Carolina at Greensboro, this project's second home, were more than generous with their time and feedback; I would particularly like to thank Gregory Grieve, Ellen Haskell, Derek Krueger and Eugene Rogers. The Interlibrary Loan Department at the Jackson Library accomplished near-impossible tasks with effortless good will. I am likewise grateful to the College of Arts and Sciences and to Candace Bernard and Robert Glickman for a fellowship award that gave me time to put the finishing touches on the book, and to members of my two writing groups, Agraphia and Write-on-Site – especially Brooke Kreitinger, Anne Parsons, Paul Silvia and Pauli Tashima –

for ensuring that I followed through. Former and current UNCG students, including Hussien Algudaihi, Noor Ghazi and Aaron Menconi, provided invaluable linguistic and technological assistance.

At I.B. Tauris/Bloomsbury, Thomas Stottor and, later, his replacement, Rory Gormley were models of editorial helpfulness as they shepherded the book through the various stages of publication. I also thank my anonymous readers for their thoughtful suggestions, and Roy Mottahedeh as series editor.

My adviser, Heshmat Moayyad, did not live to see this book in print, but his memory is imprinted upon its every page. I would also like to acknowledge Ruth Moayyad and members of the Department of Near Eastern Languages and Civilizations at the University of Chicago, especially Orit Bashkin, Frank Lewis, Holly Shissler, John Perry and John Woods, for their continued interest in and support of my doings. Jafar Fallahi, Christiane Gruber and the Chester Beatty Library in Dublin helped tremendously with images. Asa Eger, Grace Huang and Barbara Moss cheered me on even when the terrain was rough and the finish uncertain. Suzanne Gabbay, Ben Quiseng, Rachel Quiseng and Bradley Quiseng reminded me regularly of the value of family.

Finally, this volume is dedicated to Wilma Gabbay and to my antecedents on both sides, who are constant reminders of the power and meaning of bilateral descent. It goes without saying that any mistakes in this book are solely the responsibility of its mother. May any virtues it possesses do its ancestors proud, and bear fruit that continues their lines, both of the East and of the West.

Transliteration, periodization and dates

This text follows the transliteration system of the *International Journal of Middle East Studies*, with the following exceptions: I have used more commonly known spellings for terms and names familiar to non-Arabic or Persian-speaking audiences (thus, Khomeini rather than Khumaynī) and have omitted diacritics for names that appear in this text with great regularity (thus, Muhammad rather than Muḥammad, Fatima al-Zahra rather than Fāṭima al-Zahrā'). To avoid extremely cumbersome terminology I use the term 'medieval' to refer to the Islamic period of 570–1500, and 'early modern' to the period from 1500 to 1800. All dates are Common Era unless otherwise indicated.

Introduction

Redrawing family trees

The problem of patrilineal descent

When Iranian mathematician and Stanford University professor Maryam Mirzakhani died of cancer at the age of forty in July 2017, newspaper tributes glowingly enumerated the gender conventions she broke during her brief life. From being the first woman to win the coveted Fields medal (regularly described as mathematics' Nobel Prize) to inspiring the country's president and Iranian newspapers to publish photos of her without hijab, Mirzakhani appeared in commemorations as a sort of Wonder Woman of science, capable of puncturing hidebound patriarchal norms with a few deft marks of her pencil.[1]

Mirzakhani's most significant legacy, however, could be the smashing of an even bigger convention, one that received far more attention in Iranian than in Western media. The mathematician reportedly wrote in her will that she wanted her young daughter Anahita to receive Iranian citizenship – something current nationality laws prevented the child from doing because Mirzakhani's widower is not Iranian.[2] A few days after Mirzakhani's death, several members of Iran's parliament pushed for speeding up reforms of these laws to allow a mother to confer citizenship upon a child, even if that mother is married to a foreigner.[3] (Current laws allow fathers married to foreigners to confer citizenship upon their children, but not mothers.) Although little movement on the issue of reforming the laws was reported in succeeding months, if this change indeed happens, it will be a sign that Iran is distancing itself from an important component of patrilineality.

Questions of lineage and descent might seem of interest mostly to anthropologists studying far-off tribes, but they have an impact on matters ranging from politics to economics to psychology in *all* societies. In cultures exhibiting extreme patrilineality, women are often deprived of full opportunities to inherit or take part in public matters, including getting an education. They may not receive custody of their children in case of divorce. Their ability to confer their identity or nationality upon their children is likely also restricted. These limitations can in turn contribute to problems such as 'brain drains' and statelessness – matters that affect societies as a whole, not just the women within them.[4]

Patrilineality has been extremely widespread throughout history, and strains of it – some more virulent than others – linger today in most countries of the world, including most prevalently perhaps in Muslim-majority countries in the Middle East and Africa.[5] Ironically, however, precedents for acknowledging bilateral descent – descent from both males and females – exist in many of these regions, especially but not exclusively in cultures influenced by Shiʿism. That is, although pre-modern Islamic societies were typically patrilineal, some showed distinct bilateral tendencies. In this book, I draw on collections of hadith (sayings of the Prophet Muhammad and other notable figures), Qur'an commentaries, historical chronicles, poems and other sources to examine episodes in pre-modern Islamic history in which individuals or societies recognized descent from both males and females. I focus on three different, interrelated manifestations of bilateral descent – transmission of lineage, inheritance and successorship – to answer the following questions: What circumstances gave rise to these episodes? How were they justified? What form did they take, and what impact did they have? Finally, what meaning might they have for us today?

I carry out this examination primarily, but not exclusively, through the lens of Fatima, the daughter of the Prophet Muhammad, as depicted in Sunni and Shiʿi texts. Fatima rarely appears as a feminist icon in Western scholarship – although that situation is gradually changing.[6] Yet as I demonstrate in this book, her example constitutes a striking precedent for acknowledging bilateral descent in Sunni *and* Shiʿi societies, with all of its ramifications for inheritance, succession, identity of children and, especially, perceptions of women.

Those ramifications are enormous, embracing as they do the very structure and development of societies. Recognition of bilateral descent in pre-modern Islamic societies restores a fundamental reproductive power to women. It facilitates a vision of women as able to create not only children but also meaning. It also helps to dislodge some of the perceptions of misogyny that cling to Islamic societies – a matter of acute importance not only to those who study gender but also to anyone interested in the relationship between Islam and social justice.[7] While this book exposes the roots of inegalitarianism as they appear in patrilineal understandings of kinship ties, it also reveals cases in which Muslims reimagined kinship networks – and, indeed, the structure of the family itself – to feature women prominently. Working at the intersection of history, religious studies, anthropology and gender, it uncovers alternative perspectives to patriarchal narratives and determines their significance. In so doing, it builds upon a tradition of studies seeking to dispel the notion that Islam is a 'monolithic religion with a singular all-embracing gender paradigm'.[8]

This book also lays bare the pervasiveness of charismatic leadership patterns in pre-modern Islamic societies – both Sunni and Shiʿi – and how these patterns, with their frequent emphasis on family dynasties imbued with special, God-given characteristics, could admit women to leadership roles, especially if an appropriate male was unavailable. Given that women were often seen as transcending their gender when they assumed positions of authority – or even becoming men – these patterns show that the boundaries between the sexes were, in some cases, more permeable than is commonly thought.

Finally, this book's findings will, I hope, provide a foundation for dialogue about reforms of the patrilineal laws that persist in many predominantly Muslim countries. In this respect, the work is both descriptive and prescriptive. That is, I am both offering more nuanced understandings of bilateral descent in pre-modern Islamic societies than those currently available to us and, at select moments, advocating for using these understandings to make changes that will improve conditions for women in contemporary societies. Like the contemporary South African scholar Saʿdiyya Shaikh in her feminist explorations of Sufi narratives, I do not claim 'dominance or exclusivity' for my readings of episodes of Islam's pre-modern, bilateral past, but merely offer them as evidence of diverse and polymorphous systems, which may be used to further egalitarianism.[9]

Patrilineality versus bilateral descent, and a search for agency

That kinship and gender are closely intertwined is a reality long recognized by anthropologists, albeit not an unproblematic one.[10] How societies conceive of kinship structures both arises from and influences the roles of men and women in those societies.[11] In its configurations of patrilineal and other forms of descent, descent theory shows how these structures operate.[12] In their starkest formations, patrilineal societies assign the right to reproduction and lineal succession to men.[13] It is fathers who reproduce themselves in their children, not mothers; or, if a woman does contribute to the making of a child, her contribution is considered of lesser or minimal value.[14] A man's role as the creator of his children endows him with a sense of ownership; in case of divorce or death, they remain with him or his relatives.[15]

In most patrilineal systems the role of successor falls to the (eldest) son – a phenomenon that traditionally invests him with great power. He may inherit the family home, succeed his father to a position of power and become the de facto head of the family. Patrilineal societies also often privilege other male relatives in the paternal line, including younger sons, uncles and cousins, over daughters, especially with regard to inheritance. (Patrilineality was, for example, the muscle behind the legal stipulations that threatened to chase Elizabeth Bennet, her mother and her sisters from their family home in *Pride and Prejudice*, and the daughters of the Earl of Grantham in the popular television series *Downton Abbey*. In both of these cases, the properties were to go to a distant male cousin. Though fictional, they are rooted in reality.)[16]

As the 'non-reproducing spouse', the role of women in patrilineal societies is characterized by metaphors of severing and detachment, both from her birth family and that of her marriage.[17] As Marilyn Strathern writes in her study of patrilineality in New Guinea, 'Where ideas of flow and transmission of substance provide idioms of relatedness …, then such systems also have to provide a symbolic counterpart: ideas of blockage and termination.'[18] A woman, after marriage, may be seen as cut off from her clan or natal family.[19] Likewise, a woman's contribution to reproduction 'may have to be [symbolically] obliterated from the children's bodies, or otherwise set against the connections traced through their father' – a matter that, as has been noted, has implications for custody.[20] The concept of detachment similarly extends to inheritance. Since both the mother and her children have been symbolically cut off from her natal family, neither she nor they would inherit their property.[21]

To be sure, patrilineality takes many forms, and the 'cutting off' experienced by women may not always be as severe as is sketched out here.[22] A woman in a patrilineal society may continue to associate with her natal family and may even live with them, as may her children (albeit with the understanding that they belong to a different clan).[23] She may continue to carry her natal identity and the name associated with it, though 'its demise with her own death has been foreshadowed'.[24] And there is also the intangible sense of protection and belonging that patrilineal societies may offer women.

Yet the costs of patrilineality can be high. It often stems from, and reinforces, a devaluing of women. I have already spoken about the frequent notion in patrilineal societies that women contribute little to reproduction. Concomitant with this concept often runs a vision of females as deficient in reason, overly emotional, and dangerously sexual, and thus needing to be relegated to 'the invisible spheres of the private and the domestic'.[25] After all, if a woman injudiciously gave herself to the wrong man, her family's honour could be imperilled – not to mention that any resulting progeny would belong to the lineage of the father, not to her birth family. By depriving women of the economic and other forms of autonomy they might otherwise achieve, patrilineal laws and practices can limit their options and abilities to live full lives.

Moreover, in contemporary societies, strict enforcement of patrilineal laws and practices contributes to numerous social and economic problems. The UN Refugee Agency (UNHCR) has identified 'nationality laws which do not grant women equality with men in conferring nationality to their children' as a 'cause of statelessness' – a major concern for the agency.[26] Less drastically, but still consequentially, inegalitarian nationality laws may curtail a country's ability to retain its citizens, especially enterprising ones who study abroad. A woman who marries a man of a different nationality may be reluctant to return to her home country if she knows that her children will not be able to enjoy citizenship there. The so-called brain drain, a pressing problem for Iran and other Middle Eastern countries, is partly the result of these and other inegalitarian laws.[27]

Patrilineal nationality, custody and guardianship laws can also have seriously negative effects upon families and social networks. Under Iran's nationality laws, for example, Maryam Mirzakhani's daughter would have to apply for a visa in order to visit her maternal grandparents in Iran – a long and difficult process for what should be her 'natural right' as the daughter of an Iranian.[28] Even more painfully, in the event of divorce, many mothers lose custody of their children in countries where patrilineal laws prevail. As the Saudi author in exile, Manal al-Sharif – who herself had to leave her son behind when she left Saudi Arabia because of threats, monitoring and harassment – wrote in an Op-Ed piece, 'Across the kingdom, mothers fight back tears as they are forced to leave the children they have raised and the homes where their babies took their first steps and said their first prayers.'[29]

By contrast, bilateral descent allows both women and societies to flourish. A bilateral society is one in which a woman as well as a man may transmit her lineage to her children, who belong both to her family and to that of her husband.[30] She may inherit property from her natal family and pass on her inheritance (and, these days, her nationality) to her children. She may also inherit, and show forth, less tangible qualities: intellectual, spiritual or leadership abilities or virtues. In this respect she may act as a successor.

All of these roles were fulfilled to some degree by Fatima as depicted in Shi'i texts. Given that the Prophet Muhammad had no surviving male heirs, Shi'is believe that Fatima perpetuated his lineage through her sons, Hasan and Husayn, and deserved to inherit his property. Many also believe that she inherited some of the Prophet's spiritual and temporal authority. Rather than representing severing or detachment, she symbolized abundance. In this book, I demonstrate that Shi'ism, with Fatima as a model, supports the notion that a daughter can carry on her father's bloodline, inherit his property and exhibit his attributes. I also show that her example was not an anomaly. Other women, both Shi'i and Sunni, were envisioned in similar capacities, sometimes with Fatima as inspiration. Analysing bilateral conceptions of Fatima thus encourages us to rethink Islamic perceptions of women and, like some of our forebears, to redraw kinship lines.

The functions and roles associated with bilateral descent are closely related and, in many cases, overlap. For the sake of clarity, however, I address them in separate sections in this book. In each section, I first examine how Sunni and Shi'i texts belonging to Islam's high textual tradition, including hadith collections, Qur'an commentaries and histories, depict Fatima fulfilling each function. I then show how this function was likewise fulfilled by other women in medieval and early modern Islamic societies. Given the richness and diversity of materials involving bilateral descent, I have cast a wide net in selecting sources and periods to examine for the non-Fatima chapters; genres range from biographical dictionaries to historical chronicles to endowment deeds to poetry, and dynasties from the Fatimids to the Delhi Sultans to the

Ottomans. This breadth is in consonance with this book's intent to act as an exploratory survey on bilateral descent in pre-modern Islamic societies, rather than the final word; it invites and welcomes future research on the topic.

To some extent, I also explore pre-Islamic precedents for recognition of bilateral descent. As many scholars have observed, Islam did not arise in a vacuum. It was founded and, later, developed by people who had earlier subscribed to various faiths and taken part in diverse practices, or whose ancestors had done so. It is not completely a surprise, then, to encounter female successorship in Islamic societies founded by groups of Turko-Mongol heritage, given the frequency with which women participated in politics among nomadic steppe peoples; or to find female inheritance emphasized in regions such as Iran where, prior to the rise of Islam, Zoroastrian daughters had some access to it. Providing historical context for the emergence of Islamic bilateral practices deepens our understanding of them. While it may be difficult to pin down actual influence or borrowing – and the implication that such phenomena existed is, in any case, highly charged – nonetheless these contextualizations form a useful backdrop for explorations of Islamic bilateral practice. They demonstrate that recognition of bilateral descent, while rare, did exist; and they gesture towards Islam's seemingly infinite elasticity and potential for taking different forms in different regions.

Although I draw on anthropological concepts such as bilateral descent, this is not a work of anthropology. Nor is it a work of conventional history or a traditional biography of Fatima, though it does invite new ways of understanding her legacy. Rather, my approach involves close reading and analysis of primary sources to discover what they may reveal about descent and kinship in pre-modern societies. I undertake this reading using the tools and perspectives of gender studies, seeking to accomplish what Shaikh has called the 'creative excavation of women represented at the borders of the texts'.[31] One of the main objectives of that search is agency, that analytical category so central to gender studies in the contemporary West. Agency as it is typically understood, however, constitutes a less-than-flexible instrument for discussing pre-modern societies.[32] Frequently conceptualized as the ability to act to secure one's own interests, agency is usually paired in feminist theory with the notion of acting *against* something, usually repressive or patriarchal structures, with the goal of freeing one's self from such structures.[33] As scholars such as anthropologist Saba Mahmood have pointed out, however, such definitions can be severely restrictive, particularly when considering non-secular societies. They fail to take into account the fact that freedom from 'repressive' norms may not be the highest aspiration for all women, especially those who place greater emphasis on 'subordination to a transcendent will (and thus, in many instances, to male authority)'.[34] Instead, researchers benefit from taking into account the multiple ways that women *inhabit* norms – and, in so doing, effect change in themselves and in others.[35]

For example, a woman who cultivates the qualities of patience (*ṣabr*) and modesty may not appear overly agentic at first glance; in fact, she may seem to embody passivity. For the woman herself, however, such cultivation may constitute a very deliberate act leading to the ultimate goal – a 'pious character'.[36] By enduring hardship without complaint, by refraining from overly bold behaviour, she may see herself (or be seen by others) as participating in a meaningful discourse of Islamic piety. In fact, both the Virgin Mary and Fatima are praised in Islamic discourses for guarding their chastity – an act which, as will be seen, had multiple implications for exerting influence, but which would not automatically fall under the purview of agency.

To extend the concept further, motherhood can be construed in a very agentic way. Scholars who recognized in Fatima and other mothers the ability to transmit their natal bloodlines were ascribing to these women a power that carried great weight in medieval societies – a sense of identity, and an ability to perpetuate it. The act of transmission may not be as thunderously impressive as that of overthrowing a patriarchal regime (and the fact that its description normally falls to male scholars, rather than the women themselves – an almost inevitable feature of pre-modern societies – may further diminish its value in the eyes of some), but in its own way, it is quietly revolutionary. In this book, I make use of this broader conception of agency to elicit more complex and nuanced portraits of women in pre-modern Islamic societies.

Defining Shiʿism

Fatima's role as a representative of bilateral descent and female agency is intimately tied to the formation of Shiʿism. Not long after the death of the Prophet Muhammad in 632, his followers divided over the issue of who should lead the Muslim community in his stead. Some felt that leadership belonged to whoever was most qualified, regardless of his kinship ties; they supported the accession of Abū Bakr (d. 634), the Prophet's father-in-law and close friend, and an early believer in his cause.[37] Others, more dynastically inclined, said that leadership rightly belonged to another close friend and early believer, ʿAli ibn Abū Ṭālib (d. 661), who also had the distinction of being the Prophet's cousin and son-in-law – kinship ties that, in their eyes, qualified him to succeed his relative. These competing ideologies produced considerable conflict, including civil wars. They eventually led to the founding of the two largest sects in Islam: the Sunnis – short for *ahl al-sunna wa al-jamāʿa*, or the People of the Sunna and the Community; and the Shiʿis – short for *shīʿat ʿAlī*, the Partisans of ʿAli. Though Sunnis have tended to dominate, both numerically and in terms of leadership of Islamic states, Shiʿism has persisted throughout the history of Islamic civilization. Sometimes Shiʿis translated their political ideas into temporal rule; the Islamic Republic of Iran is a contemporary manifestation of such a society. More frequently, they refrained from involvement in politics, but remained nevertheless influential.

Like Sunnis, Shiʿis developed extensive ideologies, literatures and juridical systems, many of which contrasted severely with those of their counterparts. Shiʿis believed that leadership, both temporal and spiritual, of the Muslim community properly belonged only to a member of the Prophet's direct family – that is, to ʿAli, or his sons Hasan and Husayn – or to one of their descendants who had been specially designated by his predecessor. These men, who became known as the imams, were seen as possessing special God-given knowledge, particularly knowledge of how to interpret the Qur'an.[38] Given their abilities, the imams were the only men capable of guiding the Muslim community. In Sunnism, conversely, any number of men could be considered legitimate leaders of the *umma*.[39] The special position of the members of the household of the Prophet in Shiʿism was to have marked consequences for the status of females within it.

Shiʿis developed and relied upon their own scriptural sources to support their conclusions. Although both Sunnis and Shiʿis derive law from the Qur'an and hadith, the hadith collections compiled by Sunnis and Shiʿis differ conspicuously in form and content. The canonical hadith collections to which Sunnis subscribe contain only sayings or actions of the Prophet. Shiʿi collections, however, contain sayings of the Prophet as well as those of the imams and, as we will see, Fatima. With regard to content, Sunni hadith tend to play down the importance of the Prophet's direct kin, whereas Shi'i hadith emphasize those individuals and the concept of the imamate.

Sunnis and Shi'is themselves have witnessed interior divisions. Sunnis tend to follow four different schools of thought in deriving law, each of which places varying emphasis on sources such as the Qur'an, hadith, reason and analogy. In Shi'ism, differences once more over questions of succession led to the formation of different ideological groups, the largest of which are the Twelver Shi'is and the Isma'ilis. In this book, I focus on Fatima's image in Twelver Shi'i texts, but I acknowledge as well how she appears in Isma'ili texts and societies. Likewise, I examine the existence of bilateral descent in both Sunni and Shi'i societies.

Defining Fatima

Shi'ism's championing of the importance of kinship in the succession to the Prophet had special implications for Fatima and women as a whole, affecting how the daughter of the Prophet appeared in the sources and opening the door for greater gender egalitarianism in Islamic societies – even if such consequences were unintended. Had the Prophet left any surviving sons, they would have been his natural successors. Instead, 'Ali followed by Hasan and Husayn (the Prophet's grandsons through Fatima and 'Ali) and their descendants came to fulfil those roles in the eyes of Shi'is. Fatima thus formed an integral link between the majority of the imams and the Prophet. Those promoting dynastic succession saw it to their advantage to exalt her status. In hadith and other literature, especially later collections, she appeared as one of the highest-ranking women in Islam, and she too was seen as enjoying some of the qualities attributed to the imams.

Unlike the later accounts, however, the earliest stories of Fatima provide little indication of her later status. What details they do contain produce the image of a pious, somewhat mournful, occasionally defiant woman who was utterly devoted to her father. One of the four daughters of the Prophet and his first wife, Khadīja, Fatima was born while the Muslims still resided in Mecca, in either about 605 or 615.[40] She wept considerably upon her mother's death in 619, crying, 'Where is my mother? Where is my mother?'; Gabriel inspired her father to tell her that God had built for Khadīja a beautiful home in Paradise, where she lived free of hardship and clamour.[41]

Like other members of the nascent Muslim community, Fatima accompanied her father on his monumental Hijra, or emigration, to the city of Medina in 622. It was there that she married ʿAli, the Prophet's cousin. Although Abū Bakr and ʿUmar ibn al-Khaṭṭāb (d. 644), another prominent companion, had reportedly asked for her hand in marriage, the Prophet refused them, 'saying that he was waiting for the moment fixed by destiny'.[42] Despite ʿAli's fears that he was too poor to press his case, Muhammad reminded him of a coat of mail that the Prophet had given him, which could serve as a dower.[43] ʿAli followed his instructions and – given Fatima's silent consent – the marriage was completed probably in the first or second year of the Hijra.[44]

Many stories in early sources describe the poverty of the young couple and the resulting hardships they suffered. Fatima developed blisters from grinding grain; Ali drew water for other people's land until his chest hurt.[45] The couple also apparently did not enjoy perfect marital felicity. Several hadith (some disputed) relate stories of arguments between them, most notably an occasion upon which ʿAli proposed to take a second wife (a venture rejected with a few choice words by the Prophet himself).[46] Nevertheless, they and their four surviving children – Hasan, Husayn, Zaynab and Umm Kulthum – were cherished by the Prophet and stood together in times of difficulty.

Though normally taciturn, even timid, Fatima could be roused to action and anger if a member of her family was attacked or threatened. After a member of the Quraysh threw the waste of a slaughtered camel upon the Prophet while he was praying, she removed it, and 'cursed the one who had done the harm'.[47] And, after the Prophet's death in 632, Fatima became drawn into the fierce struggle over the caliphate, the leadership of which had been claimed by Abū Bakr. Two incidents stand out in the narratives. In one, she bravely confronted Abū Bakr and ʿUmar after they tried to gain entry to her and ʿAli's home in the quest of forcing the allegiance of dissidents who had gathered there. According to one account, ʿAli went forward to meet Abū Bakr with sword drawn. After ʿUmar disarmed him and the group of men were gaining entry, Fatima emerged and angrily told them that if they did not leave, she would uncover her hair – a threat so bold it convinced them to withdraw.[48] Other early accounts portray ʿUmar as intending to burn down the house, and Fatima's resulting fury.[49]

Another story revolves around Fatima's quest to regain Fadak, a property she said the Prophet had bequeathed to her as an inheritance, or (in other accounts), had been given to her as a gift, but which Abū Bakr said belonged to the caliphate. The account of Fadak, which receives detailed attention in this study, likewise portrays Fatima as mounting a claim against those whom she believed usurped her rights and those of her family, and were leading the Muslim community astray.

Not long after her father's death, Fatima herself fell ill, dying just a few months after he did. Some sources report that she never reconciled with Abū Bakr, remaining angry with him until her death.[50] Given the antipathy between himself and the rulers of the Caliphate, 'Ali did not publish news of her death and buried her at night.[51]

Her passing had been predicted by none other than her father himself. While attending to her father on his deathbed, Fatima had cried and then laughed as he said a few words to her. When 'Ā'isha asked her what those words had been, she said that he had told her that he would die soon, and that she, Fatima, would be 'the swiftest of my family to join me'. Then Fatima had wept. Then the Prophet said, 'Are you not content to be the mistress of the women of this community, or the women of the worlds?' At that, Fatima had laughed.[52]

Though she is greatly admired by Muslims today of all ideological and sectarian affiliations, Fatima holds a special place in the hearts of Shiʿis, who celebrate her birthday and other holy days associated with her and recount the travails of her and her family in lovingly staged pageants. Craftsmen in the northeastern Iranian city of Mashhad weave her name into rugs and tapestries, and government administrators issue postage stamps in her honour. To her, moreover, is assigned a host of powers and virtues, including that of heavenly intercession. It is one of the aims of this book to decipher how she came to be portrayed in such an exalted manner, and what the impact of this portrait has been for women, for female agency and for the understanding of family structure.

How this book is organized

This book is divided into three main sections, each of which addresses a different aspect of bilateral descent: 'Mothers', 'Heiresses' and 'Successors'. Within each section, pairings of chapters address how Shiʿi (and some Sunni) texts acknowledged a particular manifestation of bilateral descent with regard to Fatima, and then explore how those manifestations resonated in pre-modern Islamic societies. Next, I give a more detailed description of the sections and the chapters within them.

Part One, 'Mothers', looks at the most basic expression of bilateral descent: the concept that a female can transmit her lineage to her children, and that her children belong to her natal family as well as to that of her husband. Through an examination of hadith and Qur'an commentaries, Chapter 1 explores the diversity of medieval views on generation and lineage, demonstrating how Shi'i (and some Sunni) depictions of Fatima fit into the less widely acknowledged 'duo-genetic' view that acknowledges contributions from both male and female. It explores possible origins for these concepts, including pre-Islamic regional influences and Qur'anic depictions of the Virgin Mary, whose son Jesus belongs to her lineage. Chapter 2 then demonstrates how recognition of bilateral descent in the case of Fatima echoed in similar acknowledgement for other, less notable women in pre-modern Islamic societies. It presents vivid examples of bilateral tendencies as evidenced in biographical dictionaries, hadith collections, historical chronicles, poems and juridical texts.

Part Two, 'Heiresses', addresses another acutely important manifestation of bilateral descent: inheritance. Laws permitting daughters to inherit property or money from their natal families – and to pass it down to their offspring – confer a degree of economic autonomy upon females, and acknowledge that they both belong to and carry on their lineages. Chapter 3 analyses how Fatima's claim to Fadak, an ancient oasis town she believed had been bequeathed to her by her father, led to Shi'i inheritance practices that acknowledged bilateral descent to a greater extent than did Sunni inheritance laws. It shows that just as Shi'ism redrew kinship lines to include daughters and their offspring, its inheritance laws recognized these dynamics by allocating money and property to daughters and their offspring in a more inclusive fashion than did Sunni. Chapter 4 looks at pre-modern societies – both Sunni and Shi'i – in which daughters and their offspring inherited to a larger degree than might be predicted by the laws in place, or in which people deployed existing legal institutions to benefit daughters specifically. Drawing primarily on *waqfiyyāt*, or endowment deeds, as source material, it explores the conditions that allowed these practices to arise.

Part Three, 'Successors', deals with the aspect of bilateral descent that possesses the most far-reaching consequences for the status of women:

successorship, or the idea that a daughter may succeed her father to a position of authority. Chapter 5 examines Shiʿi portrayals of Fatima in which she appears not merely as a receptacle or transmitter of authority but also as a woman who embodies her father's mission and is capable, at least in some degree, of leading his community. In these portrayals, appearing largely in hadith collections, she transcends the trappings of traditional femininity to emerge as a powerful, outspoken activist. Chapter 6 draws on historical chronicles and poems to investigate many pre-modern Islamic societies – both Sunni and Shiʿi – that witnessed females succeeding their fathers and other male relatives to positions of public importance. It throws light on the multiple solutions to the thorny problem of how women could combine the all-important virtue of chastity (which was often predicated upon hiddenness) with sovereignty (often associated with visibility). As an exemplar of both of these qualities, Fatima figures prominently in these narratives.

Finally, the Epilogue brings the discussion into the present by examining recognition of the various aspects of bilateral descent in contemporary Muslim-majority societies. Ultimately, I aim to show that the steps nations such as Iran are taking to free themselves from the shackles of patrilineality are in line with the precepts of their pre-modern pasts.

Part One

Mothers

1

Umms and wombs

How and (maybe) why Shiʿis reckoned descent through Fatima

The so-called 'mother' is not a parent of the child, only the nurse of the newly-begotten embryo. The parent is he who mounts; the female keeps the offspring safe, like a stranger on behalf of a stranger.

(Aeschylus, *Oresteia*)[1]

I am the tree, and Fatima is its branch. 'Ali fertilizes it, and Hasan and Husayn are its fruits.

(The Prophet Muhammad)[2]

My mother, myself?

Are mothers related to their children? The question may seem odd today, given that science has told us for decades that females as well as males transmit their genes to their offspring. But in the not-too-distant past, in both Islamic and non-Islamic societies, scholars and laypeople often downplayed or even ignored female contributions to generation.[3] Instead, women served as 'incubators'; they supplied the 'material substance for the child' while men supplied the seed containing the child's essence.[4] This perspective both stemmed from a concept of women as inferior and helped reinforce it. If unable to transmit her bloodline and her characteristics, a woman was of less import to her natal family; she likewise possessed less autonomy and creative power, and, naturally, enjoyed less claim to her children. In Marjane Satrapi's brilliant graphic novel *Persepolis 2*, a character, observing that custody in cases of divorce in Iran is often awarded to men, complains, 'I heard a religious man justify this law by saying that man was the grain and woman, the earth in which the grain grew, therefore the child naturally belonged to his father!'[5]

Yet some medieval Muslim scholars – both Sunni and Shiʿi – envisioned a greater role for women in transmitting their own bloodlines. Women as well as men contributed something essential and enduring to the making of a child. This chapter examines the diversity of medieval views on generation and lineage (*nasab*), demonstrating how Shiʿi (and some Sunni) depictions of Fatima fit into the less widely acknowledged 'duo-genetic' view that acknowledges contributions from both male and female. It also explores possible origins for these concepts, including pre-Islamic regional influences and Qur'anic depictions of the Virgin Mary, whose son Jesus belongs to her lineage. Finally, it analyses how passing on one's bloodline in many of these cases signifies agency, for it attests to a sense of identity and stature for these women, even within a patriarchal structure. Recognition of the ability to transmit one's bloodline has marked significance for the status of women today. It has implications for laws dealing with a wide range of matters, from nationality to custody of children to inheritance.

Medieval views on generation

Theories of generation play a key role in determining the status of women in any given culture. By determining and describing how life is generated, scholars tell us how humans and other beings are related to 'each other, the non-human world, and the cosmos'.[6] As in so many other areas, medieval (Sunni) Muslim thinkers who expressed themselves on these matters by no means came to a consensus about them. Rather, drawing from Greek sources (who themselves disagreed on important matters) and their own research, they developed a plethora of views about how generation takes place.[7] This diversity of opinion gave rise to a certain flexibility regarding the status of women, and in particular mothers, in Islamic societies – a flexibility that (like mothers themselves) often does not receive its appropriate due.

As in so many matters, Greek thought – chiefly as espoused by Hippocrates, Galen and Aristotle – formed the foundation for theories of generation developed by Muslim scholars.[8] These earlier men differed drastically on the roles played by males and females in generation, with Hippocrates and Galen maintaining that both sexes possess a semen-like substance that plays an equal role in the forming of an embryo, and Aristotle rejecting that notion.[9] According to Aristotle, the role of the female is far less consequential and has little to do with creating the identity of a child: lacking semen, she provides 'only the passive material which the male semen, as carrier of the soul, fashions into the new individual'.[10]

To elaborate, taking into consideration the fact that children could resemble either their mothers or their fathers, Hippocrates 'argued that both male and female must contribute similar reproductive material to the foetus' – that is, semen, a substance that 'comes from all parts of the body of each parent, and goes to all parts of the body of the child'.[11] Similarly, Galen, who wrote at a time after which the ovaries had been discovered, believed that both men and women possessed semen and that the 'female semen, just like the male semen, contributes both to the matter and to the form of the foetus'.[12] Aristotle, on the other hand, believed that 'semen was a residue of nutriment in its final form – that is, blood'.[13] Males possess sufficient body heat to transform the blood into semen. In women, who lack the sufficient heat, it remains blood. Thus, men contribute semen to the making of a child, and women contribute menstrual blood.[14] But the contributions are not equal: the male contributes the soul and the form of the child whereas the female contributes only the material. As contemporary scholar B. F. Musallam observes, the 'male semen fashions the female menses into a new individual very much as a carpenter fashions wood into a bed, or a builder bricks into a house'.[15] Ideally, the male principle should 'master the matter' and the child will 'be a male and will look like his father'.[16] Cases in which such mastery does not occur – in which, for example, a male resembles his mother – represent a deplorable ineffectiveness of the semen.[17]

Concomitant with Aristotle's understanding of how generation works is the concept of women as inferior and defective. Because woman is 'merely a receptacle' who cannot generate a soul for her child during procreation, Aristotle regarded the state of being female as a deformity, even as he acknowledged it as a necessary evil.[18] Her inferiority destines her to serve man, 'he who provides the essence of life.'[19]

Muslim thinkers followed Aristotelian thought to varying degrees. Abū al-Walīd Muhammad ibn Rushd (d. 1198) 'held fast to the letter of Aristotle' with regard to conception.[20] Abū 'Ali al-Husayn ibn Sīnā (d. 1037), known in the West as Avicenna, incorporated the notion of female semen rather than menstrual blood into his ideas of conception (given the discovery of the ovaries, he was obliged to accept this argument), but otherwise his ideas about male and female contributions bore a striking resemblance to those of Aristotle: he argued that the female semen contributed to the 'matter' of the foetus, but not the principle of movement, or the soul, which was the male's (superior) contribution.[21] In fact, we can decisively speak of Ibn Sīnā's views on this matter as Aristotelian, for the scholar gave to female semen 'exactly the same role that Aristotle had assigned to the menstrual blood'.[22]

Some scholars argue that the majority of Muslims have always adhered to some form of this essentially 'monogenetic' view and continue to adhere to it today.[23] The contemporary anthropologist M. E. Combs-Schilling, for example, claims that Islam is an extremely patrilineal system, in which

> essential being and essential affiliation pass down through the patriline – that is, from great-grandfather to grandfather to father to son. Enduring biological essence is seen to transfer from father to progeny and creates an inalienable tie, written in the life-blood itself (in much of the Muslim world, patrilineal ties are known as 'blood ties'). … *Daughters as well as sons receive their basic definition from their fathers, but only sons are capable of passing it on to future generations. Females are dead ends for their patrilines – important, but ephemeral additions.*[24]

Likewise, drawing on her fieldwork conducted in an Anatolian village between 1979 and 1982, anthropologist Carol Delaney writes evocatively about the villagers' conceptualization of procreation as an event in which the man contributed the seed, and the woman, the soil in which the seed grew – an understanding that drew on the Qur'an for support: 'Women are given to you as fields, go therein and sow your seed (2:233).'[25] The contributions, though both important, were by no means seen as equal. The man's role is the 'primary, essential, and creative' one; he gives the 'seed which encapsulates the potential child'.[26] As a villager from another study stated, 'If you plant wheat, you get wheat. If you plant barley, you get barley. It is the seed which determines the kind of plant which will grow.'[27] The woman, on the other hand, merely 'provides the nurturant context for the foetus' – a context to which she brings little individuality:

> The nurture that women provide – blood in the womb and milk at the breast – can be supplied by any woman. This nourishment swells the being of

> the seed-child and while it affects the growth and development of the child, it does not affect its essential identity; that comes from the father. Women's nurturant capacity is valued, but it must also be remarked that the substance they provide ultimately derives from men since men are thought to engender both males and females. The substance women contribute pertains only to this world – it is temporal and perishable and does not carry the eternal identity of a person. The child *originates* with the father, from his seed.[28]

In this sense, the woman is identified with earth, soil and land – a concept that found expression in comparisons of marriage and sex with men's purchase of land and sovereignty over it.[29] Even if a woman does contribute a 'seed' to the making of a child, it is usually considered to be a 'distillate of menstrual blood (matter), not generative, formative and creative material'.[30] This monogenetic theory of procreation had far-reaching ramifications for gender roles in the Turkish village.[31] Men are 'imagined to have a creative power within them, which gives them a core of identity, self-motivation or autonomy. Women lack the power to create and therefore to project themselves'.[32] Similarly, because of man's role as the 'author/creator' of his child, 'children belong to their father; they are his seed. In case of divorce, the children stay with him; in the case of death, they stay with his relatives. If his ex-wife or widow remarries, the children remain behind'.[33]

Indeed, to a rather large extent, these ideas populated pre-modern Muslim (and non-Muslim) societies; and continue to find expression today.[34] In a treatise on a sura from the Qur'an, Abū al-Khayr Rashīd al-Dīn Faḍl Allah (d. ca. 1318), the famous Persian historian and vizier, cited a centuries-old Arabic poem that denied a daughter's ability to transmit her lineage. Rather, it attributed all children to their fathers: 'Our sons are the sons of our sons,/ [but] the sons of our daughters are the sons of distant men'.[35] Muslim scholars today promote similar ideas via popular means such as websites. In an entry called 'The Protection of the Lineage', a website explaining the precepts of Islam speaks of a child as inherently belonging to his or her father, making no mention of the mother: the child is an 'extension of his father and the bearer of his characteristics. … [The child] inherits his features and stature as well as his mental qualities and traits … from his father. The child is a part of his father's heart and a piece of his body'.[36] As I mentioned in the Introduction, these concepts manifest in contemporary laws that greatly affect female stature in many Muslim-majority countries.

But not all Muslim thinkers embraced, or embrace, the monogenetic theory of conception, just as not all Islamic societies were (or are) exclusively patrilineal.[37] The fourteenth-century Ḥanbalī (Sunni) thinker Ibn Qayyim al-Jawziyya, a student of the renowned Taqī al-Dīn Aḥmad ibn Taymiyya (d. 1328), rebutted the arguments of Aristotle in his treatise *Al-Tibyān*, adducing Galen and Islamic religious sources to prove that both men and women have semen, and that the function of this substance is similar.[38] Ibn Qayyim cited a hadith in which both

> 'Ā'isha and Umm Salama, two wives of the Prophet, asked him [whether women have semen], and in his answer the Prophet 'established the female semen': … 'Should a woman wash after a nocturnal emission …?' The Prophet said that she should do so if there is a trace of the fluid. They asked again: 'Do women have nocturnal emission?' The Prophet retorted: 'How else would their children resemble them?'[39]

The scholar next cited another version of the hadith, adding, 'Do you think that there is any other reason for the resemblance? When her semen dominates the man's semen the child will look like her brothers, and when the man's semen dominates her semen the child will look like his brothers.'[40] Ibn Qayyim rejected the Aristotelian idea that male contributions to generation were different from those of the female – the claim that 'the male semen does not contribute to the body of the foetus, but is like the soul (*al-rūḥ*) that animates the organs.'[41] Rather, he cited another hadith to show that the foetus is 'formed of both the male and female semina', and opines that 'the organs, parts, and form of the child are the combined and equal contribution of both, that both semens mix and become one':[42]

> The fact that the child in some cases resembles the father, and in other cases the mother, confirms this point of view. God's words in the Quran also point [to] this interpretation, when He addresses humanity and says: 'We created you of a male and a female.' (Qur'an 49:13)[43]

Likewise, Ibn Qayyim's view that 'male and female contributions were equal in value and quality' had an impact on his ideas about matters such as custody.[44] The scholar

> considers it impossible to decide on the basis of biology whether the father or the mother has more of a right to the child. While the father has precedence

> and the child takes his name, the child follows the mother in freedom and slavery because, in addition to the original share she contributes, it is formed in her womb and fed by her milk. In case of conflict, Ibn Qayyim suggests that perhaps the more religious of the two should have the child. This is as clear a statement of the biological equality of male and female as Aristotle's was of their biological inequality.[45]

These ideas convey conspicuous support for the concept of bilateral descent, with its corollary implications for female custody, inheritance and even succession.

Beyond biology

In fact, the ways in which many Islamic societies – both Sunni and Shi'i – conceptualized of *nasab* (filiation, lineage) as a legal concept indicates a considerable amount of leeway in matters of descent. Traditionally, as I have indicated, children were attributed to their fathers – a reality borne out by their names, which were typically composed of patronyms rather than matronyms: a man would be known as Aḥmad ibn Muhammad (Aḥmad son of Muhammad) rather than Aḥmad ibn Maryam (Aḥmad son of Mary). The Qur'an itself adjured this attribution, and specified that it derived from biological kinship: in a passage addressing the status of adopted sons, it commands, 'Call them by [the names of] their [biological] fathers: that is juster in the sight of God' (33:5). But biology did not always determine paternity, at least not legally.[46] Paternity, as typically conceived, was manifestly a social construct. For example, the dower that a Muslim woman receives upon marriage was usually regarded as representing a modification of a pre-Islamic practice of delivering compensation to a 'bride's family in exchange for considering her offspring part of the husband's tribe rather than that of her father and brothers'.[47] Here, paternity is a matter that can be transferred from one group to another, rather than a biological imperative. Similarly, according to most schools of Islamic law, legal institutions such as marriage or concubinage often determine paternity, rather than biology – a reality reflected in a 'pre-Islamic Arab maxim, later adopted in Islam, *al-walad li 'l-firāsh* ... "the child belongs to the bed"' – that is, the owner of the bed.[48] In some cases, a child sired by someone other than his mother's husband would still be attributed to her husband, as long as the marriage was intact and legitimate.[49] The *firāsh* doctrine thus amplified the importance of legitimate institutions over biological filiation.[50]

Moreover, conceptions of *nasab*, especially in the early years of Islam, made room for children to be attributed to their mothers. At times this attribution took on a negative cast: since a child born outside of wedlock or concubinage was linked to its mother (in this case, she is the 'owner' of the bed), maternal filiation indicated illegitimacy and sexual impropriety.[51] In other instances, however, a mother's prominence, nobility or good reputation caused her son to be called by her name.[52] Indeed, evidence from early biographical dictionaries and other sources indicates that the use of maternal *nasabs* was not an unusual feature of early Islam.[53] I will take up these matters at greater length in Chapter 2. For now, though, it is important to note that, contrary to popular views, bilateral descent has been a part of Islamic societies from a very early period. Nowhere is this more evident than in how scholars depicted the place of Fatima within her lineage.

How Fatima carried on her lineage

As many scholars have noted, Fatima did not immediately enjoy universal prominence within Shiʿism.[54] In fact, a proto-Shiʿi living in the tumultuous first century of Islam might be forgiven for thinking she was of little importance, for with Shiʿi-allied groups – especially after the martyrdom of Husayn at Karbala in 680 – promoting the candidacies of men ranging from Muhammad ibn al-Ḥanafiyya (d. ca. 700), the son of ʿAli by a woman he married after the death of Fatima to Muhammad ibn al-Ḥanafiyya's son, Abū Hāshim (d. ca. 776) to Muhammad ibn ʿAli (d. 743), a great-grandson of the Prophet's uncle, al-ʿAbbās, patrilineal ties threatened to engulf bilateral ones.[55] As the ʿAbbāsids solidified their split from Shiʿis, however, Fatima's place in the Shiʿi pantheon became better established. By the tenth, or 'Shiʿi' century, when Shiʿi dynasties ruled major parts of the Islamic world, her position was secure and her image acquiring a saintly lustre.

Even before then, however, hadith scholars, Qur'an commentators and poets were already beginning to depict Fatima as able to receive and transmit her father's bloodline. They did so in a variety of ways: by narrating hadith that showed that she manifested her father's characteristics; by invoking symbolism and imagery such as the Prophet's cloak, his flesh and blood, the paradisial river al-Kawthar, and radiance and light to indicate that her father's properties transferred to her offspring with her as a conduit; and by comparing her to the Virgin Mary and her sons to Jesus. In many of these discussions, verses from the Qur'an come into play. Naturally, these ideas receive great emphasis and elaboration in Shi'i collections, where the political impetus to see Fatima's children as the successors to the Prophet was strong, but they also appear in Sunni texts. Taken together, these depictions attribute to Fatima a creative power that is traditionally denied to females, recognizing in her a form of agency. Like Mary in both the Gospels and the Qur'an, to whom she is often compared, Fatima constitutes an irruption of the female into kinship lines of spiritual power and authority – an irruption that frequently imbues her with those very qualities.[56]

A prerequisite for being able to transmit one's lineage is, of course, being *part* of that lineage: inheriting a parent's characteristics and identity, or what we would call today his or her genes. Many hadith contained in canonical collections, both Sunni and Shi'i, give clear indications that Fatima belonged to her father's lineage and showed forth his characteristics. In a tradition appearing in a collection of the renowned Sunni scholar Muhammad al-Bukhārī (d. 870), for example, 'Ā'isha reported, 'I have not seen anyone who more resembled the Prophet in words or speech or manner of sitting than Fatima';[57] the wife of the Prophet likewise observed that Fatima's gait was very similar to that of the Prophet.[58] In a famous hadith contained in many ninth-century Sunni collections and supposedly uttered upon the occasion of 'Ali wishing to take a second wife, the Prophet declared, 'Fatima is a part of me; what hurts her, hurts me' – again, a striking claim of identification.[59]

A later Shi'i collection compiled by the eminent scholar Abū Ja'far ibn Bābawayh, also known as al-Shaykh al-Ṣadūq (d. 991), the author of one of the 'four books' comprising the Shi'i hadith canon,[60] reveals a more elaborate version of the same hadith that serves to further exalt the status of the Prophet's daughter: 'Indeed, Fatima is a part of me, the light of my eye, and the fruit of my heart. Whatever hurts her hurts me, and whatever makes her happy, makes me happy.'[61] (Another version contained in a different work by the same compiler extends the parallels even further, noting that 'God becomes angry when Fatima is angry and is happy when she is happy' – thus closely linking Fatima not only with the Prophet but also with God.[62] And in yet another collection, the Prophet adds that Fatima is his 'spirit [*rūḥ*] which is between my two sides'.[63]) As will be seen in the chapter on succession, some scholars have interpreted this hadith to mean that Fatima could act as the Prophet's deputy or even that she 'received some of his gnostic knowledge'.[64] On the most basic level, however, the tradition reinforces that concept of identification between father and daughter which is a prerequisite for transmission of lineage.

The idea of transmission itself emerges within a host of traditions defining Fatima, 'Ali and their sons, Hasan and Husayn, as the *ahl al-bayt* – the family of the Prophet (or, more literally, 'people of the house') to whom respect, honour, and love is due. Tremendous debate has swirled around who exactly should be considered the *ahl al-bayt*, and scholars continue to argue this point.[65] But according to some reports, at least, the meaning is relatively straightforward. In the 'Hadith of the Cloak', versions of which are found, among other places, in *Saḥīḥ Muslim*, 'Ā'isha narrates that the Prophet

> went out one morning wearing a striped cloak of black camel's hair. Hasan ibn 'Ali came along. [The Prophet] wrapped him under [the cloak]. Then came Husayn and he wrapped him under it along with the other one. Then came Fatima and he took her under it, then came 'Ali and he also took him under it and then said: 'God wishes to keep uncleanness away from you, people of the [Prophet's] House [*ahl al-bayt*], and to purify you thoroughly.' (Qur'an 33:33)[66]

For Sunnis, the hadith confirms that Hasan and Husayn (along with 'Ali and Fatima) are part of the Prophet's household, as symbolized by the enveloping cloak. For Shi'is, it had even more profound implications. It meant that Fatima and her family partook in the Prophet's infallibility, for they had been 'purified' of any abominations (*rijs*).[67] Just as significantly, being gathered under the Prophet's cloak meant that they received some of the 'universal *walayah* [that is, the "power of spiritual guidance and initiation"] of the Prophet in the form of the partial *walayah* (*walayat-i fātimiyyah*), which descended to Fatimah and through her to the imams who were her descendants'.[68] From the Shi'i perspective, then, the tradition serves to exalt the stations of Fatima and 'Ali and their sons and to show that Fatima is able to transmit her father's legacy – the legacy of prophecy. Once again, Fatima forms an essential link in the chain.

A related tradition found in both Sunni and Shi'i collections, and once again associated with a verse from the Qur'an, ties 'Ali, Fatima, Hasan and Husayn to the Prophet even more firmly. Referring to the episode of the Mubāhala, or mutual cursing, it describes an event occurring when a Christian deputation to Medina from Najrān (a region in the southern portion of the Arabian peninsula) argued with the Prophet about Jesus's stature.[69] At that point, the following verses were revealed: 'If anyone disputes this with you [Muhammad] now that you have been given this knowledge, say, "Come, let us gather our sons and your sons, our women and your women, ourselves and yourselves, and let us pray earnestly and invoke God's rejection on those of us who are lying"' (Qur'an 3:61). Following these instructions, the Prophet invited the Christians to meet the next day and undertake the prescribed praying and cursing.

What happened next differs considerably according to which version of the story you are reading, but many Sunni traditions report that upon the revealing of this verse, the Prophet 'called 'Ali, Fatima, Hasan and Husayn and said, "O God, they are my family."'[70] The significance here is that the Prophet recognized Fatima as 'our women' and Hasan and Husayn as 'our sons' (and 'Ali as 'our selves'). Indeed, several eminent Sunni Qur'an commentators, including Abū Ja'far Muhammad al-Ṭabarī (d. 923), Fakhr al-Dīn al-Rāzī (d. 1209) and 'Imād al-Dīn Ismā'īl ibn Kathīr (d. 1373), interpreted the phrase 'our sons' in Qur'an 3:61 to refer to Hasan and Husayn.[71]

This event naturally appears as well in Shi'i hadith collections, where it takes on a highly symbolic meaning, one often linked to the hadith about the Prophet's cloak.[72] According to the usual Shi'i versions of the story, the event begins when Christians of Najrān, invited by Muhammad to accept Islam, had gathered to consult upon the matter:

> After some discussion it was pointed out that Jesus had prophesied the Paraclete or Comforter, whose son would conquer the Earth. However, it was felt this could not refer to Muhammad who had no son. Then a great book called *al-Jāmi'* was consulted which contained the writings and traditions of all the prophets. In this book reference was found to how Adam had seen a vision of one brilliant light surrounded by four other lights and was told by God that these were five of his descendants. Similar things were found in the writings of Abraham, Moses and Jesus.[73]

Wishing to explore the matter further, the Christians sent a deputation to Medina; it was then, after much discussion, that the verses concerning the Mubāhala were revealed. According to this version of the story, when the two groups met the next day, Muhammad had brought with him 'Ali, Fatima,

Hasan and Husayn, all of whom stood under a cloak. In some accounts, Muhammad then recited Qur'an 33:33, which emphasizes the family's purity. At that point the Christians 'remembered what they had read in *al-Jāmiʿ* and became convinced that Muhammad was the figure prophesied by Jesus'.[74] The event has become a central one in Shiʿism for the manner in which it shows the purity and the 'primal rights' of leadership of the *ahl al-bayt*, as well as their descent from Adam, Abraham, Moses and Jesus: all of these are symbolized in Muhammad's spreading of his cloak over his family.[75] The event is also significant, however, for its insistence upon the filial relationship of Hasan and Husayn to Muhammad.

Indeed, accounts of the events preceding and after the birth of Husayn (and, to a lesser extent, Hasan)[76] further underline the flesh-and-blood relationship of the boy to the Prophet (while sometimes, interestingly enough, omitting Fatima and 'Ali from the equation). In one tradition found in both Sunni and Shiʿi collections, Umm al-Faḍl, a woman who was close to Muhammad, had a disturbing dream in which one of the Prophet's limbs had been left in her house.[77] The Prophet comforted her, saying, 'You have had a good dream. Fatima will bear a boy and you will nurse him.'[78] Indeed, the account continues, Fatima gave birth to Husayn and Umm al-Faḍl looked after him. The story serves to collapse the boundaries between the imam and the Prophet; Husayn is not just *close* to the Prophet, he (like Fatima) is *part* of the Prophet, which qualifies him to succeed his forebear.

These identifications continue once Husayn is born. One hadith relates that as soon as the child was delivered into the hands of a midwife, the Prophet 'called out, "O aunt, give me my son."'[79] The Prophet immediately adopted a fatherly role with Husayn, naming him, shaving his head and giving the weight of the hair in silver in alms, and performing the ritual sacrifice on his behalf.[80] Fascinatingly, along with eliminating 'Ali from the picture, in some instances the Prophet even pre-empts Fatima's role as mother. The noted Shiʿi scholar Abū 'Abd Allah Muhammad ibn Shahrāshub (d. 1192), author of one of the most prominent biographies of the twelve imams, maintains that

> the Prophet suckled Husayn himself by putting his thumb or tongue into the child's mouth; which became for the child a source of nourishment. This the Prophet did immediately after the child's birth, forbidding his mother to nurse him herself and continuing thus to feed the suckling infant for forty days.[81]

As Mahmoud Ayoub observes, this tradition is meant to indicate that Husayn's 'flesh and blood grew out of the flesh and blood of the Prophet'.[82] Indeed, in a sermon to his companions and the Muslim community of Medina, the Prophet calls Husayn 'flesh of my flesh and blood of my blood; he is my son, my child, and the best of creatures after his brother'.[83] Considered alongside the hadith in which the Prophet calls Fatima 'a part of me', these statements affirm that the Prophet's grandson is as closely related to him as is his daughter, and that both enjoy the Prophet's exceptional qualities.

Water is a potent symbol in many religious traditions: it cleanses iniquities, heals illnesses, quenches spiritual thirsts and represents fertility and the outpourings of God's heavenly bounty. Divine females are often associated with water; Anāhitā, a pre-Islamic Iranian goddess, 'was the goddess of the waters, specifically rivers and lakes';[84] she is, in fact, 'first and foremost a river, possibly originally a heavenly river, symbolized by the Milky Way'.[85] It is perhaps unsurprising, then, to find Fatima associated with water, and to discover imagery of it as yet another means by which both Sunni and Shi'i scholars supported the notion of descent via Fatima. They did so via a brief Qur'anic sura known as al-Kawthar, or 'Abundance', which reads, simply, 'We have truly given abundance (al-Kawthar) to you [Prophet] – so pray to your Lord and make your sacrifice to Him alone – it is the one who hates you who has been cut off' (108:1–3).

At first glance, the sura may appear to have little to do either with Fatima or with water. Revealed, according to Sunni Qur'an commentators such as Ibn Kathīr and 'Ali ibn Aḥmad al-Wāḥidī (d. 1075), after an opponent spoke of the Prophet as a 'man who is cut off [*abtar*], having no [male] descendants. So when he dies, he will not be remembered', the sura was meant to reassure the Prophet and to act as a rebuttal to his enemies.[86] Understanding how it accomplishes this feat requires a delicate unfolding of the many layers of meaning contained within the term 'al-Kawthar'. The most widely accepted meaning of it is that of a river in Paradise whose 'scent is finer than musk' and whose 'water is sweeter than honey and whiter than milk', or a pool to which the Prophet's community 'will be brought on the Day of Judgment'.[87] Without rejecting this interpretation, however, some Sunni and Shi'i commentators identified al-Kawthar with the *ahl al-bayt* and, in some cases, Fatima herself.[88] According to al-Rāzī, for example, some scholars interpreted the sura to mean that God 'gave the Prophet offspring, which will be everlasting'.[89] The Shi'i scholar Faḍl ibn Hasan al-Ṭabarsī (d. 1153), known for his commentary on the Qur'an, likewise observed, 'It was said that al-[K]awthar means abundant benevolence. It has also been said that it means the multiplicity of a given person [i.e. Fatima], and the descendants of Fatima have enormously multiplied in a way that they will exist until the Day of Resurrection.'[90] Thus, Fatima and her descendants are the abundance that had been thought denied the Prophet. Rather than representing the severing or 'dead end' of the patriline – the role typically assigned to daughters – she symbolizes its fruition.

Of course, the 'abundance' represented by Fatima and her descendants does not merely consist of plenitude in numbers. The identification with the river or pool in Paradise remained part of the Shiʿi tradition, and this association amplifies the holy and miraculous nature of these blessed figures. Whoever drank of this pool's cool, fragrant, sweet, soft and clear waters, according to the sixth imam, Jaʿfar al-Ṣādiq (d. 765), would 'never thirst again for all eternity'; all of his sorrows and sufferings would be washed away – just as he who pledged devotion to Fatima and her descendants on earth would find redemption.[91]

Even more prominent than the symbol of water in Shiʿism is that of light; and the concepts of descent described in the preceding pages found frequent expression in descriptions of the divine, prophetic light with which Fatima (and many other holy figures) is associated, *nūr Muhammadī* (the Muhammadan light).[92] This primordial light – sometimes seen as the physical manifestation of *ʿilm*, or spiritual knowledge, as well as the 'spermatic substance' of which Muhammad is made – is essential to the well-being of humanity, for it illumines the world, guiding its inhabitants.[93] Hadith graphically depict Fatima as one of the chief vessels of this light, as well as the light itself, a matter exemplified in her most frequent honorific, al-Zahra, 'the Radiant'. In many traditions, when asked why she was called by this name, Muhammad explains that God created Fatima from His own divine light – and that her light then illumined the very heavens and the earth, overwhelming the eyes of the angels. They prostrated themselves before God and asked, 'What is this light?' God responded: 'This is light from My light', which He drew forth from the loins of the Prophet, whom He preferred over all the prophets. God made the imams from the same light in order to guide humanity to His truth; they would inherit the leadership of the earth after the conclusion of divine revelation.[94]

Some traditions about the Muhammadan light that appear in both Sunni and Shiʿi collections connect it explicitly to notions of descent, and assign women and men equal roles in its transmission. For example, Muhammad's father, 'Abd Allah, had a blaze of light shining on his forehead. After he married Āmina, the Prophet's mother, she was invested with this light – some traditions say it 'came to rest between [her] breasts' – and 'Abd Allah no longer possessed it.[95] Indeed, when pregnant with Muhammad, Āmina 'saw a light proceeding from her which showed her the castles of Syria'.[96]

What is compelling for the purposes of this discussion is the idea that women are capable of receiving and transmitting this light; it wanders, according to one tradition, from 'the pure loins into the purified immaculate wombs'.[97] Āmina both accepts it and passes it on; some traditions even state that after 'Abd Allah's marriage to Āmina, the light 'came to rest with the clan of Zuhra, i.e., Āmina's clan'.[98] One poem by Kumayt (d. 743), a pro-'Alid poet from Kufa, even emphasizes the Prophet's female antecedents:

> When your lineage is mentioned, your long branched tree blooms [spreading out] between Eve and Āmina
> You were transmitted from generation to generation,
> And you have got from her [i.e. from Āmina] white silver and gold [i.e. you have got your light from your mother at your birth][99]

And, unsurprisingly, Fatima transmits this light to her descendants, the imams. One hadith appearing in the collection of Ibn Bābawayh, after describing how Fatima's radiance in thrice-daily prayer miraculously lit up the rooms of the people of Medina, whitening their walls at dawn, yellowing them at noon and reddening them at sunset, observes that her light ceased after she gave birth to Husayn, when it brightened his own face. That light would continue to shine on the faces of the following imams until the Day of Judgement.[100]

Although some hadith explain that God created the light of Fatima after that of Muhammad, 'Ali, Hasan and Husayn, others spell out a different order of events, indicating that she herself was the origin of the divine light that was later passed down to her descendants.[101] According to a tradition related by Ibn Bābawayh, the 'light of Fatima was created before the earth and the heaven were shaped. … God, powerful and lofty, created her from His light before He created Adam or there were spirits.'[102] After being presented to Adam, she remained 'in a hollow under the leg of the Throne' of God until Muhammad was created. Then God placed her in an apple in Paradise that was given to the Prophet by Gabriel. He split it open 'and saw a brilliant light, and was frightened by it', but Gabriel reassured him that it was Fatima and described the help and intercession she would provide for believers.[103] In a similar hadith found in the collection of the eleventh-century scholar Husayn ibn 'Abd al-Wahhāb, Fatima's light was placed in a tree of Paradise, a fruit of which was picked by the Prophet: 'God caused its juice to pass into the throat of 'Ali, and then placed Fatima in the loins of Muhammad, who deposited her in Khadīja ...; the latter bore Fatima, who was of that light: she knew what was, what would be and what was not'.[104] These hadith begin to assign to Fatima a different kind of stature, one that potentially even eclipses that of her father – a matter I will take up at greater length later.

In many ways, Fatima's prominent role is encapsulated in Ja'far al-Ṣādiq's interpretation of the renowned 'Light Verse' of the Qur'an (24:35), as set forth by the prominent scholar Muhammad ibn Ya'qūb al-Kulaynī (d. 941), author of *Al-Kāfī*, the earliest of the 'four books' forming the Shi'i hadith canon.[105] The verse, omitting commentary, reads as follows:

> God is the Light of the heavens and earth. His Light is like this: there is a niche, and in it a lamp, the lamp inside a glass, a glass like a glittering star, fueled from a blessed olive tree from neither east nor west, whose oil almost gives light even when no fire touches it – light upon light – God guides whoever He will to His Light; God draws such comparisons for people; God has full knowledge of everything.

In his exegesis, Ja'far al-Ṣādiq explains that Fatima is the niche[106] who holds within her Hasan (the lamp) and Husayn (the glass); she is also the 'glittering star, fueled from a blessed olive tree (Abraham)'.[107] In his brilliant exposition on this commentary, contemporary scholar David Pinault observes that in

> this womb-like metaphor [Fatima] is described as the birthplace and source of the light of the Imāms. ... She is a celestial being ... linked in a kind of mystical genealogy with her spiritual forefather Abraham: starfire kindled from olivewood. Fāṭima the Radiant, conveyer of illumination to her future offspring, unites celestial hierarchies, light upon light, with their earth-origins from the Abrahamic past.[108]

Once again, this interpretation graphically illustrates that Fatima, though female, is able to convey her prophetic lineage, which extends back to Abraham. She is both the hollow enveloping the light (the niche) and the light itself (the glittering star).[109] Purified of menstruation, this unearthly being transmits illumination rather than blood as her inheritance.

Jaʿfar al-Ṣādiq's interpretations would have resonated with readers accustomed to hearing about descent reckoned through another holy female – the Virgin Mary. Although this matter will be developed further later in this chapter, it is worthwhile noting here that yet another means by which Shiʿi hadith collections demonstrated that Fatima's sons belonged to their grandfather's lineage (and thus were capable of succeeding him) consisted of comparing Fatima, Hasan and Husayn to Mary and Jesus.[110] The Qur'an explicitly recognizes matrilineal descent in the case of Jesus (ʿIsā). It identifies him multiple times as 'son of Mary' (in sharp contrast, of course, to the Christian concept of him as Son of God) and portrays him as part of Mary's (fore)father's lineage, the family of ʿImrān, which (as Fatima, Hasan and Husayn later appear in Shiʿi depictions) itself descended from Abraham.[111] Shiʿi supporters and scholars seized upon this identification as evidence of legitimacy for the imams, for if Jesus could trace his origins to his mother's (prophetic) family, why not Hasan and Husayn and their descendants? This association of Fatima with Mary and Hasan and Husayn with Jesus both raised the offspring of the Prophet to the stature of Mary and Jesus and established an airtight precedent for matrilineal descent. A perhaps unintended by-product was the introduction of a female element to the sacred cosmology and genealogy associated with Shiʿism.

Umm Abīhā

The previous discussion leads us to perhaps the most mysterious and evocative hadith associated with Fatima: the traditions referring to her as *umm abīhā*, mother of her father, which appear in Sunni and Shiʿi hadith collections as early as the tenth century.[112] Normally, a mother derives her *kunya*, or paedonymic, from her relationship to her first-born son; under ordinary circumstances, then, Fatima's *kunya* would have been Umm Hasan. Why the exception here? While medieval scholars remain largely silent on the matter, contemporary scholars offer many explanations. Some say that it emerged because she cared for her father as a mother cares for a child.[113] (That the Prophet, conversely, treated his daughter with the honour accruing to a mother seems possible as well, for he reportedly visited her last among his family before leaving for a trip and first when he returned.[114] Indeed, Ibn Shahrāshūb remarked that this behaviour showed Fatima's great favour with God, 'for He ordered the child to honor the parent, not the parent to honor the child' – an interpretation which seems to suggest that the parent and child have exchanged roles.[115])

Contemporary scholar Fāḍl al-Husaynī al-Mīlānī proposes that Fatima reminded the Prophet of 'Ali's mother, Fatima bint Asad, to whom he had been much attached and whom he used to address as 'Mother'.[116] Other scholars suggest the *kunya* reflects the now-familiar concept that descent is reckoned through Fatima – that the Prophet's lineage continued through a daughter rather than a son, and, further, that 'the Prophet's law and practices were preserved through the descendants of Fatima' – an affirmation, again, that Fatima's sons are her father's successors in prophecy and guidance as well as in blood.[117] One Twelver Shi'i explanation, indeed, argues that Fatima 'learned through a revelation that the name of her very last descendant would be Muhammad, like that of her father' – referring to the Twelfth or Hidden Imam, Muhammad al-Mahdī.[118]

Yet some scholars (particularly those engaged in esoteric interpretations) have conjectured even broader implications for the name, including those of Fatima as the *source* of her father and of prophecy – thus assigning her a station that exceeded even his.[119] Noting the aforementioned hadith that portray Fatima as the first light created by God, the Italian scholar Laura Veccia Vaglieri remarks that this account would 'explain [Fatima's] *kunya*'.[120] Indications of creative power and a superior station likewise emerge in one of the names attributed to Fatima: (the masculine) Fāṭir, or Creator, found in Ibn 'Abd al-Wahhāb's hadith collection.[121]

These notions of a superior station, primacy and creativity reside in the concept of *umm*, a word bearing multiple valences, many of which extend well beyond the notion of giving birth to and nurturing a child. Of course, motherhood in its most literal sense constitutes a highly honourable role in many Islamic societies: hadith contained in revered Sunni collections quote the Prophet saying that 'paradise lies beneath [your mother's] feet'[122] and repeatedly stressing that one's mother is 'the most worthy of [one's] good companionship'.[123] Yet on a more metaphorical level, *umm* connotes 'archetype or origin of something', or the 'main, principal, or original instances of something', as some early uses of it demonstrate.[124] Some commentators, for example, maintained that the pre-Islamic tribe of the Banu al-Azd called the 'chief of their qawm (fighting men of the tribe) a mother (umm)'.[125] And the

Qur'an itself uses the word *umm* in a manner that has been interpreted in a similarly lofty fashion. For example, one verse 'refers to Mecca as the "mother of cities" (*umm al-qura*)' (Qur'an 42:7) – an epithet explained by Ibn Kathīr to mean that 'it is the most honored of all cities'.[126]

Likewise, scholars such as Ibn Kathīr interpreted Qur'an's references to *umm al-kitāb*, 'mother of the book' (Qur'an 3:7, 13:39, 43:4), to mean the celestial eternal tablet (*al-lawḥ al-maḥfūẓ*) from which it was derived, a book that remains with God and is the source of the Qur'an's lofty wisdom.[127] Conversely, others such as al-Ṭabarī and al-Rāzī saw *umm al-kitāb* as 'the fundamental source of Divine Revelation from which the Qur'an and other Divinely revealed books are transcribed or simply as "God's Knowledge"'.[128] Although differing slightly in meaning, these interpretations share a sense of the origin, primacy and womb-like all-encompassing nature of *umm*. Contemporary scholar Yusuf Ali describes *umm al-kitāb* (which, like Ibn Kathīr, he identifies with *al-lawḥ al-maḥfūẓ*) as the

> the core or essence of revelation, the original principle of fountain-head of God's Eternal and Universal Law. From this fountain-head are derived all streams of knowledge and wisdom, that flow through Time and feed the intelligence of created minds. The Mother of the Book is in God's own Presence, and its dignity and wisdom are more than all we can think of in the spiritual world.[129]

Other interpretations of *umm al-kitāb* also emerged, as will be seen below. Given these connotations, however, it is not difficult to see how Fatima's *kunya* could have led to (or even been prompted by) a sense of her as 'producing' her father or even prophecy, and surrounded her with an aura of majesty and sanctity. (Indeed, according to esoteric Shaikhism, Fatima herself is *al-lawḥ al-maḥfūẓ* from which the prophets derive 'all their knowledge, revelations, and [miraculous] powers'!)[130] At the very least, her designation as *umm abīhā* among Shi'is lent a stamp of approval to the concept of the continuity of the prophetic lineage through her offspring.

Challenges to bilateral descent

To be sure, recognition of bilateral descent was at times tenuous and limited, even within Shi'i circles. We have already seen how some pro-'Alid groups discounted the importance of the daughter of the Prophet in the first century of Islam. Some Shiʿi hadith downplay her role as well, including those that show the Prophet supplanting Fatima's role of nursing her son. Hasan and Husayn are generally known as 'son of 'Ali' rather than 'son of Fatima' (although a visitation prayer attributed to the Twelfth Imam does call Husayn the 'son of Fatima al-Zahra, [and] Khadīja al-Kubra', and many other exceptions exist).[131] Moreover, Fatima's role in transmitting her lineage sometimes appears as an anomaly, one befitting a woman cast as a 'human houri' whose origins lay in paradise,[132] who neither menstruated nor bled while giving birth,[133] and who (according to some extremist hadith) even gave birth from her thigh.[134] Acknowledging the typical dynamic of patrilineal descent, the Prophet is quoted as saying, 'All mothers' sons are attributed to their paternal relatives except for the children of Fatima, for I am their father and their paternal relative.'[135] Perhaps even more significantly, neither of Fatima and 'Ali's daughters was included in the Hadith of the Cloak, an indication that Fatima's status was, indeed, an anomaly within Shiʿism.

Even more formidable challenges to bilateral descent came, naturally, from external groups. 'Abbāsids strove to downplay the rights of daughters and their descendants while exalting those of paternal uncles and their descendants (the *ʿaṣaba*) – a category that traditionally assumed importance in Arabian societies. Some 'Abbāsid caliphs denied altogether that the sons of daughters belonged to their maternal grandfathers' lineages.[136] Others admitted 'close kinship' but said it signified little. For proof of the 'Alid's claim to leadership, Muhammad ibn 'Abd Allah, known as al-Nafs al-Zakiyya ('the Pure Soul'), an 'Alid who co-led a revolt against the 'Abbāsid caliph al-Manṣūr (r. 754–75) in 762, pointed to their descent from 'Ali as well as from the Prophet's mother and to Fatima, arguing, 'No one from the Banū Hāshim [the Prophet's clan] has the sort of bonds we can draw upon through kinship, precedence, and superiority.'[137] Al-Manṣūr, who traced his own claim to the caliphate to his descent from 'Abbās, a paternal uncle of the Prophet, was not convinced. He responded:

> My, how you pride yourself on kinship through women, as to delude the uncouth and the rabble! But God did not make women equal [in such matters] to uncles and fathers or [even] to paternal relations and guardians. God gave the uncle status equal to a father, giving him [legal] precedence in His book over the less significant mother. … You are the descendants of

> [the Prophet's] daughter, which is a close kinship. But it does not legitimate inheritance, nor does it bequeath [political and spiritual succession or authority], neither does it confer the [imamate] on her. So how could it be inherited from her?[138]

Against these types of arguments, however, Shiʿi scholars massed an arsenal of proofs, ones that – at least on paper – they did not hesitate to use. The eminent scholar Muhammad Bāqir al-Majlisī (d. ca. 1699) devoted many pages in his monumental hadith collection, *Biḥār al-anwār*, including an entire section in his volume on Fatima, to affirming Hasan and Husayn's descent from the Prophet, often depicting debates about this subject in which Shiʿis and their supporters emerged victorious over their opponents. Many of the hadith he cites suggest universal recognition of daughter's sons as part of their maternal grandfathers' lineages – directly contradicting the notion that Fatima's status is an anomaly. Given the frequent tracing of Jesus to Abraham's lineage, the hadith also confirm that (contrary to al-Manṣūr's argument) spiritual authority may indeed pass through a daughter and mother. Though they were doubtless aimed at demonstrating the legitimacy of Shiʿi claims to leadership, and not at acknowledging the contribution of women to reproduction, when taken together the traditions nonetheless suggest strong support of bilateral descent and the implications therein for spiritual and political succession.

One such account, for example, reports an exchange between the Umayyad governor al-Ḥajjāj ibn Yūsuf (d. 714) and his prisoner, the eminent jurist and hadith transmitter Saʿīd ibn Jubayr (d. 714). As al-Majlisī writes, al-Ḥajjāj told an observer, 'This old man claims that Hasan and Husayn are the Prophet's children; he shall prove this from the Qur'an, or I will cut his head off.'[139] Saʿīd thought for several moments and then cited Qur'an 6:84–5, which enumerates the descendants of Abraham, including Jesus.

> Then Saʿīd said: 'How does Jesus fit in here?' Al-Ḥajjāj replied: 'He is one of [Abraham's] descendants [*dhuriya*].' Saʿīd said, 'Jesus was one of the Abraham's descendants. He did not have a father, but he descended from Abraham because he was his daughter's [Mary's] son. Therefore, Hasan and Husayn are more worthy of being called the Prophet's children especially since they are closer to him [the Prophet] than Jesus was to [Abraham].' When al-Ḥajjāj heard this, he granted [Saʿīd] ten thousand dinars, and set him free.[140]

Similarly, al-Majlisī, narrating from the *Iḥtijāj*, a collection compiled in the twelfth century, reports a conversation between Muhammad al-Bāqir (d. 735), the fifth imam and, a close companion, Abī al-Jarūd, in which the former asks the latter what people are saying about Hasan and Husayn. 'They denied our belief that they are sons of the Messenger of God,' Abī al-Jarūd responds. The imam inquires with what proofs he is arguing his point, and Abī al-Jarūd cites Qur'an 6:84–5, as well as Qur'an 3:61, 'Come, let us gather our sons and your sons.' When al-Bāqir asks how the opponents responded to that verse, Abī al-Jarūd says, 'They said, "It could be correct that a daughter's son is considered a son, but not from the loins [*ṣulb* – that is, not a real descendant]."' At that point al-Bāqir arms his friend with what he claims is unassailable proof:

> 'I swear to God, O Abū al-Jarūd, I will give you a verse from the book of God that declares that they are from the loins of the Messenger of God, and only the infidels will deny it.' I said, 'Which one?' He said, 'Where God said, "You are forbidden to take as wives your mothers, daughters, sisters ..." to his saying, "[also forbidden are] wives of your sons who are from your loins" [4:23]. So ask them, O Abū al-Jarūd, is it permissible for the Messenger of God to marry [Hasan and Husayn's] wives? If they say yes, they are lying to God, and if they say no, then this is the proof that they are the sons of the messenger of God from his loins, and this is why it is forbidden him to marry them.'[141]

The imam thus proves that sons of daughters are sons 'from the loins' by observing that, according to Qur'anic law, Muhammad would have been forbidden from marrying his grandsons' wives *because they were the wives of your sons who are from your loins* – a prohibition that even opponents of Shi'ism would have upheld.

The seventh imam, Mūsā al-Kāẓim (d. 799), made a similar argument in a discussion with the caliph 'Abbāsid caliph Hārūn al-Rashīd (d. 809). The caliph asked the imam, 'Why did you permit people to trace your ancestry back to God's Messenger and call you sons of God's Apostle while you are descendants of 'Ali? Men are traced to their fathers; Fatima was not but a vessel and her father, The Prophet, your maternal grandfather!'[142] The imam then cited Qur'an 6:84–5 declaring, 'Therefore, [Jesus] is considered among [Abraham's] offspring through Mary; likewise, we are the offspring of the Prophet through our mother, Fatima' – an assertion that the caliph, apparently, found compelling.[143]

In a similar vein, al-Majlisī cites the arguments of 'Abd al-Ḥamīd ibn Abī al-Ḥadīd (d. 1258), the pro-'Alid scholar and author of a famous commentary on the sayings of 'Ali.[144] He countered Sunni arguments that the Qur'anic verse, 'Muhammad is not the father of any one of you men' (33:40) meant that Hasan and Husayn could not be considered his sons by stating that the 'men' referred to in the Qur'anic verse was Zayd ibn al-Ḥāritha, whom Muhammad had adopted.[145] The verse, 'Abd al-Ḥamīd wrote, should be read 'Muhammad is not the father of any one of the *grown* men among you,' and should not be applied to children such as Hasan and Husayn (or, for that matter, any of the Prophet's sons who had died while young), who could, indeed, be considered his sons.[146] 'Abd al- Ḥamīd argued forcefully that it was permissible to consider Hasan and Husayn the sons and descendants of the Prophet, citing, like many other scholars, Qur'an 3:61, 'Come, let us gather our sons and your sons,' as well as verses about inheritance and Jesus:

> Certainly He meant Hasan and Husayn. And if He put it in His will to give [inheritance] money to the sons of whomever, the sons of the daughters will be included. And God named Jesus Abraham's offspring. *The linguistics agree that the sons of the daughters belong to a man's lineage.*[147]

Clearly, the scholar is referring not just to Jesus, Hasan and Husayn, but to sons of daughters in general – a strong indication that he did not consider Fatima an anomaly. Al-Majlisī himself concurred, stating, 'The evidence to consider them sons is plentiful.'[148]

Why was Fatima seen in this way?

As I have already suggested, political expediency likely played a major role in the shaping of Fatima's image and the demarcation of kinship. Passionately committed to the concept that Hasan, Husayn and Husayn's descendants deserved to lead the Muslim community, Shi'is needed to acknowledge the place of Fatima in the lineage. Thus, they had to incorporate 'the feminine' and 'the daughter' and 'the mother' into their idea of religious hierarchy – and, naturally, to recognize that prophetic and other qualities could be transmitted through women as well as men.[149]

Regional influences may also have played a part in Shi'i depictions of Fatima and bilateral descent. Critics and admirers alike often see Shi'ism as an Iranian phenomenon, even calling it an 'Iranian Islam'.[150] (Indeed, Sunni polemics often malign Shiʿism by saying that the sect is not true Islam but rather an amalgam of foreign influences, including those of Iran, absorbed after the conquests of the seventh century and after.)[151] In fact, many aspects of Shiʿism's construction of Fatima and bilateral descent bear striking resemblances to practices and beliefs prevalent in pre-Islamic Iran. While daughters certainly did not enjoy full rights under the rule of the Sassanian Empire (224–651), they could carry on their father's bloodlines in the absence of a male heir.[152] Likewise, Zoroastrianism, the most widespread religion in pre-Islamic Iran, counts among its deities and spirits several whose qualities sound remarkably similar to those of Fatima – another circumstance that has given rise to speculation that borrowing or adaptation occurred. Like the daughter of the Prophet, the female divinity Spenta Armaiti 'represents the pious, devoted female who will serve god and man as wife and mother working to ensure that cosmic order is upheld'.[153] In her roles as daughter of Ahura Mazda, the supreme god, house-mistress of paradise and mother of creation, she foreshadows Fatima's later functions, as does her status as a 'being of light' whose radiance illuminates souls.[154] Another divine female, Anāhitā, is, as we have seen, closely associated with water (including a heavenly river) and abundance, just as Fatima became linked to al-Kawthar.[155] It is small wonder, then, that some scholars identify Shiʿism's Fatima as a syncretic figure who replaced Zoroastrian female spirits as an object of devotion for Iranian converts to Islam.[156]

Zoroastrianism is not, of course, the only Near Eastern religion featuring a strong mother figure. Striking parallels also exist between Christian depictions of Mary and some esoteric (and even non-esoteric) depictions of Fatima – giving rise, yet again, to the question of borrowing. Indeed, Massignon saw in esoteric Shiʿism 'extensive assimilation of the themes of the Christian devotion to Mary, the Mother of God'.[157] Of Fatima's *kunya*, *umm abīhā*, Vecca Vaglieri has observed, 'given the connexions between the cult of Mary among Christians and that of Fatima among Muslims … it is possible that the title arose as a counterpart to that of "Mother of God"'.[158]

Both the opportunities and the rationale for such assimilation certainly existed. Christians lived and worshipped in both the Sassanian and Byzantine empires, regions partly or completely conquered by Muslims during the early centuries of Islam. Given Mary's exalted status among many Christians and the devotion directed toward her (not to mention her stature in the Qur'an), Muslims likely felt the need to prove that Fatima occupied a similarly lofty station, or an even higher one.[159] To do so, they met claim with claim.[160] If Mary was chaste and pure, so was Fatima.[161] If Mary was the morning star, so was Fatima.[162] If Mary was the queen of all women of her time, Fatima was 'the queen of the women of [her] world and [Mary's] world, and queen of women from the beginning to the end'.[163] If Mary was a virgin – conveniently defined by Shi'i commentators as someone who never menstruated rather than someone who had never had intercourse – so was Fatima, and the birth of her children constituted a miracle akin to the birth of Jesus.[164] Indeed, some sources refer to Fatima as *Maryam al-kubrā*, 'Mary the Greater'.[165] Once again, these similarities lend credence to the notion that Shi'ism's idealization of Fatima had a foreign birth.

Yet it is just as likely that influences closer to home found their ways into Shi'i notions of kinship and images of Fatima. Bilateral descent was almost certainly recognized in pre-Islamic and early Islamic Arabia, as was the purity or superiority of certain families.[166] An example is that of the Prophet's own family. Even after her marriage to the Prophet's father, the Prophet's mother, Āmina, lived with her own clan; 'Abd Allah would visit her there. Muhammad's care was transferred to his paternal kin only after his mother's death, not after that of his father, who passed away before he was born – all indications of matrilocality, if not matrilineality.[167] The Prophet himself acknowledged descent from both clans. He is quoted in a Sunni collection as stating that 'a whore has never given birth to me since I came out of Adam's loins; the nations have never ceased to transmit me from father to son, till I emerged from the best two Arab clans – Hāshim and Zuhra' (i.e. his father's clan and his mother's clan).[168] Although the hadith lays emphasis on the purity of women and transmission from 'father to son', the mere naming of his mother's clan is significant, for it propels it into the spotlight. Like his father's clan, it acted as a superior vessel for the prophetic substance that passes from generation to generation.

That mothers and fathers played a somewhat equal part in generation during pre-Islamic times is likewise borne out by poetry composed prior to the advent of Islam. A well-known poem celebrating the author's tribe speaks of a 'primordial spermatic substance' (similar to the concept of light, above) that moves from male body to female body:

> We are pure, not turbid; our hidden essence was purely preserved
> By women who carried us well [i.e. conceived us] and by men;

We ascended the best backs [i.e. loins] and descended
For a while to the best wombs.[169]

As in the depiction of the Prophet's birth, women play an important role in reproduction here: their wombs, like men's loins, function as protective vessels for the 'hidden essence' that passes through generations.

Finally, pre-Islamic Arabian religion, like Zoroastrianism, numbered among its deities many female spirits. According to the early Muslim historian Hishām al-Kalbī (d. ca. 821), pre-Islamic Arabs regarded three of these goddesses, Allāt, al-ʿUzzā and Manāt, as the 'Daughters of Allah' and believed they possessed the ability to intercede with God on behalf of humans.[170] Indeed, the so-called Satanic Verses, which, according to some stories, Satan whispered to the Prophet – and which the latter duly transmitted as part of the Qur'an before God corrected the mistake – give credence to the power of these deities: 'Consider Allāt and al-ʿUzzā and the third one, Manāt; / Those are the high-flying cranes / Whose intercession is to be hoped for.'[171] These characteristics bear more than passing similarity to Shiʿi images of Fatima in her capacities as exalted daughter and as interceder – a role that will be explored at greater length in the chapter on succession.

Of course, the advent of Islam strove to put a definitive end to goddess worship among the people of the Arabian Peninsula. The Qur'anic verses that mention Allāt, al-ʿUzzā and Manāt sharply criticize the Quraysh for attributing daughters to God when they themselves despise female offspring, and concludes, 'They are but names which you and your fathers have invented: God has vested no authority in them' (Qur'an 53:19–23). Even as the Qur'an condemns goddess worship, however, its incorporation of many traditionally 'feminine' concepts often associated with it, including motherhood, wombs and matrilineal descent, fosters an interpretive environment ripe for magnifying the roles of women – an environment duly made use of by Shiʿi commentators. Nowhere is this more apparent than in the story of Mary.

A closer look at Mary, Fatima and 'the family of ʿImran'

The only named woman in the Qur'an, Mary emerges as a central figure in the text. Her devotion and purity place her on a par with the many prophets whose stories populate the Qur'an. Her importance – apart from the sheer number of verses devoted to her (about seventy) – manifests in the fact that the titles of two suras are directly related to her story (and that of Jesus): 'Mary' and 'The Family of 'Imrān' – the latter referring to her paternal forebears.[172] Several contemporary Western scholars, including Angelika Neuwirth, Carl Ernst and Kathryn Kueny, have remarked upon the extensive female imagery and symbolism that appear in 'The Family of 'Imran', and, in particular, with regard to Mary.[173] Of most interest to this book, the Qur'an deploys arguments for descent in the female line in order to challenge patrilineal descent. As we have seen, Shi'i commentators took up these arguments to make similar claims about Fatima and her children. Their contentions link scripture, interpretation, legitimacy and motherhood in a manner that gives females and feminine imagery leading roles in the ongoing drama of prophecy and revelation.

Revealed in Medina 'during a prolonged debate with Jews and Christians about fundamental beliefs', 'The Family of 'Imran' contains a great deal of material aimed at defining the 'status of the People of the Book' and the relationship between Muslims, Jews and Christians.[174] It begins with an invocation of God as the revealer of scripture, observing that He sent the Torah and the Gospel earlier as guides for people. The Qur'an confirms these scriptures but also, implicitly, in its capacity as the *furqān* – the 'Criterion' or 'Distinction' – clarifies some of their corrupted verses or erroneous interpretations.[175] The next verses emphasize the need of humans to acknowledge God's revelations upon pain of suffering terrible torment, and speak compellingly of God's might and omniscience. Feminine imagery erupts into the next verses:

> It is He who has formed you in wombs, as He wishes; there is no God but He, the glorious, the wise. It is He who revealed to you the scripture, part of which is definite verses; these are the mother of the book [*umm al-kitāb*]. Other [verses] are ambiguous. Those with deviation in their hearts are the ones who follow the ambiguous part of it, desiring seduction and desiring its interpretation. But none knows its interpretation except God. And those who are rooted in knowledge say, 'We believe in it, all is from our Lord.' But only those who understand take notice. (Qur'an 3:6–7)

Given that they constitute 'perhaps the most direct discussion in the Quran of the science of Quranic interpretation', scholars usually focus upon these verses for their instructions about interpretation.[176] Indeed, much ink has been spilled attempting to determine what the Qur'an means when it speaks of 'definite' and 'ambiguous' verses, and how they should be approached.[177]

Even more, perhaps, has been sacrificed to a discussion of whether a single mark of punctuation – a period – belongs after the word 'God' – a point that utterly changes the meaning about who is capable of interpreting the text.[178]

As both Neuwirth and Ernst have noted, however, analysing these verses from a perspective of gender also yields substantial dividends, for they brim with feminine imagery in a manner that defies typical characterizations of the Qur'an as a text that erases women from associations with divine tasks.[179] First, the passage speaks about God forming humans in wombs – a tribute to His role as Creator of all.[180] Next, in parallel construction, it announces that God has revealed scripture, and associates the 'definite verses' with the *umm al-kitāb*, 'mother of the book'. As mentioned previously, *umm al-kitāb* is often identified with *al-lawḥ al-maḥfūẓ*, or the Preserved Tablet, which remains with God (Qur'an 13:39). Some scholars have also interpreted it to mean the so-called definite verses mentioned here, those that yield clear interpretations.[181] Finally, the verses condemn those 'with deviation in their hearts' who follow the ambiguous verses, desiring 'seduction'. As Ernst observes, the 'term seduction or temptation [*fitna*] commonly has negative gender connotations in Arabic'.[182] Scripture and its correct interpretation, then, are here associated with wombs and motherhood – or, to put it another way, motherhood carries the connotations of correctness, correct interpretation, definiteness and legitimacy.[183]

This symbolism reappears in the story of Mary a few verses later.[184] The account begins with a typically patrilineal rehearsal of Mary's forebears, including her (fore)father, 'Imrān: 'God chose Adam, Noah, Abraham's family, and the family of 'Imran, over all people, in one line of descent.'[185] Normally, the next link in the chain of prophecy would be a male. But a surprising irruption of the female occurs in the form of Mary:

> 'Imrān's wife said, 'Lord, I have dedicated what is growing in my womb entirely to You; so accept this from me. You are the One who hears and knows all,' but when she gave birth, she said, 'My Lord! I have given birth to a girl' – God knew best what she had given birth to: the male is not like the female – 'I name her Mary and I commend her and her offspring to Your protection from the rejected Satan.' Her Lord graciously accepted her and made her grow in goodness, and entrusted her to the charge of Zachariah. (Qur'an 3:33–37)

The verses here echo the feminine imagery of the prologue, with its invocation of God, the All-Powerful, who forms beings in wombs, both male and female, and knows all hidden secrets. Even though (or, according to some interpretations, *because*) she is female, Mary is accepted into the service of God and prophecy.[186] She can 'grow in goodness', she can serve and she can carry on her family's prophetic lineage, even if she herself is not a prophet. The Qur'an confirms this capacity in a later passage describing the birth of Jesus:

> The angels said, 'Mary, God gives you news of a Word from Him, whose name will be the Messiah, Jesus, son of Mary, who will be held in honour in this world and the next, who will be one of those brought near to God. He will speak to people in his infancy and in his adulthood. He will be one of the righteous.' She said, 'My Lord, how can I have a son when no man has touched me?' [The angel] said, 'This is how God creates what He will: when He has ordained something, He only says "Be," and it is.' (Qur'an 3:45–7)

Once again, these verses mirror themes and symbols of the introductory verses of the chapter. Just as the first verses refer to God both forming humans in wombs as He wills and creating scripture, these verses speak of his authoring of a 'Word' – that is, Jesus, who is both human and scripture – and designating Mary as its pure receptacle. Just as the first verses exalt mothers (and elucidate the connection between mothers and their offspring) by referring to the 'definite' verses as the 'mother of the book', these verses exalt the mother, Mary, and elucidate the connection between her and Jesus, by stating that Jesus (the 'Word') is to be known as the son of Mary.[187]

This parallelism, and its accompanying symbolism, potentially scores several points in debates with the People of the Book. First, within the context of disputes with Christians about the status of Jesus, the Qur'an makes clear that while God may be the Creator of Jesus, He is not Jesus's father. Jesus, a human, is not to be known as the Son of God; he is to be known as the son of his mother.[188] This concept is implicit in the association of the 'definite verses' with *umm al-kitāb* – once again, correctness and legitimacy are linked to the mother. As a necessary corollary, the text establishes women, and particularly mothers, as firm links within genealogies – links that earlier scripture (including both the Torah and the Gospels) had tended to downplay or even erase in the interest of constructing a patrilineal line of descent.[189]

For example, the female-centred family of 'Imrān featured in the Qur'an, and made up of 'faithful and submissive individuals who renounce power', serves as a counter to the 'firmly established patriarchal [f]amily of Abraham' who represent the dominant Jewish tradition.[190] And though the Gospels of both Matthew and Luke include a few women in their genealogies of Jesus, they present ambivalent images of Mary's biological relationship to him. Both trace Jesus's human lineage not through Mary but through Joseph from Abraham in the case of Matthew (1.1) and from Adam in the case of Luke (3.38). In Luke, moreover, spiritual identity passes to Jesus through Mary, and she is the one who gives the child his name; but Jesus is also 'thoroughly installed in the patriline' as the 'Son of God' (in addition to his status as the son of Joseph).[191] Also in Luke, Mary alludes to the centrality of the patriline when she exclaims, in the Magnificat, '[God] has come to the help of Israel his servant, / as He promised to our forefathers; / He has not forgotten to show mercy / to Abraham and his children's children for ever' (1.54–5) – thus, linking Jesus securely to the chain of men that stretches both back and forward in time.

Once again, the Qur'an's use of the womb- and mother-related imagery in the prologue – particularly with regard to issues of interpretation – lays the groundwork for better understanding of the deep meanings embedded in its story of Mary and Jesus. In fact, identifying the 'ambiguous' verses subject to misinterpretation as those contained in the Torah and the Gospels – as some scholars have done – allows the following ideas to emerge: The Qur'an is the 'mother of the book', the archetype of other scripture, including the Torah and the Gospels. It is the best and most reliable of these texts, the 'definite' or 'strong' text, which clarifies and distinguishes true from false in the earlier texts or their interpretations. In its clarification, it exalts mothers and, in particular, demonstrates that Jesus belongs to his mother's line. The 'decisive reinterpretation' provided by the Qur'an is, thus, surprisingly female-centred.[192]

A corollary is the sense of agency attributed to Mary in this chapter and others. Mary acts as a vessel for the Word, but as Kueny points out, she is far from passive.[193] Rather, she is *actively* good, even if it is in the manner typical of how a virtuous woman behaves in patriarchal societies: by guarding her chastity (Qur'an 21:91). By this means, she is able to be 'chosen … above all women' and to receive the Spirit breathed into her, and thus to become, with her son, a 'sign for all people' (Qur'an 21:91).[194] Moreover, although the Qur'an suggests that God created Jesus, like Adam, from dust, its attributing of him to his mother and her lineage indicates that she did, in fact, contribute something to his makeup. Like Fatima, she is both the niche holding the light and the light itself. By this means she demonstrates the ability to both act and create change in herself and her surroundings that the conditions of agency require.[195]

The concepts appearing in these passages resonate profoundly in Shiʿi depictions of Fatima. In addition to drawing parallels between Mary and Fatima, Shiʿi scholars often applied Qurʾanic verses about Mary to Fatima, 'in keeping with Shiʿi belief that the *ahl al-bayt* are the living exegesis of the Qurʾan' – that is, that the members of the family of the Prophet embody in a living sense the concepts and stories of the Qurʾan and thus shed light on their meanings.[196] Ibn Bābawayh, for example, reports that angels recited verses 3:42–3, beginning, 'Mary, God has chosen you and made you pure: He has truly chosen you above all women,' to Fatima after her father's death, substituting her name for Mary's.[197]

Similarly, as we have seen, Shiʿis used the account of Mary and Jesus to legitimate Hasan and Husayn as the Prophet's successors. Just as the Qurʾan's discussion of Mary establishes a lineage that challenges Israelite patriarchal claims, later Shiʿi discussions of Fatima establish a lineage that challenged Umayyad and ʿAbbāsid claims to sovereignty and leadership. In both cases motherhood and 'feminine discourse' act as keys to legitimacy. The mother – who, in the case of *umm al-kitāb*, constitutes the Qurʾan's definite verses whose interpretation is clear – forms the firm bedrock of prophecy and revelation. Feminine imagery and concepts of matrilineal descent thus manifest in Shiʿi discourse in a markedly similar manner to ways they appear in the Qurʾan – a matter with implications for Sunnis and Shiʿis alike. The image of Fatima grows in stature as a result, for like Mary, she emerges as an exemplary being endowed with identity, piety and the ability to transmit her lineage.

Conclusion

Though children born in pre-modern Islamic societies were typically attributed to their fathers, and though, according to many traditional understandings of generation, women's contributions to the creation of a child paled in comparison to those of men, Shiʿi (and some Sunni) depictions of Fatima's relationship to her sons Hasan and Husayn display a very different dynamic. Through use of symbolism and imagery such as the Prophet's cloak, water and light; through evocative titles such as *umm abīhā* (mother of her father) and interpretations of Qur'anic verses dealing with kinship and through comparisons to the Virgin Mary, whose own son was attributed to her lineage, scholars painted Fatima as a conduit for the prophetic bloodline. Such depictions likely emerged partly for reasons of political expediency among those seeking legitimacy for the leadership of the Prophet's descendants; they may also bear traces of influence from pre-Islamic societies, including Sassanian Iran and the Byzantine Empire. By attributing her sons to her, scholars imbued Fatima with a sense of identity, agency and stature that, as a woman, she might otherwise have lacked, just as the attribution of Jesus to the Virgin Mary invested her with similar characteristics. Both Mary and Fatima were highly unusual women, however. Could the relationship dynamics recognized between them and their offspring translate into similar recognition for other women and their children, or were they inimitable? The answers to these questions form the subject of Chapter 2.

2

Other mothers, other sons

'A better claim to the throne'

When court historian Iskandar Beg Munshī took up the task of writing the chronicles of his patron, the great Safavid king, 'Abbās I (r. 1588–1629), his goal was to depict that ruler's reign with as much lustre and legitimacy as possible. Tracing Shāh 'Abbās's noble lineage constituted one means of achieving that aim. In so doing, Iskandar Beg was careful to include the king's antecedents from both the male *and* female sides. He dwelt considerably upon Shāh 'Abbās's mother, Khayr al-Nisā' Begum (also known as 'Mahd-i 'Ulya', the Elevated Cradle), who was the 'revered daughter of the siyyid Mīr 'Abdullāh Khān', who himself traced his lineage back to the fourth Shi'i imam, Zayn al-'Ābidīn.[1] The king, Iskandar Beg concluded, 'was of distinguished and God-fearing stock on both his father's and his mother's side, *and for this reason had a better claim to the throne than the other royal princes*'.[2]

As enthusiastic adopters of Twelver Shi'ism, the Safavids were natural advocates of bilateral descent. Recognition of it formed part of their ideological heritage; it allowed them, moreover, to bolster their own legitimacy in cases where they could find (or forge) maternal links to the imams. Yet if textual evidence is any indication, they were far from the only pre-modern or early modern Islamic society to envision sons as belonging both to their mothers and to their fathers' lineages. Despite a strong predilection for patrilineality, Muslim religious scholars, historians and poets writing from the ninth to the seventeenth centuries – both Sunni and Shi'i – laced their texts with mentions of matrilineal ties. These mentions weave throughout the diverse genres of the Islamic intellectual and cultural tradition: biographical dictionaries, hadith collections, historical chronicles and poems. They also feature in legal texts. Viewed from this perspective, Fatima and her sons are hardly anomalies; they are rather a consummate (and, in some cases, guiding) example of a pattern in which men traced their ancestries to their mothers as well as to their fathers, or daughters transmitted their lineages. Prominent aspects of their story, such as a huge emphasis on chastity, as well as an ambivalence that sometimes set limits on a mother's contribution (or even cast it in a negative light), reappear in other examples. Though ambiguity certainly characterized bilateral descent, and though the benefits actual women accrued from it may have been limited, it nevertheless functioned as an important tool of legitimation and a meaningful symbol of perpetuation.[3]

Bilateral descent continues to be recognized today, even in highly patrilineal societies. In Saudi Arabia, where custody and nationality laws favour fathers, maternal lineage plays a significant role in politics.[4] Just like his Safavid counterparts hundreds of years ago, a Saudi prince whose mother belongs to an important tribe or family stands a better chance of gaining power than does one whose mother is of lesser lineage. Two contemporary Saudi kings, Fahd and Salman, were part of a group of full brothers known as the Sudayri Seven – a name deriving from that of their mother, Hassa al-Sudayri, a favourite wife of their father and the member of an influential clan in Najd.[5] Studies of King Faysal (r. 1964–75) often observe that he learnt religious ideals from his maternal grandfather, a direct descendant of Muhammad ibn ʿAbd al-Wahhāb, and tribal values from his mother.[6] While with one hand they erase or downplay the ties between mothers and their children, then, with the other Saudis highlight these links – a discrepancy with deep roots in the pre-modern past.

Biographical dictionaries

Despite their stodgy mien, biographical dictionaries constitute one of the most compelling and influential literary genres of Islamic civilization.[7] A sort of pre-modern *Who's Who*, the typical biographical dictionary consists of accounts of the lives and deeds of groups of notable people, whether hadith transmitters, poets or Sufis. Having one's name included in a dictionary was the equivalent in pre-modern Islamic society of being considered important enough to merit a Wikipedia page today. That a strong sense of hierarchy pervades these texts is evident in their very name: they are frequently called, in Arabic, *kutub al-ṭabaqāt*, the 'books on classes', and are sometimes arranged according to precedence, with the most important people appearing first.[8]

Genealogy was of paramount importance in biographical dictionaries, especially early ones, which traced several generations of individuals' family trees. Who you were related to helped to determine who you were, and vice versa; a noble lineage was a sign of prestige, just as your own admirable traits (bravery in battle, or closeness to the Prophet) reflected favourably upon your ancestors and descendants. Interestingly, Sunni biographical dictionaries, particularly those dealing with the early days of Islam, name women in genealogical tracings with some regularity, providing abundant evidence of acknowledgement of bilateral descent and the importance of female kinship, even in societies where patrilineal tendencies dominated.[9] For example, in his entries on significant figures who lived during the time of the Prophet and his companions, as well as the next generation, the prominent scholar Abū 'Abd Allah Muhammad ibn Sa'd (d. 845) metaphorically depicts bloodlines flowing from both fathers and mothers: he lists not only an individual's paternal forebears but also, often, the names of his (or her) mother and her paternal ancestors (albeit after those of the males).[10] In some cases, moreover, he goes so far as to name the maternal grandmother.[11] His biography of the Prophet lists no fewer than eight generations of female antecedents and devotes several pages to female ancestors related to the Prophet, including their full names and tribes.[12] His entry on Khadīja traces six generations of female antecedents.[13]

Even more strikingly, in Ibn Sa'd's dictionary some sons are ascribed to mothers rather than to fathers, or fathers given *kunyas* that referred to their daughters rather than to their sons – a phenomenon also found in a much later dictionary authored by the Sha'fi'ī scholar Shams al-Dīn al-Dhahabī (d. 1348).[14] Usually, maternal ascription occurs when a mother is prominent or exceptional in some way, or to distinguish children born of different mothers. The companion 'Ammār ibn Yāsir (d. 657) is also known as Ibn Sumayya in tribute to his mother, the first martyr in Islam – a designation that the Prophet himself bestowed upon him.[15] The aforementioned Ibn al-Ḥanafiyya, the son of 'Ali by Khawla, a woman belonging to the tribe of the Banū Ḥanīfa, is likewise attributed to his mother, a move presumably made to clarify that he was not the son of Fatima.[16]

Ibn Sa'd's collection also regularly names daughters, their marriages and their children – a phenomenon contemporary scholar Ruth Roded aptly terms 'the Fatima syndrome', in acknowledgement of the influence of the model of the daughter of the Prophet.[17] In a volume devoted entirely to entries on women, complete with mentions of their mothers, for example, the scholar includes accounts of the lives of the daughters of 'Ali and Abū Bakr (other than 'Ā'isha, who would have warranted an entry in any case as wife of the Prophet) and of Husayn, the son of 'Ali and Fatima.[18] His biography of Umm Kulthum, one of the daughters of 'Ali and Fatima, is particularly revealing. In it, he reports that 'Umar, the second caliph, asked 'Ali for her hand in marriage when she was still a young girl. After initially refusing, saying he wished his daughters to marry the sons of his brother, Ja'far, 'Ali agreed; and 'Umar went to share the good news with an assembly of Emigrants:

> 'Umar came and said, 'Congratulate me [on my marriage].' They congratulated him and said, 'To whom, Amīr al-Mu'minīn?' He said, 'To the daughter of 'Ali ibn Abī Ṭālib.' Then he told them that the Prophet said, 'Every lineage and means will be cut off on the Day of Resurrection except my lineage and means.' Then he added, 'I accompanied [the Prophet], and I wanted to have this as well.'[19]

The account graphically demonstrates that 'Umar saw Umm Kulthum as a conveyer of her grandfather's lineage – which, far from being cut off, would persist, presumably eternally – and wished to reap the benefits on the Day of Resurrection. Similarly, the entry on Asmā' (d. 692), a daughter of Abū Bakr, conveys a clear sense of bilateral descent, yet shows how maternal ascription could be used as a two-edged sword. As the account relates, Asmā' helped the Prophet and her father prepare for the emigration from Mecca to Medina under desperate circumstances. Finding nothing with which to tie the Prophet's bag or water skin except for her belt or scarf (*niṭāq*), she tore it in two, tying the water skin with one and the bag with the other. From then on Asmā' was known as 'She of the Two Belts', Dhāt al-niṭāqayn.[20]

Years later, the account continues, when Asmā's son Ibn al-Zubayr rebelled against the Umayyads, his opponents insulted him by shouting at him during battle, 'Son of the Woman of the Two Belts!' 'So they reproach you by it?' Asmā' asked her son. 'Yes.' 'By God, it is true,' she responded.[21] The story poignantly illustrates the Umayyads' attempt to smear Ibn Zubayr by ascribing him to his mother and associating her with an incident that they take to be an embarrassing one. Asmā's response is one of devastating economy. The event happened, she seems to be saying to her son, and it is one of which to be proud.

Not all attributions of men to their mothers in the dictionaries improved their reputations.[22] Muʿāwiya, the first Umayyad caliph (r. 661–80), was sometimes known disparagingly as Ibn Hind or, worse, Ibn Ākilat al-Akbād (the Son of the Liver Eater) – both references to his mother, the infamous Hind bint ʿUtba, who featured as one of the more memorable Meccan opponents to Islam during the time of the Prophet.[23] After a battle against the Muslims in which the latter lost many men, Hind and other women took part in the grotesque exercise of mutilating their opponents' corpses. She reportedly cut out the liver of Ḥamza, a paternal uncle of the Prophet, and chewed it, later boasting of her act – thus earning her infamous moniker.[24] In Ibn Saʿd's entry on the Prophet's granddaughter, Umāma (daughter of his daughter, Zaynab), the woman confided in an adviser that Muʿāwiya had proposed to her. The adviser, al-Mughīra ibn Nawfal, responded: 'Will you marry the Son of the Liver-Eater?' Umāma turned the caliph down (and married al-Mughīra instead.)[25]

Despite its numerous references to women, Ibn Saʿd's dictionary remains a predominantly patrilineal text. The volume on women contains separate sections on the paternal aunts and cousins of the Prophet, but not his maternal relatives.[26] Naming of women in entries on men may have functioned not to celebrate the women themselves, but rather to differentiate among the children born to different mothers of the same father, or to provide veracity to links in the chains of transmitters of hadith.[27] Another consideration may have been the aid these mentions provided to readers who wished to understand exactly which members of society were excluded as marriage candidates to them, due to close kinship ties.[28] But their inclusion nonetheless demonstrates that women were envisioned as entities in their own right, who brought their own identities to their marriages and children.

Mention of women and matrilineal ties dropped off sharply in Sunni biographical collections dealing with later periods of Islamic history, but did not disappear altogether.[29] The Egyptian scholar Shams al-Dīn al-Sakhāwī (d. 1497) devoted the last volume of his huge compendium of fifteenth-century notables to women of the central Islamic lands, including many female scholars.[30] In his dictionary, al-Sakhāwī frequently mentions women's mothers' names, sometimes to the exclusion of fathers'; he names daughters as well as sons, and in one case a granddaughter.[31] Perhaps of most interest is al-Sakhāwī's ascription of a dozen sons to their mothers rather than to their fathers, most frequently referring to these sons as 'Ibn al-Shaykha', which, as Roded points out, 'attests to the prominence of learned woman and female heads of Sufi lodges'.[32] Did women find more secure toeholds in Sufi family trees than elsewhere, and if so, why? I will address this matter at greater length later in the chapter, but for now it is worthwhile noting that other biographical dictionaries dealing with Sufi orders also mentioned women.[33] A compendium detailing the birth of the Rifāʿiyya order included three generations of the founder's maternal relatives.[34] Significantly, after the demise of that founder, Aḥmad al-Rifāʿī, in 1183, a sister's son succeeded him – a clear sign that a female could transmit her paternal lineage.[35]

Shiʿi hadith collections

Biographies of important personages are not exclusive to Sunnism, of course. Shiʿi hadith collections likewise give accounts of illustrious people, most notably the imams.[36] Al-Kulaynī, for example, includes brief biographies of the Prophet, Fatima and the twelve imams in his compilation, *Al-Kāfī*. Al-Majlisī dedicates separate volumes of *Biḥār al-anwār* to many of these figures, and another single work, *Jalāʾ al-ʿUyūn*, just to them. These accounts, like their Sunni counterparts, invest mothers with great importance, frequently tracing the lineages of the maternal forebears of the imams, emphasizing their nobility and purity, and stressing that the imams' identities flowed from both sides. Though the female contribution was of less significance than that of the males – women ordinarily did not transmit the imamate to their sons, as fathers did; and, notably, the *daughters* of Fatima and 'Ali did not produce imams – it consisted of more than mere matter; it was spirituality and nobility.[37] These conceptions of motherhood, often shaped by political exigency, left their mark on Shiʿism, irrevocably braiding into it women and their lineages. (See Figure 2.1)

In his account of 'Ali, al-Kulaynī devotes considerable space to the imam's mother, Fatima bint Asad, attributing to her an exalted stature indeed. Not only was she a Hashimite – a reality that allowed 'Ali to enjoy the honour of being the first person whose 'parents both belonged to Hāshim',[38] she was 'the first woman who migrated … from Mecca to Medina on foot', a signal distinction.[39] The scholar cites reports about Fatima that paint her closeness to the Prophet with precise, deliberate strokes: she was the 'kindest person to [him]', who if

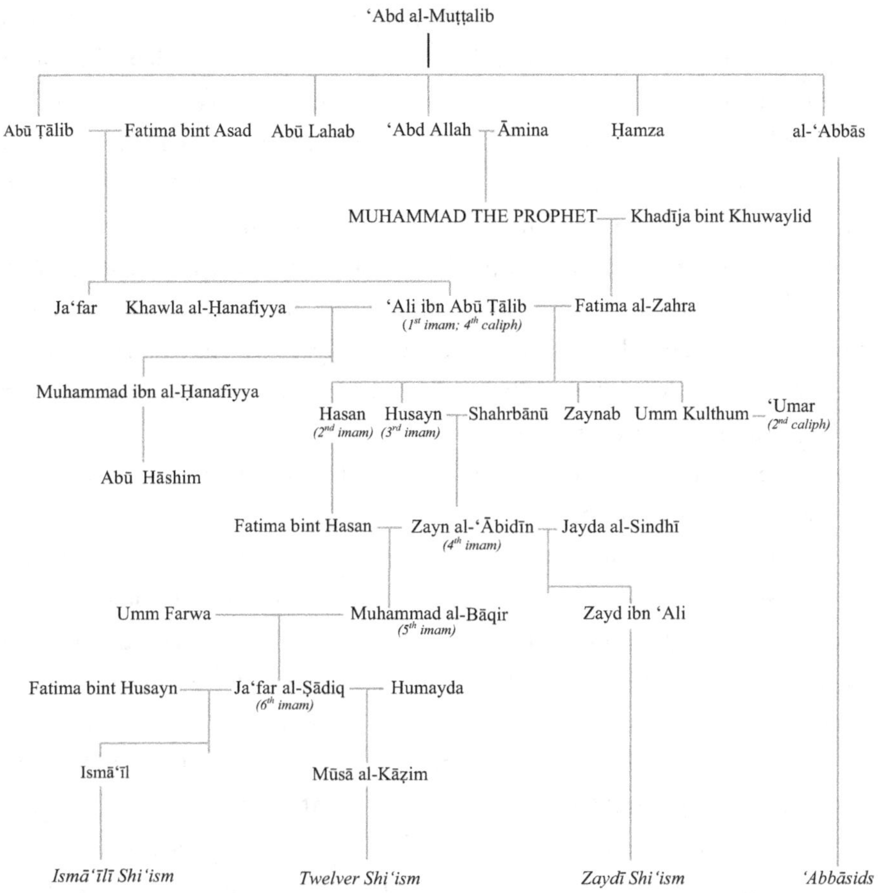

Figure 2.1 Genealogy chart showing lines of descent among early Shiʿi and Shiʿi-affiliated groups.

she 'ever had anything good in her possession … would make it available to [him] before herself and her own children.'[40] In fact, the Prophet repeatedly referred to her as his mother, mourning her death with great sadness.[41] This emphasis on metaphorical kinship serves to create a bond of brotherhood between the Prophet and 'Ali, one dependent on a female forebear in addition to their shared paternal grandfather, 'Abd al-Muṭṭalib.

Miraculous stories about the conception and birth of 'Ali that closely resemble those of the conception and birth of Fatima populate hadith collections, as though to highlight their similarities. Just as Muhammad announced to Khadīja that she would bear a child who would give birth to the imams, who would act as his leaders after the termination of revelation,[42]

Abū Ṭālib announced to Fatima bint Asad that she would 'conceive a child who will be the executor of the will and the Vizier of [the Prophet]'.[43] As with Khadīja, Fatima bint Asad is sometimes described as being impregnated not with ordinary semen but through the transfer of a heavenly light, via fruit, to the loins of Abū Ṭālib, who then passes it on to his wife.[44] She gave birth in no less prestigious a space than the Ka'ba, the holiest spot on earth, where God provided her with heavenly food to sustain her, just as He did with Mary at the temple (Qur'an 3:37).[45] None of these similarities are incidental: apart from demonstrating that Fatima bint Asad is a very holy woman, they provide legitimacy for 'Ali's caliphate. Her nobility and closeness to the Prophet transfer to 'Ali, amplifying his claim to succession.

An even more striking example of bilateral descent, and one equally related to politics, emerges in traditions about the parents of the fourth imam, Zayn al-'Ābidīn, whose lineage devolves from Husayn and Shahrbānū, the daughter of the last Sassanian king. Surfacing at a time of enormous tension over what it meant to be a Muslim (and who was fit to lead the *umma*), these reports deploy matrilineal ties to envision a joint heritage for Shi'is: Arab and Persian. Though contemporary scholars have previously sifted these stories to show how they helped solidify the connection between pre-Islamic Iran and Shi'ism, the evidence they present with regard to matrilineal descent is also persuasive.[46]

Starting in the second half of the eighth century, and reaching its fullest development in the ninth to twelfth centuries, a story began to circulate in hadith and other collections stating that the mother of Zayn al-'Ābidīn was the daughter of the last Sassanian king, Yazdigird III, who died while fleeing the Muslim invaders.[47] Although first it consisted of mere mentions, the account grew and developed until it reached quite elaborate proportions. According to accounts appearing in collections by Ṣaffār al-*Qummī* (d. ca. 902) and al-Kulaynī, and attributed to Muhammad al-Bāqir, the fifth imam, when the captured Persian princess (the Imam's grandmother) was brought into the mosque in Medina where the caliph, 'Umar, presided, she illuminated it.[48] Shahrbānū spoke in Persian, which angered 'Umar. 'Ali intervened, stating that the caliph had no right over her, and requesting that she be given the opportunity to choose 'whichever of the Muslims she likes'.[49] Shahrbānū placed her hand on the head of Husayn. 'Ali then informed his son that she would 'give birth to a son for you who will be the best of the inhabitants of the earth' – that is, an imam.[50]

Most significantly, Muhammad al-Bāqir then reports that the offspring of Shahrbānū and Husayn, the fourth imam, was called 'the Son of the Two Treasures. For God's treasure among the Arabs is the tribe of Hāshim [the family of the Prophet Muhammad and his descendants], and from among the non-Arabs, the Persians.'[51]

As contemporary scholar Mohammad Ali Amir-Moezzi suggests, the story accomplishes two important goals. First, through the figure of Shahrbānū (and, especially, her acceptance and validation by 'Ali), it highlights the importance and sacredness of Persian royalty, represented by Shahrbānū's ability to illuminate the Prophet's mosque.[52] (This phenomenon likewise recalls Āmina's pregnant belly's illuminating of the castles of Syria as well as other stories of the Muhammadan light, including those involving Fatima.) Second, it firmly joins pro-Shi'i and pro-Persian tendencies by making the point that henceforth the imams will trace their ancestry to both Persian and Arab nobility.[53] After Shahrbānū, 'Shi'i imams will be the bearers of a twofold light: that of *walāya* from 'Ali and Fatima (thus of Mohammad) and the glorious light from the ancient kings of Persia, as transmitted by S[h]ahrbānū.'[54]

That the quest to portray Zayn al-'Ābidīn, Husayn and Shahrbānū in this light met with success is borne out by later stories told about them. Hadith collections in succeeding centuries continued to feature Shahrbānū prominently and to emphasize her Persian ancestry.[55] Later Shi'i passion plays include Shahrbānū among their casts of characters and display ready acceptance of her and of her lineage – a phenomenon that attests both to the effectiveness of the Shi'i propaganda machine and to a general acknowledgement of bilateral descent.[56] Plays recounting the events of 'Ashura, for example, sympathetically describe the capture of the princess and her mourning at the later martyrdom of her husband, Husayn. Many show great sympathy for Persia and its pre-Islamic past.[57]

Given that most of the legends about Shahrbānū are likely ahistorical (the mother of Zayn al-'Ābidīn was, according to the oldest sources, a slave 'originally from Sindh,' not a Persian princess), it is likely that they developed in the way they did in order to meet certain politico-religious needs.[58] Only a few decades before Ṣaffār al-Qummī began to circulate the story, al-Nafs al-Zakiyya, who was a descendant of Hasan, had led his unsuccessful revolt against the 'Abbāsid Caliph al-Manṣūr – a rebellion that appears to have 'evoked great sympathy' among both Shi'is and non-Shi'is.[59] By revealing that

ʿAli himself had sanctioned the union between Shahrbānū and Husayn, and claimed that the imamate would inhere in their child, those who disseminated the story of the Persian princess may have sought to discredit the legitimacy of the Hasanid Shiʿis in favour of the Husaynids.[60] (Interestingly, some accounts of Shahrbānū's encounter with the Muslims in the mosque at Medina include reports of a sister who marries Hasan, a possible device for adding legitimacy to the elder brother's line.)[61]

The popularity of Persian culture and identity at the court of the ʿAbbāsid caliph al-Maʿmūn (r. 813–33) – who himself was sometimes known as the 'Son of the Persian Woman', given his ancestry – likely also played a part in the shaping of the story of Shahrbānū. At the time that these narrations gained popularity, Persian intellectuals at court were championing the *shuʿubiyya* movement, which celebrated Persian language, literature and culture and sought to dispel the hegemony of an 'Arabo-centrist orthodoxy'.[62] A Persian woman of royal blood who spoke in the language of her ancestors radiated light and had the freedom to choose her own husband – all of which were associated with Persian culture and identity – and who formed an integral part of Shiʿi ancestry would prove a formidable weapon in this battle.

A desire to pave the way for Zoroastrians to convert to Islam may have also contributed to the development of the legend. By the mid-ninth century, Zoroastrians still outnumbered Muslims in the regions of the Islamic empire that had previously belonged to the Sassanian Empire, though their political power was gone.[63] By demonstrating that Shiʿism celebrated Persian royalty and language, and counted a Persian princess among its ranks – indeed, by stating that the murdered Sassanian king's lineage continued through the line of the Shiʿi imams – Shiʿis would have added immeasurably to the appeal of their faith to Zoroastrians in Iran and removed obstacles to their conversions.[64] The princess' status reflects backwards, serving to endow the 'kings of ancient Persia with the status of maternal ancestors of the imams, thus revalidating the sovereigns and the culture of a nation of which she is the Lady'.[65] Similarly, in the noble figure of Shahrbānū and the shrines and rituals that became dedicated to her, Zoroastrians found an alternative to the popular female deity Anāhitā.[66]

Apart from laying bare the complex struggles for identity during the ʿAbbāsid period, the story of Shahrbānū also serves to show that, in a milieu in which fortunes and lives rose and fell depending on ancestry and lineage, mothers and daughters could be effectively pressed into service and incorporated, as needed, into family trees. Indeed, it indicates a certain predilection among Persians for romantic stories involving young women of royal birth – one that is reflected in the many stories involving such women in the *Shāhnāma*, or Persian book of kings.[67] That Shiʿis embraced the dual heritage of their imams is evident in Zayn al-ʿĀbidīn's honorific, 'Son of Two Treasures'. Legitimacy inhered in both females and males.

Of course, for Shahrbānū to be made wholly acceptable to Shiʿis, she needed to be Islamicized. As related by al-Bāqir, the legend of the princess's appearance at the court of ʿUmar suggests that she was already on a par with (if not better than) Muslims, given that she radiated light illuminating the Prophet's mosque and that ʿAli treated her with deference. But proof was necessary. It came in the form of a dream that a twelfth-century scholar, Quṭb al-Dīn Saʿīd ibn ʿAbd Allah al-Rāwandī (d. ca. 1177), reported Shahrbānū had prior to the Muslim conquest of the Sassanians. In the princess's words,

> Before the Muslim army arrived, I dreamed that Muhammad, God's messenger, entered our house and sat with Husayn and proposed to me on Husayn's behalf and married me to him. When morning came this matter stirred my heart and I could think of nothing else. The next night I saw Fatima, Muhammad's daughter, who came to me and introduced me to Islam. So I became Muslim, and then she said, 'Victory will go to the Muslims, and soon you will come unhurt to my son Husayn. No one will harm you.'[68]

The princess thus receives the ultimate seal of approval: no less a personage than the Prophet marries her to Husayn, and no less a figure than Fatima converts her to Islam. The mention of Fatima – to whom Shahrbānū is often compared in these stories – would also have resonated in readers' minds as the quintessential mother and someone who transmitted her father's ancestry to her offspring.[69] Thus groomed, Shiʿis would have welcomed Shahrbānū as a perfect *Muslim* bride for Husayn, even as they saw her as one who retained her identity as a Persian – and passed it on.

Interestingly, just as Zayn al-ʿĀbidīn traced his lineage to two illustrious groups, thereby uniting them, so did his son, Muhammad al-Bāqir. Zayn al-ʿĀbidīn married Fatima bint Hasan, the daughter of his uncle, the second imam. Thus, 'subsequent imams were both Husaynid and Hasanid in genealogy' or, as al-Majlisī said, 'doubly honored'.[70] Muhammad al-Bāqir himself relates a miraculous tale of his mother, whose spiritual power was such that even objects obeyed her command. As he reports,

> Once, my mother was sitting next to a wall. The wall began to break apart and we heard an intense crumbling noise. She pointed with her hands saying, 'No, for the sake of [the Prophet], God has not granted you permission to fall.' The wall remained hanging in the air until she moved away from that place. My father gave one hundred dinars as charity in appreciation and as an expression of gratitude for God's favor.[71]

Al-Bāqir's son, Jaʿfar al-Ṣādiq, reportedly said of his grandmother, 'She was a truthful person. No woman was ever found in the descendants of Hasan like her [in excellence].'[72]

Other mothers, though of lesser lineage, were likewise acknowledged and celebrated in the hadith collections. The mother of the seventh imam, Mūsā al-Kāẓim, was a slave woman named Humayda; yet, in al-Kulaynī's telling, she enjoyed high spiritual stature. According to the story, Muhammad al-Bāqir ordered a companion, Ibn al-ʿUkkasha, to buy a slave girl for his son. When the companion went to the trader indicated by the imam, he had sold 'all of his slave girls except two of them who were ill, and one of them was more beautiful than the other'.[73] The companion purchased the more beautiful girl for seventy dinars and brought her back to the imam, who asked her if she were a virgin. 'Yes,' she responded.

> He asked, 'How can that be true? The traders corrupt whatever may come in their hands.' She said, 'He would come to me and sit next to me just as men and women do but God would make a man with gray hair and gray beard appear and force him to go away from me. This happened several times between him and the man with gray hairs and beard.' The imam said, 'O Jaʿfar take her for yourself.' She then gave birth to the best person on earth who was Mūsā' ibn Jaʿfar.[74]

Jaʿfar al-Ṣādiq himself said of Humayda that she was 'clean of uncleanliness like purified gold. The angels continuously guarded her until she reached me due to God's regard for me and the possessor of the imamate after me.'[75] The story of necessity lays less emphasis on Humayda's lineage than do other narratives, but it nevertheless identifies the imam's mother by name, indicates that she is protected by the angels and attributes to her a pure character, which she presumably can transmit to her son.

Like Khadīja and Fatima, mothers of imams also experience miraculous conceptions and births. They receive glad tidings informing them of the coming births of their sons: a man's voice tells them, 'You have conceived with goodness, you are changing into goodness and you have come up with goodness. Congratulations to you for a son who is very forbearing and knowledgeable.'[76] They feel no pain from their pregnancies, and their deliveries are accompanied by lights that only they and the fathers of the imams can see.[77] Their vaginas permit their sons to be born in a seated position, their legs folded, and to immediately face Mecca. The boys emit light like 'flowing gold'; they emerge from the womb pre-circumcised and with their umbilical cords pre-cut.[78]

Of course, the role that the mothers of imams play after birth is often circumscribed. Just as Muhammad supplanted his daughter's role with Husayn, imams often supplant their wives in mothering their sons: sleeping by their sides, carrying them and suckling them with their tongues – the last a sign of the 'transmission of spiritual knowledge'.[79] And it is hardly insignificant that, according to a leading Shi'i scholar, Abū 'Abd Allah Muhammad ibn al-Nu'mān, known as al-Shaykh al-Mufīd (d. 1022), the Prophet informed 'Ali: 'When the Day of Reckoning will dawn, all people will be called by their mothers' names, except your Shi'as, who will be called by the names of their fathers, confirming their legitimacy.'[80] The association of illegitimate birth with matrilineal attribution in this report casts a negative light indeed upon bilateral (or matrilineal) descent.[81] In fact, Hasan himself is supposed to have insulted an Umayyad opponent, Ziyād ibn 'Ubayd, by ascribing him to his mother, thus casting doubt on his legitimacy.[82] Yet the hadith collections belie these aspersions by entering these women's identities and virtues in the books of record *about their sons*, their names irrevocably attached to those of their offspring. This attention, even if it does not rise to official attribution (*nasab*), suggests that these women act as linchpins in the saga of the imamate: necessary for its evolution, intrinsic to its success.[83]

Historical chronicles

Similar patterns of bilateral descent emerge in pre-modern historical chronicles, those action-packed accounts of the rises and falls of dynasties, their fortunes, travails and triumphs. Such is the case with chronicles documenting the rise of the three so-called 'Gunpowder' empires – Ottoman, Safavid and Mughal – which came to prominence in the early 1500s and dominated the Middle East and South Asia for the next two centuries.[84] Shaped once again by the necessities of politics and legitimation, recognition of bilateral descent among these dynasties owed much to Turko-Mongol precedent, and (in the case of the Shi'i Safavids in particular) a debt as well to the model of the Prophet and Fatima.

All three empires traced at least part of their ancestry to peoples of Turko-Mongol origin – former nomads of the Central Asian steppes who eventually migrated to Islam's heartlands (often laying waste to them as they did so), settled, converted to Islam and set about conquering new lands.[85] This ancestry is relevant, for Turko-Mongol nomads regularly acknowledged the transmission of lineage (and legitimacy) from both their mothers' and their fathers' sides.[86] One early pre-Islamic Turkish ruler praises the heavenly god (Tanrı), 'who had raised my father, the khakan, and my mother, the khatun, and who had granted them the state,' thus presenting himself as inheriting political authority from both parents.[87] This acknowledgement sometimes translated into actual political power for women, as I will explore in the chapters on succession. In any case, many of these concepts and ideals reappeared (albeit less emphatically) in the empires themselves.

The founding story of the (Sunni) Ottoman Empire, for example, emphasizes matrilineal ties to a rather large extent. According to the late fifteenth- and sixteenth-century chronicles that recount the legend, Osman (d. 1326), the leader of a principality in northwest Anatolia, was having some success in battling the Byzantines when he had a dream in which

> a moon rose from the breast of a widely revered dervish sheikh, Edebali, and entered Osman's own breast. From Osman's navel sprang a great tree, which grew to shade the entire world. Under the branches of the tree were mountains, from which flowing water served to quench the thirst of some and to irrigate the fields of others.[88]

Edebali explained to Osman that the dream symbolized 'God's grant of sovereignty to him and his descendants. The moon … represented [Edebali's] own daughter, to whom Osman was forthwith united in marriage.'[89] What is particularly interesting here is the transmission of the holy man's charisma *through his daughter*, and the importance of this element in the founding of the dynasty.[90] Here, as with Fatima, a daughter figures as a crucial element in a union that gives rise to an empire; her ability to disseminate her father's charisma is a key part of the equation.

During the heyday of the empire itself, however, particularly after the fourteenth century, the Ottomans took apparently deliberate steps to efface or suppress the importance of matrilineal descent, believing that it interfered with the patrilineal 'sons of Osman' narrative that they were promoting.[91] Though they continued to marry women of royal blood, rulers deliberately bore children through their slave-concubines in a way that discouraged perpetuation of the noble lineages to which their wives belonged (thus diminishing their prestige).[92] Despite their bilateral origins, then, the Ottomans took care to ensure that fathers' blood legitimized a child as royal, not mothers'.

Nevertheless, some acknowledgement of matrilineal ties still existed during this period in the form of sultans' treatments of their mothers, who became known as *valide sultan*, and their daughters. Like slave mothers of imams, concubine mothers of sultans enjoyed the reflected glory of their sons in a sort of 'reverse lineage bestowed upon them through having given birth to a member of the Ottoman dynasty'.[93] For example, they were accorded great prestige in the form of ceremonial processions that wound up with the sultan's paying obeisance to them.[94] At times, they even took matters of the state into their own hands, in some cases ruling in the stead of their (incompetent or minor) sons – a sign, albeit a sometimes controversial one, that they belonged to the royal lineage.[95] Great care was taken in marrying daughters, an indication that these women could transmit the charisma of the royal family.[96] Women of the Ottoman household, moreover, were often addressed with nomenclature such as '"Ā'isha of the age" or "the Fatima of the era"', thus linking them to the Prophet's family – the ultimate honour.[97]

Acknowledgement of matrilineal ties likewise surfaced in the Safavid Empire (1501–1736), which at its height encompassed all of today's Iran, Azarbaijan, Armenia, Bahrain and parts of surrounding states. As with the Ottomans, the Safavids' founding story involves a marriage between the daughter of a great Sufi shaykh – Zāhid Gīlānī (d. 1301) – and the shaykh's disciple, Ṣafī al-Dīn Isḥāq Ardabīlī (d. 1334), after whom the eventual empire was to take its name. As Safavid historians later reported, after 'some years of meditation and contemplation, Ṣafī was made Shaykh Zāhid's spiritual successor, whereupon the great shaykh gave to his disciple a daughter, 'of the same name as [Fatima] Zahra' – peace be upon her, who was nourished within the veil of chastity'.[98] The similarities did not end there. Like her namesake, this Fatima was imbued with her family's charisma, which she then transmitted to her husband and children.[99]

Indeed, many Safavid men acquired prestige by becoming connected to their wives' lineages, and members of the royal house consequently used marriages to cement political ties – a sign that women not only could represent their own lineages and natal families but could augment those of their spouses.[100] And as in the Ottoman Empire, mothers were often highly respected and sometimes enjoyed great power. Khayr al-Nisā' Begum not only gave birth to the future Shāh 'Abbās but also became extremely powerful on her own; as will be seen in the section on succession, for a time, she ruled the entire state.[101]

Moreover, in what constitutes explicit recognition of bilateral descent, in the Safavid Empire 'all male members of the family, *including those descending from the female line*, had in theory the right to the throne'.[102] Sons of princesses were called by royal titles and seen as part of the ruling family.[103] By educating their daughters as well as their sons, Safavids recognized that not only could females transmit their royal lineage to their progeny but also could themselves embody its ideals and virtues.[104] Though Turkic tradition may have influenced these practices, the empire's embracing of Shi'ism as its state religion (and the rulers' tracing of their heritage to the Prophet) may also have played a part, for it brought the family dynamics of the Prophet, 'Ali, Fatima and their descendants to the fore. In fact, similar to the Ottomans, Safavid chroniclers and poets called prominent royal females by titles such as 'the Fatima of the age' and associated these women with characteristics of the daughter of the Prophet such as radiance and chastity, indicating that Fatima al-Zahra was not far from peoples' minds.[105]

Similarly, Mughal emperors in India listed both paternal and maternal ancestors, daughters as well as sons in genealogies (in addition to wives and slave-concubines). In Bābur's memoirs, for example, the emperor (r. 1526–30) traced his lineage to the Mongolian conqueror Chinggiz Khān through his mother and to Timur (founder of the Timurid dynasty, which ruled much of Iran and Central Asia between the fourteenth and the sixteenth centuries) through his father.[106] Members of the royal family took care to marry within noble households, for a good lineage (whether from the male or female side) increased the likelihood of producing successful children.[107] Marriages were contracted in order to build 'connections with prestigious families' – another indication that women were able to represent and transmit their lineages.[108]

As with the Ottoman and Safavid empires, matrilineal ties feature prominently in this (Sunni) empire's founding story, although here they are perhaps even more pronounced. The scribe and statesman Abū al-Faḍl (d. 1602) interrupts a rather dry rehearsal of the distant male forebears of Emperor Akbar (r. 1556–1605) to wax eloquent about Ālanquwā, a princess whose story bears rather remarkable similarities to that of the Virgin Mary, as the author himself observes.[109] Beautiful and wise, Ālanquwā was married off at maturity to a cousin who was the king of Mughulistan. But since 'he was not her match, he hastened to annihilation and Her Majesty Ālanquwā who was the repose of the spiritual world, became likewise the ornament of the temporal world and … the sovereign of her tribe'.[110]

Then an even more unexpected event occurred. Ālanquwā was resting in bed one night when 'suddenly a glorious light cast a ray into the tent and entered the mouth and throat of that fount of spiritual knowledge and glory. The cupola of chastity became pregnant by that light in the same way as did her Majesty Miryam [Mary] the daughter of 'Imrān.'[111] She subsequently gave birth to triplets, one of whom was Būzanjar Qāān, the ancestor of Akbar. Abū al-Faḍl then resumes the list of subsequent patrilineal ancestors, but the point has been made: if Ālanquwā is Mary, Akbar, her 'son', is akin to Jesus, even if he must wait twenty-one generations to be born.

Indeed, Ālanquwā enjoys semi-divine qualities that place her on a rank similar to that of Mary. As Abū al-Faḍl writes, the 'lights of theosophy shone from her countenance, the Divine secrets were manifested on her forehead'.[112] Like Mary, she is particularly noted for her chastity; it can be assumed that it was for this virtue that she was chosen to receive the divine light. And Abū al-Faḍl makes an explicit connection between her, Akbar and Akbar's actual mother, Ḥamīda Bānū Begum (d. 1604), known by the epithet of 'Maryam-makānī' (Mary-makani). Ālanquwā's impregnation, he writes, marked 'the beginning of the manifestation of his Majesty, the king of kings, who after passing through divers stages was revealed to the world from the holy womb of her Majesty Maryam-makānī for the accomplishment of things visible and invisible'.[113] Graced with divine seed from several generations past, the holy womb of a third Mary, Akbar's biological mother, thus delivers its Jesus to the world in the form of the Mughal emperor. Once more, legitimacy resides in the female.

Though little connection with the Prophet's family appears in Abū al-Faḍl's recounting of the story of Ālanquwā, interestingly, in another version found on an inscription on the tomb of Timur in Samarqand, it is a son of ʿAli who impregnates the princess in the form of light.[114] The change is a significant one, for it weakens some of the prestige Ālanquwā possessed as the sole ancestor of her dynasty (with God or an angel as impregnator), ascribing it instead to the descendants of ʿAli (who, not coincidentally, occupied a hugely important role among the Timurids, great devotees of ʿAli).[115] The merging of these families eventually produces Timur, and, as with the other empires examined here, a dynasty that exhibits significant glimmers of bilateral descent.

Poetry and Sufism

Long before the Mughal Empire was established, the Indian poet Amīr Khusraw (d. 1325) summoned the spectre of Fatima as he identified daughters as progenitors of their fathers. Khusraw, a historian, musician and Sufi as well as a court poet, achieved lasting fame for weaving together Indic and Islamicate influences to form a new culture later known as Indo-Persian. Though forming only a small part of his voluminous oeuvre, his poems about and to daughters demonstrate that by the thirteenth century, echoes of the Islamic concept of bilateral descent – and, in particular, the model of Fatima as her father's mother – had reverberated as far as India. Judging from Khusraw's example – admittedly a small sample size – Sunnis were as likely as Shiʿis to embrace this concept, and non-royals as well as nobility. What is particularly interesting about these poems is the shifting, fluid nature of their attitude towards female offspring. In them, the poet consistently enquires into the status of daughters – are they better than, equal to or worse than sons? – and offers up very different answers, even within the same poem. From a perspective of structuralism, he raises daughters up only to cast them down, and then raises them up again. Likewise, in his hands, Aristotelian concepts of blood and semen are malleable categories that take on multiple shades of meaning. More than anything, his poems exemplify the inherent ambiguity of bilateral descent in medieval Islamic societies – its limits as well as its symbolic promise.

By the end of the thirteenth century, Khusraw was well established as a poet at the court of the Delhi Sultanate in northern India. His next step, designed to secure his place in history, was to compose a series of lengthy rhymed poems in imitation of the *khamsa* (quintet) of Niẓāmī Ganjavī (d. c. 1209), the great Persian poet who lived in what is present-day Azarbaijan. These poems often told romantic, colourful tales of bygone kings and queens, princes and princesses, adventurers and lovers. Like Niẓāmī, Khusraw included benedictions in his poems addressed to God, to the Prophet, to the king and to his spiritual mentor, the Sufi saint Niẓām al-Dīn Awliyāʾ. And like Niẓāmī, he directed a message in each poem to one of his children and filled it with admonitions and expressions of affection. Khusraw differed from Niẓāmī in that he addressed two of these messages to his daughter, Mastūra, rather than to one of his sons. As we will see, he voices a typical father's concern with his daughter's chastity and well-being, but also confirms her ability to carry on her lineage.

The first of these long poems, *Maṭlaʿ al-anwār* (*The Dawning-Place of the Lights*), completed in 1299, responded to Niẓāmī's *Makhzan al-asrār* (*Treasury of Mysteries*).[116] Khusraw dedicated the twentieth *maqāla*, or chapter, to Mastūra, then age seven, and spent most of it warning her to be chaste. But he also praised her qualities, openly professed his affection for her and predicted that he would be reborn through her. The poem opens:

O you, whose face is the light and lamp of my heart
 the best fruit of the garden of my heart (1)
Though your brothers are of good fortune
 they are not better than you, in my eyes (2)
The noble cypress and the lily
 are equal in the heart of the gardener (3)
If there is no daughter, how can a son appear?
 Without the beautiful oyster, how can the pearl appear? (4)
That luck which made you royal
 gave you the name, the fortunate Mastūra [lit., chaste or veiled] (5)
My hope is that with luck
 your name will gain luster from your behavior. (6)
But you must also strive so that from your doings
 You make straight the foundations of your name (7)
Your age is now seven; after age 17
 you will know what happiness is (8)

When you reach that age,
you will also renew my life. (9)
Live thusly, so that from your life
you'll bring to life your relatives (10)
So that, when my fallen body disintegrates
I'll be born from you, because I'm your child .... (11)[117]

In the very first hemistich, Khusraw introduces echoes of the relationship of the Prophet and Fatima, for as we have read in Chapter 1, the Prophet is said to have referred to Fatima as 'the light of my eye and the fruit of my heart'.[118] He likewise begins to make the case that even though daughters and sons are different – as different as the cypress and the lily – they are equally lovely and worthy of being beloved (2-3).

The next verses, however, destabilize the equilibrium. Here, Khusraw again points out the differences between daughters and sons – one is the oyster, the other is the pearl – but the pearl is manifestly superior to the oyster. The oyster, though beautiful, is valuable only in that it permits the pearl to emerge – a reference to the idea, popular in antiquity, that pearls resulted when a drop of dew or rain 'impregnated' an oyster and solidified.[119] Nevertheless, the female does contribute *something* to the equation by providing the safe harbour (or womb) in which the seed may develop. Khusraw continues to allude to the metaphor of the oyster, which hides its secrets, in the next verses, by challenging his daughter to live up to her name, 'Mastūra' – literally, chaste woman, also veiled, hidden, covered.

The unusual portion of the message follows. Telling Mastūra that she will know happiness after she turns seventeen – when, presumably, she will have married and given birth – Khusraw informs her that when she reaches that age, she will also rebirth him (probably through her children, possibly through her good reputation and deeds).[120] With this reference, Khusraw inevitably conjures up the Fatimid concept of *umm abīhā*, 'mother of her father', and similarly envisions Mastūra as capable of transmitting her natal lineage to her children.

In the remainder of the chapter, however, Khusraw delivers detailed instructions about what it means for a woman to live rightly: Mastūra must wear the veil, seclude herself and avoid makeup, mirrors and combs, because they are all forms of downfall for women. In this sense, from a twenty-first-century perspective at least, he demotes her once again to the status of a vessel that must be guarded from public view if it is to retain its value.

A similar dynamic occurs in Khusraw's *Hasht bihisht* (*Eight Paradises*), a poem completed in about 1302 in response to Niẓāmī's *Haft paykar* (*Seven Beauties*).[121] Widely regarded as the poet's masterpiece, *Hasht bihisht* recounts the adventures of the Sassanian king, Bahrām Gūr and, especially, his marriages to seven princesses from different regions.[122] Khusraw's message to his daughter, which appears as one of the opening chapters of the poem, sounds many of the same themes as his address to her in *Maṭla‘ al-anwār*, but develops them further. The message opens:[123]

O you over whom has been thrown a veil of light, from chastity
  'Afīfa in name, and also Mastūra (1)[124]
Your years have not reached more than seven[125]
  you are bright like a fourteen-day-old moon (2).
If only your moon were also in a well
  if only in the womb, you had been an eight-month child (3)
Yet since the bestowals of God are correct
  it is a sin to quarrel with what He has given (4)
I accept what God has given
  for what He gave, one cannot return (5)
...
After all, my father's of mother too;
  After all, my mother's a daughter too (6)
If the oyster veiled not the pearl, once more
  the watery drop, to water would turn. (7)
Can an unplanted seed bear any fruit?
  Can the sky be of use, without the ground? (8)
It's clear that one can be born without a father
  like the Messiah from the Virgin Mary (9)
But no one ever said a child was born
  without a mother of blessed existence (10)
O you, whose body is joined to my soul
  for you are both a mother to me, and a child (11)
You, in this rank that Fate has bestowed upon you
  if you place your foot on my eye, it is proper (12)
Lift your head by virtue of your lucky star
  for you are even more blessed than your origin. (13)[126]

In this highly complex poem, Khusraw – within the space of a few verses – both exalts and debases his daughter. After celebrating her bright, moon-like visage, the poet takes the ominous step of casting the moon into a well: wishing that she had been born an eight-month foetus, with no chance of survival (1–3).[127] He then accepts her existence, stating that whatever God gives must be good and, in any event, cannot be returned (4–5). In these verses, then, Mastūra begins in an exalted position, as the moon; falls to a debased position, wished dead in a well; and then arrives at an in-between station, as a burden (or gift) bestowed by God.

Khusraw then reconciles himself to his daughter's existence by stressing the necessity of female existence: were it not for mothers and daughters, neither he nor any other male would ever have been born (6). As in *Maṭlaʿ al-anwār*, he brings the metaphor of the oyster into play, which, when seeded with a drop of water, gives birth to the pearl. Without the womb in which to grow, semen would never form a child but would once more turn to water (7). To this conceit he adds the metaphors of females as earth or fields, men as the sky (8). In these typically Aristotelian images, women do play a necessary, but limited role, and are clearly inferior to men. Mothers provide the raw material – blood – for the making of a child and a safe harbour for its development. But it is men who provide the vital spark that fashions the blood into a child and endows it with its soul.

The poem then takes a new turn by introducing Mary and Jesus. Observing that the Messiah's conception proves that one can be born without a father, but not without a mother (see Qur'an 3:47 and 3:59), Khusraw dignifies females above males: no longer do they serve merely as the soil or a sheltering medium for the seed provided by a male, but can, with God's help, produce a child on their own.

It is then that Khusraw radically shifts gears, telling his daughter that she is both his mother *and* his daughter, and observing that he will be 'reborn' through her (11). These verses and those immediately following (12–13) subvert the original hierarchy: here the female's station exceeds the male's. It is appropriate if Khusraw prostrates himself before Mastūra and she steps on his eyes (a Persian expression indicating great respect). Her blessedness is greater than that of her father. The honour Khusraw indicates is owed to Mastūra echoes that shown by the Prophet to Fatima, who, as will be recalled, visited her first when he returned from trips and last before leaving – the honour shown by a child to a parent.

Yet, once again, Khusraw re-inverts the hierarchy, launching into a set of devastating restrictions for his daughter that essentially sentence her to a life in prison-like conditions.[128] In fact, his future rebirth through her requires, chillingly, the sacrifice of herself, as he makes clear later in the chapter:

Strive so that from killing your own youth
  you become a dead person to your life.
So that I, from your life, in secret
  return to life from death.[129]

These verses, echoing Qur'an 30:19 – 'He brings the living out of the dead and the dead out of the living' – confine Mastūra to the earth so that Khusraw may be resurrected.

A short poem from a much later collection, *Nihāyat al-kamāl*, completed not long before the poet's death in 1325, revisits the theme of daughters but casts them in a far less ambiguous light.[130] Here Khusraw, rather than equivocating, declares explicitly that daughters are better than sons:

The offspring of a son and the offspring of a daughter – both are descendants, without a doubt.
Since the Prophet's grandsons were born from his daughter, prefer descendants from a daughter.
[Even if] the son demonstrates some likeness [to his father], that doesn't hurt the right of the girl.
From the father there's only a drop of water; but see how much blood of the mother is in a child.
In short, a daughter is better than a son, for this one's from water, while that one is connected by blood.[131]

Khusraw begins the poem by making a controversial point: a grandchild born from either a son or a daughter belongs to the paternal lineage. Next, he reasons that since the Prophet's line continued through his daughter's sons, one should prefer grandsons produced by daughters to those produced by sons. He further justifies this stance by referring to Aristotelian-influenced medieval Muslim views on conception, but adapts them significantly to suit his argument. Since blood – the mother's contribution to generation – connects a child more powerfully to his parent than the father's contribution of semen (which is, after all, only 'a drop of water'), resemblance to the mother is stronger. Therefore, a grandson produced by a daughter will more closely resemble his maternal grandfather than a grandson produced by a son – and therefore, 'a daughter is better than a son'. In a departure from Aristotle's analysis, blood is the more substantial and influential contribution, and the one more capable of transmitting likeness.

It is difficult to know what factors induced Khusraw to embrace these views (assuming we can accept them as his own and not merely rhetorical arguments). As we will see in the chapter on succession, Delhi Sultanate India did foster a certain openness towards women and officials even accepted a female, Raḍiyya, as a sultan. Perhaps Khusraw's daughter, who would by then have been in her early twenties, had produced a grandson who resembled the poet more than offspring produced by his sons. Moreover, as a Sufi and a poet, Khusraw was accustomed to upending hierarchies (including hierarchies of gender) and confounding traditional expectations. His statements regarding the offspring of daughters, and daughters themselves, may simply reflect a larger tendency of subverting norms. Certainly they fit into the broader patterns of his work, in which Hindus take precedence over Turks, poets over scholars, Persian (and Hindi) over Arabic.[132]

The influence of Sufism, sometimes defined as the mystical branch of Islam, must be given particular weight. Sufism is not, as Sadiyya Shaikh has cogently observed, a panacea for sexism.[133] Many ugly attitudes towards women can be found in Sufi writings. Yet in many cases Sufism provided opportunities for women to flourish as devotees, saints and leaders of communities.[134] And while in some cases Sufis configured women and the feminine negatively in their poetry and other writing, elsewhere they depicted them in a positive light. For example, Sufis sometimes portrayed themselves as 'brides' yearning to unite with God, or figured God as a beloved, beautiful female towards which the male soul is striving – sometimes represented in idealized human form as Fatima or Mary.[135]

Sufi poets and saints also exhibited a marked tendency to explode the boundaries between men and women, or otherwise to de-emphasize gender as a determining marker of superiority or inferiority – a matter with striking implications for Khusraw's attitudes. The body, whether male or female, is of less importance than one's inner state.[136] Thus the Sufi poet 'Aṭṭār (d. c. 1220) wrote, in defence of including Rābiʿa, an eminent woman, in his biography of saints, 'The Prophet himself said, "God does not regard your outward forms. … When a woman becomes a 'man' in the path of God, she is a man and one cannot any more call her a woman."'[137] The category of 'man', here, refers not to a particular gender but rather to those who strive sincerely on the path of God.[138] Elsewhere the same poet says, evocatively, 'A woman will become a man, a man/A sea whose depths no mortal mind may scan.'[139] According to these verses, a woman is able to transform herself into a fully realized spiritual being – a 'man'. A woman may also 'become' a man by giving birth to a son. The boundaries separating male and female fade and sometimes disappear altogether.

Centuries earlier, the martyred Sufi saint Manṣūr al-Ḥallāj (d. 922) gave voice to similar ideas when he wrote:

> My mother gave her father birth
> which was a marvel I perceived
> And my own daughters whom I made
> became my sisters in this way to me.[140]

The author 'perceives' his mother giving birth to her father through his own birth, indicating that he is a reproduction of his grandfather. By this logic, he is brought to the same level as his daughters. The poem explicitly recognizes that a daughter is able to carry on her father's lineage, and likewise demonstrates the sort of playfulness with gendered hierarchies that frequently marks literature written by Sufis, including that of Khusraw.[141]

Finally, it is worth noting that many Sufi brotherhoods held the family of the Prophet in very high esteem and even traced their lineages to them, including, in some instances, to Fatima herself. Some groups placed her in the role of *quṭb*, the very apex of the hierarchy of saints.[142] Most Sufi genealogies, however, including that of the Chishtiyya, to which Khusraw belonged, identified 'Ali as the first conveyer of Sufism from the Prophet.[143] Moreover, the cloak with which the Prophet invested his family, including Fatima, transformed into an important symbol within Sufism; initiates typically received cloaks from their masters in a physical representation of the transmission of spiritual ability.[144] Khusraw, who must have received a cloak of his own from his master, would have been well aware of these matters and likely subscribed to many of them. In any event, he clearly found the concept of Fatima as conveyer of her father's lineage a compelling one.

Legal texts

Last but hardly least, legal scholars deliberated bilateral descent, with some throwing their weight solidly behind it. In his discussions of filiation in his work of *fiqh*, or jurisprudence, *Kitāb al-mabsūṭ*, the prominent Hanafi jurist

Muhammad ibn Aḥmad al-Sarakhsī (d. ca. 1090) gives clear indications that children belong to both parents, and that ascribing children to their mothers in addition to their fathers benefits them.[145] For example, in a case where a child is left without a maternal filiation because of contested claims to it, al-Sarakhsī rules that it is his right to claim it when he becomes older, even if he already has paternal filiation, for 'if his *nasab* is [also] established to his mother, he will be noble on both sides (*karīm al-ṭarafayn*)'.[146]

Al-Sarakhsī deploys similar arguments in cases where a man has successfully defeated a paternity claim due to adultery, but then wishes to re-establish lineage ties after the child has died in order to inherit from his or her estate. Ordinarily, the jurist rejects this attempt, except if the deceased child himself (or herself) had offspring.[147] In those cases, it is useful for the grandchildren to have that affiliation, so the *nasab* is admitted. It is done so uncontroversially when the original (now deceased) child was male. Things get muddier when the original child was female. Two students of the renowned jurist Abū Ḥanīfa al-Nuʿmān (d. 767), as al-Sarakhsī acknowledges, deny lineage in those cases, for the remaining child's '*nasab* is through his father and not through his mother'.[148] But, al-Sarakhsī continues, 'Abū Ḥanīfa said: the absence of maternal *nasab* reviles (*yataʿayyar*) the child, just like the absence of the paternal *nasab* reviles the child. Thus, the child needs the establishment of his maternal *nasab*, so that he can become noble on both sides (*karīm al-ṭarafayn*).'[149] Here, al-Sarakhsī – in contrast to Abū Ḥanīfa's students – strikes a decisive blow in favour of bilateral descent. Like Amīr Khusraw, he connects offspring to their paternal and maternal grandfathers, and supports rulings that recognize this affiliation.

Similar disputes arose in legal texts over the status of the *ashrāf*, or descendants of the Prophet, usually through ʿAli.[150] Some legal scholars said that the son of the marriage of a female *sharīf* with a non-*sharīf* was not a *sharīf* – that is, that a female could not transmit her noble status. Others, however, disagreed – once more indicating that patrilineal practices were by no means universal in pre-modern Islamic societies.[151]

Conclusion

The sampling of genres investigated here demonstrates that pre-modern Muslim scholars and poets of many stripes acknowledged bilateral descent, and often invoked the Prophet and Fatima when doing so. From biographers to historians to hadith collectors, from litterateurs to legal scholars, people writing in far-flung parts of the Islamic world envisioned women as well as men as capable of transmitting their lineages to their offspring. Factors influencing this acknowledgement may have included political expediency, Sufi tendencies and a sense of propriety and fairness. Recognition of matrilineal descent by no means automatically translated into egalitarian conditions for women and their offspring; ambiguity often blurred or dampened the recognition, diminishing its practical implications.[152] For example, even though Khusraw saw his daughter as capable of carrying on his lineage, and in some cases, as occupying a station above his, he nevertheless prescribed for her a drastically curtailed existence. And children in many Muslim-majority countries were (and in some cases still are) seen as legally belonging to their fathers – a matter that often had deleterious effects upon societies, especially in cases of divorce. What did seem to accompany such acknowledgement was an often-romantic sense of women as noble legitimators in the mould of Mary and Fatima. They inherited their natal identities – in many cases, depicted as a sort of radiance – and transmitted them to their offspring. Though the benefits it provided may have been intangible ones in the past, this conception nevertheless stood as a forceful rejoinder to the image of women as inferior and defective. Today, it harbours within it the potential to be translated into more material gains for women – and societies as a whole.

Part Two

Heiresses

3

Heiress to the Prophet

Fatima, Fadak and female inheritance

Dust in the jaws of the ʿaṣaba

(Attributed to Jaʿfar al-Ṣādiq)[1]

Carving out a more prominent place for daughters

Not long after the death of her father, Fatima, daughter of the Prophet, covered her head with her veil and left her home, accompanied by a group of her female friends and family members. Walking exactly in the manner of her father, her robes trailing on the ground, she approached the spot where Abū Bakr, the caliph, was seated among a crowd of Emigrants and Helpers. She groaned in sadness, causing those gathered to burst into tears. When their agitation had quieted, she delivered an impassioned sermon that castigated the Muslim community and its leaders on several counts. Satan had duped them, Fatima said, into acting against the teachings of the Prophet, presumably by usurping the caliphate from ʿAli, its proper possessor. Avowedly seeking to avoid sedition, they had fallen into it instead, and were, in effect, stabbing the members of the Prophet's household with sharp daggers. Moreover, by depriving her of a piece of property, Fadak, that she had inherited from her father, Muslims were transgressing the laws of the Qur'an and placing the Book of God behind their backs – a devastating charge indeed.[2]

'Is it in the Book that you inherit from your father and I do not inherit from my father?' Fatima asked sarcastically. 'You have certainly done a thing unprecedented. So go ahead and take it [Fadak] like a bridled and saddled camel that will meet you on the Day of Gathering.'[3]

The occasion precipitating Fatima's khutba, as it has become known, was Abū Bakr's decision to deny the Prophet's daughter her claim to Fadak, an ancient oasis town about two or three days' journey from Medina.[4] Inhabited by a colony of Jewish agriculturalists, and producing dates and cereals as well as handicrafts such as woven blankets with palm-leaf borders, Fadak had come under Muslim control after a series of expeditions launched by the Prophet beginning in about 627.[5] Frightened by news of his victories, the Jews of Fadak made a pact with the Prophet in which they were allowed to 'remain in Fadak while giving up half their lands and half the produce of the oasis'.[6] This produce was allocated to the Prophet, who gave the revenues of it to needy travellers.[7]

After the Prophet's death, and after Abū Bakr had become the first caliph over the protests of those who supported 'Ali, different parties laid claim to it.[8] Fatima argued she had inherited it from her father.[9] According to other accounts, she said that the Prophet had given it to her as a gift before his death.[10] Al-'Abbās, a paternal uncle, said it rightly belonged to him as a member of the *'aṣaba*, or male agnate relatives.[11] Meanwhile, Abū Bakr said that it belonged to the treasury of the Islamic state and was to be distributed to the poor and needy.[12] Traditions (disputed by Shi'is) say the Prophet had stated that he 'would have no heirs … what he left would be *ṣadaḳa*' – public property used for charity.[13] Abū Bakr famously quoted the Prophet as saying, '*lā nūrathu, mā taraknāhu ṣadaqatun*' – 'No one inherits from us [prophets]; what we leave is for charity.'[14] In her khutba, Fatima vehemently challenged that assertion, noting that several prophets had designated inheritances for their heirs.[15]

Bilateral descent does not manifest solely in the recognition that a woman's children belong to her and her natal family as well as to that of her husband. It also appears in her ability (and, consequently, the ability of her children) to inherit from her family of birth. Enormously fraught and complex, the subject of inheritance is also enormously important, for the ability to inherit from her natal family invests a woman with stature and agency, and provides her with autonomy she may otherwise lack. Significantly, just as they portrayed her as able to receive and transmit her lineage, pre-modern Shi'i scholars envisioned Fatima as deserving to inherit tangible things such as land. Though political and spiritual leadership, not gender egalitarianism, were likely foremost in these scholars' minds, their attitudes nevertheless led to benefits for women in the form of more favourable inheritance schemes for daughters and their offspring, and maternal relatives in general. This chapter discusses inheritance in patrilineal societies and Sunni attitudes towards inheritance before turning to an examination of Shiʿi attitudes. It pays particular attention to portrayals of Fatima's claim to Fadak. This claim, as will be seen, exerted a huge influence upon Shiʿi inheritance laws – an influence allowing property and money as well as blood to move along female lines, and thus carving out a larger role for females in the structure of the family. Acknowledgement of the implications of such understandings has powerful ramifications for today, when unequal inheritance practices persist in both Shiʿi and Sunni-majority countries.

The stark patrilineal model

In their starkest forms – forms in which they probably have never existed – patrilineal societies afford women no rights to inherit from their family of birth. If a woman, upon marriage, no longer belongs to her family of birth, how can she receive money or property from them? She no longer exists; her identity disappears into that of her husband. Even in cases in which a woman retains her natal identity, her inability to project it prevents her from inheriting, since these valuable possessions would slip from the hands of the natal family. Rather, she herself is property that can be handed on to another. As Simone de Beauvoir writes, speaking in a general sense,

> If she could inherit, she would ... wrongly transmit her paternal family's riches to that of her husband: [so] she is carefully excluded from the succession. But inversely, because she owns nothing, woman is not raised to the dignity of a person; she herself is part of a man's patrimony, first her father's and then her husband's.[16]

Patrilineality in its starkest form, then, implies the 'transmission of economic resources along the male line' – a transmission that can include women themselves.[17] It privileges the male agnatic relatives – uncles, brothers, grandfathers, sons descended from the same male ancestor – and envisions the most important kinship ties in terms of the larger tribe, rather than what we would call today the nuclear family comprising parents and their children, both male and female.

Land is a potent symbol in inheritance schemes; women's relationship to it is consequently an uneasy one. Keeping the land belonging to a tribe intact is of paramount importance. It constitutes the family holding, the property upon which it bases its identity. It may even hold the 'tomb of [a tribe's] eponymous ancestor … to symbolize the appropriation of the soil by his lineage'.[18] Land is therefore one of the things that is particularly withheld from women in rigid patrilineal schemes, especially women who marry outside the tribe, for women 'as heirs alienate property from the agnatic group by passing it to the husband and his children'.[19] Instead, in the strictest patrilineal schemes females themselves constitute fields or parcels of land: they can be purchased, owned, fertilized and sown, and the fruits of their soil belong not to them but to those who plant the seeds and reap the harvests.[20]

Inheritance and the advent of Islam

These concepts and themes echo throughout the history of inheritance laws in Islam – a history that, in many ways, plays out as a rhetorical drama featuring a tug of war between the rights of the male agnates – known as the *'aṣaba* – and the rights of daughters and their offspring.[21]

Female inheritance features in the writings of many Qur'an commentators, including al-Ṭabarī and al-Rāzī, and the image they paint of pre-Islamic society is one that conforms to a rigid patrilineal model.[22] Not only could women of the *jāhiliyya* not inherit but they themselves were also property to be inherited – a reality acknowledged in hadith as well as in Qur'anic legislation stating: 'O believers, it is not lawful for you to inherit women against their will.' (4:19)[23] Inheritance was limited to the 'active, male members of the tribe' – those who fought, managed families and protected property, and seized booty – in a system 'designed to keep property within the individual tribe and maintain its strength as a fighting force'.[24]

Not only did females not inherit from their natal families but their children (both male and female) were also excluded. According to these accounts, the inheritance almost always went to the male agnate relatives – a group that included brothers, paternal cousins and uncles, fathers and paternal grandfathers. As the contemporary scholar Coulson observes,

> Women occupied a subordinate and subjugated position within the group whose bond of allegiance was that of *'asabiyya* – descent through male links from a common ancestor. A woman who married into another tribe belonged henceforth, along with her children, to the tribe of her husband. The

> maternal or uterine relationship, therefore, lay outside the structure of tribal ties and responsibilities. In these circumstances the proper exploitation and preservation of the tribal patrimony mean, *inter alia*, the exclusion of females and non-agnate relatives from inheritance and the enjoyment of a monopoly of rights of succession by the male agnate relatives, or *'aṣaba*, of the deceased.[25]

Indeed, the Qur'an itself substantiates this image with its evocative depictions of the ways in which women – particularly daughters – were devalued by the pre-Islamic Arabs, who burned with shame when a daughter was born and sometimes buried infant girls alive (see Qur'an 43:17–18; 81:8–9). Girls – who were 'brought up amongst trinkets' and could not 'put together a clear argument', much less fight – counted for little.

According to the commentators, the Qur'an transformed this patrilineal system in designating both men and women as inheritors and specifically assigning shares to them – thus recognizing the 'capacity of women relatives to succeed'.[26] As another consequence (not necessarily one noted by these commentators, but by later scholars), it also effected a structural change in society and family, one in which the 'individual family ... replaced the tribe as the basic unit' – and weakened the power of the *'aṣaba*.[27]

Yet male believers also vigorously resisted the new laws, if we are to believe the commentators' reports.[28] The first verses revealed on this subject (Qur'an 2:180 and 2:240) 'encourage men to leave legacies for, *inter alia*, mothers and wives'.[29] However, not everyone listened. A widow, Umm Kuḥḥa, complained to the Prophet in 624 that her husband's paternal cousin had seized the inheritance, leaving none for her and her daughter. The cousin justified himself by saying, 'O Messenger of God, she does not ride a horse, manage a family, or wound an enemy. *She is acquired but does not acquire.*'[30] It was then that Qur'an 4:7, which clearly states that 'men shall have a share in what their parents and closest relatives leave, and women shall have a share in what their parents and closest relatives leave, whether the legacy be small or large: this is ordained by God', was revealed.[31] That verse, as Powers notes, 'establishes that both men and women are entitled to inherit. But this verse still fails to specify the exact entitlement of females, and soon after God revealed Qur'an 4:11–12, which award specific shares of the estate to daughters, mothers, sisters, and wives'.[32] The verses read, in part,

> Concerning your children, God commands you that a son should have the equivalent share of two daughters. If there are only daughters, more than

> two should share two-thirds of the inheritance, if one, she should have half. Parents inherit a sixth each if the deceased leaves children; if he leaves no children and his parents are his sole heirs, his mother has a third, unless he has brothers, in which case she has a sixth.

Other men also fought the new laws, sometimes in creative ways. The commentators document cases of widows who complained to the Prophet because their stepsons wanted to inherit them in the traditional pre-Islamic fashion, or men who were angry that 'women and children, who do not work and do not earn their living', would inherit.[33] As Mernissi writes, early Muslims

> began first of all by rejecting these new laws, wishing to continue to apply the customs of the jahiliyya despite their conversion to Islam. Then they complained to the Prophet and tried to put pressure on him to change the laws. Finally, in desperation, they took to interpreting the text as a means of escaping it.[34]

Indeed, in his commentary on the Qur'an, al-Ṭabarī addresses interpretations of a Qur'anic verse, 4:5, 'Do not entrust your property to the feebleminded. God has made it a means of support for you: make provision from it, clothe them, and speak to them kindly,' which try to deprive women of their rights.[35] As Mernissi observes, some early believers interpreted the Arabic word for 'feebleminded' (or, in Pickthall's translation, the 'foolish'), *sufahā'*, to mean 'women and children' – and as giving them leeway to exclude them from inheritance.[36] Al-Ṭabarī himself comes to the conclusion that *sufahā'* does not specifically designate women, proving it grammatically.[37] As we will see, the resistance – and attempt to give precedence to the *'aṣaba* over female relatives – continued, but took other shapes.

Contemporary scholars such as Powers have attempted to cast doubt upon these accounts of inheritance in pre- and early Islamic Arabia and to argue, for example, that the stories explaining the Qur'anic revelations – given their inconsistencies – are an unreliable basis for understanding how Islamic law took shape.[38] Other scholars have likewise attempted to complicate the idea of pre-Islamic Arabia as a monolithically patrilineal society in which inheritance was utterly denied to women. For example, the contemporary scholar Leila Ahmed points to the wealth of Khadīja, the first wife of the Prophet, as evidence that 'women's inheritance … may have been a custom in Mecca'.[39] Without entering into all of the arguments, given that matrilineal practices likely existed in pre-Islamic Arabia, it is probable that female inheritance also existed at least to some degree. Yet it is also very likely that patrilineal practices dominated and that early believers resisted changes to inheritance laws, even if their resistance did not take the exact shape outlined by the commentators.

Attempts to defy these injunctions continued after the time of the Prophet, as did the tension between the rights of the *'aṣaba* and the rights of female members of the deceased family. One way to deprive daughters of their rights involved bureaucratic sleight of hand that diverted property from daughters to trusts (waqfs), where it could be kept in perpetuity, or distributed to a male heir.[40] Technically, then, the testators obey the Qur'an, but they violate the spirit of the law. In fact, some scholars have identified the undermining of Muslim inheritance laws as the 'main reason for the early rise and rapid spread of waqfs' – and note that this institution continues to be used for this reason today.[41]

Even when family members did not resort to creating endowments, some pressured daughters into renouncing their inheritance rights, especially to land, or the daughters themselves might feel expected to do so, despite the Qur'anic laws. Such renunciation kept land from passing outside the paternal family and ensured the 'unity of the holding'.[42] (The laws also helped encourage endogamy, in which paternal cousins married, as a means of keeping land within families).[43] In exchange, a daughter might receive partial compensation from her birth family in the form of gifts, or promise of support in the case of divorce or widowhood.[44] These practices continue today. In Jabal Nablus, for example,

> A daughter in a small property-owning household often prefers to give up her share in the estate in order to reaffirm and strengthen her ties with her brothers. … By not claiming her share, a woman enhances the status of her brothers … and accentuates their obligation toward her, as they are in a position of owing their sister. If, in contract, a woman demands her share in the estate, she may receive this, but then is often no longer able to invoke her brother's help and support, which in turn undermines her position vis-à-vis her husband.[45]

Inheritance in Sunni and Shi'i law

The laws of inheritance that developed within the four major Sunni schools likewise inhibit, to a certain degree, the rights of daughters and their offspring. These laws acknowledge not only the heirs mentioned in the Qur'an – known as the *ahl al-farā'id*, or literally, 'those entitled to prescribed portions' (here I will simply call them, after Coulson, the 'Qur'anic heirs') – but also another category of heirs – the *'aṣaba*, or agnate relatives of the deceased, who would receive the 'remains of shares after the distribution to heirs that are stipulated by the Qur'an'.[46] This scheme sometimes meant that a daughter or a daughter's son would receive less than they might have were the *'aṣaba* not recognized. This matter has led some scholars (particularly Shi'i and those disposed to view Shi'ism favourably) to argue that Sunni systems and practices diverge from the intent of the Qur'an and that under Sunni law, women did not receive their due. The contemporary scholar Liyakat Takim, for example, sees this system as a throwback to 'pre-Islamic customary tribal laws' which emphasize the rights of the male agnates and the 'tribal concept of an extended family'.[47]

To be sure, Sunni laws delivered benefits to female relatives that they otherwise would have lacked. Women *did* inherit, and (if we accept the accounts of commentators such as al-Ṭabarī) they inherited more than they would have in pre-Islamic times.[48] Sunni law added the (maternal and paternal) grandmothers and the agnatic granddaughter to the list of Qur'anic heirs even though these women were not specifically mentioned as such in the Qur'an.[49] Females could even be considered members of the *'aṣaba*, as long as they belonged to the paternal side of the family.[50] Even waqfs, those instruments purportedly developed to deprive women of their inheritances, could be turned to their benefit; as will be shown in Chapter 4, some women endowed waqfs, using them to promote their own charitable projects and personas or to benefit their children, both male and female.

Moreover, some scholars see evidence in the Qur'an and hadith to support the claims of the *'aṣaba*. For example, the Qur'an's granting of double the shares to a son versus a daughter (see 4:11–12) indicates to some that the text does not intend to discard the male agnatic system entirely but 'merely to modify it, with the particular objective of improving the position of female relatives, by superimposing upon the male agnates an additional class of new heirs'.[51] Likewise, Sunni scholars cite a hadith in which the Prophet says, 'Give the *farā'id* [the shares of the inheritance that are prescribed in the Quran] to those who are entitled to receive it. Then whatever remains, should be given to the closest male relative of the deceased.'[52]

In theory if not in practice, however, Shi'ism sweeps many of these qualifications aside to feature daughters and their offspring much more prominently. Shi'ism treats male and female relatives more equally, and places a greater emphasis on closeness to the deceased, or *qaraba*, in determining rights of inheritance, thus privileging the nuclear or immediate family over the extended 'tribal' (and patrilineal) family, and 'collateral' relatives such as brothers and sisters.[53] Twelver Shi'i laws also recognize descent from both daughters and sons to a far greater degree than do Sunni – a practice that can be traced directly to Fatima.

To recapitulate, in Sunni law after all shares delegated by the Qur'an have been distributed, the remainder goes first to the agnates, relatives of the male line. In Shi'i law, however, after the distribution of the property to the Qur'anic heirs, both male and female relatives, from male *and* female lines, have the right of inheritance.[54] Moreover, in Sunni law, 'collateral' male relatives – such as the grandfather of the deceased, or an even more distant male relative – will sometimes nibble away at a daughter's claim. If there is only a daughter and no sons, for example, the daughter may still only receive a daughter's share, and the rest will go to agnates, even distant ones. In Shi'ism, she gets it all.[55]

The Shi'i defiance of the *'aṣaba* is encapsulated in a remark attributed to Ja'far al-Ṣādiq, the sixth imam, who is 'alleged to have peremptorily dismissed [the claims of the male agnate relatives] with the remark: "Dust in the jaws of the *'aṣaba*."'[56] Likewise, when asked who would inherit if a man died and left behind a daughter and a brother, Mūsā al-Kāẓim reportedly replied, 'The legacy belongs to his daughter.'[57]

To present a hypothetical contemporary case that will help to illustrate this concept, let us assume that a deceased has left behind $100,000, and that his remaining relatives are a paternal grandfather, a wife and a daughter. Under Sunni law, the paternal grandfather will claim $37,500 (3/8), the wife $12,500 (1/8) and the daughter $50,000 (1/2). Under Shi'i law, the paternal grandfather will receive nothing, the wife will still receive $12,500 (1/8) and the daughter will receive $87,500 (7/8) – a substantially larger proportion (see Table 3.1).[58]

Most significantly for our purposes, the sons of daughters, often excluded by distant male relatives by Sunni law, fare better under Shi'i. Let us again assume that the deceased leaves behind $100,000, but this time his remaining relatives are a paternal uncle, a uterine brother (i.e. a brother by the same mother but different fathers), and a daughter's son. Under Sunni law, the uncle would

Table 3.1 Inheritance Divisions for Deceased Who Leaves Behind a Paternal Grandfather, a Wife and a Daughter

Total inheritance to be distributed: $100,000	Sunni law ($)	Twelver Shiʿi law ($)
Paternal grandfather	37,500	0
Wife	12,500	12,500
Daughter	50,000	87,500

Table 3.2 Inheritance Divisions for Deceased Who Leaves Behind a Paternal Uncle, a Uterine Brother and a Daughter's Son

Total inheritance to be distributed: $100,000	Sunni law ($)	Twelver Shiʿi law ($)
Paternal uncle	83,333	0
Uterine brother	16,666	0
Daughter's son	0	100,000

receive a generous $83,333 (5/6), the brother $16,666 (1/6) and the daughter's son – nothing. Under Shiʿi law, the entire inheritance of $100,000 would go to the daughter's son (see Table 3.2).[59] Thus we can see how Shiʿi laws of inheritance envision kinship lines to allow greater recognition of propagation and perpetuation through daughters and their offspring.

To be sure, Shiʿi law hardly advocated full gender equality. Under it, daughters and other females still inherited less than males – generally one-half.[60] Most interestingly, Muhammad al-Bāqir, the fifth imam, and his son and successor, Jaʿfar al-Ṣādiq, reportedly prohibited women from inheriting land or fixed property such as houses.[61] Instead, the imams directed, a man's property should be appraised and the woman should receive her share in a liquid form. When asked for the reason, Jaʿfar al-Ṣādiq declared that the woman did not belong to the lineage. If she married and had children, she would 'spoil the legacy of the heirs'.[62]

What are we to make of this injunction, which seems to run counter to everything analysed thus far about women and lineage in Shiʿism? A close reading of the hadith – which appear in several versions, each of which differs slightly from the next – reveals that they apparently refer to widows, not to all women. For example, one version of it, cited from Muhammad al-Bāqir, reads: 'A woman does not inherit anything of the towns, houses, arms … that *her husband* leaves behind.'[63] Another reads, 'A woman does not inherit from the legacy of *her husband* in the form of land of his house or land.'[64] This provision would make a great deal more sense than if the hadith also applied to daughters, who clearly were seen as belonging to their fathers' lineages.[65]

The Isma'ili scholar Abū Ḥanīfa al-Qāḍī al-Nu'mān (d. 974), a leading jurist of the Fatimid Empire, likewise rejected the supposed prohibition on women inheriting land, averring that the report's apparent meaning 'contradicts the Book of God, the sunna, and the consensus of the opinions of the imams and the community'.[66] He maintained that a brief explanation must have been missing. Then he supplied it. The report, he asserted, referred only to certain lands which had been endowed as waqfs specifically for men and not for women; thus, in those special cases, women were 'only entitled to their share when liquidated'. 'As for land that is the private property of the deceased', al-Qāḍī al-Nu'mān continued, 'women have a share in it just as God has said. This is the only lawful course.'[67]

The Fatima connection

The semi-egalitarianism of Shi'i laws – and the emphasis placed on female inheritance by scholars such as al-Qāḍī al-Nu'mān – derived at least partly from Fatima's stature within the family of the Prophet. Given that Shi'is hold Hasan and Husayn and their descendants as the rightful political and spiritual successors to the Prophet and 'Ali, it followed that Fatima and her children should receive precedence in inheritance schemes.[68] In particular, the claim made by Fatima for Fadak symbolized many of these matters for Shi'is and, in many cases, acted as a catalyst for inheritance laws.

The history of Fadak is a tortured one. Shi'is and Sunnis alike tell many different versions of its dispossession, some varying in just a few details, some in many.[69] The property itself apparently changed hands a multitude of times. This discussion, while acknowledging the complexity of the issue, aims to highlight those elements that relate to female inheritance. One of most straightforward versions of the story – and one that brings the issues of inheritance to the fore – appears in al-Ṭabarī's *Tārīkh* in an account attributed to 'Ā'isha:

> Fāṭimah and al-'Abbās came to Abū Bakr demanding their [share of] inheritance of the messenger of God. They were demanding the Messenger of God's land in Fadak and his share of Khaybar['s tribute]. Abū Bakr replied,

> 'I have heard the messenger of God say: "Our [i.e. the prophets' property] cannot be inherited and whatever we leave behind is alms [i.e. to be given in charity]. The family of Muhammad will eat from it." By God, I will not abandon a course which I saw the messenger of God practicing, but will continue doing it accordingly.' Fāṭimah shunned him and did not speak to him about it until she died. 'Alī buried her at night and did not permit Abū Bakr to attend [her burial].[70]

Indeed, 'Ali was reportedly so incensed over Abū Bakr's treatment of his wife that he withheld the oath of allegiance to the caliph until after Fatima's death.[71]

Other versions of the story bring different details to light. In one, Fatima justified her claim to Fadak by saying that it was not an inheritance, but that the Prophet had given it to her as a gift before his death; she brought both 'Ali and Umm Ayman, the Prophet's wet-nurse, as witnesses. Abū Bakr refused this testimony based upon the Qur'anic rules requiring two males or a male and two females.[72] In another, instead of responding '*lā nūrathu*', Abū Bakr reported that he heard the Prophet say, 'This is but something assigned by God as a means of subsistence to use during my life; on my death it should be turned over to the Muslims.'[73] The upshot in most cases was the same, however: Abū Bakr (or, in some cases, 'Umar) denied it to Fatima and her family, and she and her supporters were outraged.

The battle over Fadak did not end with the demise of Fatima. As we have already seen in al-Ṭabarī's version of the story, al-'Abbās, the Prophet's paternal uncle, apparently also laid claim to the property after the Prophet's death. That he continued to do so during the reign of 'Umar, the second caliph, is evidenced by accounts related by the Sunni scholar Yāqūt al-Hamawī (d. 1229), who reported that al-'Abbās and 'Ali brought their dispute to the caliph. "Ali', the scholar wrote, 'said that the Prophet had bestowed it on Fatima during his life time. Al-'Abbās denied it and said, "This was in the possession of the Prophet, and I am his heir."'[74] The caliph refused to judge between them, saying, 'You are more knowledgeable about your family affairs, so I am giving it to both of you.'[75]

This story illustrates the tug of war between agnatic and cognatic claims on inheritance, or claims between paternal relatives and immediate descendants, including females. By laying claim to Fadak on behalf of Fatima, 'Ali asserted his belief in a cognatic system that recognizes the rights of the female (even though he introduced the notion of a gift), whereas al-'Abbās favoured the agnatic system that privileges and gives a share to paternal male relatives, even distant ones.

Meanwhile, Fadak's fate hung in the balance. Over the next few centuries, the property (or administrative rights over it) continued to change hands between many parties, including the ʿAlids and the *ʿaṣaba*. The ʿAbbāsids – descendants, of course, of al-ʿAbbās – took very different positions on the property, reflecting their varying attempts to both conciliate and repress the ʿAlids, whom they regarded as threats.[76] The first caliph, al-Saffāḥ (r. 750–4), returned Fadak to Fatima's descendants; but his successor, al-Manṣūr, no doubt prompted by the rebellion of al-Nafs al-Zakiyya and his brother, Ibrāhīm, re-confiscated it for the ʿAbbāsids.[77] After a few more changes of hand under succeeding leaders, the caliph al-Ma'mūn, known for his attempts at conciliation, once more restored the property to the descendants of Fatima.[78] The account of the ninth-century historian and geographer Aḥmad ibn Abū Yaʿqūb, known as al-Yaʿqūbī, shows the caliph debating the matter at length with the descendants of Fatima and with experts in jurisprudence:

> A group of descendants of Hasan and Husayn petitioned al-Maʿmūn, mentioning that the Prophet gave Fatima Fadak as an endowment, and that she asked Abū Bakr to return it to her after the death of the Prophet. He [Abū Bakr] asked her to bring witnesses for her claim, and she brought ʿAli, Hasan, Husayn and Umm Ayman. Al-Maʿmūn brought forth scholars and asked them about the incident. They agreed [on the particulars of the claim and the witnessing], but that Abū Bakr rejected their witness. Then al-Maʿmūn asked [the scholars]: 'What is your view about Umm Ayman?' They replied: 'She is a woman of whom the Prophet bore witness that she is an inhabitant of Paradise.' Al-Maʿmūn talked about the matter for a long time and forced them to accept the arguments put forth by proofs until they confessed that ʿAli, Hasan, Husayn and Umm Ayman had witnessed only the truth. With this agreement, he restored Fadak to the descendants of Fatima.[79]

This account represents yet another iteration of the version of the story in which Fatima brought forth witnesses to support her claim. Here, the testimony is clearly sufficient since far more than the two witnesses required are present; moreover, Umm Ayman – a woman – is celebrated as an inhabitant of Paradise, whose testimony must be regarded as acceptable. The Shiʿi poet Diʿbil al-Khuzāʿī (d. 860) commemorated the caliph's surrender of Fadak with a poem that began: 'The face of time smiled, when Maʿmūn gave back Fadak to the Hāshimites.'[80] Yet Fadak was to continue to change hands between the 'Alids and the 'Abbāsids for many more years – a potent symbol of, among other things, shifting visions of family structure and the rights of women within it.[81]

Fatima's khutba

As can be seen from the above accounts, Shiʿi-allied scholars who wrote about Fadak did so in a way that clearly sympathized with Fatima's claim to the property against those of the *ʿaṣaba* or others who would seek to deprive her of it – a move that ran parallel to the (relatively) gender-egalitarian inheritance laws jurists were formulating. Along the same lines, beginning in the ninth century, scholars – both Sunni and Shiʿi – began to report accounts of an impassioned speech given by Fatima in which she drew on Qur'anic principles to assert her right to Fadak. Fatima's khutba exerted a significant impact on Islamic history for a number of reasons, prominent among them the fact that in it, the daughter of the Prophet herself eloquently made the case for her stature within her family and her ability to inherit – and, by extension, that of other daughters.

While several sources present iterations of Fatima's khutba,[82] the earliest extant version appears to be that contained in the work by the Baghdadi litterateur Abū al-Faḍl ibn Abī Ṭāhir Ṭayfūr (d. 893), *Balāghāt al-nisā'* (the Eloquence of Women).[83] This account actually comprises two versions differing somewhat in their *isnāds* and content; most later sources cite the second version, which, according to a notation within it, is intended to include the first.[84] In the first, shorter version, after arriving at the gathering of Abū Bakr, the Emigrants and Helpers, Fatima begins her speech by praising God and remembering the abject state in which the Arabs lived before the coming of the Prophet.[85] She reminds her audience of how the Prophet defeated polytheism and the 'Arab wolves and the rebellious of the People of the Book'.[86] She lauds 'Ali as the defender of the faith and notes that after the Prophet's death, the Muslims have returned to their evil ways.[87] She criticizes them for their usurping of the caliphate and of Fadak, and warns them that an evil day awaits them.[88] She concludes by addressing a mournful poem to her father's tomb, an act provoking great weeping among those gathered.[89]

In the second version, Fatima likewise begins by praising God, elaborating at greater length upon His attributes.[90] God sent Muhammad, she says, 'as a fulfillment of His mandate, a means of implementing His decree'.[91] She informs the crowd that they are 'the servants of God, appointed to enforce His commands and prohibitions, the bearers of His religion and revelation, entrusted by God to keep yourselves virtuous, His messengers to the nations'.[92] She observes that following the Qur'an leads to redemption, for in it 'the brilliant proofs of God are realized, His intentions explained, His prohibitions warned against, His signs presented, His attributes ... made apparent; His allowances granted; His laws written'.[93] Fatima then presents the major edicts and principles of Islam and provides reasons for them, including fasting, prayer and pilgrimage.

Fatima then turns her attention to the injustice that has been perpetrated against her. She notes the Qur'anic verses that support leaving an inheritance to close relatives, including daughters, and points to others to dispute the idea that prophets do not leave inheritances.[94] For example, she invokes Qur'an 27:16, 'Solomon inherited David' (*wa waritha Sulayman Dāwūd*) (or, in some translations, 'Solomon succeeded David') and 19:5–6, in which Zachariah calls upon God, saying, 'So give me from yourself an heir who will inherit me and inherit from the family of Jacob [Ya'qūb].'[95]

Fatima then says:

> And you claim I have no right and no inheritance from my father, and that there is no blood relationship between us! ... 'Then is it the judgment of [the time of] ignorance they desire? But who is better than God in judgment for a people who are certain [in faith]' [Qur'an 5:50]. Am I to be unjustly vanquished with regard to my inheritance?[96]

Fatima spends the remainder of khutba directing severe criticism at the Emigrants and Helpers who had betrayed her and the Prophet. She concludes, ominously, 'God witnesses what you do and "soon those who have wronged are going to know to what [kind of] return they will be returned" [Qur'an 26:227]. I am the daughter of a warner, with news of a severe punishment. So, do as you will; and indeed, we will do as we will. Wait; indeed, we are waiting.'[97] Many versions then record a response from Abū Bakr, in which he variously acceded to her request (a decision later foiled by 'Umar) or rejected it. He also accused 'Ali of 'fomenting disorder through Fatima'.[98]

Fatima's khutba clearly stresses the Qur'an's and the Prophet's support of the notion of egalitarianism and bilateral descent. For example, she points to those verses that direct believers to bequeath their belongings to their descendants, both male and female, and accuses Muslims who would deprive her of her inheritance of abandoning the Book of God.[99] Likewise, she cites the Prophet saying, 'Man is preserved through his children' – a clear indication that she perpetuates his lineage.[100] In this regard, then, the khutba (which can also be read as a political document, as we will see below) stands as a proto-feminist text that declares a daughter's rights to inherit against those who would deprive her of it.

How historically accurate are the accounts of Fatima's khutba? After all, Ibn Abī Ṭāhir Ṭayfūr's *Balāghāt al-nisā'* – though we lack an exact date for its composition – was most certainly written more than two centuries after the actual events were supposed to have occurred, and Ibn Abī Ṭāhir Ṭayfūr himself acknowledged doubts surrounding its authenticity, stating that certain people claimed it was taken from a speech by Abū al-'Aynā', a ninth-century poet and litterateur.[101] Shi'is naturally denied this claim, saying the elders of the family of Abū Ṭālib had reported it from their fathers and taught it to their sons, and that Shi'i scholars had transmitted it and studied it before the birth of the grandfather of Abū al-'Aynā'.[102]

Given the different versions that appear, the likelihood exists that scholars inaccurately transmitted at least some parts of Fatima's khutba or even fabricated some portions. For example, the part of the sermon cited by Ibn Bābawayh in his *'Ilal al-sharā'i'* differs in wording from that of Ibn Abī Ṭāhir Ṭayfūr. Versions cited by other early medieval scholars also differ slightly from each other and from that of Ibn Abī Ṭāhir Ṭayfūr, primarily in the responses given by Abū Bakr to the sermon.[103] The poem Fatima addresses to her father's grave also varies in length and wording among different authors, as well as in attribution.[104] These differences, as well as the different *isnāds* cited by each author, produce the image of a text with a complex history – or, rather, of multiple texts with multiple antecedents. Even if parts of it were fabricated, however, the khutba's very composition, and its later inclusion in collections of hadith, demonstrates the urgency with which Shi'i scholars approached the issue of Fadak – an urgency that spilled over into their attitudes towards female inheritance.

More Shiʿi support for Fatima and Fadak

Scholars supported Fatima's claim to Fadak not only by citing her khutba but also by reporting hadith that linked specific passages in the Qur'an to her ownership of the oasis. For example, al-Kulaynī cited a tradition in which Mūsā al-Kāẓim, the seventh imam, in yet another attempt to win reparations from the 'Abbāsids, told the caliph al-Mahdī (d. 785) that after Fadak and its surrounding regions came under the Prophet's control, God revealed Qur'an 17:26 ('And give the relatives their rights.') Because the Prophet did not immediately recognize to which relatives the verse referred, he

> turned to [the angel] Gabriel to find out, and Gabriel turned to his Lord for the answer. God then sent a revelation telling the Prophet to give Fadak to Fatima. The Prophet then called Fatima and said to her, 'O Fatima, God has commanded me to give Fadak to you.' She said, 'O Messenger of God, I have accepted the offer from God and from you.'[105]

The emphasis on Fatima as the rightful owner of Fadak reverberates in Shiʿi rhetoric throughout the centuries. A prayer by the jurist and theologian 'Ali ibn Ṭāwūs (d. 1266), for example, depicts her as 'the wronged, the vanquished, the one whose rights were usurped, the one whose inheritance was denied her.'[106] Addressing Fatima, an anonymously authored poem cited in a thirteenth-century work by Ibn Abī al-Ḥadīd harshly criticizes Abū Bakr and 'Umar for rejecting

> … the provision for your
>   inheritance when they pushed you away.
> You were subjected to a paltry rank
>   and they drove you away.
> You claimed [it as] a gift
>   witnessed by documents.
> So they became enraged. Then no sooner
>   had they lied when they accused you of lying.
> God will remove from His mercy
>   any unbeliever who masters you.
> And He will expel from His wide door
>   any devil who rejects you.[107]

Similarly, in his tract on the beliefs of the imams, in a section on 'Evil-Doers', Ibn Bābawayh notes that Fatima 'left the world displeased with those who had wronged her and usurped her rights, and denied her the inheritance left by her father'.[108] Citing the hadith in which the Prophet called Fatima 'a part of myself; he who angers her has angered me, and he who gladdens her has gladdened me', the scholar clearly indicates that Abū Bakr and 'Umar have incurred God's severe displeasure, for God 'is wroth with him who evokes [Fatima's] anger'.[109] Likewise, nineteenth- and twentieth-century *taziyihs* (passion plays) also feature the denial of Fadak and Fatima's insistence of her rights to it as subject matter.[110]

Of course, in many of these discussions the real issue is the caliphate, not Fadak or female inheritance. Granting Fadak to Fatima and her family would have implicitly recognized their right to succession – hence Abū Bakr, 'Umar and many 'Abbāsids' determined opposition to it, and Shi'i emphasis on obtaining it. Indeed, the jurist al-Qāḍī al-Nu'mān argued that Fatima's khutba 'was not specifically about Fadak and its environs, but about "the Imamate from her and the progeny of the Prophet"' – an 'interpretative key' endorsed by many medieval and contemporary Shi'i scholars.[111] For example, Muhammad Bāqir al-Ṣadr (d. 1980), the renowned Iraqi ayatollah, portrayed Fadak as an essentially political matter:

> He who closely examines the stages of the dispute and its successive forms does not regard it as a case of asking for a piece of land. Rather he understands it as a much greater mission, a spur to revolt in order to regain a stolen throne, a lost crown and a great glory, and to revive the inverted umma. Hence Fadak exists as a symbol that represents a great concept, not that confiscated piece of land in the Hijaz. This symbolic meaning transformed Fadak from an ordinary dispute confined to a limited circle to an enormous revolution with a wide horizon.[112]

One wonders, in fact, whether Shi'i scholars and polemicists would have fought so vigorously for female inheritance rights had the Prophet's offspring been named 'Faḍl' rather than 'Fatima'. Yet fight they did. Al-Qāḍī al-Nu'mān, in his discussion of inheritance laws, explicitly justified gender-egalitarian statutes by referring to the case of Fatima and Fadak. Citing several imams who stated that an only daughter should exclude any agnates from inheritance, he wrote,

> It is not as our opponents say to those who are in similar circumstances as Fāṭima. … They wish to deny the right of Fāṭima in the inheritance of the Messenger of God. God has clearly repudiated their opinions, for they said,

> 'The daughter is not entitled to more than half as mentioned in the Book of God. The second half goes to the agnatic heirs (*'aṣaba*).' But they turned away from the Word of God.[113]

Referring to the concept that a deceased's grandchildren can substitute for his or her children if no children remain, al-Qāḍī al-Nu'mān further declared,

> The son's sons represent the sons when there is no son surviving, and male and female descendants have the same rights as male and female children. The son of a son represents the son *and the son of a daughter represents the daughter*. Those who oppose us deny that the sons of daughters come under the general term … *walad* [child]. They say that they are descendants of another people, i.e. they [belong] to their fathers [not to their mothers]. God has declared their falsity in His Book, by the tongue of His Messenger, and even through their own arguments. They manifested the ugliness of their undue assumption clarifying what they really intended, namely, invalidating the inheritance of Fāṭima.[114]

Al-Qāḍī al-Nu'mān echoed Fatima's implicit cry – 'Am I not my father's child?' – when he inveighed against the Sunni laws that would cut a daughter's inheritance in half if the deceased left a sister as well, but would give it all to the son if he left a son and a sister. He passionately declared, 'How is this? Is not the daughter a child (*walad*)?'[115]

Likewise, al-Kulaynī invoked Fatima when discussing the inheritance rights of daughters and their offspring. In a long exposition attributed to Abū Muhammad Faḍl ibn Shādhān (d. 873), a companion of the tenth imam 'Ali ibn Muhammad al-Hādī (d. 868), al-Kulaynī noted that in many circumstances, such as marriage and testimony, people do consider the son of a daughter to be a legitimate offspring. When it comes to inheritance, however, 'They say that the son of a daughter is not considered as one's son and he is not considered his father, because they follow their ancestors who wanted to invalidate [the claims of] Hasan and Husayn and Fatima. But God is the Supporter.'[116] Like other Shi'i scholars, al-Kulaynī, in citing Ibn Shādhān, stresses the precedent offered by Jesus and Mary. Citing Qur'an 6:84–5, the verses that enumerate the many prophets guided by God, he notes that God 'has identified Jesus as one of the descendants of Adam and Noah when he is the son of a daughter because Jesus had no father; then why is it that the children of a daughter of a man are not considered as one's children?'[117] Fairness and truth dictate that they are blood relatives who inherit.[118] Citing Ja'far al-Ṣādiq, al-Kulaynī declared,

'Fatima … inherited [the Prophet's] household assets and all that belonged to him.'[119]

Long before gender equality emerged as an issue in global discourse, then, Fatima's struggles for her legacy helped solidify Shi'i determination to place a greater emphasis on female inheritance than did Sunnis and envision a bigger role for close relatives, especially daughters and their sons, in the family structure. Since these roles decisively contradict the concept of 'transmission of economic resources along the male line', they suggest a more egalitarian image of kinship and family – perhaps an unintended consequence, but a consequence nonetheless.[120]

Outside influences and Qur'an 8:75

As with descent, it is possible to look to pre-Islamic regional influences – in addition to the factors already analysed – to explain Shi'i inheritance patterns. Certainly Sassanian Iran, though extremely repressive towards women in many respects, provided some inheritance rights to daughters.[121] A Sassanian juridical text, the seventh-century *Mādayān ī Hazār Dādestān* (Book of a Thousand Judgments), shows that both married and unmarried daughters inherited from their fathers; in some circumstances, a daughter acted in official capacity as an 'heiress' (*āyōkēn*), in which she 'undertakes to produce an heir and namesake for the deceased'.[122] A daughter could also 'inherit the family- or hearth-fire from her father. If she married, her husband would assume responsibility for the fire.'[123] Similarly, though females were often considered as 'chattels to be bought and sold rather than as individuals with rights' in pre-Islamic Central Asia, they still enjoyed relatively liberal inheritance rights.[124]

Matters seem to have been even more egalitarian in the Byzantine Empire, where sources – though limited between the seventh and eleventh centuries – show strong bilateral leanings. As the scholar Angeliki Laiou notes, 'The family never seems to have been patriarchal or patrilineal in the Byzantine empire. That is, the father did not have the extensive rights of a Roman pater familias over the members of his household, nor was status or property transmitted only through the male line.'[125] Both 'Byzantine succession law and … practice was based on bilateral succession, so that property traveled along both the male and the female line'.[126]

Yet Shi'i scholars, disavowing any un-Islamic influence, built their arguments on the foundation of no less an authority than the Qur'an itself. Indeed, a closer look at interpretations of one verse, Qur'an 8:75, throws light on how they advanced their case. This verse, contained in a sūra that is thought to have been revealed after the Muslims' emigration to Medina, reads: 'As for those who believe after you and migrate and strive with you, they are [to be counted] among you. But family relations [*ūlū al-arḥām*] have the strongest claim on one another in the Book of God.' (See also Qur'an 33:6 for a very similar verse.)

The claims referred to here are often believed to be those of inheritance. Commentators who wrote about this verse observed that Muslims who emigrated to Medina (Emigrants) became close to the Muslims they met in their new city (Helpers) – so close that they could inherit from each other. This verse, however, nullified that practice and affirmed that inheritance should go to those related by ties of blood.[127]

Interpretation of just who qualified as family relations (*ūlū al-arḥām*) varied wildly among jurists, however. Did it mean the *'aṣaba*, or female relatives, including those in the maternal line, or both?[128] The Sunni commentator Abū 'Abd Allah al-Qurṭubī (d. 1272), for example, noted that some Muslims interpreted 8:75 to mean that some typically non-agnate relatives who were not specifically mentioned in the Qur'an – including children of daughters, children of sisters and mothers' relatives – inherited, while others negated that notion.[129] Al-Qurṭubī observed in his commentary on the verse that Abū Dāwūd (d. 889), the famous Sunni hadith scholar, quoted the Prophet saying that if someone dies and does not leave a (Qur'anic) heir, the maternal uncle may inherit – but this was by no means a universal opinion.[130]

Unsurprisingly, Shi'is took a much less ambivalent approach. Scholars such as al-Kulaynī and his contemporary, Abū al-Naṣr Muhammad al-'Ayyāshī (d. 932), cited many traditions in which the imams, in particular Muhammad al-Bāqir, referred to 8:75 to bolster the claims of relatives in the female lines – including the maternal aunt and uncle – instead.[131] The inheritance is particularly meaningful when no other heirs exist; in all of those cases, the imam specifies that the maternal uncle and aunt (who, as non-Qur'anic heirs, would otherwise have been deprived) inherit.[132] Al-'Ayyāshī also cites a report attributed to Ja'far al-Ṣādiq describing a disagreement between 'Uthmān ibn 'Affān (d. 656), the third caliph and 'Ali about the inheritance of a man who died without leaving any *'aṣaba*, and yet had relatives who did not inherit from him, no doubt because they were maternal relatives. 'Uthmān reportedly denied that a God-given ordinance existed which directed distributing inheritance to these relatives. 'Ali disagreed, citing 8:75. Yet, according to the hadith, 'Uthmān persisted and directed that the inheritance be given to the state treasury rather than to the man's relatives – a move that the scholar clearly repudiates.[133]

Likewise, as we have seen, al-Qāḍī al-Nu'mān wrote that those who denied the rights of females and their descendants to inherit 'turned away from the Word of God'. He then cited 8:75. Though he recognized the *'aṣaba* as part of the *ūlū al-arḥām*, he nevertheless maintained that female relatives constituted it as well.[134] And Fatima herself cited 8:75 in her argument for Fadak.[135]

Once again, then, in interpreting this verse Shi'i scholars threw their weight solidly behind distribution to members of the female line, explicitly recognizing them as part of the family. The verse itself, with its use of the word *arḥām* – plural of *raḥim*, womb – opens up this possibility for them. Often the term *ūlū al-arḥām* is translated merely as 'blood relatives' or 'kindred' or 'consanguine relations', just as *dhawu al-arḥām*, another frequent term in inheritance discussions, is often translated as 'blood relations' or 'cognates', without any reference in particular to female relatives, or, indeed, to uteruses. Yet in the original Arabic, as with Qur'an 3:6–7, the feminine imagery of wombs draws the reader's attention to the role of women in society, bringing them front and centre. Those seeking to deny the emphasis on the *'aṣaba* thus found plentiful support in the Qur'an itself.

Conclusion

As this chapter has demonstrated, inheritance laws and practices constitute a material embodiment of a society's conceptions about bloodlines and kinship ties, or the very structure of the family.[136] The movement and distribution of property and money follows the unwritten, ethereal map of the bloodline, and then itself shapes and draws the bloodline. Despite Qur'anic efforts to diminish the inheritance rights of distant male agnates in favour of those of more immediate relatives, both male and female, and their offspring, Sunni law restored some of their previous influence to the *'aṣaba*. Shi'i law, in theory if not in practice, envisioned a bigger role for close relatives, especially daughters and their sons, in the family structure – a role that emerged at least partly from Fatima's quest to inherit Fadak. In her capacity as (in Shiʿi scholars' eyes) the rightful inheritor of the property, Fatima palpably embodied her ability to carry on her father's bloodline. She also enjoyed a status far beyond that of an inferior vessel. Other women partook in these benefits, as Chapter 4 will show.

4

Endowing agency

Daughters, waqfs and semi-matrilineal inheritance

Deeds that speak

In her endowment deed for the so-called Blue Mosque (*masjid-i kabūd*) in Tabriz, Iran, the fifteenth-century Qarā Quyūnlū queen Khātūn Jān Begum, wife of the enormously powerful ruler Jahān Shāh (d. 1467), made a highly significant stipulation.[1] She directed two-thirds of the proceeds from the extensive properties she was endowing to go to the support of the magnificent mosque complex. The remaining third was to go to her two daughters, Ṣāliḥa-Sultan and Ḥabība-Sultan – and, after them, to *their* daughters and the daughters of their daughters, as well as to other female descendants. Moreover, the queen herself and, after her death, her daughters were to act as trustees for the waqf, or endowment. It was, as contemporary scholar Chrisoph Werner has observed, an act with an apparently 'spectacular' intention on behalf of the queen: to protect the female members of her family by providing them with economic means of support and authority.[2] And it was fully in line with the persona of a woman who, despite her husband's prestige, was an influential political leader in her own right.[3] That the Qarā Quyūnlū were very likely Sunni (albeit with Shiʿi leanings) makes the queen's stipulation especially interesting from the perspective of this study, for it demonstrates that female acquisition and distribution of wealth did not fall in neat lines according to sectarian divisions.[4]

Indeed, given the inheritance laws sketched out in Chapter 3, it would be logical to assume that throughout history, daughters in predominantly Shiʿi societies inherited more than their Sunni counterparts. But evidence paints a far messier picture. Fatima herself, according to one report, bequeathed all her earthly goods, including land, to ʿAli. Next in line was Hasan; after him, Husayn and his descendants. Her daughters do not appear in her will.[5] Both Sunni and Shiʿi women could be, and were, deprived of their inheritances, especially land, or pressured into renouncing them.[6] In some cases societies followed customary laws rather than Islamic ones. In others people found elaborate ways to circumvent Islamic laws, or simply ignored them. Loss of inheritance cannot, of course, always be interpreted as unfavourable to women.[7] Some women seem to have willingly given up their inheritance rights in exchange for protection and financial help from their brothers. Others, even if they did not inherit, received family property in other forms, such as gifts or trousseaux.[8]

Yet in both Shiʿi and Sunni societies women did receive substantial, and clearly beneficial, inheritances – inheritances that testify to bilateral descent patterns and to the enhancement of female agency. Eleventh-century obituary records from Cairo, the capital of the (Ismaʿili) Fatimid Empire, suggest that fathers and mothers alike passed on money, land and other property to their daughters, to the exclusion of agnates, in accordance with the precepts championed by al-Qāḍī al-Nuʿmān.[9] Court records of estate divisions from fifteenth-century (Sunni) Grenada show women inheriting a great deal from their relatives, including property, in practices that often take on a distinctly matrilineal character.[10] One 'blessed old woman', for example, left her house to her granddaughter, who subsequently went to court with her husband to register it as a 'gift to their infant daughter' – thereby completing 'a cycle of four generations of interrupted ownership of the family home by its female members'.[11]

Alongside obituary notices and estate division records, another type of document speaks even more eloquently of female inheritance practices in pre-modern Islamic societies: the deeds, or *waqfiyyāt*, that women used to create trusts (waqfs), often for the benefit of public institutions, and the institutions themselves that they commissioned, expanded or maintained with these endowments. Like genealogical charts and biographical dictionaries, these deeds tell us much about how people viewed family structure; but instead of blood, the networks they unveil are built of money, property and power. This chapter considers selected examples of female waqf activity, particularly among elite women, in the pre-modern Middle East and Central Asia. Though far from a comprehensive account – an impossible feat, in any case, given the still-emerging state of the field – it nevertheless shows that elite daughters received massive amounts of wealth and property from their parents, and that many used existing legal institutions to benefit their descendants and create opportunities for power and prestige. The examples contained in this chapter, then, furnish a particularly material type of evidence for the existence of bilateral practices in medieval and early modern Islamic societies.

A popular method of transferring wealth from one generation to another without the necessity of adhering to Qur'anic distribution requirements, waqfs or trusts allowed property to be made 'inalienable in perpetuity', and the revenues from it diverted to certain beneficiaries.[12] In Chapter 3, I mentioned that waqfs often served to exclude women; in fact, some scholars have suggested that their most frequent use was by men who sought to avoid giving women their inheritance shares.[13] But waqfs could also enhance female autonomy and wealth, and could even be used to create semi-matrilineal systems of inheritance; and that usage is what many records reveal.[14] Not only did daughters inherit from their fathers and mothers – an indication that they carried on their bloodlines – but they also generated systems whereby wealth and authority travelled along female-centred lines.

Waqfs are usually divided into two basic types: private and public, with private ones meant to benefit an individual's family and descendants, and public ones intended to create or support charitable institutions that could be used by everyone, including mosques, mausolea, madrasas and Sufi lodges.[15] However, these forms often overlapped: in both cases, founders 'often stipulated that a portion of the income from the endowment should benefit needy Muslims'.[16] Moreover, even public waqfs could benefit an individual's family through the office of the *mutawalli*, or trustee, which usually carried an income. A founder who designated herself, her descendants and their descendants as trustees – as many women did in the pre-modern Islamic world – was effectively giving all a permanent source of income.[17]

She was also adding to their status and power, for in addition to the income provided, acting as a *mutawalli* constituted a position of leadership, one that increased 'control over the property' and potentially involved many business transactions.[18] For women, trusteeship could be a significant means of enhancing (or recognizing) their autonomy; it 'testifie[d] to the perception of women as independent legal actors with requisite skills and knowledge'.[19] (Of course, a secluded waqf manager whose husband or other male relative necessarily acted as her agent in court – as often happened – would reap fewer rewards from the position than others; but many women did, in fact, personally manage their waqfs.[20])

Endowments benefited women in other ways. Waqfs could be used to protect wealth or property from encroachment or confiscation, either by 'unscrupulous rulers' or by relatives (a matter of particular relevance to women).[21] They often offered certain tax benefits.[22] And simply creating a public trust conferred recognition and status upon a woman; by endowing her properties to benefit a mosque or shrine, a female patron signalled to the world that she was wealthy, generous and pious.[23]

These usages are revealed in public trust records from the pre-modern Middle East and Central Asia, which show Sunni and Shiʿi women inheriting substantial wealth from their parents, identifying with and honouring their natal lineages, benefiting their descendants as well as the public and exhibiting significant autonomy and power by acting as their own trustees – all features that run counter to typical perceptions of patrilineality. At times, they even explicitly invoke Fatima, the patron saint of female inheritance and bilateral descent.

Women and waqfs in pre-Safavid Iran and Central Asia

From the thirteenth to the sixteenth centuries, royal and other elite women in Iran and Central Asia who were of Turkic or Turko-Mongolian background frequently created waqfs, including some that were used to support significant structures such as mosques, mausolea or madrasas, and sometimes named female descendants as their trustees. Several cases exist in which royal Turkic women drew up endowments that either outright appointed their daughters as trustees or used the gender-neutral term *awlād* (children, offspring) in their deeds – indicating that either males or females could be appointed trustees.[24] As contemporary scholar Florian Schwarz notes, in the thirteenth century, the Qarā Khiṭāʾī queen Quṭlūq Terken khātūn (d. 1282) 'in at least two cases specifically appointed her daughter Pādishāh khātūn as trustee of one of her extensive [w]aqfs. This suggests that in other cases where she is said to have designated her "offspring" (*awlād*) as successors, female descendants were included.'[25]

Similarly, Khātūn Jān Begum's limiting of beneficiaries in her endowment deed for the Blue Mosque to female descendants testifies to bilateral tendencies among the Qarā Quyūnlū, the Turkic dynasty that ruled parts of western Iran (as well as portions of Anatolia and present-day Iraq) in the fourteenth and fifteenth centuries.[26] Indeed, the queen herself took active part in the dynastic struggles between her husband and their sons, and, after Jahān Shāh's death, helped quash a revolt led by two of her husband's nieces.[27] As an 'influential leader of her own faction within the Qarā Quyūnlū confederation', the queen 'pursued an independent political agenda'.[28] Her endowments for the Blue Mosque must be viewed in the same light, as a sign of her 'independent and autonomous role' within the confederation, and her desire to see her female descendants enjoy the same rights.[29]

At about the same time that Khātūn Jān Begum was exercising her power in western Iran, female endowment activity was flourishing to the east under the Timurid Empire, the dynasty that dominated much of Iran and Central Asia between the fourteenth and the sixteenth centuries (and to which the Qarā Quyūnlū at times paid tribute). True to its Turko-Mongol roots, the empire itself evinced many bilateral features. Though its founder, Timur, was not directly descended from the Mongol emperor Chinggiz Khan, he claimed some of Chinggiz' charisma by marrying his descendants. In fact, as contemporary scholar Priscilla Soucek observes, the 'Čingizid wives of Tīmūr, and of his sons Jahāngīr and Mīrānshāh, not only gave their husbands increased prestige and entitled them to use the special title *güregen* [son-in-law], but they themselves were treated with particular deference by the entire family.'[30]

One important figure in the lineage was Sawin Beg bint Aq Sufi, known as Khānzāda-Begum. A descendant of Juči, the son of Chinggiz Khan, through her mother, Shakar Beg bint Jānī Beg, Khānzāda was married first to Tīmūr's son Jahāngīr, then to another son, Mirānshāh.[31] The meticulous attention with which Timurid historians chronicled her life (and that of other Timurid wives descended from Chinggiz) demonstrates the respect with which she was regarded.[32] It is clear that Khānzāda's merit derived partly from her lineage, which was thought to strengthen Jahāngīr's claim to the throne.[33] One biographer of Timur, in fact, identified her as 'Khānzāda bint Shakar Beg Khānim' – linking her to her mother's (more prestigious) lineage, rather than that of her father.[34]

A recognition of the significance of females in the lineage continued into the next generation. A genealogical scroll now housed in the Topkapı Sarāyi Museum in Istanbul traces the ancestry of Khalīl Sultan ibn Mirānshāh, the grandson of Timur, to Chinggiz Khan through Khānzāda (his mother) and Shakar Beg bint Jānī Beg (his grandmother).[35] Similarly, the scroll documents Khalīl Sultan's descent from a far more distant figure, Ālanquwā, that princess impregnated by a ray of light whose story appeared in the description of Mughal founding history in Chapter 2.[36] The Timurids – from whom the Mughals descended – and the Chinggizids both claimed her as an ancestress.[37] Women, once again, take up decisive positions in the patriline.

These bilateral tendencies likewise manifest in endowment practices, which reached unprecedented levels under the Timurids, especially in the latter half of the fifteenth century.[38] A tremendous public building boom coincided with an upsurge in endowment activity to create one of the most prolific periods in medieval Islamic history.[39] The waqfs paid for upkeep of buildings – whether shrines, mosques, khanaqahs or madrasas – and supported the activities that occurred within them.[40]

Through establishment of waqfs, elite Timurid women took an active role in building and patronage, with domed funerary structures in particular a popular object of funding.[41] By decorating the landscape with monuments associated with their names, this type of philanthropy enhanced these women's images as female agents of piety and power. Moreover, many of their endowment deeds show an inclusive attitude towards women, freely acknowledging them as donors, witnesses and trustees. For example, Ḥabība-Sultan Begum, the young wife of the son of the Timurid ruler of Samarkand of the time, Sultan-Abū Sa'īd, used the gender-neutral term *awlād* in her endowment for a mausoleum in Samarkand built for Sultan-Abū Sa'īd's daughter, Khvānd-Sultan Bike, in 1464, indicating that female descendants as well as males could be considered as successor trustees.[42] Moreover, the endowment deed 'bears numerous imprints of the seal of Sultan-Abū Sa'īd himself as well as those of several of his sons and daughters', attesting not only to the close connections between Ḥabība-Sultan Begum and her husband's family but also to the inclusion of females in verifying a legal transaction.[43] Though Ḥabība-Sultan Begum's motives for establishing the waqf are unclear, contemporary scholar Maria Subtelny speculates that she had come into an inheritance after the death of her father (who is named as deceased in the *waqfiyya*) and conveyed it to the waqf 'as a long-term investment for herself'.[44]

With no fewer than two congregational mosques to her name, Gawhar-Shād Begum (d. 1457), the wife of the Timurid sultan Shāh Rukh (r. 1409–47), and daughter of a prominent amir, was a major architectural patron by any standard.[45] Her crowning achievement was the mosque built at Mashhad in the tomb complex of the eighth Shi'i imam, 'Ali al-Riḍā.[46] Completed in about 1418, the structure is known for its 'luxurious internal decoration'; featuring arches within arches, and enamel brick and mosaic faience in a full range of colours, it has come to be seen 'as the culmination of the Timurid style'.[47] Patronizing the construction of a congregational mosque was traditionally a sultan's role; in building the mosque that came to be known by her name, Gawhar-Shād Begum was flexing her philanthropic, economic and political muscles, and, perhaps, aiming to secure a place for herself in heaven, for the 'foundation inscription of the … mosque read: "Whoever builds a mosque for God, so likewise God will build a house for him [or her!] in paradise."'[48] Nor were her efforts without economic effect: as Subtelny notes, it was Timurid patronage, chiefly at the hands of Gawhar-Shād Begum and her son Baysunghur, that helped Mashhad, as a pilgrimage destination, develop into one of the biggest cities of Khurasan in the early fifteenth century.[49]

Significantly, Gawhar-Shād built the mosque from her private funds – an indication of her wealth.[50] She later established a waqf to support it, one that included as endowed property a bathhouse, orchards, gardens and five hundred sheep.[51] In it, she named herself and her offspring as trustees, along with another individual, Mawlana 'Alā' al-Dīn 'Ali Ḥamīd al-'Alavī and his descendants, who may have acted professional administrators.[52] The *waqfiyya* does not specify gender in its discussion of trustees; it merely names her offspring (*awlād-i awlād*) in perpetuity, 'from womb to womb, from age to age', adding, 'and may God forbid that her progeny ever be cut off'.[53] The deed speaks of semi-matrilineality in many forms: the establishment of the trust by a powerful and wealthy woman; the notion that the trust will continue to be managed by *her* descendants, attributing to her the honour and creative power of a lineage; and the authority devolving upon her offspring through management of the trust.

In addition to completing another congregational mosque in Herat, together with her husband, Shāh Rukh, Gawhar-Shād set up a waqf to benefit the shrine of a Sufi saint, Aḥmad-i Jām, west of the city.[54] The deed endowed the shrine with income from lands, canals, mills, shops and villages that were part of waqf property at the mosque in Mashhad.[55] It was not unusual for Timurid royalty to patronize Sufi establishments; several commissioned khanaqahs (lodges) or presented endowments to shrines.[56] These moves benefiting different types of religious groups helped to balance 'the power of rival religious establishments' at the same time that it created useful 'networks of alliances' for Timurids – a venture in which women were very much involved.[57]

The vast holdings enumerated in a *waqfiyya* of another elite Timurid woman, Afaq Begum (d. ca. 1527–8), one of the wives of the ruler Sultan-Husayn (r. 1469–1506), attest to her immense wealth and stature.[58] They included no fewer than 236 individual pieces of land and many other sorts of properties, including both commercial and residential, and ranging from mills to shops to vineyards to irrigation canals.[59] After her husband's death, Afaq Begum moved her portions of these holdings into an endowment for 'her own mausoleum located in the royal madrasa complex in Herat', probably as a means of protecting her property from confiscation.[60] The deed names her as trustee while she was alive; since she had no children, the position would then be taken over by whomever she appointed as successor.[61]

Waqfs are often perceived as economic engines, and the *waqfiyya* of Afaq Begum is suggestive of this.[62] It supported numerous individuals, providing stipends for a professor, eleven students, a shaykh, a prayer leader, a muezzin, five Qur'an reciters, a kitchen staff and a four-member financial team.[63] It also made provisions for feeding the poor and celebrating holidays. Throughout the deed, and in her signature, the donor is identified as 'Afaq Beki, daughter of Amīr Hasan'.[64] Despite the prominence of her husband, the donor is attributed (in typical fashion) to her natal family in a manner that gives honour to her father, who had been an early supporter of Sultan-Husayn, a member of his household guard and one of his most important amirs.[65] The image ultimately emerging from the document is that of a powerful woman who moved at ease in the world of philanthropy and business dealings, and whose identity had not become absorbed into that of her husband's lineage, but rather remained that of her own.

'Gunpowder' waqfs

Perhaps not surprisingly given their partly Turko-Mongol roots, the three 'Gunpowder' empires mentioned in Chapter 2 also witnessed significant waqf activity among royal women. Elite women in all three empires inherited or were given vast sums and properties from their fathers and mothers, and conveyed them into waqfs that supported prominent monuments and complexes. The case of Mihrümah Sultan (d. 1578), daughter of the most celebrated Ottoman sultan, Süleyman (r. 1520–1566), and his favourite concubine Hürrem (d. 1558) exemplifies many of these features. Süleyman adored Mihrümah Sultan, presenting her with so many state lands that his actions later drew criticism from a seventeenth-century Ottoman reformist, who scornfully observed that the properties 'would have provided funds for a minor king'.[66] The sultan also granted his daughter unlimited access to Topkapı Palace and married her to a favoured minister, Rüstem Pasha, who later became his grand vizier.[67] Mihrümah used her money in splashy ways. She bought huge amounts of jewels.[68] She spent 500,000 gold coins to build an aqueduct bringing water from Mount 'Arafat to the Ka'ba in Mecca.[69] She offered to outfit 400 ships for a siege of Malta.[70] And, like other royal men and women, she decorated the city of Istanbul with enormous mosque complexes designed by the celebrated architect Sinan (d. 1588), personally commissioning two of them.[71]

Unlike those constructed by earlier Ottoman women, the complexes commissioned by Mihrümah bear witness to immense wealth and a propensity to display it; she clearly wanted to assert herself on the landscape of Istanbul in a monumental way.[72] The first, completed in 1548, when Mihrümah would have been twenty-six, was located at Üsküdar, a neighbourhood where she had a terraced garden palace leading down to the sea.[73] Two minarets and a dome surrounded by three half-domes towered over the nearby Bosphorus; a guest house and caravanserai, as well as other facilities, were provided for travellers arriving by sea or by land.[74] Two porticoes bordering on the mosque lent a 'palatial touch'.[75] An inscription over the marble gate left visitors in no doubt of the complex's benefactor:

> The foundation was laid for the construction of this strong-pillared Friday mosque by the patroness of pious foundations and good deeds, the pearl of the crown of the sultanate, the greatly renowned honor of the state and the world and the faith, Hanım Sultan[76] – may God, the Exalted, distinguish her with the utmost beneficence – the daughter of the sovereign of sovereigns of the East and West.[77]

The complex's endowment deed likewise testifies to the importance of female inheritance, linking Mihrümah closely to her father and evoking Fatima and other important female figures in ways big and small. Although already married to Rüstem Pasha, by now the grand vizier, the princess is identified in the deed not as her husband's wife but as her father's offspring; she is 'the sultan's favored daughter "Mihrümah Sultan Hanım," a "Fatima in innocence, a Khadija in chastity, an 'A'isha in intelligence, a Bilquis (Queen of Sheba) in natural disposition," and the "Rabi'a of the epoch"'.[78] The deed is, moreover, 'suffused with light imagery', in what may be a tribute to the princess's proper name, which means 'Sun and Moon', but also to Fatima's epithet, al-Zahra; it portrays the dome as 'resembling in light and luminosity the roof of the Ka'ba's celestial prototype and its illuminated surface bright like the heavenly spheres'.[79] Anyone reading it would be reminded that Mihrümah was a woman of consequence who derived her importance from her father – traits she shared with Islam's most eminent female.

Fatima likewise receives attention in the *waqfiyya*'s stipulation 'that the Friday preacher of [the] mosque should be an upright shaykh who will conduct his sermons with prayers to the souls of the prophets and saints, especially to the Prophet's daughter Fatima, and to the Ottoman sultans'.[80]Although the Ottomans were, of course, Sunni, they nevertheless revered the Prophet's family; in the deed, the princess emphasizes Fatima's importance and encourages remembrance of her in a way that, again, implicitly creates a connection between the two women, thus bolstering Mihrümah's own status.

Female connections also appear in an updated version of the deed drawn up in 1558. In addition to distributing stipends to the daughter of Mihrümah and Rüstem Pasha, Ayşe Hümaşah Sultan, and to her children, the deed names Ayşe Hümaşah Sultan's descendants as the beneficiaries of extra funds from the endowment, and as its overseers and administrators.[81] When the lineage ended, the funds were to pay for improvements to imperial highways, including fountains and pavements.[82] Mihrümah thus ensured Ayşe Hümaşah Sultan's continued wealth and status by providing for her and her children, whether male or female.

These provisions were to be complemented by many others. Years later, Ayşe Hümaşah Sultan was named administrator of Mihrümah's endowment for another magnificent mosque complex she commissioned, Edirnekapı, celebrated for its innovative 'single-domed baldachin flooded with light';[83] and for a waqf set up by her father, Rüstem Pasha, for an exquisite mosque complex he had built in Tahtakale.[84] (At her husband's request, Mihrümah oversaw the construction of the latter mosque, built after Rüstem Pasha's death; and received much praise and recognition for it.[85]) Ayşe Hümaşah Sultan inherited her father's palace at Mahmudpaşa, and in 1612 turned it into a waqf to benefit herself. Upon her death, her daughter (and her daughter's descendants) would inherit it; whenever the lineage ended, it would be put up for sale and any profits turned over to the poor in Mecca and Medina.[86] She also inherited three other palaces built for her parents and one-third of her mother's fabulous wealth, with the other two-thirds going to Mihrümah's nephew, then the reigning sultan, Murad III.[87] And at her mother's instigation she married an official, Aḥmed Pasha, who, like her father, was to become grand vizier.[88] And Ayşe Hümaşah Sultan's daughter subsequently also was married to an official who became a grand vizier – a chain of marriages that 'indicate the continuing prominence of female descendants of Mihrimah'.[89] So do their abilities to inherit and pass on wealth and property.

Like their Sunni neighbours to the west, Safavid women saw the patronage of monumental buildings or public gardens as a valuable use of their wealth, for it was both a 'consecrated way of leaving a good name' and the 'means of manifesting one's importance and status in a most evident and visible way'.[90] Maria Szuppe records several instances of royal Safavid women, including Tājlū Khānum (d. 1540) and Shāhzāda Sulṭanum (d. 1562), whose waqfs financed the expansion or upkeep of prominent buildings such as shrines.[91] The example of Tājlū Khānum, the favourite wife of Shah Isma'il I, is particularly illuminating.[92] The queen, who herself hailed from a noble lineage, owned villages, land and gardens in central Iran that she converted into waqfs to benefit various mausolea.[93] A major beneficiary was the shrine in Qum of Fatima al-Maʿṣūma, the daughter of the seventh imam, Mūsā al-Kāẓim; she was buried in that city after falling ill on her way to Khurasan in 816 to visit her brother, 'Ali al-Riḍā, the eighth imam.[94] Not only did Tājlū Khānum apparently fund the construction of a new entrance for the shrine that featured two monumental minarets, and the rebuilding of the tomb chamber as a 'domed octagon' but she also endowed villages and properties outside Qum – where her natal family had extensive ties – to benefit the mausoleum.[95]

As contemporary scholar Kishwar Rizvi has noted, Tājlū Khānum's endowment deed of 1523 reflects and promotes a considerable degree of female stature.[96] After beginning with praises of God, Muhammad and 'Ali, the *waqfiyya* identifies the donor as

> the great lady, the mistress, queen of the world, leader of the chosen [pure] people, … [she is] affluent, beneficent, pure, … the just, the ruler, the sultana of the chosen women. … Builder of great, charitable works, founder of benevolent foundations, the signs of sanctity and rectitude from the tent of her high position (and) the lights of purity from the (bridal) canopy of her greatness are dazzling. The virtuous one of the world and of the religion, Shāh Begī Begum [Tājlū Khānum], daughter of the great Amir, Mihmād Beg, son of Hamza Bektash Mausillu, may her greatness and chastity be eternal.[97]

The deed implicitly invokes Fatima in many ways – by speaking of Tājlū Khānum's chastity, her exalted position among the women of the world, and by associating her with brilliance and dazzling lights. Similarly, like Fatima in many Shiʿi texts, the deed identifies Tājlū Khānum with her father's prestigious lineage rather than that of her husband.[98] The connection to Fatima is made more explicit in the deed itself, which directs that 'a large portion of the endowment was for the shrine of Fatima al-Maʿsuma', that is, the one with the same name as the 'leader of the women of the world', – Fatima al-Zahra.[99] Tājlū Khānum's deed thus underscores the parallels between the queen and the daughter of the Prophet and, by ensuring the upkeep of an important Shiʿi shrine dedicated to a female descendant of Fatima and 'Ali, emphasizes the centrality of women to Shiʿism.[100] In case that message was insufficiently clear, the *waqfiyya* cited a hadith from the eighth imam saying that whoever made pilgrimage to the shrine of his sister, Fatima, in Qum, would earn paradise.[101]

Beyond those accomplishments, however, the deed signifies female power and lineage in a more temporal sense. As Rizvi notes, Tājlū Khānum likely inherited her property and money from her natal family. She made the endowment in honour of her deceased sister and, as we have seen, identified herself in it as the daughter of her father (not the wife of her husband). The deed also calls attention to her roles as 'patron, builder, and founder of pious charities', and calls her 'the just ruler ('adila) and sultana, feminized versions of the titles shared by her husband, Shah Isma'il'.[102] By emphasizing her own lineage and sovereignty, the queen was 'asserting her autonomy as a powerful political player' at court – as, indeed, were all royal women who built big.[103]

Not many endowment deeds have survived from Mughal India, but architectural and other records attest to significant building activity among royal women, much of which must have been supported by waqfs, which in turn would have been based upon inherited properties and other wealth.[104] Ḥamīda Bānū Begum, also known as 'Ḥājī Begum' and 'Maryam Makānī', a title given to her by her son, Emperor Akbar, commissioned a resplendent tomb for her husband, Emperor Humāyūn (r. 1530–40; 1555–6), in Delhi in about 1569, using her own funds to do it.[105] Nearly seventy years later, the fabulously wealthy Jahānārā Begum (d. 1681), favoured daughter of the Emperor Shāh Jahān (r. 1628–58) (himself no mean builder), received permission from her father to construct a Friday mosque in Agra, the imperial capital of the Mughal Empire.[106] Two years later the same princess commissioned a second mosque in Srinagar, dedicated to her Sufi pīr, Mulla Shah Badakhshī.[107] In the 1650s, complementing structures funded by her father, she 'laid out the famous central bazaar of Mughal Shahjahanabad, Chandnī Chawk', a 40-yard wide street that extended for nearly a mile and featured more than 1,500 shops and porticos, frequented by traders from far-flung nations.[108] A canal, a mosque and a beautiful caravanserai, or inn with a central courtyard, also formed part of the Chandnī Chawk complex; of the inn, the princess wrote, 'I will build a serai, large and fine like no other in Hindustan. The wanderer who enters its courts will be restored in body and soul and my name will never be forgotten.'[109]

Much of Jahānārā's building fever appears to have been funded by her imperial allowances, as well as generous revenues from Surat, a well-frequented and international port on the western coast of India, bestowed upon her by her father in gratitude for the first stage of her recovery after she had been badly burned in 1644.[110] Like her Ottoman and Safavid counterparts, Jahānārā used her building programme to make a name for herself as a philanthropist and a princess who was very much present on the public stage.[111] That she was able to do so is an indication of her father's willingness to turn exceedingly valuable property over to her – a decidedly unpatrilineal move.

Sufi waqfs

Female participation in waqfs also occurred outside of royal circles, albeit with less prominent outcomes. Schwarz has documented an unusual phenomenon among two Sufi brotherhoods in Samarkand in the mid-sixteenth century. As he notes, many Sufi *waqfiyyāt* of the fifteenth and sixteenth centuries around Samarkand and Bukhara limit future trusteeship to males. One even states explicitly that male descendants should be the trustees, 'whereas no female descendant shall interfere'.[112] Yet a striking change occurs in two mid-sixteenth-century *waqfiyyāt* for Sufi lodges in Samarkand, both of which also include female descendants as candidates for trusteeship.[113] In one, a 1547 *waqfiyya* for a Kubrawī khanaqah in Samarkand, the endower and shaykh, Kamāl al-Dīn Husayn Khwārazmī, stipulates that if 'there is no male heir the trusteeship passes through the female line of descent. In the event of a disruption of the direct line the trusteeship devolves to the most qualified paternal and (then?) maternal relative (*'aṣabāt wa dhawī l-arḥām*)'.[114] Of course, women needed to 'possess chastity' in order to be considered – and had to appoint a male relative who would actually administer the waqf.[115]

Female descendants are likewise included, albeit somewhat reluctantly, in the line of succession in the Aḥrārī *waqfiyya* of 1546, which states:

> [Upon the death of the endower], whoever (*har yek*) is the most savant, pious, and qualified from among the children of that Excellency and the children of the children of that Excellency and the children of the children of the children of that Excellency, generation after generation and century after century, shall be the trustee. Men shall be preferred over women.[116]

The succession, as Schwarz observes, 'then continues through paternal relatives followed by maternal relatives'.[117] Including female succession as an option in both of these deeds represents a shift from an agnatic to an agnatic–cognatic system.[118] But why did the shift occur? Unstable political conditions, including military conflict, seem to have forced the endowers' hands. Nearly half a century earlier, Uzbek amirs almost wiped out all of the men of the Aḥrārī family in the midst of dynastic conflict over Samarkand, and portions of the family's holdings were temporarily lost.[119] Fear that control over the waqfs would permanently slip from their grasp may have triggered these families to adopt more flexible system of successions, which would help to ensure that the endowment would remain whole.[120] The two endowers, as Schwarz notes, clearly hoped to improve their chances for keeping control over the waqfs within the family. By including females, they could dramatically increase the pool of available candidates for trusteeship, thereby delaying the moment when the role would pass to someone outside the order.[121]

At the same time, making this change induced a shift in the orders' concepts of family, expanding it to include females and, potentially, their descendants.[122] And the move in at least one of the cases bundled spiritual authority into the legacy that could be inherited by females, for apparently in the Kubrawī-Husaynī order, 'charisma as well was perpetuated through succession of trusteeship'.[123]

A matter of debate

To be sure, not all scholars agree that waqfs – even female-founded ones – benefited women. In a study of endowments in mid-sixteenth-century Istanbul, historian Gabriel Baer found that they did more harm than good. Though waqfs founded by women accounted for more than a third of all of those established in the city for the period under study (a percentage in alignment with Ottoman Aleppo and other towns and periods), and though that number definitely indicates that women held property, women remained a minority as founders of waqfs – an indication that their holdings were much smaller than those of men.[124] Moreover, the waqfs they established were typically much smaller than those of men and, significantly, were lacking either urban or rural land, as well as income from land.[125] Administration of waqfs also indicated gender inegalitarianism: far fewer women than men acted as *mutawallis*, especially in proportion to the number of those women who established waqfs, and most waqfs that started out being controlled by women eventually passed to the control of men.[126] The result, Baer concluded, was that waqfs established to protect female property in the long term 'returned to male beneficiaries and to the control of male managers. Thus, the waqf in fact weakened the economic position of women as a group.'[127]

In specific response to Baer's findings, however, Margaret Meriwether's two studies of eighteenth- and nineteenth-century Ottoman Aleppo waqfs offer a far rosier outlook with regard to endowment impact upon women.[128] Though women in Aleppo, like those in Istanbul, did not often endow land, and though female-established waqfs were typically smaller than those set up by men, Meriwether found that women nonetheless 'played a greater role as administrators of endowments and were more frequently beneficiaries of these endowments' than did Baer in his study of Istanbul.[129] Moreover, rather than losing their rights to long-standing endowments, or being deprived of opportunities to serve as administrators over time, the women she studied often maintained both.[130]

Indeed, although the periods they cover are largely outside of the scope of this study, it is worthwhile taking a closer look at Meriwether's analyses of 104 *ashrāf*, or notable, families residing in eighteenth- and nineteenth-century Aleppo. Though the society was nominally patrilineal, waqf records paint a picture of relatively egalitarian family structures in which women and their children were frequently designated beneficiaries by their natal families, and sometimes were appointed as trustees.[131] Those *waqfiyyāt* stipulating the fate of notables' family residences are particularly revealing, since their large, gracious homes embodied the presence of the elite family in the city both symbolically and physically – and, in some ways, represented the family itself.[132] As Meriwether observes, in fifty-two of seventy-nine endowment deeds in which the endower's residence was included as part of the endowment, shares in the home were divided equally among all children – with the exception of married daughters, who were sometimes excluded. Even in those cases, however, daughters could often recoup their shares in the household in the event of widowhood or divorce; sometimes this right was extended to their male descendants as well.[133] Daughters (especially those who lacked spouses) were thus envisioned as belonging to and possessing a claim on the natal family, as were their male children.

Conversely, larger waqfs tended to discriminate against women more frequently, giving women half the share of men, for example, and setting stricter limitations upon their rights to live in the home or receive endowment income, as well as upon the rights of their descendants.[134] However, exceptions did exist. The very unusual endowment deed established by ʿUthmān Pasha, governor of Aleppo in 1737, named several females as potential *mutawallis*, including his sister and his sister's daughters, 'preferring female descendants to male descendants'.[135]

Women in Aleppo also frequently created endowments, including some that aimed to provide for the needs of women specifically in what has elsewhere been called a 'limited form of matrilineal inheritance': income accrues to a daughter and then to the daughter's descendants.[136] Women were often included in the list of possible *mutawallis* in smaller endowments, less frequently in larger ones.[137] One woman who set up a large endowment for both male and female descendants specified that the *mutawalli* should be 'the most worthy of these descendants, without regard to gender'.[138]

Although worthiness was sometimes the reason for appointing a female *mutawalli* over a male, demographics also played a part.[139] Political turmoil in early modern Aleppo wiped out the men in many families, leaving administrators no choice but to appoint women as successors.[140] For example, in the eighteenth century the Kawākibīs, one of the elite families of Aleppo, controlled several important waqfs, some of which were long-standing public endowments, others family waqfs that they themselves had set up.[141] When Hasan Kawākibī, a leading member of the family, died in around 1814, only daughters survived him.[142] Although a male cousin took control of the long-established public endowments, Hasan's daughter Hibbat Allah assumed management of the considerable family waqfs that had been set up by her father and grandfather, Aḥmad.[143] Once she had died, her son took over management of her father's endowment, while her female cousin's son took over that of her grandfather's.[144] In this case, the preference for direct descendants to serve as *mutawalli* over collateral ones – including agnates – created openings for women.[145] Closeness of kin trumped gender. Meanwhile, the nomination of a daughter and, later, her son to the post expanded the understanding of family to include female descendants and their children as active, contributing members.

Naturally, Aleppo remained a patriarchal and patrilineal society. Despite the incidence of female involvement, it was men who administered most waqfs.[146] Yet many inheritance and endowment structures exhibited flexibility that afforded women the opportunity to play prominent roles in Aleppan economic society.[147] Waqfs, in the end, proved assets.

Conclusion

As this chapter has demonstrated, numerous examples exist of both Sunni and Shiʿi nobility in the pre-modern Middle East and Central Asia transmitting large amounts of money and property to their daughters, thereby recognizing them as carrying on their lineages and endowing them with prestige and autonomy. Many of these daughters then created waqfs (public trusts) supporting the construction or maintenance of public monuments – moves that enhanced their personas as philanthropic and powerful people. In their *waqfiyyāt*, or deeds, these women frequently named their own children, both male and female, as the beneficiaries of the waqf's income in what constituted a form of matrilineal descent. They sometimes also named female descendants as *mutawallis*, or trustees. Together, these examples indicate that the structure of the family in pre-modern Islamic societies was by no means fixed in firm patrilineal lines, but could reserve important spaces for women.

The potential consequences of appointing female descendants as *mutawallis* are, of course, even greater than transforming the concept of family, as important as that is. As has already been suggested, the position is replete with implications for female agency, including economic autonomy, influence and spiritual or political authority; it unfolds striking possibilities for the roles women could play in society. As with patronage, a woman who manages her family's endowment – and who is not compelled to hand off the responsibilities to a male agent, as often happened – is seen as able to not only transmit her lineage but also manifest her forebears' qualities herself.[148] As such, the position represents the last piece of the puzzle of bilateral descent: succession. As Part Three demonstrates, succession marks the final transition from veiled to openly active agency. Instead of merely relaying their bloodline or the family's property to the next generation, successors themselves guided and led, emanating the charisma they inherited from their natal families. In this, too, Fatima stands as a shining example.

Part Three

Successors

5

Speaking in her father's name

Fatima as successor to the Prophet Muhammad

From mute to outspoken

A sixteenth-century Ottoman miniature painting of the Prophet Muhammad uniting Fatima and ʿAli in marriage depicts these three personages in a revealing tableau (Figure 5.1).[1] Robed in a long green cloak, his face veiled, an aureole of divine flames emanating from his head, the Prophet towers over his daughter and his son-in-law, whose clasped hands he brings together. ʿAli stands to the Prophet's left. Like his soon-to-be father-in-law, he is dressed in a green cloak; he also wears a green turban, and his face is visible. Fatima stands to her father's right. A white robe draped over her entire body allows the cuffs and hem of a blue dress underneath to peek out, but shows no traces of flesh. Her veiled head, like that of her father, emits flames. Unlike ʿAli, and unlike the unveiled females to her right, however, Fatima's entire attitude is one of shrinking submission, as though she were attempting to be invisible. Her head bends towards her father, and her right arm draws protectively up to her body. The sleeve of her robe is so long that it extends several inches beyond her hand, dangling modestly towards the floor. The only aspect of her form that indicates transcendence consists of the aureole surrounding her head, which ʿAli noticeably lacks.

As this painting suggests, Fatima is often portrayed as a woman who would rather fade into the background than take centre stage. Indeed, except when confronting Abū Bakr, the Fatima of traditional Shiʿi piety is quiescent: she receives and transmits her blood, gnostic knowledge and property, but she does not speak out in her own right, and she does not act as a religious authority or temporal leader in the same way as do the imams. Her powers tend to recede

Figure 5.1 The Prophet Muhammad presiding over the marriage of Fatima and ʿAli, from the *Siyer-i Nebī*. CBL T 419, 1594–5, fol. 24v. © The Trustees of the Chester Beatty Library, Dublin.

before those of the men in her family. Painted in largely monochromatic tones, she remains muted and veiled – the ideal female who is as hidden from view as possible.[2]

By closely examining texts, however, we can reconstruct other Shiʿi portraits. These metaphorical images, some of which are modern, some medieval, show a Fatima draped in bolder colours and acting far more assertively. Here she is not merely a receptacle or conveyer of authority, but a woman who embodies her father's mission and is capable, at least to some degree, of leading his community. In these portraits, she appears distinctly imam-like – in some cases, even prophet-like.

Just as medieval Shiʿi sources presented Fatima as inheriting her father's property, they also in some instances portrayed her as his spiritual and even political heir: a woman able to act as his successor, to show forth his qualities and to speak and guide in his stead. This Fatima shares in the 'political and religious authority' typically ascribed to the imams, including legal authority.[3] In the twentieth and twenty-first centuries, Shiʿi scholars have expanded upon this concept, producing images that contrast sharply with the traditional ones of Fatima as retiring, overly emotional and weak.[4] After analysing the factors traditionally working against female successorship, this chapter explores textual portraits of Fatima as successor, examining the circumstances that likely contributed to their creation as well as their implications. For example, these portraits underline the degree to which Shiʿism embraced the concept of bilateral descent, for by portraying the daughter of the Prophet as successor, scholars acknowledged that she possessed other of her father's qualities than those typically associated with women. The portraits also help to demonstrate the means and mechanisms by which women could become imbued with authority in predominantly patriarchal societies – means and mechanisms by no means limited to Islamic cultures. As such, they open up important lines of inquiry about female leadership. The matter is one of great relevance for today, when the ability of Muslim women to act as religious and other types of authorities is hotly contested.

Female successorship in Islam

Conditions in pre-modern Islamic societies – as indeed in most pre-modern societies – tended to militate against outright female successorship. Even when they recognized that a daughter could inherit, transmit and to some degree show forth her father's attributes, medieval authors, both Shiʿi and Sunni, tended to stop short of the radical notion that a female could act as an actual successor. For example, as we saw in Chapter 1, Sunni and Shiʿi sources clearly portray daughters as manifesting their father's attributes. Fatima, according to hadith, spoke, sat and walked like the Prophet, and the Prophet himself called her 'part of' him. One narration of this tradition even depicts Fatima as her father's deputy in a case in which the Companion Abū Lubāba had tied himself up in penitence for betraying the Prophet. Though Fatima offered to untie him, he had sworn to allow only the Prophet to release him. The Prophet then pronounced, 'Fatima is a part of me', and Abū Lubāba permitted her to untie him.[5] Thus, under certain circumstances Fatima appeared as an extension of her father, able to act on his behalf; for some Muslims, indeed, the notion that she was 'part of' her father implied that she 'received some of his gnostic knowledge'.[6] (In fact, upon her birth God is supposed to have said, 'I have bestowed knowledge upon you, and safeguarded you from menstruation.'[7])

But normative Muslim thought placed limits on the degree to which a daughter – even the daughter of a Prophet – could act as her father's successor, and in practice if not always in theory that limit often seemed to be the threshold of the home, or that of the woman's womb. For various reasons, temporal successorship, which required women to act in the public realm, remained largely out of bounds. In many ways, 'Ā'isha's disastrous participation in the first *fitna* became the cautionary example for what happens when women are allowed too much latitude. By taking part in the Battle of the Camel against 'Ali and his supporters, 'Ā'isha claimed temporal authority based on her ties both to the Prophet and to her father, the former caliph. Her goal was apparently not to rule, but simply to act according to her values and, indeed, to help determine the fate of the leadership of the Islamic community.[8] Yet the move ended badly and was later widely condemned. As contemporary scholar Denise Spellberg writes,

> 'A'isha's posthumous medieval depiction transformed her political defeat into an object lesson for both Sunni and Shi'i scholars on the inevitable disasters of female participation in politics. Her example would be utilized consistently by male authors of the medieval communal record to prove their retrospective rule: all women, by definition of their gender, were a threat to political order.[9]

Although the Qur'an 'does not explicitly forbid women from exercising direct political rule', scholars adduced many hadith after the Battle of the Camel to support the contention that women had no place in politics, thereby excluding them from successorship in the conventional sense.[10] One of these proved especially powerful. According to the Companion Abū Bakra (not to be confused with Abū Bakr), after learning that the 'Persians had named a woman to rule them', the Prophet stated, 'Those who entrust their affairs to a woman will never know prosperity.'[11] As contemporary feminist scholars have observed, this hadith – which Abū Bakra did not narrate until decades after the Prophet reportedly said it – has served as 'the sledgehammer argument used by those who want to exclude women from politics'.[12] It was, for example, 'utilized in later medieval Islamic political theory to exclude women from government positions such as that of prime minister'.[13]

Sunni jurists were not the only scholars to exclude women from participating in politics. Shi'i jurists condemned 'Ā'isha even more vociferously for her involvement in the Battle of the Camel, depicting her as even more active and vocal in her attack upon 'Ali; like their Sunni brethren, they generally discouraged women from taking part in public affairs.[14] For example, Shi'i jurists forbade women from being judges because it was seen as inappropriate for a woman to 'mix with men and raise her voice amongst them'.[15] Safavid ulama generally counselled that the ideal woman was one who obeyed her husband, brought up her children and guarded her chastity – while giving to her husband in sex 'all that he wanted'.[16] Associating with men who were not close relatives was frowned upon, and even 'learning to read and write was considered reprehensible in classical texts'.[17]

Both Shi'i and Sunni medieval scholars justified their exclusion of women from the public sphere by arguing that women's supposed inferiority and deficiency disqualified them: 'Women are regarded as weak, of poor judgment, not worth any substantial education, too emotional to be trusted with important decisions, and liable, if unveiled, to lead men astray by arousing sexual desires.'[18] Even 'Ali reportedly called women 'deficient in faith, deficient in shares and deficient in intelligence' and counselled men to be on their guard against them.[19] In many ways, the views set forth by Niẓām al-Mulk, the eleventh-century Seljuk vizier, exemplify the typical medieval views. 'The king's underlings', he wrote,

> must not be allowed to assume power, for this causes the utmost harm and destroys the king's splendor and majesty. This particularly applies to women, for they are wearers of the veil and have not complete intelligence. Their purpose is the continuation of the lineage of the race, so the more noble their blood the better, and the more chaste their bearing the more admirable and acceptable they are. But when the king's wives begin to assume the part of rulers … their commands are the opposite of what is right, and mischief ensues.[20]

In Niẓām al-Mulk's eyes, then, women were a 'source of trouble, turmoil, and temptation'.[21] Lacking complete intelligence, they were liable to cause 'chaos in political affairs' if given too free a hand – a state of affairs exemplified by

'Ā'isha, who stood as a prime example of the 'capacity of all women to destroy political order'.[22] To support his case, Niẓām al-Mulk cited a hadith: 'Consult them and oppose them.'[23] Conversely, feminine virtue, when it existed, lay primarily in a woman's capacity to behave obediently, subserviently, and to remain in the domestic sphere.

The manner in which Shiʿi scholars typically depicted Fatima demonstrates graphically the domestic parameters within which female authority – such as it existed – resided. By highlighting her roles as daughter, wife and mother, scholars celebrated her chiefly for typically 'feminine' virtues such as obedience, domesticity, devotion to her family and, especially, chastity.[24] These qualities came to be the 'preeminent ideal categories for the feminine in Qur'anic exegesis'.[25] By possessing them – or having these qualities ascribed to them – Fatima and her mother, Khadīja – as well as Mary – came to symbolize a 'unified Islamic vision of an idealized feminine gender' – in sharp contrast to the more controversial 'Ā'isha.[26] (Indeed, these women are often portrayed in hadith, along Āsiyā, the wife of the Pharaoh, as the 'best of women'.)[27]

Thus Fatima, notwithstanding her ability to inherit and to transmit her lineage, figures most prominently in Shiʿi lore not as an activist or public figure but as a 'model of female Muslim piety' known more for her reticence than her outspokenness.[28] Though devoted, she was weak and extremely emotional: ready, it seems, to break into tears at any provocation.[29] Indeed, according to many sources, Fatima cried almost incessantly after her father's death.[30] Numerous traditions, elegies, plays and *rawḍa-khwānīs* (recitals commemorating significant events in Shiʿism) describe her copious weeping; according to one tradition she 'cried so much that she annoyed the people of Medina when they came to the mosque and thus had to go to the graveyard to cry'.[31] From a political perspective, this weeping served to rouse anger among Shiʿis at those who unjustly hurt the daughter of the Prophet. But for some, it also enhanced the image of Fatima as a passive creature of sentiment who lacked the strength of character and mental firepower that would allow her to function as a temporal leader or activist.[32]

Other leadership qualities were equally lacking. For example, 'Unlike the Imāms, [Fatima] rarely displays knowledge of Islamic law, considered to be the purview of men by medieval Muslims.'[33] Even when Fatima did display some degree of authority, it was traditionally limited to the next world. She was envisioned playing a significant role on the Day of Judgement, where, according to some traditions, she would appear as a queen accompanied by thousands upon thousands of angels and houris – in consonance with her stature as Queen of Women.[34] There, she would intercede with God on behalf of her descendants and the Shiʿis who had loved her and her progeny.[35] Despite these tremendous powers in the Hereafter, however, she could not manifest them in the temporal abode – a condition that contemporary scholar Denise Soufi attributes to the general disinclination among men towards seeing women as temporal leaders, as well as a care to distinguish Fatima's role from that of the imams.[36] Although Fatima could in some instances be raised to 'the ranks of the infallible Imams', for the most part she could not be seen as possessing their full, glorious status, which included temporal authority.[37] As Soufi says, Fatima's 'sovereignty was manifested not on earth, where it could be confused with an Imamate, but rather on the day of Judgment'.[38]

Yet, as indicated, alongside this image of Fatima – which most definitely continues to exist – scholars have begun both to unearth and to paint strikingly different portraits in recent decades. This 'new' Fatima appears as an activist and public figure. Not only familiar with the law, this Fatima also elucidates and even embodies it. As a divinely inspired woman seeking to restore the revolutionary order established by the Prophet, this Fatima acts in no small measure as a temporal successor to her father.

Fatima as successor: The khutba

As some twentieth- and twenty-first-century Shiʿi scholars and activists have striven to loosen restrictions upon female authority – including in the arena of law – they have simultaneously demonstrated greater willingness to attribute temporal authority to Fatima.[39] In 'Remembering Fāṭimah: New Means of Legitimizing Female Authority in Contemporary Shiʿi Discourse', Matthew Pierce discusses the work of several Shiʿi scholars who have presented or are presenting the 'authoritative model of Fāṭimah as evidence of the right of women to assume positions of religious and political authority', among them ʿAli Sharīʿatī, Monir Gorgi, Āzarī-Qummī, Jamīla Kadīvar and Javādī Āmūlī.[40] Several focus on Fatima's role as a revolutionary who perpetuated the social ideals instituted by her father. In his famous essay 'Fatima Fatima Ast' ('Fatima is Fatima') and other writings on women, for example, the Iranian sociologist Sharīʿatī (d. 1977), depicted the daughter of the Prophet as one who bore 'the responsibility of reflecting within herself the newly created revolutionary values' brought into being by her father.[41] Fatima, Sharīʿatī wrote,

> became the owner of the values of her father, the inheritor of all the honors of her family. She was the continuation of the chain of great ancestors, the continuation which began with Adam and passed through all of the leaders of freedom and consciousness in the history of mankind. It reached Abraham and joined Moses and Jesus to itself. It reached Muhammad. The final link in this chain of divine justice, the rightful chain of truth was Fatima, the last daughter of a family who had anticipated a son.[42]

In fact, in Sharīʿatī's eyes the essence of the revolution brought by Islam lay in the massive change it wrought in how females (and, particularly, daughters) were to be regarded, as exemplified by Fatima. In a ringing endorsement of bilateral descent (Sharīʿatī suggests), God chose a daughter, not a son, to inherit her family's glory and continue the ancient prophetic chain begun by Adam. God thus delivered a clear message to the misogynistic men of the Hijaz: treat women and girls with respect.[43]

Similarly, Muhammad Bāqir al-Ṣadr, the Iraqi ayatollah, envisioned the daughter of the Prophet as the formidable fomenter of a 'Fatimite revolution', one aimed not only at securing her rightful inheritance but also at removing those who had usurped the leadership of the Muslim community and installing its rightful ruler – that is, her husband ʿAli. As he wrote, it was a revolution 'by which Fatima wanted to pluck out the cornerstone [upon] which history was built after the day of the *saqīfa*', the meeting in which Abū Bakr (illegitimately, according to Shiʿis) was appointed caliph.[44] As contemporary scholar Rachel Feder notes, al-Ṣadr's portrait of Fatima diverges sharply from the typical depictions of an incessantly weeping, weak woman whose sadness paralyses her. Rather, her tears galvanized her to anger and action: 'In Ṣadr's version it is her grief that procures her inspiration to embark upon revolutionary action. Ṣadr's Fatima is emotionally and mentally stable; her thoughts are lucid and determined, and she is in a suitable condition to undertake decisive action.'[45]

Other Shiʿi scholars have focused on Fatima's role as an impeccable model for humankind – an indication that, like the imams, she herself functions as an 'actual embodiment of the law'.[46] Arguing that Fatima was 'not only infallible (*maʿṣūma*) but also authoritatively infallible (*maʿṣūma muṭlaqa*)', the senior cleric Javādī Āmūlī maintained that 'her sunna is just as authoritative as ʿAli's'.[47] This reasoning, as Pierce observes, both supports the argument that 'the use of Fāṭimah as a role model is grounded in the *sharī'ah*' and implies that 'the potential for women's authority is no less than men's'.[48]

During an interview in Qum, the home of the most significant Shi'i scholarship in Iran, the prominent Shi'i cleric Mihdī Mihrīzī cited Fatima's arguments about Fadak as described in al-Kulaynī's *Al-Kāfī*, to support the idea that a woman's testimony is equal to that of a man. (Often, jurists have cited Qur'anic verses such as 2:282 to say that a woman's testimony is worth half that of a man.) As he noted, Fatima 'went to Abū Bakr and said that Fadak is ours. She went, not 'Ali, and said that Fadak is ours, and Abū Bakr judged in favor of Fatima' (according to this version of the event). The cleric concluded, 'If Fatima did not believe, and Abū Bakr did not believe, that the testimony of women was worth that of half of a man' – why should people today accept that precept?[49]

As indicated in this example, even the medieval sources depict her as an authority, though they do so in a manner that is less pronounced than her other roles. Such a portrait particularly emerges in evocations of Fadak. As previously noted, beginning in the ninth century, hadith began to appear about the impassioned speech given by Fatima in which she publicly defended her right to Fadak. Though inheritance of property was the ostensible reason for the khutba, the speech served many different, interrelated functions. In claiming to inherit Fadak, Fatima also claimed her right to a less quantifiable substance from the Prophet: religious authority for herself and her family. The khutba both made this argument and, as will be seen, has been used by scholars to make it.

As noted in Chapter 3, in the khutba Fatima repeatedly cited Qur'anic verses in support of her arguments to inherit Fadak, and accused Abū Bakr of intentionally turning his back on the Qur'an by ignoring its precepts regarding inheritance. 'Are you so special', she asked sarcastically,

> that God specified a verse for you from which he excluded my father? Or are you saying that my father and I are of two faiths so we do not inherit from each other? Are not my father and I of one faith? Or perhaps you think you are more knowledgeable of the specifics and generalities of the Qur'an than the Prophet?[50]

In these statements, Fatima maintains that Abū Bakr lacked the understanding of the Qur'an possessed by the Prophet and that she is following the more knowledgeable lead of her father – an argument represented in the ironic questions, 'Did God specify a verse from you from which he excluded the Prophet? … Or are you more knowledgeable in the specifics and generalities of the Qur'an than my father?' However, Fatima's words also convey the notion that she *herself* has a better understanding of the Qur'an than does Abū Bakr – and that she inherited this understanding from her father. By citing Qur'an 27:16, for example, 'Solomon succeeded (or inherited [from]) David', Fatima suggests that she 'succeeds' the Prophet by inheriting some of his spiritual insight and authority. (Commentators often interpret acting as an heir as implying more than material inheritance; in one commentary on the Qur'an, for example, one translator and editor glosses 27:16 thus: 'The point is that Solomon not only inherited his father's kingdom but his spiritual insight and the prophetic office.')[51]

Fatima underlines this concept elsewhere in the khutba. As we have already seen, she quotes the Prophet saying, 'Man is preserved through his children' – suggesting that she perpetuates his lineage as well as his characteristics.[52] Repeatedly emphasizing that she is the daughter of the Prophet, Fatima implies that this kinship tie cloaks her with prophet-like authority – 'I am the daughter of a warner, with news of a severe punishment.'[53] Together, these statements convey the concept that she inherited not only her father's property but also his characteristics and spiritual authority.

This idea likewise appears in the way in which medieval and early modern Shi'i scholars deployed Fatima's khutba. Not only did they refer to it when making rulings upon inheritance but they also incorporated parts of it into other legal treatises and discussions, thus placing Fatima on a level similar to that of the imams, and invoking her as a spiritual authority.[54]

A case in point is Ibn Bābawayh's *'Ilal al-sharā'i'*. As its title indicates, this text provides justification or reasons for divine ordinances in the form of hadith. Like other Shi'i hadith collections, this text treats the imams as a source of hadith in addition to the Prophet – and, it accords a similar status to Fatima. That is, it cites Fatima not merely as a transmitter of hadith about the Prophet, but as a model, herself, for behaviour.

The section citing Fatima falls in what is arguably the most important part of the book – a chapter called *'Ilal al-sharā'i' wa usūl al-islām*, or 'The Reasons for Laws and Ordinances, and the Fundamentals of Islam', which explains such measures as prayer, charity and fasting during the month of Ramadan. Section 1 of the chapter cites 'Ali. Sections 2, 3 and 4 cite Fatima's khutba. Following is a translation of the parts explaining God's edicts:

> God ordained faith a purification for you from polytheism, prayer an elevation from arrogance, alms a source of prosperity, fasting a confirmation

> of sincerity, pilgrimage an establishment of religion, justice a harmony of the hearts. Obeying us brings order to the nation and our leadership is a safeguard from disunity.
>
> Jihad brings honor to Islam, patience is the best means for obtaining rewards, enjoining good is for the welfare of the public, kindness to parents is a safeguard from God's wrath. Maintaining relations with kin increases your numbers, and the law of retribution reduces bloodshed. Fulfilling vows is a way toward forgiveness, fairness [in business dealings] with weights and measures eliminates injustice, avoiding slander is a barrier from damnation. Abandoning theft brings about integrity, banning the unjustified consumption of orphans' wealth is a protection from injustice, and fair rulings bring happiness to the community. God, the exalted, prohibited polytheism so that one can be devoted to Him only. 'So fear God as He should be feared' [Qur'an 3:102] in that which He has commanded you to do and that which He has forbidden.[55]

Fatima appears, here, as a confirmer and explainer of the laws and principles of Islam – including prayer, charity, fasting, pilgrimage, fairness, fulfilment of vows and avoiding theft and polytheism – and the reasons behind them. The khutba is, as the contemporary Iranian scholars Gorgi and Massoumeh Ebtekar note, 'more than a discourse in defense of her personal rights to inheritance. It provides a strong philosophical and logical background on the foundations of Islamic religion and thought.'[56] Ibn Bābawayh's use of Fatima's khutba thus stands as an example of how one of the most prominent medieval Shiʿi hadith scholars depicted the daughter of the Prophet as a figure of temporal authority.

Several centuries later, in Safavid Iran, the Shiʿi scholar al-Majlisī likewise cited Fatima's khutba in *Biḥār al-anwār*, his monumental collection of hadith. Like Ibn Bābawayh, al-Majlisī drew on the text to elucidate the reasons for God's implementation of certain laws. For example, in a section on upholding the ties of kinship (*ṣilat al-raḥm*), he writes: 'Fatima in her khutba said: God enjoined upholding the ties of kinship [as a means of increasing your numbers].'[57] In a chapter on slander and obscene language, he writes: 'Fatima in her khutba said: God enjoined refraining from slander as a barrier from damnation.'[58] In a chapter on the benefits of prayer and the penalty of abandoning it, he writes: 'Fatima in her khutba said: God enjoined prayer as a means of avoiding arrogance.'[59] Finally, in a section on the benefits of fasting during the month of Ramadan, al-Majlisī writes: 'Fatima in her khutba about Fadak said: God enjoined fasting as a means of confirming sincerity.'[60] Again, Fatima herself appears here as a model for behaviour. She is not merely transmitting hadith – she herself is a source of hadith. In this sense she occupies a status similar to that of the imams: a temporal religious authority.

Likewise, Isma'ili jurists such as al-Qāḍī al-Nuʿmān, in his interpretation of Fatima's khutba, 'linked the inheritance issue to that of the succession of the Imamate and concluded that Fatima had acted as a witness (*ḥujja*, lit "proof") to her contemporaries'.[61] *Ḥujja* is a term that possesses many valences, but in Isma'ilism indicates a representative of a prophet or imam – an extremely exalted position.[62] Al-Qāḍī al-Nuʿmān's acceptance of Fatima's stature, as we have already seen, led him to promote the more gender-egalitarian inheritance statutes that we witnessed in the previous chapters. Even in a pre-modern setting, then, Fatima's words carried legal weight and (in the case of the Fatimid Empire) decisively contributed to better inheritance conditions for women.

Still, it is in modern times that Fatima's role as both a spiritual and a temporal authority has flourished. Contemporary Shi'i scholars have adduced Fatima's khutba to portray her as a model of a politically active woman of acute understanding. A scholar in Hyderabad, India, M. M. Taqui Khan, published a translation and commentary on Fatima's khutba as an 'act of devotion to Fatima' as well as a 'feminist act of consciousness-raising to teach the Shi'a of Hyderabad about the strength of the women of the [*ahl al-bayt*]'.[63] Likewise, al-Ṣadr cited Fatima's khutba to support his argument about the proper succession to Muhammad. Al-Ṣadr attributed to Fatima a clearer understanding of the attempt among interlopers to seize the caliphate than perhaps that of 'Ali himself, writing that 'Fatima was the first … to declare the partisan nature of the ruling party. She accused them of political plotting, then she was followed, in this thought, by some of her contemporaries like Imam 'Ali and Muʿāwiya ibn Abū Sufyān.'[64]

He likewise wrote,

> How wonderful you were, O daughter of the Prophet, when you took the mask off the bitter truth and predicted for your father's ummah a terrible future, in whose skies red clouds would glimmer – How shall I put it? [Rather], rivers would overflow with blood and be filled with skulls! You reproached the 'good' ancestors for their deeds by saying, 'Unquestionably into sedition they have fallen, and indeed, Hell will encompass the disbelievers.' (Qur'an 9:49)[65]

To Fatima, then, is attributed the divine foreknowledge of the fate of the *umma* and an infallible sense of how the caliphate should be structured – a clear indication that she has inherited her father's ability to lead and guide.

Fatima as successor: The *muṣḥaf* and other miracles

The concept of succession also materializes in the many traditions describing Fatima's *muṣḥaf*, or book – a divinely inspired text that she is supposed to have received, and which is imbued with extraordinary wisdom and powers – as well as in many other miracles and events that link her directly to prophets and imams.[66] According to traditions reported by the Shi'i hadith collectors al-Kulaynī, Ṣaffār al-Qummī and others, Gabriel visited Fatima to comfort her after her father's death. The angel told her 'about her father, his place, of the future events and about what would happen to her children. At the same time Ali, peace be upon him, would write all of them down and this has come to be the *muṣḥaf* of Fatima.'[67] (Some traditions which may refer to a different book – known as the *kitāb* of Fatima rather than the *muṣḥaf* of Fatima – are said to contain a list of kings who would rule.)[68] Although distinct from the Qur'an – which it exceeds in size by about three times – the *muṣḥaf* of Fatima bears close similarities to it.[69] For example, it is said to have been divinely inspired. Like the Qur'an, according to some traditions the *muṣḥaf* contains legal rulings. One tradition cites the sixth imam, Ja'far al-Ṣādiq, saying of it, 'I do not believe that in the *muṣḥaf* there is anything of the Qur'an. Rather it contains what makes people need us and makes us in need of no one. It even mentions [the legal punishment for] a lashing, half a lashing, one fourth of a lashing, and the indemnity for a scratch mark.'[70] (However, another tradition records the same imam saying, 'There is nothing in it of the knowledge of the lawful and unlawful matters but it has knowledge of things that had happened and things to happen in the future.')[71]

The references to the *muṣḥaf* of Fatima associate it with considerable authority and power, qualities that reflect back upon the daughter of the Prophet. Some traditions state, for example, that because an angel spoke to Fatima to deliver the book, she became known as *al-muḥaddatha* – a term meaning 'those who are inspired, or whose expectations are accurate, and directed by divine power'.[72] All of the imams are known as *muḥaddathun*, and the arrogation of the title to Fatima places her among their ranks.[73]

Second, traditions indicate that the text functioned as a source of 'extraordinary *'ilm*', or knowledge; it was passed, along with other scrolls, from imam to imam. These scrolls 'authenticate the imam's claim to authority … [and] point to where the authentic *'ilm* is located, for it is only the possessor of the scrolls who has the authoritative divinely inspired knowledge'.[74] As we have already seen, according to Ja'far al-Ṣādiq, the book contains 'what makes people need us and makes us in need of no one'. In this capacity, the book bestows a rank upon Fatima that transcends even that of the imams, for she constitutes a source of their power and authority. Though Shi'i commentators are careful to clarify that Fatima was not a prophet and that the *muṣḥaf* is not the Qur'an, the story of a text transmitted to her via divine inspiration, and possessing extraordinary powers and qualities, enhances the image of the daughter of the Prophet as prophet-like – and, hence, as a successor to her father.[75]

Other miracle tales identify Fatima closely with prophets and imams. I have already discussed the hadith that identify her as the first light created by God and as a human houri – thus giving her heavenly origins like those of (or even more exalted than) the imams and prophets. Fatima's precociousness also testifies to her high status. Stories of her birth bear remarkable similarities to stories of the Prophet's birth: like him, she emitted a light that illumined the East and the West, and like him, she fell on the earth in a prostrating position, already worshipping God.[76] According to al-Ṭabarī, Fatima even extended her finger upon falling to earth from the womb – a testimony to the oneness of God – and Shi'i scholars report that she immediately uttered the shahada, including in it 'Ali and her offspring.[77] The miracle of early speech is akin to that of Jesus, who, according to some interpretations of the Qur'an, addressed his mother shortly before or soon after birth.[78]

Even Fatima's weeping, so often characterized as a feminine attribute, can be seen as both prophet- and imam-like. Several contemporary scholars, including Mahmoud Ayoub, Christopher Clohessy and Matthew Pierce, have devoted considerable attention to the theme of sorrow in Shi'ism, demonstrating that lamentation over the fate of the *ahl al-bayt*, especially Husayn, can be a deliberate, positive and even powerful act in the face of oppression.[79] For example, several imams affirmed that weeping for the *ahl al-bayt* leads to redemption and Paradise for the mourners;[80] sorrow for the chosen ones of God brings down His wrath upon the people of earth.[81] The weeping of the prophets, the imams and Fatima is thus emblematic of the weeping to be undertaken by all Shi'is. Seen in this light, Fatima – accounted one of the 'five weepers', along with Adam, Jacob (Ya'qūb), Joseph (Yūsuf) and Zayn al-'Ābidīn – is no longer a weak reed; rather, she belongs to a noble heritage whose model is worthy of imitation.[82] She may appear more than ever as a quiescent individual in her patient, if tearful, enduring of suffering; but so do the great men who preceded and followed her. Spiritual and temporal authority, these images suggest, spring from emotion; weeping is, as Pierce notes, a 'feminized form of protest' that took hold among Shiʿis, men and women alike.[83]

Just as weeping and lamenting the fate of the *ahl al-bayt*, or praising them and visiting their shrines, can earn people a place in paradise, tormenting them can do the opposite – and Fatima's powers in determining a sinner's fate often take on a prophetic cast. Shiʿi depictions of a deathbed encounter between the daughter of the Prophet, Abū Bakr and ʿUmar convincingly demonstrate this concept. As reported by Ibn Bābawayh, the pair came to ask forgiveness for their misdeed in withholding Fadak. After some tense discussion, Fatima asked them if they remembered hearing the Prophet say, 'Fatima is part of me and I am from her; he who offends me offends God. He who offends her after my death is the same as he who offends her during my life, and he who offends her during my life is that same as he who offends her after my death?' 'Yes, by God, we remember', they said. Fatima then said: 'O God, I hold You witness, so you who are present testify to this: surely they have offended me when I am living and after my death. By God, I shall not speak a word to you until I meet my Lord, and complain to Him about you and that which with you have inflicted me.'[84]

Abū Bakr and ʿUmar reacted very differently to this appalling statement, which so directly defied and challenged the authority of the caliphate. The former burst into loud laments, saying, 'I wish that my mother had not borne me!' to which ʿUmar retorted, 'It is strange how people appointed you as guardian of their affairs while you are not but a foolish old man! You become anxious at a woman's anger, and you rejoice at her satisfaction. What is wrong with he who angers a woman?' The pair then left the house.[85] (In a version of the hadith contained in Sunni collections, Fatima forgave Abū Bakr before her death.)[86]

According to the logic of the hadith, Fatima's torment, resulting from Abū Bakr and ʿUmar's actions, afflicts not only her but also the Prophet – and will bring down God's wrath upon them. The story thus substantiates her spiritual authority, which is closely correlated to her emotions. Female anguish is hardly a typical construction of authority; thus, it is hardly surprising that ʿUmar remains almost blissfully unaware of their transgression: Why should Abū Bakr, or any man, worry that they have offended a mere woman? he wonders. Yet the narrator conveys that the wound is mortal – to them.

Likewise, the manner in which Fatima is portrayed as a martyr links her closely to Husayn and his death at Karbala. According to some particularly polemical accounts of the story in which ʿUmar and others tried to force their way into Fatima and ʿAli's house to obtain ʿAli's oath of allegiance to Abū Bakr, Fatima bravely confronted a man, ʿUmar's companion, Qunfudh, who then whipped and pushed her. The assault led to a miscarriage and, ultimately, to Fatima's death.[87] These acts, along with the denial of Fadak, all contributed to the popular image of Fatima as someone whose death represented 'the culmination of endless suffering and oppression', no less than Husayn.[88]

Even Fatima's chastity – the very thing that defines her as a woman – sometimes propels her to imam- or prophet-like stature. Fatima was reportedly hyper-vigilant about veiling: from birth to death, and even beyond, she desired to be hidden from view. One hadith says that she was instantly veiled upon emerging from Khadīja's womb.[89] Another claims that she veiled even before a blind man.[90] In the hadith cited earlier describing Fatima's deathbed encounter with Abū Bakr and ʿUmar, she refused to turn towards them until ʿAli had covered her with his garment; she also washed and dressed herself in her best clothes before she died so that friends would not need to uncover her corpse prior to burial.[91] And she was reportedly deeply troubled by the idea that people would be gathered naked before God on the Day of Resurrection, until the Prophet reassured her that she would rise privately from her grave and would adorn herself with three garments of light handed to her by an angel, thus being protected from the eyes of people.[92] She is even quoted as saying that what is best for women is 'that they do not see men and that men do not see them'.[93] That Fatima was reportedly unveiled when ʿUmar and his men entered her house to obtain ʿAli's oath of allegiance – according to one version of the events after the Prophet's death – sharpens the sense of violation committed by the men.[94]

From a twenty-first-century secular feminist perspective, Fatima's preoccupation with chastity and veiling hardly shouts 'agency'. Rather, it sets her firmly within a patriarchal structure that aims to control female bodies and to keep them hidden.[95] Indeed, the use of the chador, a enveloping garment that covers most of a woman's head and body, excluding her face and hands, has even been traced to Fatima.[96] Without discounting those types of interpretations, however, reading further into hadith with a more flexible understanding of agency generates meanings less redolent of passivity. One oft-repeated hadith asserts, 'Fatima has guarded her chastity and God has forbidden her offspring to the Fire' (or, more literally, 'Fatima kept chaste her private parts [*farjaha*] and

God has forbidden her offspring to the Fire').[97] The terminology in the first part of the hadith is the same as that used for Mary in the Qur'an, and it endows her with similar powers.[98] As noted in Chapter 1, thanks to her vigilance, Mary was chosen by God to be the vessel for His Spirit, and she and her son are made 'a sign for all people' (Qur'an 21:91). Fatima was likewise chosen by God to achieve eternal redemption for her children (and, according to some hadith, for all of those who love them).[99] Her self-discipline and self-renunciation produces a weaponized chastity capable of achieving the ultimate reward. As with Mary, her guarding of her body is an act replete with agency, albeit in a different form from that more recognizable in secular societies; and it places her on a spiritual level above that of the imams, whose redemption she secures.

The hadith is especially interesting when juxtaposed to another chastity-related report mentioned earlier, in which God is said to have told Fatima, 'I have bestowed knowledge upon you, and safeguarded you from menstruation'. This tradition is often cited in explanation of one of Fatima's names, 'al-Batūl', the Virgin, which means, as noted earlier, that she did not menstruate rather than that she did not have sexual intercourse.[100] The hadith does little to cast women's bodies in a favourable light. To menstruate was, according to one report of the Prophet, 'reprehensible in the daughters of the prophets';[101] it was polluting or, at the very least, led to deficiency in faith because menstruating women cannot pray or fast.[102] By being purified of menstruation, Fatima transcends the 'defective' female body to occupy, as Pierce puts it, a 'distinct ontological category'.[103] Indeed, in one hadith the Prophet told 'Ā'isha (rather pointedly, it seems) that Fatima was 'not like the women of the children of Adam: she is not deficient as they are deficient'.[104] Thus, though the hadith may show Fatima occupying a singularly high station – an imam-like one in which masculine knowledge replaces female menstruation – it does so by maligning more ordinary women and their (bleeding) bodies.

By contrast, the hadith about Fatima's chastity and the redemption of her progeny sets a different tone. Here, her purity is not the result of a spectacular, miraculous and possibly unrepeatable gift from God; it derives from her own self-discipline and restraint. And rather than depicting the vagina as polluted/polluting, defective or deficient, this hadith portrays that organ as capable of great power if properly used. Though it may have been an attempt to corral women's sexual proclivities, the hadith nevertheless puts unlimited power into women's hands (not to mention other body parts).

The path to seeing Fatima in the light of a temporal leader in her own right – one who transcended the limitations placed upon her by her femaleness – is widening in both scholarly literature and Shiʿi piety. Alongside images as a nurse, mother or 'shimmering white image that brings consolation to … grieving women', Iranian posters produced since the Islamic Revolution depict her as a soldier who leads other women to the battlefield – or protest.[105] One such poster shows Fatima clad in a black chador, her hand 'lifted high in a mingled gesture of exhortation and direction', a rifle barrel over her shoulder (see Figure 5.2).[106] A prominent Western scholar has gone so far as to suggest that Fatima rather than ʿAli was the 'legitimate successor to supreme leadership'.[107] Without venturing to that extreme, a website closely affiliated with the Islamic Republic of Iran and dedicated to women and the family states that although Fatima is not an imam, 'in God's eyes, and among the

Figure 5.2 Twentieth-century poster by Iranian artist Mohammad Khazāʾī depicting Fatima as a soldier. © Peter J. Chelkowski.

Muslims, and especially the Shi'is, not only is she not less than the rest of the imams but she is equal to 'Ali, and of greater stature than the remainder of the Pure Ones'.[108] Blessed alongside 'Ali by the Prophet's sacred saliva, recognized with her husband as one of the two Qur'anic seas from which pearls come forth, Fatima stands next to her husband as both a repository and a fount of spiritual and temporal leadership.[109]

The role of pre-Islamic practices

As with the images of her perpetuating her lineage and inheriting her father's property, a number of factors likely played a part in medieval and early modern Shi'i depictions of Fatima as an authoritative figure and successor. Given her close ties to the imams, exalting her status was a necessary corollary of dignifying her children.[110] Yet, just as with lineage and inheritance, pre-Islamic practices likely also paved the way for Fatima to be seen in this light. In this section, I look at concepts of female succession in Iran, the Byzantine Empire and pre-Islamic Arabia as a means of exploring potential influences.

As has already been suggested, daughters held a rather ambiguous status in pre-Islamic Iran. On the one hand, they were encouraged to be submissive and obedient, as evidenced by Zoroastrian scripture. On the other, women did possess many rights, and several famous examples exist of daughters who were lauded for their bravery and virtue, and who either represented their fathers well in the public sphere or succeeded their fathers to important positions. Tracing direct influence from these cases upon Shi'i depictions of Fatima is difficult, but it is likely that they smoothed the path among Iranians and others for acceptance of the idea of a daughter as more than merely a paragon of domesticity.

Like many later Islamic texts, Zoroastrian scripture tended to look upon females with a somewhat wary eye, seeing them as deficient in reason and therefore more prone to falling prey to evil than men: they were considered 'weak willed, easily tempted, and led astray by the devil's horde'.[111] Though not inherently evil, women had to conform closely to the standards set by the virtuous feminine spirits in order to be good, which entailed being pious, devoted and obedient to the dominant men in their lives. Consequently, their ability to act as fully fledged successors and as competent entities in the public sphere was limited. For example, their inherent deficiency and greater susceptibility to pollution rendered them unfit to rule or take part in many priestly activities. Indeed, women who stepped out of the domestic sphere to take on public roles could be associated with the 'evil female spirits who spread disorder'.[112] Inevitably, disasters 'were thought to occur when the female gender was permitted to exercise authority and make decisions'.[113] The ideal role of woman as subservient to men emerges in an early Zoroastrian text which has been identified as a possible wedding sermon delivered by Zoroaster for his daughter, Pouruchista, to a seer. It states, 'Indeed, I shall unite in marriage her among you, she who will serve father, husband, pastor, and family.'[114]

Despite their secondary status and inherent deficiencies as presented in Zoroastrian texts, however, in practice women enjoyed some rights, and at times royal women took on notably public and powerful roles. The Sassanian period presents a typically mixed portrait. Sassanian women were traditionally subordinate to men, whether their fathers, brothers or husbands, and found contentment in domesticity rather than seeking 'public recognition, secular authority, or clerical positions'.[115] The optimal woman combined beauty with amiability towards men, submissiveness and a sense of 'each gender's religiously-assigned role and purpose in the world'.[116]

Yet Sassanian women did possess some rights and responsibilities and enjoyed some freedom of activity outside of the home.[117] Some girls at least were taught to play music, for one text describes the best musician as a 'beautiful girl who plays the *chang* [harp] in the harem and whose voice is high and melodious'.[118] Some women had knowledge of legal matters and were 'recognized as being legally competent'.[119] The seventh-century Sassanian juridical text, *Mādayān ī Hazār Dādestān*, shows that in addition to having access to inheritance, freeborn women 'could enter into contractual agreements and commercial transactions … they had to fulfill debts, and they were held responsible for violations of law'.[120] Because their legal capacity was not equivalent to that of males, however, their 'public actions, such as trading, often would have been mediated by adult males with whom the women had statutory relationships'.[121]

Normally girls were married off at the age of fifteen to husbands chosen by their fathers. Yet, a 'daughter could declare to her father that she did not want to marry, and could not be compelled to do so. She was not punished in any way for this decision, nor did she lose her allowance.'[122] She could also enter into an unapproved relationship without necessarily losing her inheritance.[123]

Most important for the purposes of this study, societies in pre-Islamic Iran acknowledged the ability of daughters to serve as successors. Apart from their ability to transmit their lineage and to inherit, daughters were occasionally seen as possessing the necessary competence to represent their fathers in the public sphere, or to replace them once their fathers had died. For example, pre-Islamic and Islamic sources speak glowingly of a semi-legendary Kayānid ruler, Humāy, who succeeded her father to the throne despite the existence of a son, and of two Sassanian princesses who followed their father to the throne, Pūrān Dukht (sometimes also known as Būrān Dukht) and Āzarm Dukht.[124] Both offspring of Khusraw II (known as Khusraw Parvīz) by his wife Maryam (the daughter of the Roman Emperor Maurice), Pūrān Dukht and Āzarm Dukht were two of the only remaining descendants of the royal line after their brother, Kavād II, massacred seventeen brothers and an eighteenth was assassinated by a usurper. Royal guards loyal to the dynasty succeeded in overthrowing the usurper and enthroning Pūrān; she seems to have ruled for sixteen or seventeen months (629–30) before dying, at which time her sister, who also reigned only briefly, replaced her.[125] As contemporary scholar Haleh Emrani notes, the decision to enthrone the princesses acknowledges their ability to not only (potentially) produce an heir who will continue the father's lineage but also rule themselves and, indeed, acknowledges the capacity to be 'considered the rightful holder of *xwarrah*', or *farr* – that is, 'the divine glory of kingship' which a deity bestows upon a ruler, who then passes it to his descendants.[126]

As when a Sassanian daughter is appointed her father's heir, as indeed these cases represent, the women's gender here was ultimately of less importance than their lineage. Indeed, it was by disregarding their femaleness – a step that, Emrani argues, involved a 'shift and an adjustment, not a revolution' – Sassanian aristocrats and religious leaders were able to preserve the 'imperial ideology and the monarchy' that otherwise would have collapsed in the absence of a male descendant.[127]

Interestingly, for these women of the imperial elite, transcending or transforming their gender involved assuming male garb and displaying traditionally masculine (especially military) imagery. In paintings, Pūrān is shown 'wearing the same type of clothing as the Sassanian kings, including a green tunic in a special pattern over sky-blue pants, a sky-blue crown, and sitting on the throne while holding a … battle-axe' – garb that differs greatly from 'outfits of royal women who were always depicted in very long dresses that cover their legs and feet'.[128] On her coinage, her crown displays the symbol of Wahrām (Bahrām), the 'deity of offensive victory', also displayed by her father, Khusraw II – interpreted by Emrani as a 'symbolic gesture to reinforce her connection to her father', and to bolster her image as a military monarch.[129] Ultimately, Emrani suggests, Pūrān's gender was 'rendered irrelevant through the use of symbols'; she 'was not viewed as the queen; she was in fact the king!'[130]

It is particularly revealing to see how these women's reigns appear in the *Shāhnāma* (Book of Kings), the enormously influential Persian epic poem completed in about 1010. Although not to be taken as an accurate historical account, the *Shāhnāma* nevertheless stands as an important record of how a (relatively) early Persian Muslim thinker, Abū al-Qāsim Firdawsī (d. ca. 1020), looked at Iran's pre-Islamic past. It also exerted a huge impact upon Islamic societies in Iran and elsewhere. Recited, copied and illustrated from India to Turkey over many centuries, it helped shape mores and patterns of behaviour in much of the medieval Islamic world.

Significantly, in the *Shāhnāma* Firdawsī presents numerous cases of women who acquitted themselves well in the public sphere, sometimes acting as deputies of their fathers, sometimes as their successors – and often displaying traditionally 'masculine' characteristics. For example, the champion Gurd Āfarīd, the daughter of the warrior Gazhdaham, fights valiantly against the champion Suhrāb and the Turanian army, defending a Persian fortress against their incursion. The *Shāhnāma*'s account of Humāy is particularly significant, even if parts of it strike the contemporary reader as extremely unsavoury. According to the epic, the ruler Ardishīr Bahman had both a son, Sāssān, and a daughter, Humāy, the latter described as 'virtuous, educated, and prudent'.[131] The father slept with the daughter, according (as Firdawsī delicately put it) to Pahlavi custom, and Humāy became pregnant.[132] Six months passed, during which the king fell ill and realized that he was going to die. Ordering Humāy and his counsellors before him, he seated her upon the throne, saying,

I have bequeathed to her my crown and high throne
  The army, and the great treasure
And my future legatee
  Will be that same soul who is born from her
Whether it be a son or a daughter
  To that heir will be given the crown and throne of the father.[133]

Upon hearing these words, Sāssān – who under ordinary circumstances would have succeeded his father – departed in a huff for other lands. Ardashīr Bahman died of his illness and in accordance with his wishes Humāy acceded to the throne. She ruled effectively for thirty-two years, surpassing her father in wisdom and justice and causing the whole earth to flourish.[134] Desiring to maintain the throne for herself, she concealed the birth of her son, later known as Dārāb, who was raised by strangers. Eventually, however, his identity was revealed and he succeeded Humāy, just as Ardashīr Bahman had commanded.

The episode, despite its distasteful aspects, nevertheless reveals much about the underlying concerns of the royal families portrayed by the epic and the means by which they construed authority. First, it shows a strong emphasis on lineage and the tendency among royalty to embrace endogamy as a means of preserving its purity, for by sleeping with his daughter, Ardashīr Bahman stood a better chance of reproducing himself than if he had allowed his son to succeed him. In this case, however, the king saw his female offspring as capable of not only perpetuating his lineage but also showing forth some of the virtues enshrined within it, including typically 'unfeminine' characteristics such as wisdom, judgement and ability to rule. Such was the implication of his appointing of Humāy and her unborn child – *whether male or female* – as his successor. Blood trumped gender in this case. Ardashīr Bahman's judgement proved correct, for Humāy carried out her kingly duties admirably. Despite its morally repugnant elements (for us), then, the episode sets forth a more positive view of women than the stereotypical one in which they appear as dangerous, reason-deficient beings fit to serve only in the private sphere.

The accessions of Pūrān and Āzarm Dukht, the two Sassanian princesses who followed their father, Khusraw II, to the throne, accomplish a similar goal via less controversial means. Though Firdawsī begins the account of Buran's rule by quoting an aphorism similar to that attributed to the Prophet – 'when a woman becomes king, matters go badly', its mention appears to be largely formulaic or obligatory, for he contradicts that message by depicting Pūrān as a wise, open-handed and just sovereign who ruled with great gentleness, and who, upon her death, took away with her a good name.[135] Likewise, Āzarm Dukht, shown as ruling only four months, is portrayed as capable, punishing the disloyal with hanging and behaving with great kindness towards the loyal. Their typically 'feminine' characteristics thus recede into the background.

Firdawsī was not the only Muslim scholar who painted favourable portraits of these queens. No less a scholar than al-Ṭabarī eulogized Pūrān as

> a queen who made her people happy. He stated that on the day of her coronation, Pūrān pledged to encourage pious conduct and justice and that she 'treated her subjects well, spreading justice, minting coins and repairing stone and wooden bridges. She excused people from payment of outstanding taxes and wrote open letters to them in which she explained how she wished to do well by them.'[136]

Al-Ṭabarī's praise of Pūrān is all the more meaningful given that, according to at least some accounts, it was her accession to the throne that precipitated the Prophet's reported remark, 'Those who entrust their affairs to a woman will never know prosperity.'[137] Known for his upstanding qualities and meticulous scholarship, al-Ṭabarī was one of the religious authorities who did not consider the hadith a 'sufficient basis for depriving women of their power of decision making and for justifying their exclusion from politics.'[138] Based on their attitudes towards these Sassanian queens, then, al-Ṭabarī and Firdawsī, two influential Muslim authors, accepted and even promoted the idea that women could successfully play an active role in the public sphere, including at the very highest levels, and that authority and charisma could be transmitted to females – ideas that must have filtered into the greater scholarly consciousness.[139]

A strong current of female authority, often exemplified by the Virgin Mary, also ran through the Byzantine Empire. Though stereotypes of women as weak, inferior in intellect and prone to evil populated early Christian doctrine as they did Zoroastrian scripture, and though texts tended to idealize the submissive woman who sat home and spun, enterprising women nonetheless found avenues through which to live full, agentic lives.[140] Byzantine women took part in a 'number of occupations, including that of doctor and midwife'; they also made and sold cloth, food and crafts in retail markets.[141] They owned and administered property, and traded.[142] While prohibited from becoming priests, women were 'ordained as deaconesses from the fourth century on and aided the bishop with pedagogic and ritual functions pertaining to women.'[143]

Asceticism – chastity's even more stringent cousin – often served as a means by which Byzantine women attained greater freedom and authority. As contemporary Byzantinist Carolyn L. Connor writes, 'Some church fathers … used Scripture to denigrate women generally, but women were met with approval if they dedicated their lives to religious activities. The church advocated celibacy as a way for women to win through asceticism the status lost through the Fall and through marriage.'[144] Thus, from the third and fourth centuries on, 'women gradually achieved through [asceticism] greater self-determination and autonomy than if they married conventionally'.[145]

One ascetic paradigm women followed was that of the sacred virgin. Modelling themselves after the Virgin Mary, sacred virgins dedicated themselves to the church at the age of sixteen or seventeen.[146] Women who chose to live as sacred virgins had access to 'literacy and learning, otherwise reserved to males', gathered at churches and shrines, and made pilgrimages to hermitages and monasteries.[147] They 'advised, ministered to, protected, and taught other women'.[148]

Another paradigm was that of the ascetic aristocrat. Wealthy women who devoted themselves to celibacy and asceticism after having been widowed (or sometimes while still married!) found 'a freedom similar to that of men'.[149] Like sacred virgins, they studied scripture and travelled on pilgrimages; they also used their wealth to sponsor 'building projects such as churches, monasteries, hospices, and hospitals'.[150] Ascetic aristocrats often moved in public circles and helped 'decisively in the success of the new religion'.[151] On occasion they were even 'known to debate or edify emperors'.[152]

Women of royalty enjoyed even more authority and agency than did their less-noble counterparts. Authority inhered in and was transmitted by imperial women in a variety of ways. For example, a man who wished to become emperor and who did 'not succeed to the throne through birth, adoption, or inheritance could attain the position only through a coup – or through marriage to the previous emperor's widow'.[153] A female partner of a ruler 'shared in the supreme authority invested in his office', even though that authority often took typically 'feminine' forms such as 'concerns for children, wifely loyalty, piety, and dynastic continuity'.[154] Yet empresses could also take on greater visibility and more 'masculine' roles. As Connor notes, women

> served as regents for their sons after an emperor's death and until the child reached majority at age eighteen. During a regency she played a direct role in government by ruling the empire while her son was being prepared to rule. The widow, or sometimes the daughter, of a deceased emperor was entitled by right to rule in her own name.[155]

Several examples of succession (or semi-succession) by daughters exist among Byzantine dynasties. Sisters Zoe and Theodora, daughters of the emperor

Constantine VIII, ruled jointly for a brief period in 1042 after various rules by husbands and sons collapsed.[156] Centuries earlier, though she did not rule in her own name, Pulcheria, offspring of the Emperor Arcadius (r. 383–408) and the Empress Aelia Eudoxia, and elder sister of the Emperor Theodosius II (r. 408–450), wielded a great deal of authority during her brother's reign, becoming the de facto ruler in the early fifth century.[157] Pulcheria acted as guardian to her brother after their father's death, grooming him for rule and teaching him correct kingly behaviour.[158] In 414, Theodosius bestowed the title of Augusta upon his sister, then only fifteen; she apparently took control of the government, leaving her brother free to pursue his more literary pursuits. Her portrait was featured both on coins and in the Senate house.[159]

Pulcheria no doubt derived much of her legitimacy and influence from her status as a member of the ruling dynasty and a direct descendant of the previous emperor. Indeed, her grandfather, Theodosius the Great, is credited with paving the way for imperial females to exercise dominion: he 'believed that his personal qualities and those of his kin, not abstract principles of law and ideology, would best strengthen and preserve the state' – a 'dynastic impetus' that 'led naturally to the enhancement of imperial women'.[160] Here we see a vivid enactment of Weber's charismatic authority, transmitted from forebears to their descendants, including, in this case, female descendants.

As with non-royal women, however, Pulcheria's asceticism and piety – which she modelled after the Virgin Mary – also strengthened her ability to exert influence.[161] Vowing to remain celibate in a public ceremony at the age of fourteen, Pulcheria 'embraced Mary as a paradigm for her own asceticism, in the belief that by emulating the *Theotokos* [Mother of God] she would receive the Divine Word in her own body'.[162] The Augusta's emphasis on Mary benefited the cult of the Virgin in the Byzantine Empire, Pulcheria herself, and the religious identity of ordinary women. Thanks in part to her patronage of monuments dedicated to the Virgin Mary as Theotokos – including three great churches in Constantinople – Pulcheria 'played a major part in establishing the new cult in the capital'.[163] Perhaps most significantly, she supported or helped to convene the councils of Ephesus and Chalcedon, in which bishops proclaimed and affirmed Mary's status as the Mother of God.[164]

The glory of the Virgin, whose lustre she helped to polish, reflected back upon Pulcheria and upon women in general, affording them more latitude in religious activities. In a newly introduced Easter rite, Pulcheria

> entered the sanctuary of the Great Church to take communion within the company of priests and of Theodosius her brother, an expression of her claim to the priestly character possessed by an Augustus. She defended this practice against the objection that she was a daughter of Eve by evoking the mystical birth of Christ in her own flesh and her consequent Marial dignity. Echoing as it did a popular new enthusiasm, this claim to Marial dignity added a potent element to Pulcheria's sacral *basileía* [imperial dominion].[165]

Likewise, the churches celebrating Mary that Pulcheria helped build 'emphasized in monumental architecture the association between the Virgin Theotokos and the virgin Augusta'.[166] Just as the Virgin Mary came to be seen as the 'protector of not only rulers but [also] the city of Constantinople and all its inhabitants', so did Pulcheria – by virtue of her virginity – come to be seen as a powerful weapon against Byzantium's enemies, the Persians.[167] In the view of the fifth-century historian, Sozomen, 'when Pulcheria devoted her virginity to God and imposed the same vow on her sisters, she secured God's favor, causing "every threat and war raised against her brother to disperse spontaneously"'.[168] Like Fatima's chastity, deployed to acquire paradise for her offspring and followers, Pulcheria's abstinence achieved enormous victories.

Finally, Pulcheria – in part due to her efforts in strengthening the status of the Virgin Mary, whose reception of the Divine Word 'confirmed the dignity of her sex' – helped to effect a change in the religious identity of women and gave them a greater role in religious rites.[169] A new memorial ceremony introduced in the liturgical cycle of the Hagia Sophia, for example, constituted a '"celebration of virginity" exalting women because the Virgin Theotokos had erased the sin of Eve'.[170] Previously 'subordinate to men in the eyes of the church', women now saw before their eyes, in some cases larger than life, two women: one, to whom was assigned the exalted status of Mother of God, and the other, identified as Augusta, taking a large role in the ruling of an empire and influencing the direction of Christianity.[171] These models must have heightened the sense of their own worth and abilities.

Though her identification with the Virgin Mary served to exalt females, in coinage, crosses and portraits Pulcheria seems to have transcended her gender.[172] Coins struck in about 420, for example, lack the ordinary distinguishing marks between imperial males and females. As Kenneth Holum writes,

> For the first time ... coin designers abandoned the traditional distinction, expressed through distinct reverse types, between male and female holders of *basileia* [imperial dominion]. The Long-Cross [coins] appeared with identical reverses from the mint of Constantinople and with obverses of Theodosius II, of his western colleague Honorius, and of Pulcheria. Like Aurelian's dedication of portrait busts in the senate house, these coins assimilated the Augusta with her male counterparts. Like the cross of the Trier Ivory, they declared that a woman might claim to be 'master of victory'.[173]

Even with the possibility of being 'master of victory', imperial women's authority fell short of that of men. Pulcheria generally remained in her brother's shadow, giving him credit for ruling even if she 'exercised real power'.[174] Following the death of Theodosius II in 450, Pulcheria 'reigned alone at Constantinople' but only for a few weeks.[175] 'Then', as Holum writes, 'since the Romans could not abide a woman reigning alone, the empress took a husband' – the tribune Marcian who 'pledged to respect Pulcheria's vow of virginity'.[176] As Judith Herrin observes, the patriarchal tradition inevitably dominated; stories such as that of Pulcheria suggest only that 'when men behave in an insufficiently imperial style, or are just indecisive or weak, women can act in their place' – not that women could be entrusted with permanent power.[177] Yet Pulcheria's embracing of her dynastic connections and the example of the Virgin Mary proved a potent combination that afforded her wide latitude at court and opened up pathways for female religious and imperial authority, not only in the Byzantine Empire but elsewhere in the region.

Finally, pre-Islamic and early Islamic Arabia yield several examples of women who succeeded their fathers or shared in their father's characteristics. As we have already seen in Chapter 1, pre-Islamic religion promoted the concept of 'daughters of God' who manifested some of their father's qualities, and were able to intercede on behalf of believers. Ordinary women in pre-Islamic Arabia likewise played considerable roles in the public sphere: they took part in warfare, traded, acted as soothsayers and priestesses, wrote poetry and gave trenchant advice on all sorts of matters.[178] Many in the early days of Islam and before its advent were identified in terms of their relationships to their fathers and are seen as exemplifying their fathers' qualities. 'Ā'isha is sometimes known as 'bint Abī Bakr', or '*al-ṣiddīqa bint al-ṣiddīq*', 'the truthful woman, daughter of the truthful man' – a designation that, as Spellberg notes, 'doubly emphasizes the paternal precedent of exemplary faith and character'.[179] One hadith recounts that Zaynab, one of the Prophet's wives, once protested to him about his preference for 'Ā'isha. 'Ā'isha 'silenced her co-wife with Muhammad's tacit support. 'A'isha defended herself with such verbal zeal and ire that the Prophet noted a family resemblance, remarking with pride, "She is the daughter of Abū Bakr."'[180] Here, 'Ā'isha manifests her father's eloquence and, like her father among most other companions, takes precedence among her co-wives in the Prophet's eyes.

Hind bint 'Utba, as seen in Chapter 2, likewise made a name for herself (albeit an unsavoury one) as an actor in the public sphere. Another Hind, bint al-Khuss, the daughter of a 'well-known member of the Iyād [tribe]', became known for her 'eloquence, quickness of repartee and perspicacity'.[181] Some sources say of her that she

> used to go to 'Ukāẓ [a western Arabian town in which competitions of poetry and music were held], serve as arbiter and give her opinion about camels, horses, men, women, and express in refined words opinions of great simplicity. Some of her answers, in rhyming prose, became proverbs, probably at an early date …; her 'sayings' have been collected by philologists and cited as *shawāhid* and as examples of very trenchant statements.[182]

Women in pre-Islamic and early Islamic Arabia also apparently held important roles with regard to the Ka'ba, a site sacred to Muslims and pagans alike – and at least in one case this role was likely inherited. Two pagan women, Ḥubba and Sulāfa, held the key to the Ka'ba at different times; it was in the hands of Sulāfa at the time of the Muslim conquest of Mecca.[183] In a society in which females acted as soothsayers and priestesses, it is possible that Ḥubba in some way succeeded her father in his role as the 'priest-king of Mecca'.[184] Far from disappearing outright, such attitudes and practices likely moulded the women and men of the first centuries of Islam.[185] It is not far-fetched to imagine that they found their ways as well into medieval Shi'i approaches to Fatima.

Conclusion

Though the predominant image of Fatima in medieval and early modern Shi'i texts is that of a woman whose spiritual authority was limited to the next world – an image whose contours were defined by suppositions about women's general lack of fitness for temporal rule – scholars are increasingly deploying her example today to support leadership roles for women. To do so, they are drawing on medieval hadith depicting Fatima as an imam-like successor to her father. In these hadith, Fatima, like the imams, interprets the Qur'an; confirms and explains the laws and principles of Islam; and pronounces on the rightness (or wrongness) of the direction of the Muslim community. She is even able to receive something akin to divine revelation in the form of the *muṣḥaf*, a divinely inspired book revealed to her by Gabriel. Conditioned on chastity and self-renunciation, and a body that, unlike that of most women, does not bleed, Fatima's authority takes a somewhat different form from that of men, but it is nevertheless powerful enough to redeem an entire community. The concept of Fatima as her father's successor – a concept that, as I have indicated here, manifests even in the pre-modern era – by no means emerged in a void. Despite a prevailing concept in many societies of women as inferior, weak and susceptible to corruption, strong precedents for female succession existed in the pre-Islamic Near East. Daughters of royal lineage typically accrued authority in the absence of an appropriate male, or when a male was too young or too weak to rule on his own. Societies dominated by charismatic authority that was transmitted along familial lines afforded greater chances for daughters to succeed, for supporters were willing to overlook gender in the quest to preserve the rule of a particular dynasty. Sometimes, ruling women embraced absolute chastity and piety as a means of enhancing their authority, and identified themselves with female icons who likewise manifested these characteristics. Given the supposed tendencies for women to be corrupt, such associations must have eased the doubts of men who worried that female rule would bring chaos. Some ruling daughters ceased, at least on some level, to be 'women' in the eyes of their followers: they transcended the constraints of their gender and became honorary men, endowed with wisdom, good judgement and military tendencies. Paintings and coinage depict them as men, or otherwise ignore the usual distinctions between males and females. As we will see in Chapter 6, many of these patterns reappear in cases in which women succeeded their fathers and other relatives in pre-modern Islamic societies.

6

Fatima's royal shadow

Muslim female rulers' quest for legitimacy and sovereignty

'The tongue of 'Ali'

Though Fatima's role as successor to her father hardly seems reproducible, evidence from Shi'i and other texts indicates otherwise. Other women closely associated with the *ahl al-bayt* likewise acted as successors – some even more prominently than their illustrious forebear.[1] Zaynab, the daughter of Fatima and 'Ali, is particularly notable in this respect. As a member of the Prophet's family who survived the Battle of Karbala, Zaynab appears in medieval Shi'i hadith collections as an outspoken advocate of her family and its cause. Many funeral orations are attributed to her, and she is also known for bravely confronting the caliph, Yazīd, and 'pronounc[ing] his imminent doom', as well as successfully defending Husayn's daughter, Fatima the Younger, from a man who wished to obtain her as a concubine.[2]

One of Zaynab's most rousing speeches, however, is a lacerating sermon delivered to the people of Kufa after the defeat at Karbala. The Kufans had invited Husayn to raise the rebellion against the Umayyads, only to betray him after they were cowed by the forces of Yazīd. According to Shi'i versions of the story, the Kufans later bitterly regretted their acts, weeping as the survivors of the Prophet's family, including Zaynab and the youthful, ill Zayn al-'Ābidīn, the fourth imam, were paraded enslaved through their streets; but Zaynab took little pity upon them.

In a version of the sermon contained in a collection of al-Shaykh al-Mufīd, the narrator, Ibn Satīr, observed as Zayn al-'Ābidīn and the women approached on their way from Karbala.[3] When the women of Kufa began to weep, the imam said, feebly, 'Beware, [if] these women are indeed weeping – then who killed us?' Then, Ibn Satīr said, 'I saw Zaynab the daughter of 'Ali, and I had never seen a lady with all her modesty being so eloquent. It seemed that she spoke in ['Ali's] voice.' After raising 'her hand towards the people to silence them, so the breathing slowed and the noises were silenced', she began by praising God and the Prophet, whom she called 'my father'.[4] Then she harshly criticized the people of Kufa as 'people of chicanery and betrayal', comparing them to 'the one who unravels her yarn after it is firmly spun' (Qur'an 16:92). Calling the Kufans cowards and violators of oaths, she declared that by forsaking and intriguing against the 'scion of the Seal of Prophethood, Master of the youths of Paradise' (i.e. Husayn), they had cemented their own humiliation and abasement. After elaborating upon this theme, she concluded:

> What you have committed is foolishness and degradation enough to fill the heavens and the earth! Are you then surprised if the heavens rain blood? 'And the chastisement of the hereafter is even more degrading' [Qur'an 41:16]. So do not take these moments of respite lightly, for He is not prompted by haste nor is it feared that He will miss the reprised. No! 'Your Lord is ever observant.' [Qur'an 89:14]

After Zaynab fell silent, Ibn Satīr saw people 'bewildered, their hands on their mouths, and I saw an old man weeping till his beard was drenched, and he said, "Their elderly are the best among the elderly people and their progeny … is never wrong, nor discredited."'[5]

The sermon conveys a clear sense of Zaynab as a temporal leader of the Shi'i community – a role she was forced to adopt given the illness of her nephew, Zayn al-'Ābidīn, who was able only to utter a few words in protest of the Kufans' remorse. The similarities with Fatima's khutba are striking. Like her mother, Zaynab delivers a harsh critique of people who have fallen off the path of virtue, one in which she adduces the Qur'an to support her views and speaks with a voice filled with outrage and righteous authority. Like Fatima, she is specifically described as resembling her father greatly – the observer says that she seemed to speak in the voice of 'Ali, who was particularly known for his eloquence. As with Fatima, her words strike deeply into the hearts of her audience; the old man who weeps, indeed, attributes infallibility to Zaynab and other progeny of the Prophet. Finally, like Fatima, Zaynab is portrayed as both eloquent *and* modest: she speaks, but nevertheless maintains her chastity.

In all of these ways, she serves as a female model of leadership – a role that has only expanded in the post-revolutionary Iran, where she has become known as the 'tongue of 'Ali' who inherited both her mother's 'feminine' chastity and her father's (and brothers') 'masculine' bravery and eloquence.[6]

Zaynab is not an anomaly. Just as many daughters in pre-modern Islamic societies, both Sunni and Shi'i, inherited and passed on characteristics, property and wealth from their natal families to their children, so did they succeed their fathers and other relatives to positions of public importance, whether as religious scholars, Sufi shaykhs, or benefactors.[7] Though they were able to accomplish it less frequently, daughters of kings, sultans and other leaders also succeeded their fathers, especially in societies in which dynastic rule prevailed and in which questions of lineage took precedence over those of gender. Female rulers stepped in for brief periods when appropriate males were unavailable, or ruled as regents on behalf of weak or incapacitated males. Less frequently, they reigned for relatively long periods on their own.

Gender-based protests were, inevitably, mounted against these women. Opponents said that women were incapable of rule and needed to be secluded, both for their honour and that of those around them. They frequently attacked women by questioning their chastity.[8] Yet also emerging from the literature describing reigning females is a surprising matter-of-factness towards female rule, an acknowledgement of female intelligence and leadership skills, and multiple solutions to the thorny problem of combining chastity and sovereignty. As an exemplar of both of these qualities, Fatima often figures in these narratives, which decisively demonstrate that women in pre-modern Islamic societies could and did lead – especially those in whose veins ran the blood of their royal fathers.

Slipping the constraints of their gender: Sitt al-Mulk (d. 1023) and Arwa (d. 1138)

Perhaps unsurprisingly considering its titular figure, the Fatimid Empire abounded with women exercising authority and influence. Indeed, the empire, which stretched across much of northern Africa and significant portions of the Middle East from the tenth to the twelfth centuries, constitutes one of the most prominent Islamic societies to acknowledge bilateral descent in its many forms. Founded by Isma'ilis, that branch of Shi'ism that traced the imamate through Ismā'īl, the elder son of Ja'far al-Ṣādiq (unlike the Twelver Shi'is, who traced it through Mūsā al-Kāẓim, Ismā'īl's half-brother), the empire not only took its name from the daughter of the Prophet but also promoted concepts of descent, inheritance and succession that acknowledged a significant role for women – often relating these concepts directly to Fatima.

Because the Fatimids sought religious and political legitimacy through their connections to the family of the Prophet, from which they claimed descent, they emphasized the importance of blood ties over marriage ties and the nobility of the mother as 'a condition in establishing a legitimate line of descent'.[9] In writing an elegy commemorating a patron's late mother, for example, the famous Fatimid court poet Ibn Hāni' al-Andalusī noted, 'To our mothers we owe half of our lineage' – thus acknowledging the 'virtues of mothers, who are to be praised in equal terms as … fathers'.[10] The poem likewise 'echoes the virtues and importance of the most noble of all mothers, Fatima, whom the poet repeatedly hails as the mother of the Fatimid Imams'.[11]

Indeed, like Mary at various times throughout the reign of the Byzantine Empire, Fatima received special attention commensurate with one associated with both spiritual and temporal authority; often, moreover, her example was used to justify the recognition that women could possess such authority. Scholars such as al-Qāḍī al-Nu'mān, as we saw in Chapter 5, designated Fatima a *ḥujja*, or 'proof'. In a major (and possibly unprecedented) sign of her significance, the daughter of the Prophet appeared on coins: the Imam-caliph al-Mu'izz inaugurated his caliphate with the minting in 953 of *dīnārs* bearing his name on the one side and reading on the other: "Ali ibn Abi Talib is the Nominee of the Prophet and the Most Excellent Representative and the Husband of the Radiant Chaste One (*zawj al-zahrā' al-batūl*) [i.e. Fatima].'[12] Though reference to the Prophet's daughter on coins proved too controversial to keep, nevertheless 'through the use of Fatima's epithets, al-Mu'izz had symbolically and publicly acknowledged … the role of a woman in the legitimisation of Fatimid power'.[13] Fatima's name was also

> included in the blessing formula adopted by the Fatimids for their khutba. When the general Jawhar conquered Egypt, he ordered the removal of any mention of the 'Abbāsid rulers from the Friday sermon, to recite instead: 'Praise be on Muhammad, on 'Ali and on Fatima the virgin, on al-Hasan

> and al-Husayn, and on the Imams, forefathers of the chief commander of believers [i.e. al-Mu'izz bi-'llāh].'[14]

Similarly, the Fatimids celebrated Fatima's 'birthday and made it into a holiday, when gifts were exchanged among the palace people'.[15] By reciting a 'rosary-like prayer known as *Tasbīḥ Fāṭima* (Fatima's glorification of God)', and combining it with the shahada, people living during the Fatimid dynasty could earn 'benefits equivalent to 1,000 good deeds' in the sight of God – another sign of the authority of the Prophet's daughter.[16] Moreover, Fatima's example in defending the rights of the *ahl al-bayt* exerted a positive influence on how people thought about women taking part in the public sphere, including politics.[17]

Indeed, many accounts indicate women enjoyed a certain degree of freedom and status during the Fatimid era. As we have already seen, Fatimid law provided for relatively egalitarian inheritance practices. Likewise, sources show Fatimid women receiving educations, taking part in (public) prayer, trade, propaganda and diplomatic relations, and sometimes acting as architectural patrons.[18] Daughters from scholarly families studied and sometimes 'succeeded' their fathers.[19] The historian Ṣalāḥ al-Dīn al-Ṣafadī (d. 1363), who spent much of his intellectual life in Damascus and Cairo, mentions the erudition of Sutayta bint al-Muhamalī (d. 987), 'the daughter of a *qāḍī* and mother of a *qāḍī*, who was well versed in the Arabic language, studied *fiqh*, learnt the *farā'iḍ* and was known as a *ḥadith* transmitter'.[20] He likewise speaks admiringly of several female calligraphers emerging from scholarly families.[21]

At court, several royal women exerted a great deal of influence, and two females, Sitt al-Mulk (d. 1023) and Arwa bint Aḥmad al-Sulayhiyya (d. 1138), acceded to the throne.[22] Sitt al-Mulk, the daughter of the Imam-caliph al-'Azīz (r. 975–96) and the sister of his successor, al-Ḥākim (r. 996–1021), ruled on her own for a month after the mysterious disappearance and presumed death of the eccentric al-Ḥākim. She then acted as regent after her nephew's accession and until her death two years later. Arwa, the wife of the Sulayhid ruler al-Mukarram Aḥmad b. 'Ali, stepped into the breach when her husband fell too ill to rule, and continued to hold the reins of power in her grasp for many years after his death in 1084. Although she was a widow who succeeded her husband, rather than a daughter who succeeded her father, her example is included here not only because her reign extended for so long but also because scholars used the model of Fatima to justify her spiritual authority. Operating under the expansive shadow of the daughter of the Prophet, both of these women benefited from a willingness among elites to see women as capable administrators and inheritors of dynastic charisma and authority.

Eldest daughter of al-ʿAzīz and his favourite concubine, the Greek al-Sayyida al-ʿAzīziya, Sitt al-Mulk (Lady of Power) grew up in highly privileged circumstances. Intelligent and beautiful, she inspired great devotion in her father, who – according to the Egyptian secretary and historian Ibn Ẓāfir (d. 1292) – 'adored her mightily and denied her nothing'.[23] In fact, her 'father singled her out by giving the western of two royal palaces in Cairo to her exclusively and creating a special guard force – a separate regiment – for her use called the Qasriya'.[24] According to some accounts, al-ʿAzīz even 'made Sitt al-Mulk a party to power by asking her opinion and encouraging her to express it'.[25] It seems likely that she was an active player in the struggle for influence between Berber and non-Berber factions that was being waged at court.[26]

Her influence and activity continued after her father's sudden death in 996 and the accession to the throne of the designated heir apparent, her half-brother al-Ḥākim, then only ten.[27] The next few years witnessed tremendous acts of generosity between the siblings, testimony either to affection or attempts at influence (or both). By the second year of al-Ḥākim's reign, Sitt al-Mulk had 'dispensed lavish donations upon' the young caliph, including horses, mules, eunuchs, fine clothing, a 'crown embedded with precious stones' and other treasures.[28] Her brother reciprocated a few years later, in 1000, giving Sitt al-Mulk 'highly profitable *iqṭāʿāt*s, land grants and real estates'.[29] As one historian wrote, she soon took on the role of adviser to al-Hakim, who was 'consulting her in the affairs [of state], acted according to her opinion, and did not oppose her advice'.[30] According to Ibn Ẓāfir, 'Sitt al-Mulk had been guiding al-Ḥākim in his best policies by pointing him in the right direction, and the Imam-caliph valued her opinion so much that he would change his mind on matters at the last moment on account of her advice.'[31]

Then the caliph began to exhibit increasingly odd behaviour. As Paul Walker writes, 'Over the final seven years of his rule, [al-Ḥākim] changed into a strange ascetic figure, ever generous and accessible, but also tyrannical.'[32] Highly suspicious of women, he enacted progressively severe restrictions against their movements before banning them from going out at all – a measure partly enforced by forbidding 'cobblers from making or selling footwear for them.'[33] Christians and Jews were also targets: 'Breaking with a tradition of tolerance, al-Hakim forbade them the purchase and consumption of wine, even for religious [ceremonies]. He destroyed their places of worship and ordered their cemeteries profaned.'[34] He also ordered all dogs in Cairo killed; forbade 'singing in public and walking along the banks of the Nile'; and banned certain types of food, including very ordinary ones.[35]

Disagreement appears to have erupted between the caliph and his sister as a result of his actions. When al-Ḥākim designated a cousin as the next caliph rather than his own son, Sitt al-Mulk 'took it upon herself to defend the direct bloodline of the dynasty by giving refuge in her residence to al-Ḥākim's wife Amina and their son 'Ali, who, according to Ibn Taghrībirdī, were both fleeing from the caliph's persecution.'[36] Ibn Ẓāfir reported that

> near the end, as a symptom of his pernicious misrule, al-Hakim began to threaten his highly competent and intelligent sister and to accuse her of having done such vile things, the likes of which had never previously occurred. Although, at the start of his reign she had offered him the best advice and he had followed her opinion, by the end he had changed, becoming more hostile which led in part to the burning and looting of Fustat.[37] According to this account, she was among those who went to him to complain and to try to stop the atrocities. Thereupon his attitude toward her soured; his deference for her seniority disappeared. Instead he castigated her for rumors he had heard about her behavior, things she should not have done.[38]

According to Ibn Ẓāfir, the caliph accused Sitt al-Mulk of fornication and planned to have her examined to see if the unmarried princess was still a virgin. If not, she would be killed; if proven innocent, she would be imprisoned. For her part, Sitt al-Mulk – who would hardly have welcomed the prospect of this inspection – feared that the dynasty was in peril and 'resolved to seize the initiative' by having al-Ḥākim killed and putting his son, 'Ali (later known as al-Ẓāhir), on the throne.[39]

Though many medieval chroniclers such as Ibn Ẓāfir claimed that Sitt al-Mulk engineered the assassination of her half-brother, no evidence of it exists, for the caliph simply disappeared after riding out of Cairo alone one night.[40] Attempts to find his body or to verify his death failed.

The void left by al-Ḥākim's absence created an opportunity for Sitt al-Mulk to seize control, and so she did, ruling the Fatimid state for the month after his disappearance and before his successor and son, al-Ẓāhir, assumed the throne.[41] Her sovereignty, moreover, extended into the announcement of her nephew's succession and beyond. The vizier Khāṭir al-Mulk 'announced on Sitt al-Mulk's authority the succession to the caliphate of al-Hakim's son: "Our Lady … says that this is your master."'[42] It was Sitt al-Mulk, too, who crowned the new caliph.[43]

Sitt al-Mulk acted as regent after her nephew's appointment, for though the young caliph was already sixteen, he reportedly 'occupied himself with pleasures, leisure and listening to music' as his aunt managed the affairs of state.[44] In this role, she undid many of the excesses of her half-brother.[45] For example, she allowed women to move about once more and people to drink wine and listen to and play music.[46] Jews and Christians were able to rebuild their synagogues and churches and thus recoup some of their lost status.[47] Sitt al-Mulk likewise tried to renew the government's economic health, in part by restoring cancelled commercial taxes and reclaiming formerly government-owned lands given away by al-Ḥākim.[48] Her efforts were not restricted to Cairo: she also 'conducted diplomatic negotiations with Byzantium'.[49]

Her activity met with approval from observers contemporary with her reign. As Walker notes, she ruled 'so effectively that, when she died two years later … her obituary notice took special note that, although a woman, she had been a patron to men'.[50]

About fifty years later and 1,300 miles to the southeast, another woman was consolidating her rule in the Yemen, an important outpost of the Fatimid Empire. The example of Arwa, known as al-Sayyida al-Ḥurra (the 'Free Lady') inevitably occupies a prominent place in modern works about female rule in medieval Islamic states.[51] Deservedly so, for she rose to a significant position of power and held it for more than fifty years. Her accession and reign likely benefited from a particularly progressive attitude towards women among the Sulayhids, the dynasty to which she belonged and which, while giving allegiance to the Fatimids, dominated the Yemen for nearly a century.[52]

Founded by the Ismaili *dāʿī* (religious propagandist or missionary) 'Ali ibn Muhammad al-Sulayhī (r. ca. 1047-1067), the Sulayhid dynasty 'took pride in educating its women to high standards and … valued their judgement'.[53] Such was the assertion of the Yemeni historian Najm al-Dīn 'Umāra (d. 1174), who provided evidence for it in his account of Arwa's life.[54] As he reports, the young queen-to-be, a member of the Sulayhid clan, was brought up in the royal palace after her father's death. There, 'Ali, her future father-in-law, showed great appreciation and support of her, and made sure she received an education.[55] 'Umāra lauded Arwa's 'knowledge of the Qur'an, her ability to read and write, to memorize chronicles, poetry and historical events, and her excellence in glossing and interpreting texts'.[56]

Married to al-Mukarram in about 1065, Arwa rose to the position of queen-consort two years later upon the death of 'Ali.[57] About ten years later, when al-Mukarram fell ill, the king 'transferred the responsibility of the affairs of government onto his wife', then in her late twenties.[58] For the next decade, Arwa

> effectively exercised power over southern Yemen, as well as overseeing the affairs of Oman and Bahrayn, With her husband's death, as queen mother, she continued to rule in the name of her son and, at his death, she remained in power until her long life (she lived to be almost ninety) came to an end in 532/1138 – and, with it, the Sulayhid dynasty as a whole.[59]

In both the medieval and contemporary eras, the female icon with whom scholars and poets most frequently linked Arwa was not Fatima but Bilqīs, the Queen of Sheba, famous in the Qur'an for her interactions with King Solomon, and often a symbol for female sovereignty in Islam.[60] As Delia Cortese and Simonetta Calderini write, in 'today's Yemen, Arwa is still remembered as a great and much loved sovereign, as attested in Yemeni contemporary historiography, literature and popular lore, where this daughter of Yemen is referred to al-Bilqīs al-sughra – that is, the junior queen of Sheba'.[61]

Yet scholars, religious leaders and, reportedly, the ruler herself also invoked Fatima in speaking of her sovereignty and spiritual authority. The fifteenth-century Isma'ili scholar Idrīs 'Imād al-Dīn quotes Arwa, in one of the codicils to her will, bearing 'witness to Fatima, the "radiant and the pure," as the fifth among the elected *aṣḥāb*, or People of the House'.[62] Political motives – particularly complex ones, in this instance – may have played a part in this mention. Idrīs 'Imād al-Dīn was, like Arwa herself, a Ṭayyibī – that is, a member of the Ismaili sect recognizing an alleged son, al-Ṭayyib, as the successor to the murdered Fatimid caliph al-Amīr (d. 1130) against the claims of al-Amīr's cousin, al-Ḥāfiẓ. Idrīs 'Imād al-Dīn was also a *dā'ī muṭlaq* – an 'absolute *dā'ī*', the highest-ranking official in the Ṭayyibi *da'wa* hierarchy, and a line established by Arwa.[63] By deliberately inserting the mention of Fatima into Arwa's will, Idrīs 'Imād al-Dīn may have sought to 'link the queen and Tayyibī leadership to the holiest of Shiʿi female figures'.[64] Highlighting Fatima's role as a female member of the *ahl al-bayt* would have underscored and legitimized Arwa's authority both as a supporter of the Ṭayyibīs and an establisher of the *dāʿī muṭlaq* line.

Likewise, at least one scholar invoked Fatima in seeking to demonstrate that Arwa enjoyed spiritual as well as temporal authority. The Ṭayyibī poet and scholar Sultan al-Khaṭṭāb (d. 1138–9), in both a collection of poetry and a doctrinal treatise, affirmed that Arwa (like Fatima) was a *ḥujja*, or 'proof' – one of the highest stations in the Ismaʿili hierarchy.[65] He justified his assertion by noting that many women 'have been in the spiritual ranks', including Fatima, Khadīja and Mary, and by elaborating upon esoteric ideas of masculine and feminine which convey that women are not bound by their biology.[66] As contemporary scholar Karen Bauer writes,

> Al-Khaṭṭāb explains that the bodily form is like a garment (*qamīṣ*) rather than the intrinsic essence of a person; what matters are good deeds rather than the bodily form. Many women have been better than men, such as the Prophet Muhammad's daughter Fatima. He then says that when a woman acquires certain excellencies, she may be considered to be masculine in the spiritual hierarchy, although her bodily form is that of a woman: 'Masculine and feminine are human garments … that do not express the truth nor do they lead to His path.'[67]

As with Idrīs ʿImād al-Dīn, political considerations likely motivated al-Khaṭṭāb, who, as Cortese and Calderini note, was preoccupied with 'defending the legitimacy of the line of the Yemeni *dāʿī*s down to his own master, Dhuʿayb. As Dhuʿayb had been appointed *dāʿī muṭlaq* on the authority of Arwa, a woman, al-Khaṭṭāb had a vested interest in arguing in favor of female spiritual attainments.'[68] Yet the upshot is the same: an exaltation of Fatima, and reflected glory for Arwa.

To be sure, Sitt al-Mulk and Arwa did not altogether escape the constraints of their gender. Coins issued during Arwa's reign – an important signifier of sovereignty – continued to mention her husband's name, not her own, long after his death.[69] Indeed, the presence of a male figurehead, however negligible his power, seemed essential to both women's rules. Apart from the brief period during which Sitt al-Mulk reigned alone after the disappearance of al-Ḥākim, both she and Arwa ruled in the name of a male. After the death of her son, Arwa was compelled by Fatimid leadership in Cairo to marry a relative, the *dāʿī* Sabāʾ b. Aḥmad al-Sulayhī, who would nominally rule.[70] (Even so, however, ʿUmāra reported that she did not 'submit to the will of her new husband; and, being "the master of her own people" … [maintained] her acknowledged high status among them'.[71])

Moreover, many elites sought to tarnish these women's reputations by accusing them of the sort of bad behaviour traditionally imputed to women who dared step out of the domestic sphere. Al-Ḥākim, as we have already seen, suspected his sister of fornication. Some chroniclers saw fit to involve Sitt al-Mulk in a romantic entanglement with a cousin and to depict both of them attempting a coup before al-Ḥākim's accession.[72] Associations with gendered traits such as devious plotting and treachery extend to the colourful descriptions of Sitt al-Mulk's supposed murder of her brother.[73] Al-Ṣabīʾ (d.1056), the 'almost-contemporary ʿAbbāsid and anti-Fatimid historian', accused the princess of planning the assassination with the Berber chief Ibn Dawwās, relating that 'after the killing, Ibn Dawwās brought al-Ḥākim's corpse to Sitt al-Mulk, who then buried it in her *majlis*, hid the whole thing and gave money and robes of honour to Ibn Dawwās', whom she later had murdered as well.[74]

No evidence exists to substantiate these reports of intrigues, however, and later (pro-Fatimid) historians rejected them.[75] Indeed, amid attempts to curb, downplay or besmirch the reigns and reputations of these women, a few matters emerge with clarity from the chronicles. First, Sitt al-Mulk and Arwa did appear to exercise sovereignty and leadership, and their entry into typically male spheres was greeted for the most part favourably. Ibn Ḥammād (d. 1230), the Berber historian, wrote of the queen that she 'protected the empire and directed the government'.[76] A poet writing after her death affirmed that 'living under the sovereignty … of Sitt al-Mulk / We have shared the comfort of its shadows.'[77] Similarly, historians called Arwa *malika* (queen) and, as we have seen, some writers affirmed her position as *ḥujja*.[78] According to some sources, the Friday khutba was even said in Arwa's name: 'May Allah prolong the days of al-Ḥurra the perfect, the sovereign who carefully manages the affairs of the faithful.'[79] Though not named on coins, both women often served as the 'signatories and the recipients of official correspondence and numerous diplomatic missives' – another sign of their authority.[80]

Second, despite the efforts to smear these women, they appear in most accounts to transcend these aspersions. Even the anti-Fatimid chronicler

Hilāl al-Ṣabī', while describing Sitt al-Mulk's supposed participation in the assassination of al-Ḥākim, called her 'intelligent and energetic'.[81] In a society in which dynastic succession was the norm, and which derived its legitimacy in part from its reported links to the daughter of the Prophet, women were seen as inheriting and displaying the charisma, authority, intellect and leadership skills of their male relatives.

Becoming a man: Raḍiyya bint Iltutmish (d. 1240)

The sense of transcending one's gender and becoming an honorary male manifests even more graphically in the example of the Indian ruler Raḍiyya (r. 1236–40), daughter of the sultan Shams al-Dīn Iltutmish, ruler of the Delhi Sultanate in northern India from 1211 to 1236. Following the death of his eldest son and presumptive heir, Iltutmish reportedly passed over his other sons to name Raḍiyya as his successor, claiming that she was the most worthy of sovereignty. Although Raḍiyya's reign lasted less than four years, she left an important legacy of female rule in South Asia. Like, to some extent, her forebears in Sassanian Iran, Pūrān and Āzarm Dukht, Raḍiyya assumed the trappings of masculinity in order to rule effectively, discarding female attire and donning the tunic and headdress of a man. Her identification as a male exploited a metaphorical space in which elite daughters could exercise greater agency within a society that normally severely restricted their actions. It also presented a means (though controversial, as will be seen) of addressing the question of chastity. Finally, though Central Asian and pre-Islamic Persian precedents almost certainly facilitated her accession, the example of Fatima, well known to the Muslim elite of India, may have played a part as well.

According to the Ghurid Juzjānī (d. ca. 1260), a historian contemporary with Raḍiyya's reign, Raḍiyya was the eldest daughter of Iltutmish, a Delhi sultan of the thirteenth century who was of Turkish stock.[82] Iltutmish intended for his eldest son, Nāsir al-Dīn Maḥmūd Shāh, to succeed him. But after that son died prematurely of illness in 1229, the sultan was obliged to make other plans. After returning from an expedition to Gwalior in 1233, the sultan designated as his successor Raḍiyya, the daughter of his chief wife, Tarkān Khātūn. The historian explains that Raḍiyya 'exercised authority, and possessed great grandeur' and because her father 'used to notice in her indications of sovereignty and high spirit, although she was a daughter, and [consequently] veiled from public gaze … he commanded [his secretary] to write out a decree, naming his daughter as his heir-apparent, and she was made his heir [accordingly]'.[83]

This designation was carried out over the complaints of his attendants, who maintained that he should not name his daughter as successor when he had 'grown-up sons who [were] eligible for sovereignty'.[84] Juzjānī records the sultan as responding that his sons were 'engrossed in the pleasures of youth, and none of them possesses the capability of managing the affairs of the country'; whereas Raḍiyya, his daughter, was the most worthy, as would be proven after his death.[85]

At a different point in the narrative, however, Juzjānī conveys an expectation prevalent among the people that Raḍiyya's half-brother, later known as Rukn al-Dīn Fīrūz Shāh, would succeed his father. Fīrūz Shāh had been granted the *iqtā*ʿ of Lahore upon Iltutmish's return from Gwalior, the same time that the sultan apparently designated Raḍiyya his successor. Upon Iltutmish's return to the capital from his final military expedition, the ailing sultan brought Fīrūz Shāh with him, 'for the people had their eyes upon him, since, after [the late] Malik Nāsir-ud-Dīn, Mahmūd Shah, he was the eldest of [Iltutmish's] sons'.[86] In fact, the day after the sultan's death, on a date corresponding to 30 April 1236, the 'maliks and grandees of the kingdom, by agreement', seated Fīrūz Shāh on the throne.[87] His brief, tumultuous reign was dominated by his mother, Shāh Terken, who ruled the kingdom while Fīrūz Shāh occupied himself in 'buffoonery, sensuality, and diversion'.[88]

Shāh Terken's use of her newfound power to settle old scores led to widespread revolt among nobles and officials in the kingdom, many of whom broke out into open rebellion. Amid the turmoil, Shāh Terken attempted to put Raḍiyya to death, upon which the people of Delhi rose up, attacked the palace and seized Shah Terken. After considerable upheaval, the Delhi forces and members of Iltutmish's personal slave group enthroned Raḍiyya, who ordered Fīrūz Shāh imprisoned. He was executed on 18 Rabīʿ al-Awwal of the Hijrī year 634 (26 November 1236).[89]

Under Raḍiyya, Juzjānī observes, 'all things returned to their usual rules and customs' and, after initial rebellions by some provincial governors and amirs who refused to acknowledge her, 'the kingdom became pacified, and the power of the state widely extended'.[90] The historian writes that from Lakhnawati to Diwal and Damrilah – that is, from western Bengal to lower Sind – 'all the

Maliks and Amīrs manifested their obedience and submission'.[91] Even if the power of the state was extended during her reign, however, evidence also exists of retrenchment from Hindu strongholds such as Ranthanbor and Gwalior – events that may have displeased Iltutmish's slave officers, who had taken great pride in the sultan's conquests of those regions.[92]

Two highly provocative statements occur about midway through Juzjānī's account. He writes that the *malik* (amir in some versions) Jamāl al-Din Yāqut, the Habashī (Abyssinian), 'who was Lord of the Stables, acquired favor in attendance upon the Sultān', and that this favour caused the Turkish amirs and other officials to become envious.[93] The historian then writes, nearly in the same breath, that the sultan put aside female dress, and 'issued from [her] seclusion, and donned the tunic, and assumed the head-dress [of a man], and appeared among the people; and, when she rode out on an elephant, at the time of mounting it, all people used, openly, to see her'.[94]

Subsequent to Raḍiyya's discarding of female attire, an act no doubt undertaken to enhance her air of authority and military power, many of the leaders who had previously supported the sultan began to rise up against her. She succeeded in crushing the first internal rebellion, instigated by ʿIzz al-Dīn Kabīr Khān, the *iqtāʿ*-holder of Lahore, but failed to do so with the second, instigated by Ikhtiār al-Dīn Altunapa, commander of the crown fortress of Tabarhindh and secretly abetted by amirs of the court.[95] As Juzjānī writes, when Raḍiyya pursued Altunapa to Tabarhindh (identified with Bhatinda in Punjab, northwest of Delhi), the Turk amirs 'rose against her, and put to death [her supporter], Amīr [Jamāl al-Din Yāqut], the Habashī, seized Sultān Raḍiyya and put her in durance, and sent her to the fortress' of Tabarhindh.[96] In the meantime, they enthroned in her place her brother, thenceforth known as Muʿizz al-Dīn Bahrām Shah. They likely hoped to exert more power during his reign by insisting on the appointment of a viceroy to the sultan, Aytegin, Raḍiyya's *amir-i hājib* (military chamberlain) and a former member of Iltutmish's personal slave troop.

Here the story takes another surprising twist. After Aytegin overstepped his bounds and was subsequently murdered on the new sultan's orders, Altunapa – who had no doubt hoped to derive favours from his now-deceased ally – came to see the expediency of marrying Raḍiyya, his prisoner, and attempting to retake the sultanate, a plan to which Raḍiyya agreed. Together they marched an army towards Delhi, aiming to dethrone Bahrām Shāh.[97] But the new sultan led out a force to rout his sister and Altunapa and succeeded. The troops accompanying the couple abandoned them, and both Raḍiyya and her husband were killed by Hindus on 25 Rabīʿ al-Awwal 638 (21 October 1240).

As valuable as it is, Juzjānī's account leaves much to be desired. His laconicism creates ample opportunity for misunderstanding and for later elaboration by less circumspect historians, as does his tendency to narrate the same events slightly differently in separate *tabaqāt*.[98] One matter that remains shrouded in ambiguity, given the markers also pointing to Fīrūz Shāh, is whether Iltutmish actually designated Raḍiyya as his successor. Jackson notes that since Juzjānī was not in Delhi at the time of the sultan's return from Gwalior, he could not have witnessed the appointment; 'In these circumstances, we have to consider the possibility that the story is apocryphal and was put about by those who made her sultan.'[99] Still, whether Raḍiyya was actually appointed by her father is perhaps not the burning issue here. She clearly manifested leadership qualities that were observed both by the sultan and by those around him – qualities that lent credence to the decision to seat her on the throne, no matter from whom it came.

Even greater confusion is engendered by Juzjānī's cryptic descriptions of the jealousy aroused among Turkish amirs by Raḍiyya's preference for Jamāl al-Din Yāqut, and the sultan's subsequent discarding of female attire. The proximity of the two statements makes it tempting to link them, and their gendered nature proves a trap into which many a medieval (and modern) historian falls. As will be seen, the fantastic, amorous speculation to which they gave rise in the middle period of Islam produced an even more luridly romantic scenario in the modern period: the transformation of this 'warlike' sultan into a beleaguered heroine whose reputation stands in need of rescuing.[100]

Precedents among Turks, Mongol-type peoples and Persians likely paved the way to Raḍiyya's accession to the throne. Many of the Turkish slave officers who brought her to power originated from the Pontic and Caspian steppes, where women were afforded significantly more latitude than they enjoyed in non-nomadic societies.[101] Other *ghulām*s were of 'Khitan or Qara-Khitan stock – Mongol-type peoples of the eastern steppes' who founded dynasties in Turkestan.[102] As we have already seen, bilateral descent was often recognized in these societies, and women often participated in assemblies, fought and sometimes ruled as successors to their fathers or other relatives.[103] Upon the death of Gur Khān, a Khitan leader, for example, his daughter Koyunk Khatun ruled Turkestan for several years in the twelfth century.[104] Similarly, one of the feudatory rulers of Khwārazm 'was succeeded early in the same century by his only child, a daughter, who even after her marriage to the founder of the Khwārizmshāhī dynasty, retained her sovereign power and title'.[105]

Pre-Islamic Persian precedent, as enshrined in the *Shāhnāma* – with which Turkish officers and other powerful figures in the sultanate would likely have been acquainted – may also have influenced those who enthroned Raḍiyya, albeit less directly, including the idea that charisma and 'divinity' resided only in the royal family, including in females.[106] And the model of Fatima may also have played a part in Raḍiyya's accession. As exemplified by Amīr Khusraw a few generations later, the Sunni Turkish elite of Delhi were well aware of the example of Fatima and even embraced the concept of dynastic succession that she represented.[107] Given these precedents, making the leap from seeing a daughter as capable of transmitting her father's lineage, to seeing her as able to rule and lead in his stead, was not an insurmountable one.

Even if pre-Islamic and Islamic precedents created somewhat favourable conditions for a daughter's succession to the throne, the prevailing attitude towards women as intellectually inferior to men, overly emotional and susceptible to evil and corruption – and therefore requiring seclusion – remained a formidable obstacle.[108] As has already been suggested, one way for a woman to circumvent this obstacle was, quite simply, not to *be* a woman, but rather a man. Either through her own efforts, those of her supporters, or both, she could transcend or transform the public perceptions of her gender to an extent that people would cease to associate her with the weaker, 'deficient' sex.[109] By associating themselves with traditionally masculine symbols, titles and imagery, Muslim women could raise their sociopolitical status and be considered worthy of achieving or maintaining sovereignty.

Raḍiyya and her supporters relied on such associations to legitimize her rule. The most obvious of these is her assumption of male attire. Cross-dressing helped Raḍiyya cultivate her popularity with the people of Delhi – some of her most fervent supporters – since it allowed her to ride out in public and undertake state business 'in the manner of kings', and helped to dispel the 'impression of effeminacy and weakness that her sex was likely to create'.[110] Writing about three quarters of a century after her death, Amīr Khusraw describes both the debilitating effect of purdah, the traditional seclusion for females, upon Raḍiyya's ability to rule, and the freedom engendered by her emergence from it:

> For several months, her face was veiled –
>   her sword's ray flashed, lightning-like, from behind the screen.
> Since the sword remained in the sheath,
>   many rebellions were left unchecked.
> With a royal blow, she tore away the veil;
>   she showed her face's sun from behind the screen.
> The [lioness] showed so much force
>   that brave men bent low before her.[111]

Her coinage also conveys a sense of male legitimacy or a striving for it. Some of her coins bore both her name and that of her father; Iltutmish was proclaimed as *al-sultān al-ā'ẓam* (the greatest sultan) and Raḍiyya, *al-sulṭān al-mu'aẓẓm* (the great sultan) and identified as *bint al-sulṭān* (daughter of the sultan). Later coins named Raḍiyya alone.[112] Perhaps significantly, she appears both on the coins and in the early histories with the gender-neutral and awe-inspiring sobriquet of sultan: the king, the leader.[113] Centuries later, in retelling the story of Iltutmish's designation of Raḍiyya as his successor, one Mughal-era historian has the sultan saying of Raḍiyya that 'although she is in appearance a woman, yet in her mental qualities she is a man and in truth she is better than [my] sons'.[114]

Raḍiyya's success in identifying as a man benefited from surprisingly flexible conceptions of gender in medieval Islamic culture – a phenomenon we have already encountered in many forms. Although, as in Western medieval societies, the categories of 'male' and 'female' were sharply delineated, with the majority of positive attributes arrogated to men and negative ones to women, one's biological sex did not necessarily determine one's gender. Women who acted as men could very nearly 'become' them, with all of the positive and powerful attributes associated with men.[115] Blame or shame did not necessarily result. Indeed, several centuries after Raḍiyya, in Mughal India, royal women who behaved in a man-like way attracted favourable attention, not scorn. In her memoirs, the Mughal princess Gulbadan Begum (d. 1603) – herself very well respected as a pious benefactress and author, the daughter of Emperor Bābur and the sister of Emperor Humayun – described two female guests at an imperial gathering held in Agra. These elites wore men's clothing, played polo and shot with the bow and arrow. Despite 'all their conspicuous unconventionality, it is noteworthy that these uncommon women were not treated as eccentric social outcasts but were … honored guests at the imperial family's Mystic Feast'.[116]

Naturally, not all medieval attempts at cross-dressing, whether in Christian or Muslim societies, met with approval.[117] It was Joan of Arc's resumption of male dress while in jail that largely precipitated her final condemnation and execution.[118] The high textual tradition of Islam condemns cross-dressing, as does that of Christianity.[119] A hadith declares that the Prophet Mohammad 'cursed the man who dressed like women and the woman who dressed like men'.[120] Indeed, some medieval historians, writing well after her rule ended, attribute Raḍiyya's deposition to her donning of male attire and 'performance' as a man.[121]

Yet the real reasons for her fall from grace are probably far more mundane. Peter Jackson observes that although the Turkish slaves who surrounded her father brought Raḍiyya to power, they likely did so with the idea that they would be able to manipulate her.[122] Meanwhile, although she showed them favour, she demonstrated no signs of being tractable. In fact, she took many steps to assert her autonomy and to break their monopoly. Her patronage of Jamāl al-Din Yāqut (who was not a Turk), her emergence from purdah and her coinage can all be seen in this light.[123] These demonstrations of autonomy proved too much for the Turks, leading them to depose her and enthrone someone they thought they might be more submissive: her brother. Scandal over perceived immorality or transgressions of gender-based mores, however, did not contribute to their decision. Jackson argues that 'however scandalous [her behaviour] might have been to the Tājik *'olamā'* of Delhi, it would surely have had less impact on the Turkish military', who were accustomed to seeing women in powerful positions.[124]

That the same fate would likely have befallen her had she been a man is demonstrated in the shortness of many of her brothers' reigns. In fact, Raḍiyya's rule stands out for its vigour and relative length, which exceeded that of both the brother who preceded her and the one who immediately followed her.[125] All came to power during a transitional period during which, even if one was male, the likelihood of remaining on the throne for more than a few months was weak.

Early assessments of Raḍiyya's rule make no mention of gender-based transgressions.[126] Juzjānī does write, somewhat morosely, that she was 'endowed with all the admirable attributes and qualifications necessary for kings; but, as she did not attain the destiny, in her creation, of being computed among men, of what advantage were all these excellent qualifications unto her?'[127] Yet I believe Juzjānī uses her femaleness here as a foil to avoid placing blame for her deposition where it belongs: on the activism of the Turkish slave group. That group was growing ever more powerful as the historian was writing his *Tabaqāt-i Nāsirī*, which he co-dedicated to his patrons, the sultan Nāsir al-Dīn Maḥmūd, son of Iltutmish[128] and Nāsir al-Dīn's deputy, Balaban the Lesser, a powerful member of the slave group and the head of the dynasty later replacing that of Iltutmish. Underlining that group's role in the removal of a popular sultan would hardly have been a politically expedient move.[129]

Amīr Khusraw adopted a more neutral tone with regard to Raḍiyya, attributing the end of her rule to the hand of an inscrutable fortune, not to her sex:

> For three years in which her hand was strong
>   No one lay a finger on one of her orders.
> In the fourth, since the page had turned from her matters
>   The pen of fate drew a line through her.[130]

Even though Raḍiyya was able to divest herself of femininity during her reign, intervening centuries have served to re-feminize her. Medieval and even modern historians present heavily gendered and even erotically charged accounts of her reign and deposition. 'Isāmi, writing in the mid-fourteenth century, is at first relatively restrained in his depiction. He writes that as the top-ranking amirs were lamenting the failings of Fīrūz Shāh as leader, Raḍiyya 'let loose her scarf from the window', declaring herself ready to rule and asserting that the king had chosen her as his heir apparent. The chiefs debated the matter and decided to enthrone her, a move that was welcomed by the populace. But 'Isāmī then adopts a distinctly gendered approach. He indicates that she had ruled successfully for three years when a radical change occurred:

> I am told that she came out of *purdah* suddenly, discarded her modesty and became jovial. One day, she put on male attire and cap and came out of the exalted palace. Then she mounted an elephant and went about publicly. Then, I heard that for another six months that daughter of the renowned king continued to hold a public durbar; everyone high and low used to enjoy the sight of her face. After a month or two, she began to ride escorted by the

> State officers. This having continued for a full six months, everybody from the lowest to the highest became suspicious of her.
>
> I am told that a slave of the Ethiopian race used to stand by her side when she mounted her horse. With one hand he used to hold her arm and help her to mount her horse firmly. … When the grandees of the State noticed the liberties he took openly, they felt scandalized and said to one another privately: 'From the way this demon has made himself more powerful in the State than other servants, it would be no wonder if he found his way to seize the royal seal.'[131]

The historian then attributes a long disquisition on the failings of women to the Turks who have become determined to remove Raḍiyya from the throne:

> All women are in the snare of the devil; in privacy, all of them do Satan's work. Confidence should not be placed in women; devils should not be relied upon. At no time can faithfulness be expected of women. Faithfulness is masculine; expect it only from men. In public women look better than a flower garden, but in privacy they are worse than a fireplace. When the passions of a pious woman are inflamed, she concedes to an intimacy even with a dog. If a man places confidence in a woman, she makes him a laughing stock. A woman is a sign of danger wherever she [may] be, since she is of devilish disposition. To wear the crown and fill the throne of kings does not benefit a woman; this is the role exclusively meant for the experienced type of man. A woman cannot acquit herself well as a ruler, for she is essentially deficient in intellect. It is better for a woman to occupy herself with the *charkha* (spindle) since attainment of high position on her part would make her intoxicated.[132]

The 'furious' Turks decide to undo their mistake since 'it would not be consistent with our manhood to bow through stupidity to a woman, particularly now when the world is suspecting her'.[133] 'Isāmī writes that they confronted Raḍiyya the very next morning as she was holding court. Killing Jamāl al-Dīn Yāqut on the spot, they seized the sultan, bound her and sent her in heavy chains to Tabarhindh. A year and a half later, Altunapa (or, as in this account, 'Latuna') depicted here as a raiding wanderer accompanied by a small band, attacked and captured that fortress. Freeing Raḍiyya without recognizing her, he married her. Subsequently, Raḍiyya revealed to him the secret of her identity. She encouraged Altunapa to march an army upon Delhi, and this stalwart official was forced to give in: 'When Latuna heard this from his wife, he had no alternative beyond giving his consent.'[134]

'Isāmī depicts the ensuing battles as humiliating defeats of Raḍiyya's forces. He writes: 'I am told that, as a result of the first attack [by the new sultan's troops], defeat was inflicted in that battlefield on the troops of [Raḍiyya] in the twinkling of an eye. She took to flight and proceeded to [Tabarhindh], her eyes shedding tears of blood at every step.'[135] A second attack launched by Raḍiyya three or four months later resulted in a complete rout of her troops; as for the sultan, 'She was dismayed in fight and fled in the direction of Kaithal where a group of Hindus, immediately as they saw such a bird fall into their trap, captured her treacherously and killed her as well as Latuna. It was in the year 638 [1240] that they killed them in a dreary desert.'[136]

Apart from the apparent inaccuracies he introduces into the account – to name but a few, the Turks did not confront Raḍiyya in court but rather lured her out of it; Altunapa was the commander of Tabarhindh, not a roaming raider; there is no evidence that Jamāl al-Din Yāqut was a slave – 'Isāmī adds lurid colour and assigns to Raḍiyya the worst traits associated with women during his era.

The traveller Ibn Baṭṭūta (d. 1368 or 1369), likewise writing about a century after the events had transpired, presents a more sympathetic but highly melodramatic version of the story. While not directly charging Raḍiyya with sexual immorality, as some later historians did, he attributes her deposition at least in part to her association with Jamāl al-Din Yāqut: 'She mounted [a] horse like [a] man armed with bow and quiver; and she would not cover her face. Then, she was accused of connections with an Abyssinian slave of hers. The army … agreed to depose her and have her marry. She was consequently deposed and married to one of her relations.'[137]

After Raḍiyya's troops suffered a defeat, the historian reports, the sultan fled and, hungry and tired, asked a peasant whom she found tilling the soil for something to eat.

> He gave her a piece of bread which she ate and fell asleep; and she was dressed like a man. But, while she was asleep the peasant's eyes fell upon a gown … studded with jewels which she was wearing under her clothes. He realized that she was a woman. So he killed her, plundered her and drove away her horse, and then buried her in his field.

The peasant then tried to sell Raḍiyya's garment, but the people at the market becoming suspicious, he confessed to her murder and pointed out where she was buried. A dome was built over her grave 'which is now visited, and people obtain blessings from it'.[138]

Ibn Baṭṭūta's narrative – no doubt based on accounts current in fourteenth-century Delhi – immerses the sultan into a universe resembling that of the tales of the so-called holy transvestites in medieval Western literature who, as John Anson observes, 'move in a world of pure erotic romance'.[139] The stories of these women, whose sexual identities are eventually revealed, turn 'on the concept of woman as ritual sacrifice'; they hinge on the moment when 'the woman's body is finally relocated in its cultural place'.[140] Likewise, the ornamenting of Raḍiyya's story reveals at work an imagination that revels, however sympathetically, in the exposure of feminine 'weakness'. Like Joan of Arc, Raḍiyya has been 'rescripted and reclad to serve the interests of God, king, country, and finally masculinity – male heterosexual desire – itself'.[141]

Raḍiyya's identification as a male in order to achieve and maintain power raises many uneasy questions. Does her relative success, based as it was upon a suppression of her femaleness, truly represent empowerment for women? If a woman conforms to androcentric models in order to succeed, is she disrupting gender hierarchies or affirming them? As Hotchkiss writes of female transvestites in medieval Europe, 'Because of the social implications of gender inversion, interpretation often remains ambiguous.'[142]

Yet Raḍiyya's example, despite its ambiguity, symbolizes a step forward for women. By showing that some flexibility towards female sovereignty existed in medieval Islamic societies, especially for sultans' daughters who identified as men, her rule reveals that gender identity was far less stable in these societies than is often thought, and that gender could be constructed by means other than one's biological sex. Such a construction perforce admits some 'femaleness' into the category of 'good' (i.e. 'male').

Ruling as a woman: Parī Khān Khānum (d. 1578)

If women such as Raḍiyya turned to identifying as men as a means for maintaining sovereignty and circumventing the issue of chastity, others found a path through chastity itself. The Safavid princess Parī Khān Khānum, another favourite royal daughter, briefly took the reins of state during times of turmoil. Poets praising Parī Khān Khānum – who, although engaged, apparently never solemnized the marriage – focused on her purity to produce an image of a unique form of female rule.[143] In so doing, they drew on figures such as Fatima and Mary, among others – once again exemplifying the power of these personalities to legitimate sovereignty.

In many ways, the Safavid Empire provided the ideal circumstances for female participation in politics. Blending Twelver (and esoteric) Shiʿi, Sufi, Turko-Mongol and Iranian influences, all of which displayed a certain degree of openness to female power, the Safavids placed great emphasis on the concept of hereditary charisma, in which women were believed to share.[144] Indeed, royal women featured prominently in early Safavid statecraft, enjoying a surprisingly large field upon which to exercise their princely ambitions.[145] Tājlū Khānum, as seen in Chapter 4, was a patron and builder. Shāhzāda Sulṭanum, the sister of Shāh Tahmāsp (r. 1524–76), the second emperor, served as the 'privileged adviser of the sovereign, who consulted her on every decision ... she also directed many state affairs', including mediating in 'negotiations between Shah Tāhmāsp and the emperor Humayun of India'.[146] The rise of her niece, the princess Parī Khān Khānum, likewise illustrates the degree to which royal Safavid women had access to the levers of power, even if ultimate authority was denied to them.[147]

According to many Safavid accounts, as a young woman Parī Khān Khānum stood out for her intelligence, distinguishing herself through her 'study of the main sciences of her day, as well as Islamic law, jurisprudence, and poetry – all of which she mastered and which ... "made her distinct from the females"'.[148] Her father, Shāh Tahmāsp, took notice of her exceptional qualities; as one historian wrote, his 'affection and admiration for his favorite daughter became so pronounced that, "despite the presence of several capable princes," he sought her blessing and advice in all decisions concerning matters "trivial or major, domestic or financial"'.[149] The Safavid chronicler Iskandar Beg Munshī wrote that Parī Khān Khānum was 'constantly in attendance on her father, who treated her with respect and esteem. People who had difficult problems asked her to intercede with the Shah, which she frequently did with success'.[150]

Given her influence and prestige with her father, it was natural that Parī Khān Khānum's star should also rise among the Qizilbāsh, those Turkmen tribesmen whose military might had helped bring the Safavids to power and who constituted a powerful element at the court of Tahmāsp (many were amirs and officers of state).[151] She formed alliances with Qizilbāsh leaders and colluded with them regarding Tahmāsp's successor after the king died in 1576.

As Iskandar Beg Munshī writes, Qizilbāsh and other factions at court disagreed over which son should succeed Tahmāsp: the second eldest son, Ismā'īl Mīrzā, or the third-eldest, Ḥaydar Mīrzā. (The very bad eyesight of the eldest son, Sultan Muhammad Mīrzā, known as Khudābanda, the most natural candidate, disqualified him in the eyes of many.[152]) Parī Khān Khānum favoured Ismā'īl Mīrzā, who, because of behaviour displeasing to his father, had been imprisoned in the Qahqaha fortress.[153] Yet proximity bred power, and the morning after Shāh Tahmāsp's death, Ḥaydar Mīrzā 'placed the royal crown on his head, buckled on Shāh Tahmāsp's personal sword, and produced the late Shāh's will', which he claimed named him as heir apparent.[154] Given her open favour for Ismā'īl, Parī Khān Khānum was briefly taken into custody; but convinced her rather naive brother that she supported him, thereby winning her release.[155] She then facilitated his execution by his enemies by giving them the keys to the palace.[156]

The path was now clear for Ismā'īl Mīrzā (now to be known as Ismā'īl II) to accede to the throne, and Parī Khān Khānum sent a messenger to Qahqaha to fetch him.[157] In the meantime, however, 'It was Parī Khān Khānum who gave the orders.'[158] According to some accounts, 'After their morning prayers every day, the Qizilbāsh leaders proceeded to her residence for an audience.'[159] They brought to 'her notice pressing administrative and financial problems. Not one of them dared to contravene her orders.'[160]

Once Ismā'īl reached Qazvin, he camped on the northern side of the city for some time and then spent two weeks in the home of a prominent amir and supporter, Husaynqulī Khulafā', awaiting 'the astrologer's advice concerning the most propitious time to enter the capital for his coronation'.[161] The notables during this time continued their practice of 'calling at the house of Parī Khān Khānum, thinking in this way to improve their standing in the eyes of the Shah and to assure him of their trustworthiness'.[162] In fact, as Iskandar Beg noted, 'Parī Khān Khānum's stewards began to act with greater pomp and circumstance than during the reign of Shāh Tahmāsp, and her doorkeepers, chamberlains, and other retainers instituted ceremonies more appropriate to the court of a king.'[163]

Such attention did not go over well with Ismā'īl, who – despite his sister's invaluable assistance in getting him made king – 'began dropping hints to the emirs about their practice of dancing attendance on Parī Khān Khānum'.[164] On one occasion, he

> came out openly and said: 'Have you not understood, my friends, that interference in matters of state by women is demeaning to the king's honor,

> and that for men to associate with the women [lit., the veiled and the chaste] of the Safavid royal house is an abominable crime?' The emirs soon understood the message, and stopped going to Parī Khān Khānum.[165]

Iskandar Beg alluded to Parī Khān Khānum's disappointment in Ismā'īl, for whom she had expected to fill a role similar to that of Shāhzāda Sulṭanum for *her* brother, Shāh Tahmāsp.[166] At one point before the coronation, she and 'other women of the royal harem were received in audience by the Shāh, but Parī Khān Khānum was not honored by the overwhelming display of royal favor she had expected'.[167] Such remarks foreshadow the next events: the Shāh's death, ostensibly of poisoning, only fifteen months after his coronation. Many theories circulated about his death, which was attributed variously to colic and to 'severe flatulence' caused by overeating and opium.[168] Unsurprisingly, Parī Khān Khānum also fell under suspicion, with some people proposing that the princess, angry at her treatment, had 'conspired with maidservants of the harem to arrange that poison be inserted in the electuary mixture' that the king consumed that night.[169]

As in the death of al-Ḥākim in Fatimid Egypt, Ismā'īl's demise left a vacuum into which his enterprising sister stepped. State officials clearly wished to maintain her in a position of power. After proposing unsuccessfully that Ismā'īl II's infant son, Shāh Shujā', succeed him, one governor then

> tried another tack. Since he knew that all the emirs would obey Parī Khān Khānum, he suggested, hoping to flatter Parī Khān Khānum, that she should be the real ruler of the state, but that coins should be minted in the name of Shāh Shujā', since it was not appropriate that a woman should sit on the throne. But he did not have any luck with this suggestion either.[170]

According to another report, a group of notables even 'approached Parī Khān Khānum and asked her to succeed her brother. She declined, maintaining that with the presence of her older brother, Muhammad Mīrzā, she could not possibly welcome such an offer.'[171] In fact, it was Sultan Muhammad Mīrzā – the nearly blind eldest son of Shāh Tahmāsp – who became the nominee, but with the expectation that his rule would be in name only. As Iskandar Beg wrote, after the discussion and decision

> the emirs ... rose and went to the private apartments of Parī Khān Khānum, both to seek her advice and to inform her of what had happened. Parī Khān Khānum considered herself to be the ruler. She agreed that, when Sultan

> Muhammad Mīrzā arrived from Shiraz, he would become the titular king, but the real power would reside in her hands.[172]

At first all went according to plan. For the ten weeks or so before Sultan Muhammad Shāh's arrival in Qazvin, Parī Khān Khānum took 'upon her own shoulders the responsibility for the conduct of state affairs. The emirs obeyed her orders, and every day presented themselves at her house.'[173] So powerful was Parī Khān Khānum's control that the notables even required her permission to leave Qazvin and visit the new king in Shiraz.[174]

Before long, however, the doomed princess's plans went awry. Messengers informed the new king and his wife, the very powerful Khayr al-Nisā' Begum (Mahd-i 'Ulya), of Parī Khān Khānum's expectations to retain control over affairs of state.[175] They were vastly displeased and voiced their anger. Support ebbed from Parī Khān Khānum, who, 'in her pride and folly, displayed no great regard for [Khayr al-Nisā' Begum]'.[176] On the same day as his arrival in Qazvin, Sultan Muhammad Shāh – no doubt egged on by his wife – ordered the princess killed. Aides to Khalīl Khān, her former tutor, strangled her on 11 February 1578, just short of her thirtieth birthday.[177] Others, including Shāh Shujā', were killed at the same time.[178]

Female rule did not collapse with the demise of Parī Khān Khānum. It merely changed hands. Having eliminated her sister-in-law and other enemies, Khayr al-Nisā' Begum consolidated her power. As Iskandar Beg writes, the new queen 'was in complete control of the state, and nothing was done without her order'.[179] She even 'took part in a military campaign against the Ottomans in the winter of 1578-9. Although her son ... was official commander-in-chief of the Safavid troops, it was she who discussed decisions with Qizilbāsh generals.'[180]

Yet Khayr al-Nisā' Begum too met a violent end before long. Chafing under her rule (as well as, according to some accounts, her criticisms and disdain), the 'self-willed amirs' determined to break her power.[181] (Some, unsurprisingly, accused her of unchastity.)[182] In a message to the king asking her to be removed, they wrote:

> Your Majesty well knows that women are notoriously lacking in intelligence, weak in judgment, and extremely obstinate. Mahd-i 'Ulya has always opposed us, the loyal servants of the crown, and has never agreed with us on matters of state policy; she has acted contrary to the considered

opinions of the Qizilbāsh elders, and has constantly attempted to humiliate and degrade us.[183]

The king attempted to placate them, but Khayr al-Nisā' Begum refused to budge. In July of 1579, a little over a year since the couple's arrival in Qazvin, Qizilbāsh amirs 'burst into the harem without ceremony and strangled [Khayr al-Nisā' Begum]. Not satisfied with that, they went to the house of her mother ... and slew her too, together with several Mazandarani notables who happened to be there.'[184]

What do the stories of Parī Khān Khānum and Khayr al-Nisā' Begum tell us? As in other medieval and early modern Islamic societies, Safavid female rule clearly had its limits.[185] Parī Khān Khānum could not claim the throne except during an interregnum, and her brother resented any attempts at influence. The Qizilbāsh, too, cited the inappropriateness of female rule in their condemnation of Khayr al-Nisā' Begum as regent, protesting that while a male king was present, 'he should rule by himself and not delegate his power to a woman'.[186]

Men presented different objections to having a woman in power, all of which conform to the traditional stereotypes set forth by Niẓām al-Mulk. Ismā'īl II, as we have seen, opined that females should be secluded and that any participation in politics brought dishonour upon them and those associating with them. The Qizilbāsh based their grievances on the idea that women were 'lacking in intelligence, weak in judgment, and extremely obstinate'.[187]

Yet women did take part in state affairs, and it is noteworthy that chroniclers such as Iskandar Beg (unlike later historians) spoke rather matter-of-factly of their participation, portraying it as 'customary and legitimate'.[188] He also praised women for their intellect and guidance. Referring to Zaynab Begum, a sister of Parī Khān Khānum, he wrote, approvingly, 'She was a highly intelligent woman, and as a member of the harem of Shāh 'Abbās I, acquired a position close to the Shāh and great influence.'[189] Moreover, the historian's account of Khayr al-Nisā' Begum's reign is largely sympathetic.[190] He portrayed her as 'reasonable' in some of her criticisms of the Qizilbāsh amirs, and severely condemns her murder.[191] Likewise, the historian Natanzī called 'necessary and proper' Parī Khān Khānum's protection of the throne 'along with the treasuries and the other accouterments of sovereignty' in the two-and-a-half-month period before Sultan Muhammad's arrival in Qazvin.[192] As in other societies, gender in early Safavid Iran may have simply been a convenient pretext for eliminating a powerful enemy.

As in India, Turko-Mongol and Iranian precedents, with their notions of 'power as vested in the ruling family', including females, likely helped bring Parī Khān Khānum and other royal women to power.[193] Indeed, both 'steppe and Iranian ideals of sovereignty' probably contributed to the rise of the princess and people like her.[194] Yet, as the contemporary scholar Maryam Sabbaghi has suggested, Islamic ideals – including evocations of Fatima – may also have played a part, as an examination of poetry written about the princess reveals.[195]

A patron of poets and a poetess herself, Parī Khān Khānum appears in a number of divans and other works written by Safavid litterateurs.[196] Often, these poets portrayed the princess as a sovereign, paying tribute to her by comparing her to such 'sacred female figures of wisdom and power' as Bilqīs and Fatima.[197] For example, Muḥtasham Kāshānī (d. 1588), the renowned Safavid poet, wrote at least five poems about Parī Khān Khānum.[198] His qasidas eulogizing her reveal a very distinct notion of Islamo-Iranian female sovereignty: one that draws upon both pre-Islamic Iranian figures and women associated with Islam (including, naturally, Fatima), and that combines within it the typically 'feminine' virtues of delicacy, chastity and hiddenness with 'masculine' characteristics such as might, justice and wisdom – and without privileging the latter over the former.[199] Through his poetry, we can catch a glimpse of what shape a specifically *female* rule might take.

At first blush, Muḥtasham's poems in praise of Parī Khān Khānum – especially when contrasted with those praising men such as her father – seem to emphasize her feminine qualities. While poems describing Shāh Tahmāsp make note of his 'blood thirsty and fearless eye', those speaking of Parī Khān Khānum play up her chastity, often linking it to Fatima or to Mary, who, of course, represented the apex of chastity and purity.[200] Speaking in typically hyperbolic terms, Muḥtasham describes Parī Khān Khānum as so chaste that she sits behind three curtains, not one; no one except family has ever gazed upon her face, even in a dream.[201] She is 'that Mary of the age', to whose immaculate doors the breeze brought the scent of no person.[202] Unlike her father, whose military might causes even the fiercest beings to tremble, the 'delicacy of [Parī Khān Khānum's] refined nature' causes the very wind to tremble like a willow before her.[203] These descriptions yield the image of a refined, delicate, chaste princess who is hidden away, not someone active in the public sphere, much less capable of ruling a state.

And yet in many of the same poems, Muḥtasham addresses Parī Khān Khānum's sovereignty and leadership abilities.[204] He speaks in several poems of her kingship, or *pādishāhī*, and in so doing compares her to earlier Iranian male kings. For example, just as the poet compares the justice meted out by Shāh Tahmāsp, her father, to that of Anūshīrvān, the Sassanian king known for his equitable ways, so he likens that of Parī Khān Khānum to the same figure.[205] He also recognizes in her military might, strength, wisdom and good judgement – all components of temporal leadership.[206] He even indicates that she has access to gnostic knowledge, a crucial element of spiritual leadership: 'You'd say that invisible divine inspiration, from the Dominion of the Secret-Knowers, arrived to that royal breast.'[207] Though her sovereignty takes a different shape than that of her father, it is sovereignty nonetheless.

A closer look at parts of a few poems lays bare how Muḥtasham combines these different elements.[208] He eulogizes Parī Khān Khānum in one qasida in the following manner:

> The princess of the era and its people, the Sun of the earth
> Radiant as Venus (*zahrā'-yi zuhra*), veiled as Mary
> Parī Khān – king of the angels and of mankind
> If Bilqīs were alive, she would acquire kingship from her[209]

In these lines, Parī Khān Khānum lords it over both worlds as the 'sun'; she is 'king of the angels and of mankind', so powerful and wise that Bilqīs herself – the symbol of female leadership – would learn kingship (*pādishāhī*) from her. (Here, as Sabbaghi notes, the Persian words for 'king' and 'kingship' seem to be stripped of associations with gender.)

The hemistich referring to Venus, Mary and, implicitly, Fatima evokes chastity in a complex and rather paradoxical manner. Venus is, clearly, a female planet who blazes forth brightly. Like her, Parī Khān Khānum is 'radiant', or *zahrā'* (a term that not-so-obliquely refers to Fatima al-Zahra, Fatima the radiant, as well as to the planet itself, known in Persian as *zuhra*). On the other hand, the princess is as veiled and hidden as Mary. How can Parī Khān Khānum be both hidden (the ideal condition for women) and revealed, both veiled and resplendent? Readers familiar with the Qur'an would have known its evocation of God as both 'the First and the Last; the Seen and the Hidden'

(57:3); such contradictions, then, would have posed no problem for them. Perhaps banking on these associations, Muḥtasham seamlessly combines these apparent contradictions to produce the image of a figure who exercises sovereignty and shines forth at the same time that she remains hidden and chaste.

In another poem, Muḥtasham makes use of similarly contradictory descriptions and further elucidates the link between chastity and sovereignty. The poet describes Parī Khān Khānum in these terms:

The foundation of strength, Venus of Jupiter rank
  The shelter and protection of culture, the Sun, Bilqīs the dignified
Parī Khān Khānum, the emperor of the dominion and people
  Before whose kingship the houris and parīs are ashamed
The chaste Maryam-Fatima, from which the honor of the world
  Possesses, from the beauty of her modesty, as dominion, the Seven
Heavens . . . .
She before whom Rābiʿa of the heavenly bridechamber
  Secretly confessed her shame.[210]

Once again, Muḥtasham praises Parī Khān Khānum's sovereignty by comparing her to Bilqīs and to Venus, both the planet and the mythological daughter of Jupiter; here, Venus is raised to her father's rank. Once again, the poet combines typically 'male' and 'female' terms to describe her: she is emperor (*pādishā*) of the dominion and people; her royalty *(shāhanshāhī)* is so great that the lovely, virtuous fairies and beautiful, chaste inhabitants of Paradise (*parīs* and houris) are abashed before it.

Then Muḥtasham addresses the theme of chastity and modesty, embodied in Mary and Fatima, of whom Parī Khān Khānum stands as a contemporary exemplar, as well as Rābiʿa, the exemplary Sufi ascetic and saint. In one sense, these comparisons can be read as a return to the veiled, passive female and thus, a potential diminishment of the princess's dominion. But the mere act of linking Bilqīs to Mary and Fatima reflects the acknowledgement that these figures (and, by extension, Parī Khān Khānum) share the queen's authority and supremacy. The poet's evocation of chastity accomplishes the same feat. As Muḥtasham writes, the honour of world, through Parī Khān Khānum's own modesty, possesses as dominion the 'seven heavens' (lit. 'seven fortresses'). Her chastity, then, confers sovereignty – a sovereignty affirmed in the final lines of the poem: 'May the shadow of the auspicious sovereigns not wane over your head/And may your shadow not wane over humanity until the Day of Reckoning.'[211] Her kingship ranks below that of the greater (male) kings, but it gathers the world of humanity under its protection.

In this case, then, chastity (a virtue most often associated with females) leads the way to sovereignty and dominion (characteristics most often associated with males). By being chaste, women could emerge from the inner realms and enjoy the prerogatives of men, including rule.[212]

The precedents for this concept, as indicated in Chapter 5, are many. Fatima's chastity afforded her great power, including that of securing paradise for her progeny and their followers. By renouncing sex and marriage, early ascetic Christian women (as well as Muslims such as Rābiʿa) claimed the freedom and authority typically reserved to men. Pulcheria, as we have seen, voluntarily adopted chastity and asceticism as a means of consolidating her spiritual authority and establishing a connection between herself and the Virgin Mary. Muḥtasham similarly deploys Parī Khān Khānum's chastity as a potent weapon that elevates her to the rank of the greatest of Islam's female holy figures and enables her to exercise sovereignty over humans.

These measures have powerful implications for concepts of female sovereignty, and, indeed, for Fatima herself. The idea of female rule becomes, somehow, less improbable, within both a Muslim and an Iranian context. The shape it takes does not precisely match that of male rule, but neither is it divorced from positive 'masculine' qualities such as intellect and good judgement.[213] Finally, by linking her so closely to Bilqīs and to kingship (*pādishāhī*), Muḥtasham enlarges the idea of who *Fatima* (and her vicegerent, Parī Khān Khānum) is and what she represents: might, wisdom and judiciousness as well as chastity.

Of course, Muḥtasham's poetic evocation of Parī Khān Khānum failed to translate perfectly into reality. With the exception of her few months' rule, the princess did not achieve total sovereignty. And pathways to power for Safavid women narrowed significantly in succeeding centuries, as prominent religious scholars such as al-Majlisī – despite his vocal admiration for Fatima – attempted to corral women, including royal females, into the harem, and to enforce a patriarchal, patrilineal scheme of succession in which females were excluded from sovereignty and, indeed, from participation in politics at all.[214] The voiceless Fatima thus moved back behind the veil, awaiting her turn to emerge once more.

Conclusion

As this chapter demonstrates, daughters as well as sons succeeded their fathers and other male relatives to roles as shaykhs, scholars, calligraphers, patrons and, less frequently, rulers in pre-modern Islamic societies. Such succession often turned upon an understanding that a daughter could both inherit and manifest her father's characteristics, including traditionally 'masculine' ones such as wisdom and reason. In cases of female dominion, women and their supporters found multiple solutions for dealing with the restrictions of chastity, which suggested that women were best hidden from men's eyes, not seated on a throne. For example, they sometimes invoked Fatima as an exemplar of both sovereignty and chastity – a move that enlarged the sphere of activity for the current female ruler at the same time that it affirmed and re-emphasized the leadership abilities of the daughter of the Prophet. Other rulers cast off femaleness altogether. Though instances of female rule were often troubled and short, and though these sovereigns were subjected to numerous attacks upon their reputations, medieval and early modern chroniclers often described their reigns with recognition of their talents and a certain degree of matter-of-factness. These characteristics suggest that rule by women, though unusual, was not an utterly outlandish concept among pre-modern Muslims.

What became of Islamic concepts of bilateral descent, including female succession, in the modern era? As concern for women's rights and women's equality mounted worldwide, many Muslims began directly addressing these issues in their own societies. At the same time, however, objections centring on questions of authenticity and Western intrusion threw up roadblocks. The Epilogue looks at how recognition of bilateral descent has fared in the tumultuous world of today.

Epilogue

Whither Fatima?

In 2012, the top clerics of Afghanistan issued a statement declaring women subordinate to men. 'Men are fundamental and women are secondary,' the statement read. 'Also, lineage is derived from the man. Therefore, the use of words and expressions that contradict the sacred verses must be strictly avoided.'[1] Renouncing 'the equality of men and women enshrined in the Afghan constitution', the statement – which banned mixing of the sexes in work and education, and required women to have a male guardian while travelling – was widely seen as being 'dangerously reminiscent of the Taliban era'.[2]

Clearly, recognition of bilateral descent – with all of its implications for full personhood and equality – is not unanimous today in Muslim-majority countries, just as it is not in countries dominated by other religions.[3] It is not difficult to find examples of movements, state-sponsored or not, that portray women as secondary and subordinate to men: guided by their emotions, deficient in reason and incapable of carrying on their own bloodlines. Denial or drastic curtailing of certain rights, including custody and inheritance rights, as well as the right to confer nationality, is a natural corollary of such understandings of the female body and mind.[4]

Yet, as in the pre-modern era, other trends also appear, whether in the arenas of nationality, inheritance or successorship – trends that, whether explicitly or not, echo the bilateral patterns found in many pre-modern Islamic societies, and envision women as far more than mere vessels. Egypt and Morocco have both undertaken reforms to allow women to pass on their nationality to their children, even when they are married to foreign nationals.[5] Saudi Arabia, while normally forbidding such transmission, permits it under 'certain circumstances such as where fathers are unknown, stateless, of unknown nationality or do not establish filiation'.[6] Similarly, reforms in countries ranging from Indonesia to Tunisia have striven to equalize inheritance practices, which includes in some cases de-emphasizing agnates in favour of the nuclear family.[7] Reforms enacted in Tunisia in the 1950s introduced, among other changes, the provision that 'daughters and granddaughters could exclude agnatic relatives of the deceased, including the brother, paternal uncle and their descendants, as heirs'.[8] As of this writing, women in Tunisia and Morocco were petitioning for equal inheritance shares for women and men, with varying degrees of success.[9]

Daughters in many Muslim-majority countries have also drawn on hereditary charisma (as well as their own talents) to succeed their fathers to positions of importance, or at least to have significant voices in political or religious matters. Benazir Bhutto, the first female prime minister of Pakistan, famously followed her father into politics. Zulfikar Ali Bhutto (d. 1979), prime minister from 1973 to 1977, began educating his daughters as well as his sons in political matters when they were still young, encouraging them to 'feel part of the greater world'.[10] The elder Bhutto was instrumental in his daughter's decision to study at Harvard, where she obtained a degree in comparative politics in 1973, and desired her to play a part in Pakistan's political life after his death. She led the country from 1988 to 1990 and from 1993 to 1996, and was campaigning for re-election when she was assassinated in 2007. Her example shows how educating daughters became not only socially acceptable but also a mark of prestige among certain elite Muslim families in the nineteenth and twentieth centuries; it also demonstrates that, like sons, daughters can enjoy dynastic privileges.

Similarly, several daughters of Iranian clerics and politicians have followed in their fathers' footsteps by achieving prominence in their fields – implicitly claiming their authority. Zahra Mostafavi Khomeini, daughter of Ayatollah Khomeini (d. 1989), the leader of the Iranian Revolution and the founder of the Islamic Republic of Iran, earned a PhD in philosophy and taught at the University of Tehran; she also leads a political party that strives to increase female participation in government. According to Mostafavi Khomeini, her father 'wanted women to play a full part in society, not just as typists or nurses. At home, he never asked his wife, even once, "give me a cup of tea," or "close the door." He did it himself!'[11] She herself has maintained that 'women must be allowed to pursue an appropriate role for themselves in politics, academics and education … and "like men, their talent must be allowed to flourish"'.[12] Likewise, Fā'iza Hāshimī Rafsanjānī, the outspoken daughter of the late president Akbar Hāshimī Rafsanjānī (d. 2017), in addition to editing the newspaper *Zan* (Woman), served as a member of the Iranian parliament for four years.[13] The name recognition and prestige she gained as her father's daughter no doubt assisted her rise to political power.

Seminary life is another arena in which women have benefited from inherited charismatic authority. According to ethnographic research conducted at the Zaynabiyya Seminary in the Syrian shrine-town of Sayyida Zaynab between 2007 and 2010, female teachers who belonged to scholarly families were often regarded as endowed with authority.[14] Another study showed that Pakistani women related to clergymen stood a better chance of obtaining administrative positions in education after they returned home from attending the female-only seminaries in Qum such as Jamīʿat al-Zahra (named after Fatima).[15]

In many cases, Fatima serves as a role model for women seeking leadership roles. Bint al-Huda (1937–1980), a prominent Iraqi activist and religious scholar, drew inspiration from the example of the daughter of the Prophet. Because Fatima had been 'active in public affairs', Bint al-Huda felt that she could be, too.[16] She named her primary schools for girls 'Zahra' after Fatima's sobriquet – testimony to the influence of the daughter of the Prophet's example in the education of women.[17] Sharīʿatī, in advocating for female education and for women entering the public realm as committed social activists, named Fatima as an exemplar.[18] The Iranian feminist scholars Ebtekar and Gorgi have also relied on the example of Fatima in justifying their right – and the right of other Muslim women – to 'speak and teach with authority'.[19] In the nineteenth century, the Babi heroine Ṭāhirih, who identified strongly with Fatima, claimed 'independent will and action' as her legacy.[20]

Naturally, not all of the ways in which Fatima's example is invoked serve to expand a public presence for women. Some contemporary Shiʿi scholars continue to emphasize her role as obedient, long-suffering housewife and mother and veiled woman par excellence.[21] And the idealization of Fatima in this role can actually lead to greater oppression for women.[22] One Iranian woman, questioned about her 'ideal role model' during a 1989 radio broadcast, was threatened with the death penalty for stating that she found Fatima to be outmoded and considered 'Oushin (a female character in a highly popular Japanese television serial) a more appropriate model for herself'.[23] Yet, as in the past, the seriousness with which Fatima is portrayed in her role as activist, and the evocative accounts of women who have been encouraged by that role, suggests that she has the potential to act more as inspiration than as flog.

Feminism is, to put it mildly, a fraught concept today in many Muslim-majority countries (as it is in non-Muslim-majority countries).[24] Objections to it often centre on the idea that it is a Western-style innovation that runs against Islamic mores. It is true that the forms modern feminism has often taken in the West – primarily secular, interested in the rights and freedoms of the individual – tend to conflict with more traditional values. Even more damning is the frequency with which Western countries have used poor treatment of women in Muslim-majority countries as an excuse for imperialism and Islamophobia.[25]

The notion that equality of men and women is a Western-style idea, however, does not hold water. As this book has striven to prove, many gender-egalitarian ideas and practices, including those involving bilateral descent, can be traced to the very advent of Islam, and manifested in different ways over centuries in Shiʿi *and* Sunni societies. They point the way forward to a more equal future, with benefits for men and women alike. Do such ideas and practices conform to 'true Islam', if we can even speak of such a phenomenon? The people espousing them surely believed they did. In their minds' eye, they saw the Fatima of the past stepping forth from the shadows to voice her plea for justice and equality. Today, we watch as many brave Muslim women do the same. Who knows to what heights they will lead us?

Notes

Preface

1 For more on the poem, see Chapter 2.

Introduction: Redrawing family trees

1 Saeed Kamali Dehghan, 'Maryam Mirzakhani: Iranian Newspapers Break Hijab Taboo in Tributes', *The Guardian*, 16 September 2017, https://www.theguardian.com/world/2017/jul/16/maryam-mirzakhani-iranian-newspapers-break-hijab-taboo-in-tributes.
2 See 'What Was Maryam Mirzakhani's Will?', 16 *Āftāb*, July 2017, http://www.aftabir.com/news/article/view/2017/07/16/1734233; Zahra Arzanī Huqūqdān, 'Law Does Not Grant Citizenship to Mirzakhani's Daughter', *Āftāb*, 16 July 2017, http://aftabnews.ir/fa/news/460963/.
3 'Iran's Parliament to Accelerate Citizenship Law for Maryam Mirzakhani's Daughter', *Euronews*, 16 July 2017, http://fa.euronews.com/2017/07/16/iran-parliament-to-accelerate-citizenship-law-for-mryam-mirzakhani-daughter; Dehghan, 'Maryam Mirzakhani'.
4 Chris Harris, 'How Death of Maths Genius Mirzakhani is Breaking Taboos for Women in Iran', *Euronews*, 17 July 2017, http://www.euronews.com/2017/07/17/how-death-of-maths-genius-mirzakhani-is-breaking-taboos-for-women-in-iran; United Nations High Commissioner for Refugees (UNHCR), 'Background Note on Gender Equality, Nationality Laws and Statelessness 2014', http://www.unhcr.org/en-us/protection/statelessness/4f5886306/background-note-gender-equality-nationality-laws-statelessness-2014.html.
5 See, for example, UNHCR, 'Background Note'; Homa Hoodfar, 'Divorce and Custody: Contemporary Practices: Iran and Afghanistan', in *Encyclopedia of Women and Islamic Cultures* (*EWIC*), ed. Suad Joseph (Leiden: Brill, 2003–2007), 2:105; Suad Joseph, 'History and Its Histories: Story-Making and the Present', *Review of Middle East Studies* 46, no. 2 (2012): 14; Manal al-Sharif, 'I Left My Son

in a Kingdom of Men', *The New York Times*, 9 June 2017, https://www.nytimes.com/2017/06/09/opinion/sunday/saudi-arabia-women-driving-ban.html; Max Fisher, 'Map: Which of the World's Monarchies Allow Female Royal Succession', *The Washington Post*, 4 December 2012, https://www.washingtonpost.com/news/worldviews/wp/2012/12/04/map-which-of-the-worlds-monarchies-allow-female-royal-succession/?utm_term=.cc3ba35c6040.

6 Several studies do exist which look at her as a model for women, but typically one relegated to the domestic sphere. See, for example, Mary F. Thurlkill, *Chosen Among Women: Mary and Fatima in Medieval Christianity and Shi'ite Islam* (Notre Dame: University of Notre Dame Press, 2007); Denise Spellberg, 'The Politics of Praise: Depictions of Khadija, Fatima and 'A'isha in Ninth-Century Muslim Sources', *Literature East & West* 26 (1990): 130–48; Firoozeh Kashani-Sabet, 'Who Is Fatima?: Gender, Culture, and Representation in Islam', *Journal of Middle East Women's Studies* 1, no. 2 (2005): 1–24. For works that make at least some allusion to her in a less restrictive role, see Peter J. Chelkowski, 'Iconography of the Women of Karbala: Tiles, Murals, Stamps, and Posters', in *The Women of Karbala: Ritual Performance and Symbolic Discourses in Modern Shi'i Islam*, ed. Kamran Scot Aghaie (Austin: University of Texas Press, 2005); Rachel Kantz Feder, 'Fatima's Revolutionary Image in *Fadak fi al-Ta'rikh* (1955): The Inception of Muhammad al-Sadr's Activism', *British Journal of Middle Eastern Studies* 41, no. 1 (2014): 79–96; Rawand Osman, *Female Personalities in the Qur'an and Sunna: Examining the Major Sources of Imami Shi'i Islam* (Abingdon: Routledge, 2015); Matthew Pierce, 'Remembering Fatimah: New Means of Legitimizing Female Authority in Contemporary Shi'i Discourse', in *Women, Leadership, and Mosques: Changes in Contemporary Islamic Authority*, ed. Masooda Bano and Hilary Kalmbach (Leiden: Brill, 2012); and Karen Ruffle, 'May You Learn from Their Model: The Exemplary Father-Daughter Relationship of Mohammad and Fatima in South Asian Shi'ism', *Journal of Persianate Studies* 4, no. 1 (2011): 12–29.

7 As Margot Badran has written, 'Islamic feminism aims to recover and implement Islam's fundamental principles of social justice and the equality of all Muslims, including gender equality. There can be no social justice without gender equality'. See *Feminism Beyond East and West: New Gender Talk and Practice in Global Islam* (New Delhi: Global Media Publications, 2007), 51. For discussions of scholarship on Islamic feminism, see Huma Ahmed-Ghosh, 'Dilemmas of Islamic and Secular Feminists and Feminisms', *Journal of International Women's Studies* 9, no. 3 (2008): 99–116; Sa'diyya Shaikh, *Sufi Narratives of Intimacy: Ibn 'Arabī, Gender, and Sexuality* (Chapel Hill: University of North Carolina Press, 2012), 21–4; and Osman, *Female Personalities*, 1–4.

8 Shaikh, *Sufi Narratives*, 5. See also Lila Abu-Lughod, *Do Muslim Women Need Saving?* (Cambridge: Harvard University Press, 2013), 6–40.
9 Shaikh, *Sufi Narratives*, 28–9.
10 Sylvia Junko Yanagisako and Jane Fishburne Collier, 'Toward a Unified Analysis of Gender and Kinship', in *Gender and Kinship: Essays Toward a Unified Analysis*, ed. Jane Fishburne Collier and Sylvia Junko Yanagisako (Stanford: Stanford University Press, 1987), 15.
11 Ibid., 30–1.
12 Jane Fishburne Collier and Sylvia Junko Yanagisako, 'Introduction', in Collier and Yanagisako, *Gender and Kinship*, 4.
13 Mina Elfira, 'Kinship, Descent Systems: East Asia, Southeast Asia, Australia, and the Pacific', in Joseph, *EWIC*, 2:333.
14 Ibid.; also Marilyn Strathern, 'Producing Difference: Connections and Disconnections in Two New Guinea Highland Kinship Systems', Collier and Yanagisako, *Gender and Kinship*, 278–9.
15 Carol Delaney, 'The Meaning of Paternity and the Virgin Birth Debate', *Man* 21, no. 3 (1986): 500.
16 Male primogeniture, a patrilineal custom that limits inheritances to the eldest male offspring, still exists in Britain. See Sarah Lyall, 'Son and Heir? In Britain, Daughters Cry No Fair', *The New York Times*, 22 June 2013, http://www.nytimes.com/2013/06/23/world/europe/son-and-heir-in-britain-daughters-cry-no-fair.html.
17 Strathern, 'Producing Difference', 276.
18 Ibid.
19 Ibid.; also, Elfira, 'Kinship, Descent Systems', 2:333.
20 Strathern, 'Producing Difference', 276.
21 Elfira, 'Kinship, Descent Systems', 2:333.
22 Strathern, 'Producing Difference', 278–9, 284.
23 Ibid., 276.
24 Ibid., 278.
25 Shaikh, *Sufi Narratives*, 9.
26 UNHCR, 'Background Note'.
27 Huqūqdān, 'Law Does Not Grant Citizenship'; Harris, 'How Death of Maths Genius'; Heshmat Alavi, 'Iran's Growing Brain Drain Disaster', *Blasting News*, 23 February 2017, http://uk.blastingnews.com/education/2017/02/iran-s-growing-brain-drain-disaster-001495453.html
28 Huqūqdān, 'Law Does Not Grant Citizenship'.
29 Al-Sharif, 'I Left My Son'.

30 Joseph B. Aceves, *Identity, Survival, and Change: Exploring Social/Cultural Anthropology* (Morristown, NJ: 1974), 127.

31 Shaikh, *Sufi Narratives*, 27.

32 For trenchant discussions of this topic, see Saba Mahmood, *Politics of Piety: The Islamic Revival and the Feminist Subject* (Princeton: Princeton University Press, 2004), 4-10; and Lucy K. Pick, *Her Father's Daughter: Gender, Power, and Religion in the Early Spanish Kingdoms* (Ithaca: Cornell University Press, 2017), 6-15.

33 Mahmood, *Politics*, 8, 6.

34 Saba Mahmood, 'Feminist Theory, Embodiment, and the Docile Agent: Some Reflections on the Egyptian Islamic Revival', *Cultural Anthropology* 16, no. 2 (May 2001): 204.

35 Mahmood, *Politics*, 14–15.

36 Mahmood, 'Feminist Theory', 221.

37 For a detailed description of the early development of Shiʿism, see Wilferd Madelung, *The Succession to Muhammad: A Study of the Early Caliphate* (Cambridge: Cambridge University Press, 1997), 29–56.

38 Imam has a far more specific meaning in Shiʿism than in Sunnism, where it can simply indicate prayer leader or leader in a general sense.

39 See Liyakat N. Takim, *The Heirs of the Prophet: Charisma and Religious Authority in Shiʿite Islam* (Albany: State University of New York Press, 2006), 24–30.

40 For disputes about her date of birth, see Henri Lammens, *Fatima et les Filles de Mahomet* (Rome: Sumptibus Pontifcii Instituti Biblici, 1912), 12–14; also Laura Veccia Vaglieri, 'Fāṭima', in *Encyclopaedia of Islam*, 2nd ed., CD-ROM, version 1.1 (*EI*[2]).

41 Aḥmad al-Yaʿqūbī, *Al-Tārīkh* [Historiae], ed. M. Th. Houtsma (Leiden: Brill, 1969), 2:35.

42 Aḥmad ibn Yaḥyā al-Balādhurī, *Ansāb al-ashrāf*, ed. Muhammad Ḥamīd Allah (Cairo: Dār al-Maʿārif, 1987), 1:402.

43 Abū ʿAbd Allah Muhammad ibn Saʿd, *Kitāb al-ṭabaqāt al-kabīr,* vol. 8, trans. Aisha Bewley as *The Women of Madina* (London: Ta-Ha, 1997), 14.

44 Ibid., 8:13-15; see also Veccia Vaglieri, 'Fāṭima'.

45 Ibn Saʿd, *Kitāb al-ṭabaqāt*, 8:17. See also Muhammad ibn Ismāʿīl al-Bukhārī, *Saḥīḥ*: *Kitāb al-Daʿwāt, bāb al-takbīr wa al-tasbīḥ ʿinda al-manām.*

46 Al-Balādhurī, *Ansāb*, 1:403; al-Bukhārī, *Saḥīḥ*: *Kitāb al-nikāḥ, bāb dhab al-rajul ʿan ibnatihi fi al-ghayrat wa al-inṣāf.*

47 Al-Bukhārī, *Saḥīḥ*: *Kitāb manāqib al-anṣār, bāb mā laqiya al-nabī wa aṣḥabahu min al-mushrikīn bi-makka* (29).

48 Al-Yaʿqūbī, *Tārīkh*, 2:141.

49 Abū Ja'far Muḥammad ibn Jarīr al-Ṭabarī, *Tārīkh al-rusul wa al-mulūk*, vol. 9, trans. Ismail K. Poonawala as *The History of al-Tabari: The Last Years of the Prophet* (Albany: State University of New York Press, 1990), 186–7, 187 n. 1291; also, Veccia Vaglieri, 'Fāṭima'.

50 See, for example, al-Bukhārī, *Ṣaḥīḥ: Kitāb farḍ al-khums, bāb farḍ al-khums* (1).

51 Al-Balādhurī, *Ansāb*, 1:402, 405; al-Ṭabarī, *Tārīkh*, 9:196. See also Veccia Vaglieri, 'Fāṭima'; and Denise L. Soufi, 'The Image of Fāṭima in Classical Muslim Thought' (PhD diss., Princeton University, 1997), 123.

52 Ibn Sa'd, *Kitāb al-ṭabaqāt*, 8:19. See also al-Bukhārī, *Ṣaḥīḥ*: *Kitāb faḍā'il al-ṣaḥābat, bāb faḍa'il Fāṭima bint al-nabī* (15).

Chapter 1

1 Aeschylus, *Oresteia*, ed. and trans. Alan H. Sommerstein (Cambridge: Harvard University Press, 2008), 439.

2 Muhammad ibn Muhammad al-Nu'mān al-Mufīd, *Kitāb al-amālī*, trans. Mulla Asgharali M.M. Jaffer as *Al Amaali: The Dictations of Sheikh al-Mufid* (Stanmore: World Federation of Khoja Shia Ithna-Asheri Muslim Communities, 1998), 234–5.

3 Cynthia Eller, *The Myth of Matriarchal Prehistory: Why an Invented Past Won't Give Women a Future* (Boston: Beacon Press, 2000), 95; Delaney, 'Meaning of Paternity', 508.

4 Eller, *Myth of Matriarchal Prehistory*, 95; Delaney, 'Meaning of Paternity', 495 and passim.

5 Marjane Satrapi, *Persepolis 2: The Story of a Return*, trans. Anjali Singh (New York: Pantheon Press, 2004), 183.

6 Delaney, 'Meaning of Paternity', 506.

7 Sherry Sayed Gadelrab, 'Discourses on Sex Differences in Medieval Scholarly Islamic Thought', *History of Medicine and Allied Sciences* 66 no. 1 (2011): 45.

8 Basim Musallam, *Sex and Society in Islam: Birth Control before the Nineteenth Century* (Cambridge: Cambridge University Press, 1983), 39.

9 Musallam, *Sex and Society in Islam*, 40.

10 Ibid.

11 Ibid., 43.

12 Ibid., 46.

13 Ibid., 43.

14 Aristotle, *Generation of Animals*, trans. A.L. Peck (Cambridge: Harvard University Press, 1942), 96–9; see also Musallam, *Sex and Society in Islam*, 44.

15 Musallam, *Sex and Society in Islam*, 44.
16 Ibid., 45.
17 Ibid.
18 Munawar Ahmad Anees, *Islam and Biological Futures: Ethics, Gender, and Technology* (London: Mansell, 1989), 66–7.
19 Anees, *Islam and Biological Futures*, 66–7.
20 Musallam, *Sex and Society in Islam*, 48.
21 Ibn Sīnā, *Ḥayawān*; quoted in Musallam, *Sex and Society in Islam*, 47–8; see also Gadelrab, 'Discourses', 66.
22 Musallam, 'Avicenna'.
23 Delaney, 'Meaning of Paternity', 511 n. 9.
24 M.E. Combs-Schilling, *Sacred Performances: Islam, Sexuality, and Sacrifice* (New York: Columbia University Press, 1989), 61. My emphasis.
25 Delaney, 'Meaning of Paternity', 496–7 and passim.
26 Ibid., 495, 497.
27 Michael Meeker, 'The Black Sea Turks: A Study of Honor, Descent and Marriage' (PhD diss., University of Chicago, 1970), 157; quoted in Delaney, 'Meaning of Paternity', 497.
28 Delaney, 'Meaning of Paternity', 497; emphasis in original.
29 See Diane E. King, 'Kinship and State: Arab States', in Joseph, *EWIC*, 2:347.
30 Delaney, 'Meaning of Paternity', 511 n. 9.
31 Ibid., 497.
32 Ibid., 499.
33 Ibid., 500.
34 King, 'Arab States', 2:347. As Delaney notes, the knowledge 'that both men and women contribute essentially and creatively to a child' was not 'widely assimilated in the West until the mid-twentieth century'; in fact, the images of seed and field were 'used to explain procreation to [her] when [she] was growing up in America in the 1940's'. See 'Meaning of Paternity', 508, 497. See also Judith Tucker, *Women in Nineteenth-Century Egypt* (Cambridge: Cambridge University Press, 1985), 56–7, for a discussion of custody versus guardianship in Hanafi law.
35 Hamed Fayazi, 'Rashid al-Din's Interpretation of Surat al-Kawthar', *The Muslim World* 102 (2012): 286. The poem, which may date to pre-Islamic times, can be found in Abū 'Uthmān al-Jāḥiẓ, *Kitāb al-hayawān*, ed. 'Abd al-Salām Hārūn, 8 vols. (Beirut: Dār al-Jīl, 1996), 1:346.
36 See 'The Rights of Parents and Children in Islam', *Islam: The Modern Religion*, accessed 16 May 2018, http://www.themodernreligion.com/family/children_rights.htm
37 Musallam, *Sex and Society in Islam*, 49.

38 Ibn Qayyim al-Jawziyya, *Al-Tibyān fī aqsām al-Qur'an*, ed. Muhammad Ḥāmid al-Fiqqī (Cairo: Maba'at Ḥijāzī, 1933), 334–5. See also Musallam, *Sex and Society in Islam*, 50–1. Likewise, the thirteenth-century thinker Ibn al-Nafis put forth the notion that both male and female semen exist, both of which 'possess specific temperaments (the male is hot and dry, and the female is cold and moist) that when mixed together in the womb attain a temperament suitable for the emanation of the new human soul from God'. See Nahyan Fancy, 'Generation in Medieval Islamic Medicine', in *Reproduction: From Antiquity to the Present*, ed. Nick Hopwood, Rebecca Flemming, and Lauren Kassell (Cambridge: Cambridge University Press, forthcoming.)

39 Ibn Qayyim, *Al-Tibyān*, 334–5. Translation by B.F. Musallam.

40 Ibid., 335.

41 Ibid., 352.

42 Ibid., 352.

43 Ibid., 352–3.

44 Musallam, *Sex and Society in Islam*, 51.

45 Ibid., 52.

46 Daniel Pollack et al., 'Classical Religious Perspectives of Adoption Law', *Notre Dame Law Review* 79, no. 2 (2004): 140.

47 Kecia Ali, *Sexual Ethics and Islam: Feminist Reflections on Qur'an, Hadith, and Jurisprudence* (Oxford: Oneworld Publications, 2006), 3.

48 Pollack et al., 'Classical Religious Perspectives', 140; Ebrahim Moosa, '"The Child Belongs to the Bed": Illegitimacy and Islamic Law', in *Questionable Issue: Illegitimacy in South Africa*, ed. Sandra Burman and Eleanor Preston-White (Cape Town: Oxford University Press, 1992), 173; Ali, *Sexual Ethics*, 66-7.

49 Adeel Mohammadi, 'The Ambiguity of Maternal Filiation (*nasab*) in Early and Medieval Islam', *The Graduate Journal of Harvard Divinity School* 11 (Spring 2016): 56–7.

50 Mohammadi, 'Ambiguity', 56–7; Ali, *Sexual Ethics*, 67. See also Ali, *Marriage and Slavery*, 87–9, for a discussion of paternity claims and maintenance.

51 Mohammadi, 'Ambiguity', 53, 60.

52 Ibid., 59.

53 Ibid., 58, 59; see also Ruth Roded, *Women in Islamic Biographical Collections: From Ibn Sa'd to Who's Who* (Boulder: Lynne Rienner, 1994), 12, 22.

54 See Denise Spellberg, *Politics, Gender and the Islamic Past: The Legacy of 'A'isha bint Abi Bakr* (New York: Columbia University Press, 1994), 218 n. 22; and Thurlkill, *Chosen among Women*, 18-22. Thurlkill also addresses scholarly disputes regarding the evolution of traditions and theologies about Fatima.

55 See Moojan Momen, *An Introduction to Shi'i Islam: The History and Doctrines of Twelver Shi'ism* (New Haven: Yale University Press, 1985), 47–8; 64.

56 See Cleo McNelly Kearns, *The Virgin Mary, Monotheism, and Sacrifice* (Cambridge: Cambridge University Press, 2008), 123; also Angelika Neuwirth, 'The House of Abraham and the House of Amran: Genealogy, Patriarchal Authority, and Exegetical Professionalism', in *The Qur'an in Context: Historical and Literary Investigations into the Qur'ānic Milieu*, ed. Michael Marx Neuwirth and Nicolai Sinai (Leiden: Brill, 2010), 506–7, 527.

57 Al-Bukhārī, *Al-Adab al-mufrad: kitāb al-'utās wa al-tathā'ub* (147).

58 Al-Bukhārī, *Saḥīḥ: kitāb al-istidhān, bāb* 43.

59 See for example Aḥmad ibn Ḥanbal, *Kitāb faḍā'il al-ṣaḥāba*, ed. Waṣī Allah ibn Muhammad 'Abbās (Beirut: Mu'assasat al-Risāla, 1983), 2:756; Abū 'Īsā Muhammad al-Tirmidhī, *Sunan al-Tirmidhī*, ed. 'Izzat 'Abīd al-Da'ās (Homs: Maktabat Dār al-Da'wa, 1967), 9:386. For a discussion of this question, and Shi'i skepticism about it, see Soufi, 'Image', 51–5.

60 For more on Ibn Bābawayh, see Momen, *Shi'i Islam*, 78–9, 313–4.

61 Abū Ja'far ibn Bābawayh, *Amālī al-ṣadūq* (Najaf: Al-Maṭba'a al-Ḥaydariyya, 1970), 437.

62 Ibn Bābawayh, *Ma'ānī al-akhbār*, ed. 'Ali Akbar al-Ghaffārī (Tehran: Maktabat al-Ṣadūq, 1959), 303; see also al-Mufīd, *Amālī*, 104.

63 Ibn Bābawayh, *Risālat al-i'tiqādāt*, trans. Asar A.A. Fyzee as *A Shi'ite Creed* (London: Oxford University Press, 1942), 109.

64 Soufi, 'Image', 33.

65 See, for example, Ismā'īl ibn 'Umar ibn Kathīr, *Tafsīr al-Qur'an al-'aẓīm*, 9 vols. (Beirut: Dār al-Kutub al-'Ilmiyya, 1998), 6:365–7. For explanations of the many interpretations given to the terms *ahl al-bayt* and *ahl al-kisā'*, see Soufi, 'Image', 3–4; Ignác Goldziher et al., 'Ahl al-Bayt', in *EI*[2]; Arthur Stanley Tritton, 'Ahl al-Kisā'', in *EI*[2]; Hamid Algar, 'Āl-e 'Abā', in *Encyclopaedia Iranica*, ed. Ehsan Yarshater (New York: Columbia University Center for Iranian Studies, 1996–), http:www.iranicaonline.org/ (*EI*[r]); Veccia Vaglieri, 'Fāṭima'; Thurlkill, *Chosen among Women*, 20–3.

66 Muslim ibn al-Ḥajjāj, *Saḥīḥ*: *kitāb faḍā'il al-ṣaḥaba, bāb faḍā'il ahl al-bayt al-nabī*. Many other versions also exist, some involving Umm Salama, the wife of the Prophet.

67 Muhammad Bāqir al-Majlisī, *Biḥār al-anwār*, 110 vols. (Tehran: Maṭba'at al-Islāmiyya, 1956–1972), 43:24; also Abū Muhammad Ordoni, *Fatima the Gracious* (Qum: Anṣāriyān, 1987?), Chapter 10: At-Taherah. One 'abomination' of which Fatima was purified was menstruation, as will be later discussed.

68 Seyyed Hossein Nasr, 'Shi'ism and Sufism', in *Shi'ism: Doctrines, Thought and Spirituality*, ed. Nasr et al. (Albany: State University of New York Press, 1988), 103–4.

69 For more about this event, see Seyyed Hossin Nasr et al., *The Study Qur'an: A New Translation and Commentary* (New York: HarperCollins, 2015), 147 n. 59, 61; Werner Schmucker, 'Mubāhala', in *EI*[2]; Momen, *Shi'i Islam*, 13–14; Mahmoud Ayoub, *Redemptive Suffering in Islām: A Study of the Devotional Aspects of 'Āshūrā' in Twelver Shī'ism* (The Hague: Mouton, 1978), 79.

70 See, for example, Muslim, *Saḥīḥ*: *kitāb faḍā'il al-ṣaḥaba, bāb faḍā'il 'Ali ibn 'Abī Ṭalib.*

71 See, for example, Ibn Kathīr, *Tafsīr*, 2:46; also Fayazi, 'Rashid al-Din', 287. Separately, in a hadith ascribed to 'Umar, and cited by many reputable Sunni *muḥaddithūn* such as Ibn Sa'd and al-Tirmidhī, the Prophet himself is said to have referred to Fatima's children, Hasan and Husayn, as 'my sons and my daughter's sons'. See Soufi, 'Image', 12.

72 Schmucker, 'Mubāhala'.

73 Momen, *Shi'i Islam*, 14.

74 Ibid., 14.

75 Schmucker, 'Mubāhala'.

76 Since the imams would ultimately descend from Husayn's line, Hasan received less attention in the texts.

77 Ibn Sa'd, *Kitāb al-ṭabaqāt*, 8:194. In some variants the woman who dreams of the Prophet's limb is Umm Ayman, who helped care for Muhammad when he was small and remained close to him and his family. See al-Majlisī, *Biḥār*, 43:242–3.

78 Ibn Sa'd, *Kitāb al-ṭabaqāt*, 8:194. The same hadith goes on to relate that sometime after the child's birth, Umm al-Faḍl took him to the Prophet, who bounced him up and down and kissed him. The child then urinated on him. The Prophet said, 'Umm al-Faḍl, take my son, he has urinated on me' – once more identifying Husayn as the Prophet's offspring, this time in very human terms.

79 Muhammad ibn al-Fattāl al-Nīsābūrī, *Rawḍat al-wā'iẓīn*, ed. Muhammad Khurāsānī (Najaf: Al-Maṭba'a al-Ḥaydariyya, 1966), 154; quoted in Ayoub, *Redemptive Suffering*, 75.

80 Al-Mufīd, *Al-Irshād*, ed. al-Sayyid Kāẓim al-Mīyāmawī (Tehran: Dār al-Kutub, 1958); quoted in Ayoub, *Redemptive Suffering*, 74.

81 Muhammad ibn 'Ali ibn Shahrāshūb, *Manāqib Āl Abī Ṭālib* (Najaf: Al-Maṭba'a al-Ḥaydariyya, 1956), 3:207; quoted in Ayoub, *Redemptive Suffering*, 75. See also Matthew Pierce, *Twelve Infallible Men* (Cambridge: Harvard University Press, 2016), 139, for implications.

82 Ayoub, *Redemptive Suffering*, 76.

83 Ibn Bābawayh, *Amālī*; quoted in Ayoub, *Redemptive Suffering*, 41.

84 Richard Foltz, *Religions of Iran: From Prehistory to the Present* (London: Oneworld, 2013), 58.

85 Ibid., 60.

86 See Nasr, *Study Qur'an*, 1568-9.

87 Fakhr al-Dīn al-Rāzī, *Al-Tafsīr al-kabīr*, 32 vols. (Beirut: Dār Iḥyā' al-Turāth al-'Arabī, [1980–?]), 32:123-4; see also Nasr, *Study Qur'an*, 1568-9.

88 Al-Rāzī, *Al-Tafsīr*, 32:124. See also Ordoni, *Fatima the Gracious*, Chapter 9: Al-Mubarakah; Osman, *Female Personalities*, 109; Ruffle, 'May You Learn from Their Model', 13; and 'Ali Sharī'atī, '*Fatimah Fatimah Ast*' (Fatima is Fatima), in *Shariati on Shariati and the Muslim Woman*, ed. and trans. Laleh Bakhtiari (USA: ABC International Group, 1996), 153, 159.

89 Al-Rāzī, *Al-Tafsīr*, 32:124.

90 Quoted in Ordoni, *Fatima the Gracious*, Chapter 9: Al-Mubarakah.

91 See Ayoub, *Redemptive Suffering*, 206.

92 See Uri Rubin, 'Pre-existence and Light: Aspects of the Concept of Nūr Muḥammad', *Israel Oriental Studies* 5 (1975): 62–119; also Rubin, 'Nūr Muḥammadī', in *EI*[2].

93 Rubin, 'Pre-existence', 67, 72.

94 Ibn Bābawayh, '*Ilal al-sharā'i*'; quoted in al-Majlisī, *Biḥār*, 43:12.

95 See Rubin, 'Pre-existence', 84-5.

96 Muhammad ibn Isḥāq, *Sīrat Rasūl Allah*, trans. A. Guillaume as *The Life of Muhammad* (Oxford: Oxford University Press, 1955), 72. For more versions, see Ibn Sa'd, *Kitāb al-ṭabaqāt al-kabīr*, vol. 1, trans. S. Moinul Haq and H. K. Ghazanfar (Karachi: Pakistan Historical Society, 1967), 111–12.

97 Al-Mas'ūdī, *Ithbāt al-Waṣiyya*, 129; quoted in Rubin, 'Pre-existence', 98.

98 Yunus ibn Bukayr, quoted in Bayhaqī, 1:84-6; quoted in Rubin, 'Pre-existence', 84.

99 Al-Kumayt ibn Zayd al-Asadī, *Hāshimiyyāt*, 84, 39 ff; quoted in Rubin, 'Pre-existence', 91. For more on al-Kumayt, see Moshe Sharon, 'The Development of the Debate Around the Legitimacy of Authority in Early Islam', *Jerusalem Studies in Arabic and Islam* 5 (1984): 79–81.

100 Ibn Bābawayh, '*Ilal al-sharā'i*', quoted in al-Majlisī, *Biḥār*, 43:11.

101 Rubin, 'Pre-existence', 102, and Ruffle, 'May You Learn from Their Model', 7.

102 Ibn Bābawayh, *Ma'ānī*, quoted in al-Majlisī, *Biḥār*, 43:4. Translated by Christopher Clohessy.

103 Ibid., 43:4-5.

104 Husayn ibn ʿAbd al-Wahhāb, *ʿUyūn al-Muʿjizāt* (Najaf: Al-Maṭbaʿa al-Ḥaydariyya), 47. Translated by Laura Veccia Vaglieri.

105 For more on al-Kulaynī, see Etan Kohlberg, 'Kolayni', in *EI*ʳ.

106 The contemporary Qur'an scholar Abdullah Yusuf ʿAli explains that the niche is 'the little shallow recess in the wall of an Eastern house, fairly high from the ground, in which a light (before the days of electricity) was usually placed. Its height enabled it to diffuse the light in the room and minimized the shadows'. See *The Holy Qur'an: Text, Translation and Commentary* (Elmhurst, NY: Tahrike Tarsile Qur'an, 1987), 907 n. 2998.

107 Muhammad ibn Yaʿqūb al-Kulaynī, *Al-Kāfī*, ed. ʿAli Akbar al-Ghaffārī, 8 vols. (Tehran: Dār al-Kutub al-Islāmiyya, 1957–61), 1:195; trans. Muhammad Sarwar, 8 vols. (New York: The Islamic Seminary, 2015), 1:174–5.

108 David Pinault, 'Zaynab bint ʿAlī and the Place of the Women of the Households of the First Imāms in Shīʿite Devotional Literature', in *Women in the Medieval Islamic World: Power, Patronage, and Piety*, ed. Gavin Hambly (New York: St. Martin's Press, 1998), 74–5.

109 For further development of this concept, see Ayoub, *Redemptive Suffering*, 57–8, and Thurlkill, *Chosen among Women*, 63.

110 A thriving cottage industry is devoted to comparisons of the Virgin Mary and Fatima, both in the pre-modern era and today. The sources are too numerous to mention comprehensively here, but for some idea of the import of their discussions, see Soufi, 'Image', 167–80; Thurlkill, *Chosen Among Women*, 1–9 and throughout; Christopher Paul Clohessy, *Fatima, Daughter of Muhammad* (Piscataway, NJ: Gorgias Press, 2013), 193–223; Osman, *Female Personalities*, 115–19; and Jane Dammen McAuliffe, 'Chosen of All Women: Mary and Fatima in Qur'anic Exegesis', *Islamochristiana* 7 (1981): 19–28.

111 For 'son of Mary', see, for example, Qur'an 43:57. For Jesus's lineage, see Qur'an 3:33–4 and 6:84–5.

112 See Soufi, 'Image', 69 n. 165.

113 See ibid.

114 Ibn Bābawayh, *Amālī*, 207; Ibn Shahrāshūb, *Manāqib*, 3:113.

115 Ibn Shahrāshūb, *Manāqib*, 3:113.

116 Fāḍl al-Husaynī al-Mīlānī, *Fāṭima al-Zahrā': Umm Abīhā* (Najaf: Maktabat al-Ṣādiq), 35. See also al-Kulaynī, *Al-Kāfī*, 1:458.

117 Soufi, 'Image', 69 n. 165.

118 Veccia Vaglieri, 'Fāṭima'.

119 Ibid.

120 Ibid.

121 Ibn ʿAbd al-Wahhāb, *ʿUyūn al-Muʿjizāt*, 46. For a gloss of Fāṭir, see Nasr, *Study Qur'an*, 1175 n. 11. For a discussion of the term's extremely esoteric implications, see Henri Corbin, *Terre Céleste et Corps de Résurrection: De l'Iran Mazdéen à l'Iran Shîʿite*, trans. Nancy Pearson as *Spiritual Body and Celestial Earth: From Mazdean Iran to Shīʿite Iran* (Princeton: Princeton University Press, 1977), 66–8; also Soufi, 'Image', 185, and Clohessy, *Fatima*, 6–8, 73–4. Todd Lawson's 'The Authority of the Feminine and Fatima's Place in an Early Work by the Bab', *Journal of Baha'i Studies* 1 (2007): 137–70 also contains a discussion of the esoteric Fatima; see especially 152–4.

122 See, for example, Ibn Sa'd, *Kitāb al-ṭabaqāt al-kabīr*, vol. 7, trans. Aisha Bewley as *The Men of Madina* (London: Ta-Ha, 1997), 19.

123 Al-Bukhārī, *Saḥīḥ:bāb man aḥaq al-nās bi-husn al-suḥbat* (2).

124 Nasr, *Study Qur'an*, 130 n. 7.

125 Suzanne Pinckney Stetkyvich, *The Mute Immortals Speak: Pre-Islamic Poetry and the Poetics of Ritual* (Ithaca: Cornell University Press, 1993), 139.

126 Ibn Kathīr, *Tafsīr*, 7:175; see also Kathryn Kueny, *Conceiving Identities: Maternity in Medieval Muslim Discourse and Practice* (Albany: State University of New York Press, 2013), 40.

127 Ibn Kathīr, *Tafsīr*, 7:200. See also Nasr, *Study Qur'an*, 1190 n. 4. The Preserved Tablet or *al-lawḥ al-maḥfūẓ* is mentioned in Qur'an 85:22.

128 See Nasr, *Study Qur'an*, 627 n. 39.

129 Ali, *Holy Qur'an*, 1324 n. 4606.

130 Corbin, *Terre Céleste*, 65.

131 See Ayoub, *Redemptive Suffering*, 255-6. Husayn is also called 'Ibn Fatima' in several poems. See al-Majlisī, *Biḥār*, 45:238, 248.

132 See, for example, al-Majlisī, *Biḥār*, 43:4, 7, 18.

133 Al-Majlisī, *Biḥār*, 43:21.

134 Ibn ʿAbd al-Wahhāb, *ʿUyūn al-Muʿjizāt*, 59; quoted in Soufi, 'Image', 174. See also Clohessy, *Fatima*, 107-16; Pierce, *Twelve Infallible Men*, 120-1; Thurlkill, *Chosen Among Women*, 43, 64; and Spellberg, 'Politics of Praise', 145, for discussions of Fatima's inimitability and, especially, how it related to her purity and chastity.

135 Al-Majlisī, *Biḥār*, 43:228. See also Ibn Ḥanbal, *Faḍā'il*, 2:658. Another version of the hadith runs as follows: 'All the sons of one mother trace themselves back to an agnate, except the sons of Fatima, for I am their nearest relative and their agnate.' See Yusūf ibn Ismā'īl al-Nabhānī, *Al-Sharaf al-muʿabbad li-āl Muhammad* (Cairo: Muṣṭafā al-Bābī al-Ḥalabī, 1961), 97.

136 See Ordoni, *Fatima the Gracious*, Chapter 9: Al-Mubarakah.

137 Al-Ṭabarī, *Tārīkh*, vol. 28, trans. Jane Dammen McAuliffe as *The History of al-Tabari: 'Abbasid Authority Affirmed* (Albany: State University of New York Press, 1995), 167–8. For more on the revolt and on al-Nafs al-Zakiyya, see Frantz Buhl, 'Muhammad b. 'Abd Allah', in *EI*^{2}; also, Marshall G.S. Hodgson, The *Venture of Islam: Conscience and History in a World Civilization,* 3 vols. (Chicago: University of Chicago Press, 1974), 1:276. For a family tree showing the relationship of al-Nafs al-Zakiyya and al-Manṣūr to their ancestors and each other, see Hodgson, *Venture,* 1:261.

138 Al-Ṭabarī, *Tārīkh*, 28:169–70, 172.

139 Al-Majlisī, *Biḥār*, 43:229.

140 Ibid. The jurist was eventually executed by al-Ḥajjāj, according to other hadith.

141 Ibid., 43:232; see also 43:233 for a similar hadith from a different collection.

142 Al-Majlisī, *Biḥār*, quoted in Ordoni, *Fatima the Gracious*, Chapter 9: Al-Mubarakah.

143 Soufi, 'Image', 13.

144 See Wilferd Madelung, 'Abd-Al-Ḥamīd b. Abu'l-Ḥadīd', in *EI*^{2}.

145 Al-Majlisī, *Biḥār*, 43:234. For more about Zayd, see Nasr, *Study Qur'an*, 1031 n. 40.

146 Al-Majlisī, *Biḥār*, 43:234.

147 Ibid. Emphasis mine.

148 Ibid.

149 Soufi, 'Image', 152.

150 For a concise discussion of how this phenomenon appears in Corbin's works, see Ehsan Yarshater, 'The Persian Presence in the Islamic World', in *The Persian Presence in the Islamic World*, ed. Richard G. Hovannisian and Georges Sabagh (Cambridge: Cambridge University Press, 1998), 83–5.

151 See Fatima Mernissi, *Sultanés Oubliées: Femmes Chefs d'État en Islam,* trans. Mary Jo Lakeland as *The Forgotten Queens of Islam* (Minneapolis: University of Minnesota Press, 1993), 122. Likewise, see Sheikh al-Sheikh, 'Saudi Arabia's Top Cleric Says Iranians are "Not Muslims"', *BBC,* http://www.bbc.com/news/world-middle-east-37287434. Centuries earlier, the prominent Hanbali scholar Ibn Taymiyya (d. 1328) took aim at Shi'is among other groups, arguing that converts 'carried over remnants of their pre-existing spiritual and ritual practices into their new religion, and in various ways brought to their new community deviant practices, customs, beliefs of "innovations"'. See Tariq al-Jamil, 'Ibn Taymiyya and Ibn al-Mutahhar al-Hilli: Shi'i Polemics and the Struggle for Religious Authority in Medieval Islam', in *Ibn Taymiyya and His Times*, ed. Yossef Rapoport and Shahab Ahmed (Oxford: Oxford University Press, 2010), 232–3.

152 Jenny Rose, 'Three Queens, Two Wives, and a Goddess: Roles and Images of Women in Sasanian Iran', in Hambly, *Women in the Medieval Islamic World*, 35. See also Kathryn Babayan, 'The "Aqā'īd al-Nisā": A Glimpse at Safavid Women in Local Isfahani Culture', in Hambly, *Women in the Medieval Islamic World*, 376–7, n. 13; Leila Ahmed, *Women and Gender in Islam: Historical Roots of a Modern Debate* (New Haven: Yale University Press, 1992), 19–22; and Anahit Perikhanian, 'Iranian Society and Law', in *The Cambridge History of Iran*, vol. 3, *The Seleucid, Parthian and Sasanian Periods*, ed. Ehsan Yarshater (Cambridge: Cambridge University Press, 1983), 649, 651–5.

153 Jamsheed K. Choksy, *Evil, Good, and Gender: Facets of the Feminine in Zoroastrian Religious History* (New York: Peter Lang, 2002), 35, 45.

154 Ibid., 45.

155 Foltz, *Religions of Iran*, 60.

156 Choksy, *Evil, Good, and Gender*, 99. Corbin, on the other hand, recognizes the similarities but resists suggesting that they represent syncretism or influence. See *Terre Céleste*, xvi, xxviii.

157 Veccia Vaglieri, 'Fāṭima'.

158 Ibid.

159 The Prophet Muhammad's image underwent a similar burnishing to demonstrate that he performed the same sorts of miracles as Jesus and was similarly infallible and pure. See Jonathan A. C. Brown, *Muhammad: A Very Short Introduction* (Oxford: Oxford University Press, 2011), 89–93.

160 As Soufi observes, the scholar Ibn Shahrāshūb 'offers a direct, point by point comparison between Fatima and Maryam in an attempt to prove that Fatima is superior to Maryam in his *Manāqib Āl Abī Ṭālib*'. See 'Image', 177.

161 Ibid., 153–8.

162 Ibid., 160.

163 Ibn Bābawayh, '*Ilal al-sharā'i*' (Najaf: Al-Maṭba'a al-Ḥaydariyya, 1963), 182.

164 Al-Majlisī, *Biḥār*, 43:15, 16; see also Soufi, 'Image', 170, and Clohessy, *Fatima*, 107-16.

165 Ibn Shahrāshūb, *Manāqib*, 3:133.

166 See Roded, *Women*, 22; also, Nikki Keddie, *Women in the Middle East: Past and Present* (Princeton: Princeton University Press, 2007), 18. Much ink has been spilled debating the degree to which pre-Islamic Arabic was matrilineal. See Leila Ahmed, 'Women and the Advent of Islam', *Signs* 11, no. 4 (1986): 667.

167 Ahmed, 'Women and the Advent of Islam', 668.

168 Jalāl al-Dīn 'Abd al-Raḥmān al-Suyūṭī, *Al-khaṣā'iṣ al-kubrā*, ed. Muhammad Khalīl Harrās, 3 vols. (Cairo: Dār al-Kutub al-Ḥadītha, 1967), 1:96. Translation by Uri Rubin.

169 Attributed to al-Samaw'al ibn 'Ādiyā, quoted in Abū Tammām, *Dīwān al-Ḥamāsa*, 2 vols. (Cairo: al-Maktaba al-Azhariyya, 1927), 1:38. Translation by Uri Rubin.

170 Hishām ibn al-Kalbī, *Kitāb al-aṣnām*, trans. Nabih Amin Faris as *The Book of Idols* (Princeton: Princeton University Press, 1952), 17.

171 For a discussion of these verses, see Carl Ernst, *How to Read the Qur'an: A New Guide, with Select Translations* (Chapel Hill: University of North Carolina Press, 2011), 98–104; Nicolai Sinai, 'An Interpretation of Sūrat al-Najm (Q. 53)', *Journal of Qur'anic Studies* 13, no. 2 (2011): 9–11; and John Burton, 'Those Are the High-Flying Cranes', *Journal of Semitic Studies* 15, no. 2 (1970): 246–65.

172 See Barbara Freyer Stowasser, 'Mary', in *Encyclopaedia of the Qur'an*, ed. Jane Dammen McAuliffe (Leiden: Brill, 2005), CD-ROM.

173 See Neuwirth, 'House of Abraham', 499–531, Ernst, *How to Read the Qur'an*, 174–86; Kueny, *Conceiving Identities*, 40–5; and Osman, *Female Personalities*, 79–83.

174 Raymond Farrin, *Structure and Qur'anic Interpretation: A Study of Symmetry and Coherence in Islam's Holy Text* (Ashland, OR: White Cloud Press, 2014), 24; Nasr, *Study Qur'an*, 126.

175 Nasr, *Study Qur'an*, 128.

176 Nasr, *Study Qur'an*, 129–30 n. 7.

177 See ibid., 130–1; Farid Esack, *The Qur'an: A User's Guide* (Oxford: Oneworld Publications, 2005), 75–7.

178 This matter is of particular significance to Shi'is. See Ernst, *How to Read the Qur'an*, 176; Diana Steigerwald, 'Twelver Shi'i Ta'wīl', in *The Blackwell Companion to the Qur'an*, ed. Andrew Rippin (Malden, MA: Blackwell, 2006), 377.

179 See Neuwirth, 'House of Abraham', 526; Ernst, *How to Read the Qur'an*, 174.

180 Wombs play an important part elsewhere in Islamic scripture; for a trenchant discussion, see Osman, *Female Personalities*, 32–6.

181 See Ernst for other analysis of why this 'gendered language' is 'employed in verses relating to the interpretation of scripture'. *How to Read the Qur'an*, 175.

182 Ernst, *How to Read the Qur'an*, 175; also Neuwirth, 'House of Abraham', 520, and Julie Scott Meisami, 'Fitnah or Azadah? Nizami's Ethical Poetic', *Edebiyāt* 1, no. 2 (1989): 55.

183 See Ernst, *How to Read the Qur'an*, 175; also Neuwirth, 'House of Abraham', 522.

184 See Ernst, *How to Read the Qur'an*, 174.

185 See Neuwirth, 'House of Abraham', 507 n. 25 for an explanation of the identity of 'Imran'.

186 See Osman, *Female Personalities*, 73–4.

187 See Kueny, *Conceiving Identities*, 41, for associations between *umm al-kitāb* and Mary.
188 Nasr, *Study Qur'an*, 266–8 n. 171; 284–5 n. 17; see also Robinson, 'Jesus', in McAuliffe, *Encyclopaedia of the Qur'an*.
189 Kearns, *Virgin Mary*, 122–3.
190 Neuwirth, 'House of Abraham', 505, 513; See also Ernst, *How to Read the Qur'an*, 186; and Osman, *Female Personalities*, 79–82.
191 Kearns, *Virgin Mary*, 150–1.
192 See Ernst, *How to Read the Qur'an*, 173; and Neuwirth, 'House of Abraham', 527.
193 Kueny, *Conceiving Identities*, 43.
194 See ibid.
195 Mahmood, 'Feminist Theory', 203, 212.
196 Soufi, 'Image', 171; see also Ayoub, *Redemptive Suffering*, 42–3.
197 Ibn Bābawayh, *Amālī*, 101.

Chapter 2

1 Iskandar Munshī, *Tārīkh-i 'ālamārā-yi 'Abbāsī*, ed. Īraj Afshār, 2 vols., 2nd ed. (Tehran: Amir Kabīr, 1971), 1:128; trans. Robert M. Savory as *History of Shah 'Abbas the Great*, 2 vols. (Boulder: Westview Press, 1978, 2 vols.), 1:209. Mahd-i 'Ulya was a common title for royal women. See Maria Szuppe, 'Status, Knowledge, and Politics: Women in Sixteenth-Century Safavid Iran', in *Women in Iran from the Rise of Islam to 1800*, ed. Guity Nashat and Lois Beck (Urbana: University of Illinois Press, 2003), 164 n. 22.
2 Iskandar Munshī, *Tārīkh*, 1:127; English tr., 1:209. Emphasis mine.
3 See Mohammadi, 'Ambiguity', 53, 59–62.
4 Joseph Kechichian, *Succession in Saudi Arabia* (New York: Palgrave, 2001), 26.
5 Ibid., 27.
6 Ibid., 251 n. 71.
7 For more information about this genre, see Wadād al-Qāḍī, 'Biographical Dictionaries: Inner Structure and Cultural Significance', in *The Book in the Islamic World: The Written Word and Communication in the Middle East*, ed. George N. Atiyeh (Albany: State University of New York Press, 1995).
8 Ibid., 94.
9 See Roded, *Women*, 12, 22, and Mohammadi, 'Ambiguity', 57, for excellent expositions on this topic.

10 Ibn Saʿd, *Kitāb al-ṭabaqāt al-kabīr,* vol. 3, trans. Aisha Bewley as *The Companions of Badr* (London: Ta-Ha, 2013), 104, 114, 128; and Ibn Saʿd, *Kitāb al-ṭabaqāt,* 7:10, 56, 60, 61, 89, 210. See also Roded, *Women,* 22.

11 Ibn Saʿd, *Kitāb al-ṭabaqāt,* 3:114, 163; see also Roded, *Women,* 22.

12 Ibn Saʿd, *Kitāb al-ṭabaqāt,* 1:54-63; see also Roded, 22.

13 Ibn Saʿd, *Kitāb al-ṭabaqāt,* 8:9.

14 Roded, *Women,* 23.

15 Al-Dhahabī, *Siyar aʿlām al-nubalāʾ,* 1:416; quoted in Mohammadi, 'Ambiguity', 57–8; Ibn Isḥāq, *Sīrat rasūl Allah,* 229.

16 Ibn Saʿd, *Kitāb al-ṭabaqāt,* 3:12; see also Mohammadi, 'Ambiguity', 60.

17 See, for example, Ibn Saʿd, *Kitāb al-ṭabaqāt,* 3:87-8, which describes the companion Muṣʿab al-Khayr. It gives the name of his daughter, Zaynab, her mother, and the daughter's daughter. See also Roded, *Women,* 22.

18 Ibn Saʿd, *Kitāb al-ṭabaqāt,* 8:176–80; 298–301; 306–7.

19 Ibid., 8:299–300. Some Shiʿis dispute that this marriage took place.

20 Ibid., 8:176.

21 Ibid., 8:176-7.

22 See Mohammadi, 'Ambiguity', 53; also Pierce, *Twelve Infallible Men,* 85.

23 For a penetrating treatment of Hind as the '*jāhiliyya* woman par excellence' who later undergoes rehabilitation as a Muslim, see Nadia Maria El-Cheikh, *Women, Islam, and Abbasid Identity* (Cambridge: Harvard University Press, 2015), 17–37.

24 Ibn Isḥāq, *Sīrat Rasūl Allah,* 385-6.

25 Ibn Saʿd, *Kitāb al-ṭabaqāt,* 8:28. For other sources, see Roded, *Women,* 37.

26 Ibn Saʿd, *Kitāb al-ṭabaqāt,* 8:293–8; see also Roded, *Women,* 22, where she notes that maternal aunts are 'not systematically recorded and are included only if they fall into some other category'.

27 Roded, *Women,* 23–4, 140.

28 Ibid., 23-24.

29 Ibid., 135.

30 See Carl F. Petry, 'Al-Sakhāwī', in *EI*²; also Roded, *Women,* 59, 68.

31 Roded, *Women,* 128.

32 Ibid.

33 Ibid., 107. She notes that Shams al-Dīn Aḥmad Aflākī (d. 1360), a chronicler of the Mevlevī order in Anatolia, lists 'sisters, wives, concubines and daughters … alongside their male relations' in his text.

34 Ibid., 108.

35 Ibid. See also Margaret L. Meriwether, *The Kin Who Count: Family and Society in Ottoman Aleppo, 1770–1840* (Austin: University of Texas Press, 1999), 52–3,

for more details about the Rifāʿiyya order and several other Aleppo families who traced descent through females.

36 For a discussion of Shiʿi collective biographies, see Pierce, *Twelve Infallible Men*, 3–6.

37 Notably, according to usage in Egypt dating from Fatimid times, descendants of ʿAli's daughters could be considered *ashrāf*, or noble descendants of the Prophet, although they did not belong to the smallest class of nobility which was reserved only for the descendants of Hasan and Husayn. See Cornelius van Arendonk, 'Sharīf', in *EI*^{2}.

38 Al-Kulaynī, *Al-Kāfī*, 1:452; English tr., 1:457.

39 Ibid., 1:453; English tr., 1:457.

40 Ibid., 1:453; English tr., 1:458.

41 Ibid., 1:453; English tr., 1:458.

42 Al-Majlisī, *Biḥār*, 12:80; quoted in Clohessy, *Fatima*, 83.

43 Al-Kulaynī, *Al-Kāfī*, 1:454; English tr., 1:459.

44 See Pierce, *Twelve Infallible Men*, 131.

45 Ibid., 134.

46 See Mohammad Ali Amir-Moezzi, 'Šahrbānu', in *EI*^{r}.

47 Ibid.

48 Al-Kulaynī, *Al-Kāfī*, 1:467; English tr., 1:472. See also al-Majlisī, *Biḥār*, 46:9.

49 Al-Kulaynī, *Al-Kāfī*, 1:467; English tr., 1:472.

50 Ibid., 1:467; English tr., 1:472.

51 Ibid., 1:467; English tr., 1:472. See also al-Majlisī, *Biḥār*, 46:4.

52 Amir-Moezzi, 'Šahrbānu'.

53 Ibid.

54 Ibid.

55 See for example Amir-Moezzi, 'Šahrbānu', and Pierce, *Twelve Infallible Men*, 135.

56 Amir-Moezzi, 'Šahrbānu'.

57 Ibid.

58 Ibid.

59 Ibid.

60 Ibid.

61 Ibid.

62 Ibid.

63 See William W. Malandra, 'Zoroastrianism: Historical Review up to the Arab Conquest', in *EI*^{r}.

64 Amir-Moezzi, 'Šahrbānu'.

65 Ibid.

66 Scholars have in fact shown some crossover between rituals and sites devoted to Anāhitā and those to Shahrbānū. See ibid.

67 See, for example, Djalal Khaleghi Motlagh, *Frauem im Schahname*, trans. Brigitte Neuenschwander as *Women in the Shāhnāmeh: Their History and Social Status within the Framework of Ancient and Medieval Sources* (Costa Mesa: Mazda, 2012).

68 Rāwandī, *Al-Kharā'ij wa al-jarā'ih*; quoted in Majlisī, *Biḥār*, 46:11. Translation by David Pinault.

69 Amir-Moezzi, 'Šahrbānu'.

70 Al-Majlisī, *Jalā' al-'Uyūn*, 850; quoted in Pierce, *Twelve Infallible Men*, 135.

71 Al-Kulaynī, *Al-Kāfī*, 1:469; English tr., 1:474.

72 Ibid., 1:469; English tr., 1:474.

73 Ibid., 1:476; English tr., 1:482.

74 Ibid., 1:477; English tr., 1:482.

75 Ibid., 1:477; English tr., 1:483.

76 Ibid., 1:387-8; English tr., 1:384.

77 Ibid., 1:388; English tr., 1:384-5. See also Pierce, *Twelve Infallible Men*, 139.

78 Al-Kulaynī, *Al-Kāfī*, 1:388; English tr., 1:384-5.

79 Pierce, *Twelve Infallible Men*, 139.

80 Al-Mufīd, *Amālī*, 292. See also Pierce, *Twelve Infallible Men*, 140, and Mohammadi's discussion of this hadith in 'Ambiguity', 63-4. The latter suggests an interpretation that downplays the shamefulness of maternal filiation in the hereafter.

81 Pierce, *Twelve Infallible Men*, 140.

82 Ibn 'Asākir, *Tārikh Dimashq*, 6:502; quoted in Rubin, 'Al-Walad li-l-Firāsh', 16-17; see also Mohammadi, 'Ambiguity', 61.

83 Pierce, *Twelve Infallible Men*, 135, 140.

84 For an explanation of this nomenclature, as well as a vivid description of the conditions that led to the formation of these empires, see Hodgson, *Venture*, 3:16–27.

85 See Hodgson, *Venture*, 3:16.

86 Szuppe, 'Status, Knowledge, and Politics', 141.

87 Takin, *Grammar of Orkhon Turkic*; quoted in Leslie Peirce, *The Imperial Harem: Women and Sovereignty in the Ottoman Empire* (Oxford: Oxford University Press, 1993), 16.

88 Aşıkpaşzāde, *Tevarikh-i Al-i Osman*, Neşri, *Kitab-ı cihan-nüma* and others; quoted in Peirce, *Imperial Harem*, 16. See also Colin Imber, 'The Ottoman Dynastic Myth', *Turcica* 19 (1987): 21-2.

89 Peirce, *Imperial Harem*, 16.

90 Ibid., 16; also Imber, 'Ottoman Dynastic Myth', 22.

91 Peirce, *Imperial Harem*, 39–41.

92 Ibid., 41.

93 Ibid., 41.

94 Ibid., 188.

95 Roded, *Women*, 135; Peirce, *Imperial Harem*, 17.

96 Peirce, *Imperial Harem*, 22.

97 Ibid., 41.

98 Qummī, *Khulāṣat al-tavārīkh*; quoted in Kishwar Rizvi, 'Gendered Patronage: Women and Benevolence during the Early Safavid Empire', in *Women, Patronage and Self-Representation in Islamic Societies*, ed. D. Fairchild Ruggles (Albany: State University of New York Press, 2000), 126–7.

99 Rizvi, 'Gendered Patronage', 127.

100 Ibid.; Szuppe, 'Status, Knowledge, and Politics', 144–5.

101 Iskandar Munshī, *Tārīkh*, 1:226; English tr., 1:338.

102 Szuppe, 'Status, Knowledge, and Politics', 147. Emphasis mine.

103 Ibid., 147–8.

104 Ibid., 149–50.

105 See, for example, 'Ali ibn Aḥmad Muḥtasham, *Dīvān-i Muḥtasham Kāshānī*, ed. Akbar Bihdārvand (Tehran: Nigāh, 2000), 326; also Rizvi, 'Gendered Patronage', 126, 148 n. 21.

106 Bābur, *Bāburnāma*, trans. Wheeler M. Thackston as *The Baburnama: Memoirs of Babur, Prince and Emperor* (New York: The Modern Library, 2002), 7–12; see also Ruby Lal, *Domesticity and Power in the Early Mughal World* (Cambridge: Cambridge University Press, 2005), 81–5.

107 Lal, *Domesticity and Power*, 171.

108 Ibid., 83, 170.

109 See Abū al-Faḍl, *Akbarnāma*, 3 vols., trans. Henry Beveridge as *The Akbarnama of Abu'l Fazl* (Calcutta: The Asiatic Socieity, 1907; reprinted 2000), 1:178–83; also, Lal, *Domesticity and Power*, 148. For more on Ālanquwā in the context of the Timurids, see Priscilla P. Soucek, 'Tīmūrid Women: A Cultural Perspective', in Hambly, *Women in the Medieval Islamic World*, 214. The mythical ancestress also appears in the famous epic chronicling the life of Chingghiz Khan. See *The Secret History of the Mongols: The Life and Times of Chinggis Khan,* trans. and ed. Urgunge Onon (Richmond, Surrey: Curzon Press, 2001), 41–3.

110 Abū al-Faḍl, *Akbarnāma*, 1:179.

111 Ibid., 1:179.

112 Ibid., 1:179.

113 Ibid., 1:180.

114 See A. Azfar Moin, *The Millenial Sovereign: Sacred Kingship and Sainthood in Islam* (New York: Columbia University Press, 2012), 38.

115 Moin, *Millenial Sovereign*, 39.

116 For a more detailed description of the poem, see Mohammad Wahid Mirza, *Life and Works of Amir Khusrau* (Lahore: Panjab University Press, 1962), 193–5.

117 Amīr Khusraw, *Maṭla' al-anwār*, ed. Ṭāhir Aḥmad Ughlī Muharramūf (Moscow: Idāra-yi Intishārāt-i Dānish, Shu'ba-yi Adabiyāt-i Khāvar, 1975), 331:1–11.

118 Ibn Bābawayh, *Amālī*, 437.

119 See Pliny, *Naturalis Historia,* trans. John Bostock and H.T. Riley as *The Natural History of Pliny* (London: George Bell and Sons, 1890), 2:431; for a famous poem recounting the story of a drop of rain that becomes a pearl, see Sa'dī, *Būstān,* ed. Ghulām Husayn Yūsufī (Tehran: Khvārazmī Publications, 2008), 115.

120 Cf. Niẓāmī, who wrote to his son: 'With your good name's die stamp your coin; / let honour raise you up to Heaven, / So that, in my confinement, I, / by your greatness, will be raised high.' Niẓāmī Ganjavī, *Haft paykar*, ed. Bihrūz S̱arvatīyān (Tehran: Intishārāt-i Ṭūs, 1998), 90:7–8; trans. Julie Scott Meisami as *The Haft Paykar: A Medieval Persian Romance* (Oxford: Oxford University Press, 1995), 31:7–8.

121 See Mirza, *Life and Works*, 201–3.

122 See Gabbay, *Islamic Tolerance: Amīr Khusraw and Pluralism* (Abingdon: Routledge, 2010), 41–61, for a discussion of the Bahram Gūr portion of the poem.

123 See Ibid., 62–5, for a discussion of this section of the poem.

124 It is possible that these are different daughters, and that saying that her 'name is also Mastūra' is just a pun. One variant giving the daughter's age as seven months, rather than seven years, supports that argument. However, I believe it is more likely that Khusraw is referring to only one daughter whose age is seven years.

125 Some variants give seven months. See note above.

126 Amīr Khusraw, *Hasht bihisht*, ed. Ja'far Iftikhār (Moscow: Idāra-yi Intisharāt-i Dānish, Shu'ba-yi Adabiyāt-i Khāvar, 1975), 36–7:354–68.

127 Fetuses born at eight months were considered nonviable. See Gabbay, *Islamic Tolerance*, 107 n.78.

128 See ibid., 62–3.

129 Amīr Khusraw, *Hasht bihisht*, 38:380.

130 For more on this collection, see Mirza, *Life and Works*, 171–2.

131 Amīr Khusraw, *Nihāyat al-kamāl*, ed. Yāsīn ʿAli Niẓāmī (Delhi: Maṭbaʿ-i Qayṣarīyah, 1913/4), 105.

132 See Gabbay, *Islamic Tolerance*, 3–5.

133 Shaikh, *Sufi Narratives*, 12.

134 Ibid., 12.

135 Annemarie Schimmel, *Meine Seele ist eine Frau: Das Weibliche im Islam*, trans. Susan H. Ray as *My Soul is a Woman: The Feminine in Islam* (New York: Continuum, 1997), 23, 99; Jamal Elias, 'Female and Feminine in Islamic Mysticism', *The Muslim World* 77 (1988): 220.

136 Saʿdiyya Shaikh, 'In Search of *al-Insān:* Sufism, Islamic Law, and Gender', *Journal of the American Academy of Religion* 77, no. 4 (2009): 790.

137 Farīd al-Dīn ʿAṭṭār, *Tazkirāt al-ʿawliyā'*, trans. A.J. Arberry as *Muslim Saints and Mystics* (London: Arkana, 1966), 40.

138 Schimmel, *Meine Seele*, 76–8.

139 ʿAṭṭār, *Manṭiq al-ṭayr*, ed. Muhammad Riża Shafiʿī Kadkanī, 3rd ed. (Tehran: Intishārāt-i Sukhan, 2006), 396; trans. Afkhan Darbandi and Dick Davis as *The Conference of the Birds* (London: Penguin, 1984), 198.

140 Manṣūr al-Ḥallāj, *Dīwān*, ed. Kāmil Muṣṭafā al-Shaybī (Cologne: Manshūrāt al-Jamal, 2007), 35–6; trans. Herbert W. Mason as *Al-Hallaj* (Richmond, Surrey: Curzon Press, 1995), 74.

141 See Gabbay, *Islamic Tolerance*, 60–2.

142 Soufi, 'Image', 75.

143 Carl Ernst, *Sufism: An Introduction to the Mystical Tradition of Islam* (Boston: Shambhala, 2011), 138.

144 Nasr, 'Shiʿism and Sufism', 104; see also Rizvi, 'Gendered Patronage', 126.

145 Mohammadi, 'Ambiguity', 65–8.

146 Al-Sarakhsī, *Kitāb al-mabsūṭ*, 17:113; quoted in Mohammadi, 'Ambiguity', 67.

147 Ibid., 7:52; 67.

148 Ibid., 7:52–3; 67.

149 Ibid., 7:52–3; 67.

150 See Arendonk, 'Sharīf'.

151 Ibid.

152 In his study of a cross-cultural sample of preindustrial societies, Martin King Whyte found that 'matrilineal descent and matrilocal residence [were] associated with modest benefits for women in certain areas', but not 'sweeping consequences'. See *Status of Women in Preindustrial Societies* (Princeton: Princeton University Press, 1978), 171.

Chapter 3

1 Al-Kulaynī, *Al-Kāfī*, 7:75; English tr., 7:68.

2 Abū al-Faḍl ibn Abī Ṭāhir Ṭayfūr, *Balāghāt al-nisā'*, ed. Barakat Yūsuf Habbūd (Beirut: Al-Maktaba al-ʿAṣrīya, 2000), 31–3.

3 Ibid., 32.

4 Yāqūt al-Hamawī, *Muʿjam al-Buldān* (Beirut: Dār Ṣādir, 1984), 238).

5 Veccia Vaglieri, 'Fadak', in *EI*[2].

6 Ibid.

7 Yāqūt al-Hamawī, *Muʿjam*, 239; see also Veccia Vaglieri, 'Fadak'.

8 Yāqūt al-Hamawī, *Muʿjam*, 238–40.

9 Al-Ṭabarī, *Tārīkh*, 9:196; Ibn Saʿd, *Kitāb al-ṭabaqāt*, 8:20.

10 Yāqūt al-Hamawī, *Muʿjam*, 239; see also Soufi, 'Image', 101–3; 105.

11 Yāqūt al-Hamawī, *Muʿjam*, 239; see also Soufi, 'Image', 93.

12 Veccia Vaglieri, 'Fadak'.

13 Yāqūt al-Hamawī, *Muʿjam*, 239–40; al-Ṭabarī, *Tārīkh*, 9:196. See also Veccia Vaglieri, 'Fadak', and Soufi, 'Image', 95.

14 Yāqūt al-Hamawī, *Muʿjam*, 239; al-Ṭabarī, *Tārīkh*, 9:196; Ibn Saʿd, *Kitāb al-ṭabaqāt*, 8:20. For full discussions of the grammatical and other implications of this statement, see David S. Powers, *Studies in Qur'an and* Ḥadīth: *The Formation of the Islamic Law of Inheritance* (Berkeley: University of California Press, 1986), 123–8, as well as Muhammad Bāqir al-Ṣadr, *Fadak fī al-tārīkh* (Beirut: Dār al-Ta'āruf al-Maṭbuʿāt, 1990), 112–43; trans. Abdullah al-Shāhīn as *Fadak in History* (Qum: Anṣāriyān, 2002), 137–76.

15 Ibn Abī Ṭāhir Ṭayfūr, *Balāghāt*, 34.

16 Simone de Beauvoir, *Le Deuxième Sexe*, trans. Constance Borde and Sheila Malovany-Chevallier as *The Second Sex* (New York: Knopf, 2010), 90.

17 Ingrid Pfluger-Schindlbeck, 'Kinship, Descent Systems and State: The Caucasus', in Joseph, *EWIC*, 2:337.

18 Germaine Tillion, *Le Harem et Les Cousins*, trans. Quintin Hoare as *The Republic of Cousins: Women's Oppression in Mediterranean Society* (London: Al Saqi Books, 1983), 144.

19 Erika Loeffler Friedl, 'Inheritance: Contemporary Practice: Iran and Afghanistan', in Joseph, *EWIC*, 2:302; see also Tillion, *Le Harem*, 144.

20 King, 'Kinship and State', 347; also Delaney, who writes, 'It is not so much that women inherit land (which they rarely do despite stipulations in the Koran) but that in the symbolic sense, women are land. The land and its fruits are for the benefit of the group; to give away a daughter would be like giving away a field.'

'Meaning of Paternity', 498. Kecia Ali also offers a cogent treatment of the concept of marriage as ownership in *Marriage and Slavery*; see especially 50–1, 164–90.

21 Powers, *Studies*, 191; also Judith Tucker, *Themes in Islamic Law: Women, Family, and Gender in Islamic Law* (Cambridge: Cambridge University Press, 2008), 138–40.

22 See Abū Ja'far Muhammad ibn Jarīr al-Ṭabarī, *Tafsīr al- Ṭabarī: Jāmī' al-bayān 'an ta'wīl āy al-Qur'an*, ed. Maḥmūd Muhammad Shākir and Aḥmad Muhammad Shākir, 16 vols. (Cairo: Dār al-Ma'ārif, 1955–), 4:262; also Powers, *Studies*, 53.

23 See Ṭāhir al-Ḥaddād, *Imra'atunā fi al-Sharī'ah wa al-Mujtama'*, trans. Ronak Husni and Daniel L. Newman as *Muslim Women in Law and Society* (Abingdon: Routledge, 2007), 45.

24 Powers, *Studies*, 191; also Noel J. Coulson, *Succession in the Muslim Family* (Cambridge: Cambridge University Press, 1971), 29.

25 Coulson, *Succession*, 29.

26 Noel J. Coulson, *History of Islamic Law* (Edinburgh: Edinburgh University Press, 1964), 16.

27 Ibid., 16.

28 Powers, *Studies*, 53.

29 Ibid., 53.

30 Al-Ṭabarī, *Tafsīr*, 7:598. Emphasis mine. Translation by David Powers.

31 Ibid., 7:598.

32 Powers, *Studies*, 53–4.

33 See Fatima Mernissi, *Le Harem Politique*, trans. Mary Jo Lakeland as *The Veil and the Male Elite: A Feminist Interpretation of Women's Rights in Islam* (New York: Basic Books, 1991), 120.

34 Ibid., 121.

35 Al-Ṭabarī, *Tafsīr*, 7:560–72; see Mernissi's penetrating discussion in *Le Harem Politique*, 126–8.

36 Al-Ṭabarī, *Tafsīr*, 7:561.

37 See Mernissi, *Le Harem Politique*, 127–8.

38 Powers, *Studies*, 190.

39 See Ahmed, 'Women and the Advent of Islam', 666; also, Powers, *Studies*, 54–5 n. 10.

40 See Keddie, *Women in the Middle East*, 43, Tillion, *Le Harem*, 148–9; al-Ḥaddād, *Imra'atunā*, 46; also, Maya Shatzmiller, *Her Day in Court: Women's Property Rights in Islamic Law and Society* (Cambridge: Harvard University Press, 2007), 72–5.

41 See Keddie, *Women in the Middle East*, 43; also Powers, *Studies*, 136, and Tillion, *Le Harem*, 148–9, for the use of waqfs in the contemporary Maghreb.

42 Tillion, *Le Harem*, 148.

43 See Moors, 'Inheritance: Contemporary Practice: Arab States', in Joseph, *EWIC*, 2:300–1; Meriwether, *Kin Who Count*, 132–40; and Tillion, *Le Harem*, 73–6.

44 See Keddie, *Women in the Middle East*, 210.

45 Moors, 'Inheritance: Contemporary Practice', 2:300. See also Friedl, 'Inheritance, Contemporary Practice', 2:302, for more discussion of the family politics involved in renouncing one's inheritance.

46 Liyakat N. Takim, 'Law: The Four Sunnī Schools of Law', in Joseph, *EWIC*, 2:444.

47 Ibid.

48 As well as more than women did in many contemporaneous European societies and in China. See Shatzmiller, *Her Day in Court*, 70–1; also Tucker, *Themes in Islamic Law*, 139–40.

49 Coulson, *Succession*, 35.

50 See Joseph Schacht, 'Mīrāth: In Pre-Modern Times', in *EI*[2].

51 Coulson, *History*, 17. See also Naṣr, *Study Qur'an*, 193–4 n.11.

52 Al-Bukhārī, *Saḥīḥ: Kitāb al-farā'iḍ, bāb mīrāṯ al-walad min abīhī wa umīhī* (5). See also *Bāb* 7 and *Bāb* 9.

53 For discussions of the differences between Sunni and Shi'i laws of inheritance, see Liyakat N. Takim, 'Law: Other Schools of Family Law', in Joseph, *EWIC*, 2:448–9; Wilferd Madelung, 'Shi'i Attitudes toward Women as Reflected in Fiqh', in *Society and the Sexes in Medieval Islam*, ed. Afaf Lutfi al-Sayyid-Marsot (Malibu: Undena Publications, 1979), 74–5; Adele Ferdows, 'The Status and Rights of Women in Ithna 'Ahsari Shi'i Islam', in *Women and the Family in Iran*, ed. Asghar Fathi (Leiden: Brill, 1985), 24–6; Coulson, *History*, 113–14; Coulson, *Succession*, 108–34; Tucker, *Themes in Islamic Law*, 138–9.

54 See Ferdows, 'Status and Rights of Women', 25; Madelung, 'Shi'i Attitudes toward Women', 74.

55 See Al-Qāḍī al-Nu'mān, *Da'ā'im al-Islām*, 2 vols., trans. Asar A.A. Fyzee as *The Pillars of Islam* (Oxford: Oxford University Press, 2004), 2:361 and al-Kulaynī, *Al-Kāfī*, 7:67; also Takim, 'Law: Other Schools of Family Law', 448.

56 Or, more colloquially, 'Let them eat dirt'. Al-Kulaynī, *Al-Kāfī*, 7:75; English tr., 7:68; quoted in Coulson, *History*, 113; Madelung, 'Shi'i Attitudes toward Women', 74.

57 Al-Kulaynī, *Al-Kāfī*, 7:87; English tr., 7:76–7.

58 I have extrapolated these examples from Coulson, *Succession*, 124–5.

59 See Coulson, *Succession*, 125.

60 See al-Kulaynī, *Al-Kāfī*, 7:84–5; English tr., 7:74–5 for justifications.

61 Ibid., 7:127–30; English tr., 7:104–6.

62 Ibid., 7:129; English tr., 7:105-6.
63 Ibid., 7:127-8; English tr., 7:104. My emphasis.
64 Ibid., 7:128; English tr., 7:104. My emphasis.
65 Ibid., 7:86-7, 90; English tr., 7:76-7, 7:80.
66 Al-Qāḍī al-Nuʿmān, *Daʿā'im*, 2:393–4.
67 Ibid., 2:394.
68 See Coulson, *History*, 115; Madelung, 'Shiʿi Attitudes toward Women', 74–5; Ferdows, 'Status and Rights of Women', 33–4.
69 For accounts of the story, see Yāqūt al-Hamawī, *Muʿjam*, 238-40; Aḥmad ibn Yaḥya al-Balādhurī, *Kitāb futūḥ al-buldān*, 2 vols., trans. Philip Khûri Ḥitti as *The Origins of the Islamic State* (New York: Columbia University, 1916), 1:50-6; al-Ṭabarī, *Tārīkh*, 9:196-7; Veccia Vaglieri, 'Fadak'; Soufi, 'Image', 91-116; Madelung, *Succession to Muhammad*, 360-3.
70 Al-Ṭabarī, *Tārīkh*, 9:196.
71 Ibid., 9:197.
72 Yāqūt al-Hamawī, *Muʿjam*, 239; al-Balādhurī, *Futūḥ*, 1:52; also Soufi, 'Image', 100-1.
73 Al-Balādhurī, *Futūḥ*, 1:53.
74 Yāqūt al-Hamawī, *Muʿjam*, 238–9.
75 Ibid., 239.
76 See Muhammad Husayn al-Ṭabāṭabā'ī, *Al-Mīzān fī tafsīr al-Qur'an*, trans. Sayyid Saeed Akhtar Rizvi as *Al-Mīzān: An Exegesis of the Holy Qur'an* (Tehran: World Organization for Islamic Services, 2014), 8:22–4 n. 1 for a cogent discussion of the 'Abbāsids, inheritance and agnacy.
77 Yāqūt al-Hamawī, *Muʿjam*, 239; see also Veccia Vaglieri, 'Fadak'.
78 Yāqūt al-Hamawī, *Muʿjam*, 239.
79 Al-Yaʿqūbī, *Tārīkh*, 2:573. See also al-Balādhurī, *Futūḥ*, 1:54-6.
80 Yāqūt al-Hamawī, *Muʿjam*, 4:239.
81 See Veccia Vaglieri, 'Fadak'.
82 These include al-Qāḍī al-Nuʿmān's *Sharḥ al-akhbār fī faḍā'il al-a'imma al-aṭhār*, ed. M.H. al-Jalālī (Qum: Mu'assasat al-Nashr al-Islāmī, 1988–92); Abū Bakr Aḥmad al-Jawharī's *Al-Saqīfa wa fadak*; ed. Muhammad Hādī al-Amīnī (Beirut: Sharīkat al-kutub, 1993), and Muhammad ibn Jarīr ibn Rustam al-Ṭabarī al-Shiʿi's *Dalā'il al*-imāma (Najaf: Al-Maṭbaʿa al-Haydariyya, 1949). See Soufi, 'Image', 109 n. 130.
83 Soufi, 'Image', 106. For more on Ibn Abī Ṭāhir Ṭayfūr, see Shawkat M. Toorawa, *Ibn Abi Tahir Tayfur and Arabic Writerly Culture: A Ninth-Century Bookman in Baghdad* (Abingdon: RoutledgeCurzon, 2005). He was apparently a Sunni, although affiliations were very flexible in the early centuries of Islam.

84 Ibn Abī Ṭāhir Ṭayfūr, *Balāghāt*, 34; see also Soufi, 'Image', 107.
85 Ibn Abī Ṭāhir Ṭayfūr, *Balāghāt*, 30-1.
86 Ibid., 31.
87 Ibid., 31–2.
88 Ibid., 32.
89 Ibid.
90 Ibid., 33.
91 Ibid.
92 Ibid.
93 Ibid., 33–4.
94 Ibid., 34–5.
95 Ibid., 34.
96 Ibid., 34–5.
97 Ibid., 36.
98 Soufi, 'Image', 109–10.
99 Ibn Abī Ṭāhir Ṭayfūr, *Balāghāt*, 34.
100 Ibid., 35.
101 Ibid., 29–30; see also Soufi, 'Image', 106–7.
102 Ibn Abī Ṭāhir Ṭayfūr, *Balāghāt*, 30.
103 See Jawharī, *Al-Saqīfa wa fadak*, 103; al-Ṭabarī al-Shi'i, *Dalā'il al-imāma*, 35-6; also Soufi, 'Image', 109–10.
104 See, for example, al-Ṭabarī al-Shi'i , *Dalā'il al-imāma*, 35; Ibn Abī Ṭāhir Ṭayfūr, *Balāghāt*, 32, and Soufi, 'Image', 108 n. 128, for how the poem appears in other sources.
105 Al-Kulaynī, *Al-Kāfī*, 1:551. Sunni scholars such as Ibn Kathīr have disputed this account, saying that the verse was revealed when the Muslims were still in Mecca, long before they had gained control of Fadak. Others, however, including al-Sūyūṭī, agreed with the interpretation. See Clohessy, *Fatima*, 62.
106 'Ali ibn Tāwūs, *Iqbāl al-A'māl* (Beirut: Mu'assasat al-Tārīkh al-'Arabī, 2004), 117. Translation by Denise Soufi.
107 Anonymous, quoted in Ibn Abī al-Ḥadīd, *Sharḥ nahj al-balāgha*, 21 vols., 2nd ed (Beirut: Mu'assasat al-A'lamī lil-Maṭbū'āt), 16:235–6. Translation by Denise Soufi.
108 Ibn Bābawayh, *Risālat al-i'tiqādāt*, 109.
109 Ibid.
110 See, for example, Iqbāl Nāmdār, 'Ghaṣb-i bāgh-i fadak', discussed in Soufi, 'Image', 132–8.

111 See Delia Cortese and Simonetta Calderini, *Women and the Fatimids in the World of Islam* (Edinburgh: Edinburgh University Press, 2006), 9.

112 Al-Ṣadr, *Fadak*, English tr., 57–8. I have corrected the translation.

113 Al-Qāḍī al-Nuʿmān, *Da'ā'im*, 2:361.

114 Ibid., 2:362. Emphasis mine. Note that *walad* in classical Arabic 'means the non-gender-specific "child" or "children," while in modern Arabic it can only mean "boy" or "son"'. See M. A. S. Abdel Haleem, *The Qur'an* (Oxford: Oxford University Press, 2010), xxxiii.

115 Al-Qāḍī al-Nuʿmān, *Da'ā'im*, 2:364. See previous footnote about the classical meaning of *walad*.

116 Al-Kulaynī, *Al-Kāfī*, 7:90; English tr., 7:80.

117 Ibid., 7:90; English tr., 7:80.

118 Ibid., 7:90; English tr., 7:80.

119 Ibid., 7:86; English tr., 7:76.

120 Pfluger-Schindlbeck, 'Kinship, Descent Systems and State', 2:337.

121 For discussions of female inheritance in Sassanian Iran, see Perikhanian, 'Iranian Society and Law', 668; Rose, 'Three Queens', 35; Choksy, *Evil, Good, and Gender*, 88.

122 Rose, 'Three Queens', 35.

123 Ibid. Fire was sacred to Zoroastrians, and each household had a hearth fire.

124 Richard N. Frye, 'Women in Pre-Islamic Central Asia: The Khātūn of Bukhara', in Hambly, *Women in the Medieval Islamic World*, 63–4.

125 Angeliki Laiou, *Women, Family and Society in Byzantium* (Farnham, Surrey: Ashgate, 2011), 57.

126 Ibid. See also very interesting articles discussing later inheritance practices in the same text, 129–60; and, for discussion of dowry, in Laiou's *Gender, Society and Economic Life in Byzantium* (Aldershot, Hampshire: Variorum, 1992), 233–60.

127 Nasr, *Study Qur'an*, 501 n. 75.

128 Ibid., 501-2 n. 75.

129 Muhammad ibn Aḥmad Al-Qurṭubī, *Al-Jāmiʿ al-aḥkām al-Qur'an*, ed. 'Abd Allah ibn 'Abd al-Muḥsin al-Turkī and Muhammad Riḍwān 'Irqsūsī, 24 vols. (Beirut: Mu'assasat al-Risāla, 2006), 10:89–91. For more on inheritance and these non-agnate relatives, sometimes called *dhawu al-arḥām*, see Schacht, 'Mīrāth'; also al-Qāḍī al-Nuʿmān, *Da'ā'im*, 2:373, especially n. 57.

130 Al-Qurṭubī, *Al-Jāmiʿ*, 91.

131 Al-Kulaynī, *Al-Kāfī*, 7:119; English tr., 7:100-2; Abū al-Naḍr Muhammad ibn Masʿūd al-'Ayyāshī, *Kitāb al-tafsīr*, ed. Hāshim al-Rasūlī al-Maḥallātī, 2 vols. (Qum: Chāpkhāna-yi 'Ilmiyya, 1961), 2:210.

132 Al-Kulaynī, *Al-Kāfī*, 7:119; English tr., 7:100-2.
133 Al-'Ayyāshī, *Tafsīr*, 2:210.
134 Al-Qāḍī al-Nu'mān, *Da'ā'im*, 2:361.
135 Ibn Abī Ṭāhir Ṭayfūr, *Balāghāt*, 34.
136 As Meriwether writes, 'In designating which family members had inheritance rights, the *shari'a* ... was in effect demarcating the boundaries of the family in the eyes of the law.' See *Kin Who Count*, 154.

Chapter 4

1 Christoph Werner, 'Ein Vaqf für meine Töchter: Ḥātūn Bēgum und die Qarā Quyūnlū Stiftungen zur 'Blauen Moschee' in Tabriz', *Der Islam* 80: 102-4.
2 Ibid., 103, 107.
3 Ibid., 107.
4 See Hans Robert Roemer, 'The Türkmen Dynasties', in *Cambridge History of Iran*, vol. 6, *The Timurid and Safavid Periods*, ed. Peter Jackson and Laurence Lockhart (Cambridge: Cambridge University Press, 1986), 166-8, for a discussion of Jahān Shāh's religious affiliations.
5 Al-Majlisī, *Biḥār*, 43:235-6. Of course, one must take into account the symbolic value of Fatima's inheritance, which represented the caliphate; hadith could be expected to reflect that reality.
6 See Meriwether, *Kin Who Count*, 166–7, especially for discussions of a Lebanese Shi'i village and the Bedouin of Cyreniea; for the Ottoman Empire, Tucker, *Themes in Islamic Law*, 151. Also see individual entries under 'Law' and 'Inheritance' in the *EWIC*, especially Friedl and Moors entries on 'Inheritance: Contemporary Practice', 2:299–303.
7 Moors, 'Inheritance: Contemporary Practice', 2:300–1.
8 Tucker, *Themes in Islamic Law*, 151.
9 Cortese and Calderini, *Women and the Fatimids*, 159, 213.
10 Shatzmiller, *Her Day in Court*, 67.
11 Ibid., 61.
12 See Peter C. Hennigan, *The Birth of a Legal Institution: The Formation of the Waqf in Third-Century A.H. Ḥanafī Legal Discourse* (Leiden: Brill, 2004), xiii; also, Timur Kuran, 'The Provision of Public Goods under Islamic Law: Origins, Impact, and Limitations of the Waqf System', *Law & Society Review* 35, no. 4 (2001): 842; Maria Subtelny, *Timurids in Transition: Turko-Persian Politics and*

Acculturation in Medieval Iran (Leiden: Brill, 2007), 148; and Meriwether, *Kin Who Count,* 179.

13 Subtelny, *Timurids*, 155. See also Hennigan, 'Birth of a Legal Institution', xvi, n. 12; Kuran, 'Provision of Public Goods', 860.

14 See, for example, Meriwether, *Kin Who Count,* 189–90; Tucker, *Women in Nineteenth Century Egypt*, 95; Kuran, 'Provision of Public Goods', 860. See also Subtelny, *Timurids*, 154-5, for discussions of female-established waqfs in Mamluk Cairo and sixteenth-century Bukhara. I have borrowed the term 'semi-matrilineal' from Roded.

15 See Subtelny, *Timurids*, 150–1; also, Shatzmiller, *Her Day in Court*, 72–5.

16 Subtelny, *Timurids*, 150.

17 The portion of the endowment's income given to *mutawallis* was typically 10 per cent to 15 per cent, but could be higher. See Kuran, 'Provision of Public Goods', 856.

18 Tucker, *Women in Nineteenth Century Egypt*, 96.

19 Ibid.

20 Ibid.

21 Hennigan, 'Birth of a Legal Institution', xv; Subtelny, *Timurids*, 180.

22 Kuran, 'Provision of Public Goods', 847.

23 Szuppe, 'Status, Knowledge, and Politics', 152.

24 Florian Schwarz, 'An Endowment Deed of 1547 (953 h.) for a Kubravi Khanaqah in Samarqand', in *Die Grenzen Der Welt: Arabica et Iranica ad honorem Heinz Gaube*, ed. Lorenz Korn, Eva Orthmann and Florian Schwarz (Weisbaden: Reichert Verlage, 2008), 197–8. As noted in Chapter 3, in classical usage *walad* had a gender-neutral meaning.

25 Schwarz, 'An Endowment Deed', 197.

26 See Clifford Edmund Bosworth, *The New Islamic Dynasties: A Chronological and Genealogical Manual* (New York: Columbia University Press, 1996), 273-4; Werner, 'Ein Vaqf', 105.

27 Werner, 'Ein Vaqf', 106.

28 Ibid., 107.

29 Ibid., 94.

30 Soucek, 'Tīmūrid Women', 200.

31 Ibid., 210.

32 Ibid., 200, 210.

33 Ibid., 210.

34 Ibid., 214.

35 Ibid.

36 Ibid.

37 See Ibid.; also Moin, *Millenial Sovereign*, 37–8.

38 Subtelny, *Timurids*, 149.

39 Ibid.

40 Ibid., 149, 151.

41 Ibid., 151–2.

42 Schwarz, 'An Endowment Deed', 197–8; see also Subtelny, *Timurids*, 249.

43 Subtelny, *Timurids*, 249.

44 Ibid., 250.

45 Beatrice Forbes Manz, 'Gowhar-Sād Āgā', in *EI*³.

46 'Azīz Allah 'Uṭāridī, *Tārīkh-i Āstān-i Quds-i Rażavī*, 2 vols. (Tehran: Sāzmān-i Chāp va Intishārāt-i Vizārat-i Farhang va Irshād-i Islāmī, 1992), 2:215; see also Subtelny, *Timurids*, 205–6.

47 Nushin Arbabzadah, 'Women and Religious Patronage in the Timurid Empire', in *Afghanistan's Islam*, ed. Nile Green (Oakland: University of California Press, 2017), 61.

48 Ibid.

49 Subtelny, *Timurids*, 205–6.

50 Arbabzadah, 'Women and Religious Patronage', 61; Subtelny, *Timurids*, 237.

51 Arbabzadah, 'Women and Religious Patronage', 62.

52 See 'Uṭāridī, *Tārīkh*, 2:752; also, Subtelny, *Timurids*, 237–8.

53 'Uṭāridī, *Tārīkh*, 2:752.

54 Manz, 'Gowhar-Sād Āgā'; Arbabzadah, 'Women and Religious Patronage', 61.

55 Shivan Mahendrarajah, 'The Shrine of Shaykh Aḥmad-i Jām: Notes on a Revised Chronology and a Waqfiyya', *Iran* 50 (2012): 146.

56 Arbabzadah, 'Women and Religious Patronage', 64.

57 Ibid., 57, 61.

58 For the entire *waqfiyya* in both Persian and English, see Subtelny, *Timurids*, 257–348.

59 Subtelny, *Timurids*, 183.

60 Ibid., 172. (Her fears were justified; Uzbeks 'captured Herat and seized the possessions of all of Sulṭān-Ḥusain's wives and daughters' about ten months after she set up the waqf. See ibid., 179.)

61 Ibid., 297.

62 According to Marshall Hodgson, waqfs replaced *zakāt* as the 'vehicle for financing Islam as a society'. See *Venture*, 2:124.

63 Subtelny, *Timurids*, 303–7.

64 Ibid., 174, 315.

65 Ibid., 174.

66 Gülru Necipoğlu, *The Age of Sinan: Architectural Culture in the Ottoman Empire* (Princeton: Princeton University Press, 2005), 299–300.

67 Ibid.

68 Ibid., 299.

69 Ibid., 300.

70 Christine Isom-Verhaaren, 'Süleyman and Mihrimah: The Favorite's Daughter', *Journal of Persianate Studies* 4, no. 1 (2011): 74–6; 83.

71 Necipoğlu, *Age of Sinan*, 296–331; Isom-Verhaaren, 'Süleyman and Mihrimah', 78–83.

72 Necipoğlu, *Age of Sinan*, 305.

73 Ibid., 300–1.

74 Ibid., 301–3.

75 Ibid., 304.

76 Mihrümah sometimes signed her letters as Hanım Sultan. See ibid., 297.

77 Ibid., 303.

78 Ibid., 302.

79 Ibid., 304.

80 Ibid., 302.

81 Ibid.

82 Ibid.

83 Ibid., 307, 539 n. 68, 314.

84 Ibid., 317.

85 Ibid., 330.

86 Ibid., 539 n. 71.

87 Ibid., 300, 299. Mihrümah's son had predeceased her.

88 Ibid., 297.

89 Isom-Verhaaren, 'Süleyman and Mihrimah', 72.

90 See Szuppe, 'Status, Knowledge, and Politics', 152.

91 See ibid., 152–3.

92 For a detailed account, see Rizvi, 'Gendered Patronage', 127, 134–42.

93 Szuppe, 'Status, Knowledge, and Politics', 152.

94 Rizvi, 'Gendered Patronage', 134.

95 Sheila R. Canby, *Shah 'Abbas: The Remaking of Iran* (London: British Museum Press, 2009), 222; Rizvi, 'Gendered Patronage', 139, 142.

96 See Rizvi, 'Gendered Patronage', 138–9.

97 Husayn Mudarrisī Ṭabāṭabā'ī, *Turbat-i pākān*, 2 vols. (Qum: Chāpkhāna-yi Mihr, 1976), 1:134–5. Translation by Kishwar Rizvi.

98 Rizvi, 'Gendered Patronage', 139.

99 Ibid., 140.

100 The shrine itself accomplishes the same feat, to some degree. An inscription at the entrance door to the tomb chamber blesses Fatima al-Ma'ṣūma as well as Muhammad, Fatima al-Zahra and the twelve imams – thus including women. Yet interestingly, 'Even at this most venerated of feminine edifices, the most visible presence was that of a man: it is Shah Isma'il's name that is inscribed in the girdling inscription of the great iwan, not that of his [wife], whose wealth most probably financed the construction.' Ibid., 138, 142.

101 Mudarrisī Ṭabāṭabā'ī, *Turbat-i pākān*, 1:138.

102 Rizvi, 'Gendered Patronage', 139.

103 Ibid., 141.

104 Gregory C. Kozlowski, 'Imperial Authority, Benefactions and Endowments (*Awqāf*) in Mughal India', *Journal of the Economic and Social History of the Orient* 38, no. 3 (1995): 359; idem, 'Muslim Women and the Control of Property in North India', *The Indian Economic and Social History Review* 24, no. 2 (1987): 169–70.

105 Kozlowski, 'Muslim Women', 169–70, n. 19; see also Abū al-Faḍl, *Ā'īn-i Akbarī*, trans. Heinrich Blochmann and Henry Sullivan Jarrett (Calcutta: The Asiatic Society, 1993), 1:518.

106 Catherine B. Asher, *Architecture of Mughal India* (Cambridge: Cambridge University Press, 1992), 189–90; Afshan Bokhari, 'Imperial Transgressions and Spiritual Investitures: A Begam's "Ascension" in Seventeenth Century Mughal India', *Journal of Persianate Studies* 4, no. 1 (2011): 91.

107 Bokhari, 'Imperial Transgressions', 93.

108 Stephen P. Blake, 'Contributors to the Urban Landscape: Women Builders in Ṣafavid Isfahan and Mughal Shahjahanabad', in Hambly, *Women in the Medieval Islamic World*, 420–1; see also Stephen F. Dale, 'Empires and Emporia: Palace, Mosque, Market, and Tomb in Istanbul, Isfahan, Agra, and Delhi', *Journal of the Economic and Social History of the Orient* 53 (2010): 225.

109 Blake, 'Contributors to the Urban Landscape', 421.

110 Bokhari, 'Imperial Transgressions', 96, 100.

111 Ibid., 101.

112 Schwarz, 'An Endowment Deed', 198.

113 Ibid., 197.

114 Ibid.

115 Ibid.

116 Ibid.

117 Ibid.

118 Ibid.

119 Ibid., 199.

120 Ibid.

121 Ibid.

122 Ibid.

123 Ibid.

124 Gabriel Baer, 'Women and Waqf: An Analysis of the Istanbul Tahrîr of 1546', *Asian and African Studies* 17 (1983): 10–11.

125 Ibid., 11, 12.

126 Ibid., 13, 16.

127 Ibid., 27.

128 See Margaret L. Meriwether, 'Women and *Waqf* Revisited: The Case of Aleppo, 1770–1840', in *Women in the Ottoman Empire: Middle Eastern Women in the Early Modern Era*, ed. Madeline C. Zilfi (Leiden: Brill, 1997) and *Kin Who Count.*

129 Meriwether, 'Women and *Waqf* Revisited', 151.

130 Ibid.

131 Meriwether, *Kin Who Count,* 52.

132 Ibid., 70.

133 Ibid., 71.

134 Ibid., 199–200.

135 Meriwether, 'Women and *Waqf* Revisited', 146.

136 Tucker, *Women in Nineteenth-Century Egypt*, 95.

137 Meriwether, *Kin Who Count,* 200.

138 Ibid., 201.

139 Following the lead of the Ottoman royal family may also have been a factor. See Meriwether, 'Women and *Waqf* Revisited', 146.

140 Ibid., 148.

141 Ibid., 149.

142 Ibid.

143 Ibid.

144 Ibid., 149–50.

145 Ibid., 150.

146 Ibid., 151.

147 Meriwether, *Kin Who Count,* 151, 209.

148 See, for example, Tucker, *Women in Nineteenth-Century Egypt*, 96.

Chapter 5

1 Muṣṭafā Darīr, *Siyer-i Nebī* (Life of the Prophet), Turkish MS 419 (vol. 4, 1594–5), Chester Beatty Library, Dublin, fol.24v. Also see Spellberg, *Politics, Gender and the Islamic Past*, 179–90 for an exposition of the *Siyer-i Nebī's* images of Khadīja, Fatima and 'Ā'isha.

2 See Pinault, 'Zaynab bint 'Alī', 73.

3 Takim, *Heirs of the Prophet*, 26.

4 For two essays documenting this phenomenon, see Pierce's 'Remembering Fāṭimah' and Feder's 'Fatima's Revolutionary Image'.

5 Abū al-Qāsim al-Suhaylī, *Al-rawḍ al-unuf fī sharḥ al-sīrat al-nabawiyya li- Ibn Hishām*, 7 vols. (Cairo: Dār al-Kutub al-Ḥadītha, 1967), 3:282.

6 Soufi, 'Image', 32–3.

7 Al-Kulaynī, *Al-Kāfī*, 1:460; English tr., 1:465.

8 Spellberg, *Politics, Gender and the Islamic Past*, 104, 107.

9 Ibid., 106.

10 Ibid., 105.

11 Mernissi, *Le Harem Politique*, 49. Also translated, 'Never will succeed such a nation as makes a woman their ruler'. See al-Bukhārī, *Saḥīḥ*: *Kitāb al-maghāzī, bāb kitāb al-nabī ilā kisrā wa qaysar* (82).

12 Mernissi, *Le Harem Politique*, 4.

13 Spellberg, *Politics, Gender and the Islamic Past*, 140.

14 Ibid., 137.

15 Fayḍ Kāshānī, *Mafātih al-Sharā'i'*; quoted in Robert Gleave, '"She Should Not Raise Her Voice When Amongst Men": Imāmī Arguments against (and for) Women Judges', in Mirjam Künkler and Devin Stewart, ed., *Female Religious Authority in Shi'i Islam: Past and Present* (Edinburgh: Edinburgh University Press, forthcoming).

16 See Babayan, 'Aqā'īd al-Nisā', 369–70.

17 Moojan Momen, 'Women: In Shi'ism', in *EI*[r]. See, for example, Majlisī's *Hilyat al-Muttaqīn*, quoted in Babayan, "Aqā'īd al-Nisā", 369–70.

18 Momen, 'Women: In Shi'ism'.

19 Al-Sharīf al-Raḍī, *Nahj al-Balāgha*, trans. Sayed Ali Reza as *Nahjul Balagha = Peak of Eloquence: Sermons, Letters, and Sayings of Imam Ali ibn Abu Talib* (Elmburst, NY: Tahrike Tarsile Quran, 1996), 204. See also Osman, *Female Personalities*, 157.

20 Niẓām al-Mulk, *Siyāsat-nāma*, trans. Hubert Darke as *The Book of Government or Rules for Kings* (New Haven: Yale University Press, 1960), 185.

21 Spellberg, *Politics, Gender and the Islamic Past*, 141.

22 Ibid., 142, 148.

23 Quoted in Babayan, 'Aqā'id al-Nisā', 355.

24 Kashani-Sabet, 'Who is Fatima?', 20.

25 Spellberg, *Politics, Gender and the Islamic Past*, 171.

26 Ibid., 178; see also Soufi, 'Image', 79, for a discussion of Fatima as the feminine ideal.

27 Al-Majlisī, *Biḥār*, 43:19. For a full discussion of feminine ideals in Islam, including 'Ā'isha's place within them, see Spellberg, *Politics, Gender, and the Islamic Past*, 151-90.

28 Soufi, 'Image', iii, 1.

29 Feder, 'Fatima's Revolutionary Image', 86; see also Kashani-Sabet, 'Who Is Fatima?', 9.

30 One tradition quotes the Prophet as saying that after his death, 'she will remain sad, depressed, and crying (*maḥzūna makrūba bākiya*)'. Ibn Bābawayh, *Amālī*, 101.

31 Ibn Bābawayh, *Amālī*, 124–5; quoted in Soufi, 'Image', 119; see also 116–45.

32 See, for example, Kashani-Sabet, 'Who is Fatima?', 9; Pinault, 'Zaynab bint 'Alī', 73, 93.

33 Soufi, 'Image', 203. For a discussion of traditions narrated by Fatima, see ibid., 69–74.

34 Al-Majlisī, *Biḥār*, 43:219-20; see also Rubin, 'Preexistence', 99-102, Soufi, 'Image', 181–2; Clohessy, *Fatima*, 168-77, 186-91.

35 Al-Majlisī, *Biḥār*, 43:14; see also Soufi, 'Image', 187–9; Clohessy, *Fatima*, 163-92.

36 See Soufi, 'Image', 198, 200–1.

37 Ibid., 152.

38 Ibid., 153.

39 See Pierce, 'Remembering Fāṭimah', 352–3; Cortese and Calderini, *Women and the Fatimids*, 6, 10; Feder, 'Fatima's Revolutionary Image', 86–7; Osman, *Female Personalities*, 126.

40 Pierce, 'Remembering Fāṭimah', 346, 353–8.

41 Clohessy, *Fatima*, 216.

42 Sharī'atī, '*Fatima Fatima Ast*', 159. To be sure, scholars such as Kashani-Sabet have looked askance at Sharī'atī, saying that his depictions of Fatima ultimately reinforced 'traditional womanly values, including chastity, religiosity, and domesticity'. See Kashani-Sabet, 'Who Is Fatima?', 20.

43 Sharī'atī, '*Fatima Fatima Ast*', 159–61; see also Kashani-Sabet, 'Who Is Fatima?', 16.

44 Al-Ṣadr, *Fadak*, 48; English tr. 58.

45 Feder, 'Fatima's Revolutionary Image', 86-7.
46 Takim, *Heirs of the Prophet*, 32.
47 'Abd Allah Javādī Āmūlī, *Zan dar āyina-yi jalāl va jamāl*, 412, 413; quoted in Pierce, 'Remembering Fāṭimah', 357.
48 Pierce, 'Remembering Fāṭimah', 357.
49 Ḥujjat al-Islam wa al-Muslimīn Mihdī Mīhrīzī, interview by Karen Bauer, Qum, Iran, 9 June 2011.
50 Ibn Abī Ṭāhir Ṭayfūr, *Balāghāt*, 34–5.
51 See Ali, *Holy Qur'an*, 981 n. 3254. Similarly, the same editor translates 'inherit' as 'represent' in 19:6, noting that 'it is true that an heir inherits property, but his higher duty is to represent in everything the personality of him from whom he inherits'. Ibid., 768 n. 2460.
52 Ibn Abī Ṭāhir Ṭayfūr, *Balāghāt*, 35.
53 Ibid., 36.
54 Osman has independently arrived at a similar conclusion; see *Female Personalities*, 123.
55 Ibn Bābawayh, *'Ilal al-sharā'i'* (Najaf: Al-Maṭba'a al-Ḥaydariyya, 1963), 248. With modifications, I have mostly cited Monir Gorgi's translation of the khutba; see 'The Sermon of Fatima Zahra (AS)', *Farzaneh: Journal of Women's Studies and Research in Iran and Muslim Countries* 3, no. 8 (1997).
56 Monir Gorgi and Massoumeh Ebtekar, 'The Life and Status of Fatima Zahra: A Woman's Image of Excellence', *Farzaneh: Journal of Women's Studies and Research in Iran and Muslim Countries* 3, no. 8 (1997): 7.
57 Al-Majlisī, *Biḥār*, 74:94.
58 Ibid., 79:111.
59 Ibid., 82:209.
60 Ibid., 96:368.
61 Cortese and Calderini, *Women and the Fatimids*, 10.
62 See Maria Dakake, 'Ḥojjat', in *EI*[3]; also Karen Bauer, 'Spiritual Hierarchy and Gender Hierarchy in Fāṭimid Ismā'īlī Interpretations of the Qur'an, *Journal of Qur'anic Studies* 14, no. 2 (2012): 29. Like others, however, al-Qāḍī al-Nu'mān stopped short of identifying Fatima as an imam, saying that she 'plays "no part in the Imamate, she being the 'Mother of the Imams'"'. See Cortese and Calderini, *Women and the Fatimids*, 106.
63 Ruffle, 'May You Learn from Their Model', 27.
64 Al-Ṣadr, *Fadak*, 100; English tr. 124–5.
65 Ibid., 102; English tr. 126.

66 See al-Kulaynī, *Al-Kafī*, 1:239-42; English tr., 1:217–20. For secondary sources, see Soufi, 'Image', 76-7; Pinault, 'Zaynab bint 'Ali', 73–4; Jean Calmard, 'Fāṭema', in *EI*[r]; Osman, *Female Personalities*, 112.

67 Al-Kulaynī, *Al-Kāfī*, 1:241; English tr., 1:220. For an interesting discussion of the Bāb's presentation of the *muṣḥaf* of Fatima, see Lawson, 'Authority of the Feminine', 147-8.

68 See Soufi, 'Image', 77 n. 211.

69 Al-Kulaynī, *Al-Kāfī*, 1:240; English tr., 1:218.

70 Ibid., 1:240; English tr., 1:219. See also Andrew J. Newman, *The Formative Period of Twelver Shīʿism: Ḥadith as Discourse Between Qum and Baghdad* (Richmond, Surrey: Curzon Press, 2000), 74.

71 Al-Kulaynī, *Al-Kāfī*, 1:240; English tr., 1:219.

72 Ordoni, *Fatima the Gracious*, Chapter 15: Al-Muhaddathah. The same author notes that it can also mean 'those who utter true and accurate words, those who are spoken to by angels, or those whose opinions and viewpoints always conform to righteousness as if they were inspired by the Kingdom of Heaven'. It is, however, distinct from a Prophet, who can both see and hear the angel while asleep or awake. The *muhaddath* can only hear the angel while awake, and cannot see the angel either while asleep or awake. Ibid.; also Ibn Bābawayh, *'Ilal al-sharā'i'*, 182.

73 See Soufi, 'Image', 77 n. 212; also Etan Kohlberg, 'The Term Muḥaddath in Twelver Shīʿism', in *Belief and Law in Imāmī Shīʿism* (Hampshire: Variorum, 1991), 41.

74 Takim, *Heirs of the Prophet*, 28; see also Newman, *Formative Period*, 73–5.

75 See Pinault, 'Zaynab bint 'Ali', 74; also Ordoni, *Fatima the Gracious*, Chapter 15: Al-Muhaddathah.

76 Ibn Sa'd, *Kitāb al-ṭabaqāt*, 1:111-12; al-Majlisī, *Biḥār*, 43:3. Similarly, both she and Husayn spoke while in the womb. See Clohessy, *Fatima*, 131-2.

77 Clohessy, *Fatima*, 86-7; al-Majlisī, *Biḥār*, 43:3.

78 See Qur'an 19:24-6; also, Nasr, *Study Qur'an*, 770.

79 See, for example, Ayoub, *Redemptive Suffering*, especially Chapters 1 and 5; Pierce, *Twelve Infallible Men*, 54-67; Clohessy, *Fatima*, 135-62.

80 Al-Mufīd, *Amālī*, 172, 316.

81 See Clohessy, *Fatima*, 160-1.

82 Ibn Bābawayh, *Amālī*, 124-5 and al-Majlisī, *Biḥār*, 43:155-6; see also Pierce, *Twelve Infallible Men*, 63, 123; Ayoub, *Redemptive Suffering*, 198; and Clohessy, *Fatima*, 148-50.

83 Pierce, *Twelve Infallible Men*, 67.

84 Ibn Bābawayh, *Amālī*, 186–7.

85 Ibid., 187.

86 Ibn Sa'd, *Kitāb al-ṭabaqāt*, 8:19.

87 Ibn Shahrāshūb, *Manāqib*; quoted in al-Majlisī, *Biḥār*, 43:233. See also Soufi, 'Image', 88–9.

88 Kamran Scot Aghaie, 'The Gender Dynamics of Moharram Symbols and Rituals in the Latter Years of Qajar Rule', in Aghaie, *Women of Karbala*, 51; see also Soufi, 'Image', 28, 88–9, 151.

89 Al-Majlisī, *Biḥār*, 43:3.

90 Al-Qāḍī al-Nu'mān, *Da'ā'im*, 2:198.

91 Ibn Sa'd, *Kitāb al-ṭabaqāt*, 8:19. Other hadith say she was ashamed of either her thinness or her bulk.

92 Al-Majlisī, *Biḥār*, 8:53–5.

93 Al-Qāḍī al-Nu'mān, *Da'ā'im*, 2:198; see also Soufi, 'Image', 74.

94 See Soufi, 'Image', 88–9 for hadith relating this version of the story; see Al-Ya'qūbī, *Tārīkh*, 2:141, for a version in which she threatened to uncover her head if they entered.

95 See, for example, Thurlkill, *Chosen Among Women*, 64; Spellberg, 'Politics of Praise', 133, 145.

96 Kashani-Sabet, 'Who is Fatima?', 3.

97 Al-Majlisī, *Biḥār*, 43:20, 231.

98 See Qur'an 21:91, 66:12.

99 Al-Majlisī, *Biḥār*, 43:219, 227.

100 Ibid., 43:15, 16. See Clohessy, *Fatima*, 109–16, for an excellent discussion of this topic.

101 Al-Majlisī, *Biḥār*, 43:15, 16.

102 Clohessy, *Fatima*, 43.

103 Pierce, *Twelve Infallible Men*, 121. See also Thurlkill, *Chosen Among Women*, 64, Spellberg, 'Politics of Praise', 145.

104 Ibn Shahrāshūb, *Manāqib*; quoted in al-Majlisī, *Biḥār*, 43:16.

105 Chelkowski, 'Iconography of the Women of Karbala', 134.

106 Ibid.

107 Wilferd Madelung, 'Introduction', in *The Study of Shi'i Islam: History, Theology and Law*, ed. Farhad Daftary and Gordofarid Miskinzoda (London: I.B. Tauris, 2014), 5.

108 'Fatima Zahra, "Umm Abīhā"', Socio-Cultural Council of Women and the Family, Supreme Council of the Cultural Revolution, accessed 12 July 2018, https://tinyurl.com/ybg3y5hu.

109 Ibn Sa‘d, *Kitāb al-ṭabaqāt*, 8:17; al-Majlisī, *Biḥār*, 43:32.
110 Soufi, ‘Image’, 207.
111 Choksy, *Evil, Good, and Gender*, 52.
112 Ibid., 103.
113 Ibid., 54.
114 Yasna 53:4; quoted in Choksy, *Evil, Good, and Gender*, 117.
115 Rose, ‘Three Queens’, 32; Choksy, *Evil, Good, and Gender*, 92. Followers of Judaism, Christianity, and religions other than Zoroastrianism of course lived in Iran during the Sassanian period.
116 Choksy, *Evil, Good, and Gender*, 56.
117 Ibid., 88.
118 Rose, ‘Three Queens’, 37.
119 Ibid., 36–7.
120 Choksy, *Evil, Good, and Gender*, 88.
121 Ibid.
122 Rose, ‘Three Queens’, 33.
123 Ibid., 33–4. This concept is evident in the *Shāhnāma*, where daughters frequently choose their own husbands against the will of their fathers but are treated sympathetically. See Alyssa Gabbay, ‘Rebels, Virtuous Adorers and Successors: The Agentic Daughters of the Shahnama’, in *Shahnama Studies III: The Reception of Firdausi’s Shāhnāma*, ed. Gabrielle van den Berg and Charles Melville (Leiden: Brill, 2018), 300.
124 See Yarshater, *EIr*, s.v. ‘Homāy Čehrzād’, ‘Bōrān’, and ‘Āzarmīgduxt’.
125 Rose, ‘Three Queens’, 44.
126 Haleh Emrani, ‘Like Father, Like Daughter: Late Sasanian Imperial Ideology and the Rise of Bōrān to Power’, *e-Sasanika* 5 (2009): 5.
127 Ibid., 7.
128 Ibid., 6.
129 Ibid., 5.
130 Ibid., 7. In further support of this idea, Emrani observes that Āzarm dukht was ‘presented with a beard on her coins … to emphasize the fact that the monarch was not a woman’. Others, however, have attributed the image of a man on her coins to the ‘reuse of older coins’ in the absence of time to mint new ones; and, alternatively, to a male co-ruler. See Touraj Daryaee, *Sasanian Persia: The Rise and Fall of an Empire* (London: I.B. Tauris, 2009), 36; and Parvaneh Pourshariati, *Decline and Fall of the Sasanian Empire: The Sasanian-Parthian Confederacy and the Arab Conquest of Iran* (London: I.B. Tauris, 2008), 206.

131 Abū al-Qāsim Firdawsī, *Shāhnāma*, ed. Evgeniĭ Ėduardovich, et al., 9 vols. (Moscow: Idāra-yi Intishārāt-i Adabiyāt-i Khāvar, 1960–1971), 6:351:165.

132 Consanguineous marriage seems to have been practiced in Elamite, and Achaemenid dynasties and in later ones as a 'means of consolidating power'. Despite many references to consanguineous marriage in magi writings, 'there is no evidence that it ever became a popular form of consummated marriage in Iran under Zoroastrian or Muslim rule' although it was indeed practiced among royalty. Choksy, *Evil, Good, and Gender*, 91.

133 Firdawsī, *Shāhnāma*, 6:352:173–5.

134 Ibid., 6:354:4.

135 Ibid., 9:305:1, 23; see also Rose, 'Three Queens', 44.

136 Rose, 'Three Queens', 44.

137 Al-Bukhārī, *Sahīh: Kitāb al-maghāzī, bāb kitāb al-nabī ilā kisrā wa qaysar* (82). The validity and interpretation of this oft-cited hadith have precipitated much debate. Does it refer to Pūrān, or is it really aimed at 'Ā'isha's participation in the Battle of the Camel (which, naturally, occurred after the Prophet's death)? How reliable was its narrator? See Mernissi, *Le Harem Politique*, 3, 49-50, 61; also Spellberg, *Politics, Gender, and the Islamic Past*, 139.

138 Mernissi, *Le Harem Politique*, 61.

139 In fact, the contemporary scholar A. B. M. Habibullah has argued that – at least partly based on Persian ideals – beginning in the tenth century Islamic constitutional theory posed no legal obstacle to female sovereignty. He further maintains that 'in the 13th and 14th centuries the idea of a woman ruler was no more repugnant to Islamic law than, for example, were the numerous Turkish Sultans who included among them, not only unmanumitted slaves but … persons with physical deformities as well'. 'Sulṭanah Rāziah', *The Indian Historical Quarterly* 16, no. 4 (1940): 751–3.

140 See Bernard P. Prusak, 'Woman: Seductive Siren and Source of Sin?', in *Religion and Sexism: Images of Women in the Jewish and Christian Traditions*, ed. Rosemary Radford Ruether (New York: Simon and Schuster, 1974), esp. 99–100; Carolyn L. Connor, *Women of Byzantium* (New Haven: Yale University Press, 2004), 15–16.

141 Laiou, *Gender, Society and Economic Life*, 246.

142 Ibid., 248–9.

143 Connor, *Women of Byzantium*, 19.

144 Ibid., 16.

145 Ibid.

146 Ibid., 17.

147 Ibid., 17–18.
148 Ibid., 17.
149 Ibid., 18.
150 Ibid.
151 Ibid., 19.
152 Ibid., 18.
153 Ibid., 48.
154 Judith Herrin, 'The Imperial Feminine in Byzantium', *Past and Present* 169 (2000): 21; Connor, *Women of Byzantium*, 50.
155 Connor, *Women of Byzantium*, 48.
156 Ibid., 215–37.
157 Herrin, 'Imperial Feminine', 13.
158 Connor, *Women of Byzantium*, 55. The fifth-century scholar Sozomen, for example, wrote that Pulcheria 'took control of the government, reaching excellent decisions and swiftly carrying them out with written instructions'. Quoted in Kenneth G. Holum, *Theodosian Empresses: Women and Imperial Dominion in Late Antiquity* (Berkeley: University of California Press, 1982), 97.
159 Connor, *Women of Byzantium*, 55.
160 Holum, *Theodosian Empresses*, 3.
161 Famously, Elizabeth I also embraced virginity (and emulation of the Virgin Mary) as a means of consolidating her sovereignty. See Sarah Gristwood, *Game of Queens: The Women Who Made Sixteenth-Century Europe* (New York: Basic Books, 2016), 242.
162 Holum, *Theodosian Empresses*, 141.
163 Herrin, 'Imperial Feminine', 13; Connor, *Women of Byzantium*, 59.
164 Connor, *Women of Byzantium*, 61, 62; see also Holum, *Theodosian Empresses*, 147–74.
165 Holum, *Theodosian Empresses*, 145.
166 Ibid., 143.
167 Connor, *Women of Byzantium*, 59.
168 Quoted in Holum, *Theodosian Empresses*, 110–11.
169 Ibid., 141.
170 Ibid., 145.
171 Connor, *Women of Byzantium*, 58.
172 Once again, interesting parallels exist between her and Elizabeth I, who declared in a speech to her troops upon the eve of an invasion: 'I know that I have the body but of a weak and feeble woman, but I have the heart and

stomach of a king and of a king of England too.' See Gristwood, *Game of Queens*, 317.

173 Holum, *Theodosian Empresses*, 110.

174 Ibid., 111.

175 Ibid., 208.

176 Ibid., 208, 209.

177 Herrin, 'Imperial Feminine', 34.

178 See Ahmed, 'Women and the Advent of Islam', 666, 681, 686, 691.

179 Spellberg, *Politics, Gender and the Islamic Past*, 33.

180 Ibid., 37.

181 See EI^2, s.v. 'Hint bint al-Khuss'.

182 See ibid.

183 Ahmed, 'Women and the Advent of Islam', 686.

184 Ibid., 686.

185 Ibid., 691.

Chapter 6

1 For excellent discussions of Zaynab, Umm Kulthum, Sukayna and others, see Aghaie, *Women of Karbala*; Pinault, 'Zaynab bint "Alī"', 69–98; Pierce, *Twelve Infallible Men*, 114–16.

2 Ayoub, *Redemptive Suffering*, 129.

3 See al-Mufīd, *Amālī*, 300–2. See also al-Majlisī, *Biḥār*, 45:108–10, for a very similar version; and Ayoub, *Redemptive Suffering*, 130–1, for a discussion of the sermon.

4 Al-Mufīd, *Amālī*, 301.

5 Ibid., 301–2.

6 'Ali Qā'imī, *Naqsh-i zanān dar tārīkh-i 'Āshūrā'* (Qum: n.p., n.d.), 19, 93; quoted in Chelkowski, 'Iconography of the Women of Karbala', 122, 127. See also Faegheh Shirazi, 'The Daughters of Karbala: Images of Women in Popular Shi'i Culture in Iran', in Aghaie, *Women of Karbala*, 109.

7 Mohammad Akram Nadwi, *Al-Muḥaddithāt: The Women Scholars in Islam*, 2nd ed. (Oxford: Interface Publications, 2014); Roded, *Women*, 65–86, 107–9. See also Mernissi's *Sultanés oubliées*, 88, Cortese and Calderini, *Women and the Fatimids*, 101–3, for power accrued through being a sister, mother, wife or consort.

8 Undermining powerful females by casting aspersions upon their sexual integrity was a frequent strategy deployed in Europe as well as the Middle East. See Gristwood, *Game of Queens*, xxix.
9 Cortese and Calderini, *Women and the Fatimids*, 5, 44.
10 Ibid., 43.
11 Ibid.
12 Ibid., 106.
13 Ibid., 107.
14 Ṣalāḥ al-Dīn ibn Aybak al-Ṣafadī, *Kitāb al-wafī bi-al-wafāyāt* (Weisbaden: F. Steiner, 1981–), 11:320:225; quoted in Cortese and Calderini, *Women and the Fatimids*, 107.
15 Ibid., 9.
16 Al-Qāḍī al-Nuʿmān, *Sharḥ al-akhbār*, 22; quoted in Cortese and Calderini, *Women and the Fatimids*, 9.
17 Cortese and Calderini, *Women and the Fatimids*, 106.
18 Ibid., 33–5.
19 Ibid., 206.
20 Al-Ṣafadī, *Kitāb al-wafī*, 9:4317:387; quoted in Cortese and Calderini, *Women and the Fatimids*, 229 n. 85.
21 Al-Ṣafadī, *Kitāb al-wafī*, 14:164:128; quoted in Cortese and Calderini, *Women and the Fatimids*,. 229 n. 86; see also ibid., 206–7.
22 Cortese and Calderini, *Women and the Fatimids*, 101–47.
23 Paul E. Walker, 'The Fatimid Caliph al-'Aziz and His Daughter Sitt al-Mulk: A Case of Delayed but Eventual Succession to Rule by a Woman', *Journal of Persianate Studies* 4, no. 1 (2011): 33.
24 Ibid.
25 Mernissi, *Sultanés oubliées*, 160.
26 Cortese and Calderini, *Women and the Fatimids*, 119–20; see also Mernissi, *Sultanés oubliées*, 161.
27 Cortese and Calderini, *Women and the Fatimids*, 119, Walker, 'Fatimid Caliph', 34.
28 Cortese and Calderini, *Women and the Fatimids*, 121; Walker, 'Fatimid Caliph', 36.
29 Cortese and Calderini, *Women and the Fatimids*, 121.
30 Ḥamza ibn Asad ibn al-Qalānisī, *Tārīkh Dimashq*, ed. S. Zakār (Damascus: Dār Hassān, 1983), 97.
31 Jamāl al-Dīn ibn Ẓāfir, *Akhbār al-duwal al-munqaṭiʿa*, ed. A. Ferré (Cairo: IFAO, 1972), 57; quoted in Cortese and Calderini, *Women and the Fatimids*, 121.

32 Walker, 'Fatimid Caliph', 37.
33 Ibid.; see also Mernissi, *Sultanés oubliées*, 169.
34 Mernissi, *Sultanés oubliées*, 172.
35 Ibid., 171.
36 Cortese and Calderini, *Women and the Fatimids*, 123.
37 One of the main sections of Cairo. See ibid., 199, for a description of the circumstances leading to its burning.
38 Ibn Ẓāfir, *Akhbār*, 57–8; quoted in Walker, 'Fatimid Caliph', 38.
39 Ibid.
40 Walker, 'Fatimid Caliph', 37.
41 Cortese and Calderini, *Women and the Fatimids*, 125.
42 Ibid., 124.
43 Ibid.
44 Walker, 'Fatimid Caliph', 39.
45 Cortese and Calderini, *Women and the Fatimids*, 125.
46 Ibid., 125.
47 Walker, 'Fatimid Caliph', 39.
48 Ibid., 39–40.
49 Cortese and Calderini, *Women and the Fatimids*, 125.
50 Walker, 'Fatimid Caliph', 39.
51 Mernissi defines her epithet as 'the noble lady who is free and independent; the woman sovereign who bows to no superior authority'. *Sultanés oubliées*, 115. See also treatments of Arwa in Farhad Daftary, 'Ṣayyida Ḥurra: The Ismāʿīlī Ṣulayḥid Queen of Yemen', in Hambly, *Women in the Medieval Islamic World*, 117–30; Cortese and Calderini, *Women and the Fatimids*, 127-40; Bauer, 'Spiritual Hierarchy', 29-46 .
52 Cortese and Calderini, *Women and the Fatimids*, 127.
53 Ibid., 128.
54 Ibid.
55 Ibid., 129.
56 'Umāra, *Tārīkh al-Yaman*, ed. Muhammad ibn 'Ali al-Akwa', 2nd ed. (Beirut: Maṭba'at al-Sa'ādat, 1976), 137; quoted in Cortese and Calderini, *Women and the Fatimids*, 129.
57 Some discrepancy exists about the dates of 'Ali's death. See Cortese and Calderini, *Women and the Fatimids*, 130, and EI^2, s.v. 'Sulayhids'.
58 Cortese and Calderini, *Women and the Fatimids*, 130.
59 Ibid., 127.

60 Ibid., 132, for a description of Bilqīs in the Qur'an, see Osman, *Female Personalities*, 66–72.

61 Cortese and Calderini, *Women and the Fatimids*, 134.

62 Ibid., 135.

63 Ibid., 239, 133.

64 Ibid., 135.

65 Ibid., 136; see Bauer, 'Spiritual Hierarchy', 29.

66 Bauer, 'Spiritual Hierarchy', 41.

67 Ibid., 42. See also Cortese and Calderini, *Women and the Fatimids*, 136.

68 Cortese and Calderini, *Women and the Fatimids*, 137.

69 Ibid., 108–9; 134.

70 Ibid., 131.

71 'Umāra, *Tārīkh al-Yaman*, 36; quoted in Cortese and Calderini, *Women and the Fatimids*, 132.

72 Walker, 'Fatimid Caliph', 34.

73 Cortese and Calderini, *Women and the Fatimids*, 124.

74 Ibid.

75 Walker, 'Fatimid Caliph', 34, 38, 40–2; Cortese and Calderini, *Women and the Fatimids*, 123–4.

76 Cortese and Calderini, *Women and the Fatimids*, 125.

77 Ibid., 126.

78 Ibid., 109, 138.

79 Mernissi, *Sultanés oubliées*, 115–16.

80 Cortese and Calderini, *Women and the Fatimids*, 107–8.

81 Ibid., 124.

82 Minhāj-i Sirāj-i Juzjānī, *Ṭabaqāt-i Nāṣirī*, ed. 'Abd al-Ḥay Ḥabībī, 2 vols. (Tehran: Dunyā-yi Kitāb, 1984), 1:456; trans. Henry George Raverty as *Tabaḳāt-i Nāṣirī: A General History of the Mohammadan Dynasties of Asia* (Calcutta: The Asiatic Society, 1881, 2 vols.), 1:635.

83 Ibid., 1:457–9; English tr. 1:638. A later medieval historian, Firishta, writes that Iltutmish left Raḍiyya in charge while he was in Gwalior, suggesting that she proved herself as a capable administrator during that period. See Habibullah, 'Sulṭanah Rāziah', 754.

84 Juzjānī, *Ṭabaqāt-i Nāṣirī*, 1:458; English tr. 1:638.

85 Ibid., 1:458; English tr. 1:639.

86 Ibid., 1:454–5; English tr. 1:631.

87 Ibid., 1:454–5; English tr. 1:631. As Habibullah notes, this appointment constituted a 'clear breach of the arrangement made in the proclamation'. He

speculates that it was 'conducted by the provincial governors and military officers who had joined the late king in his last expedition and were present at the capital at the time of his death'. Fīrūz Shāh's mother likely also advocated strongly for her son. See Habibullah, 'Sulṭanah Rāziah', 757.

88 Juzjānī, *Ṭabaqāt-i Nāṣirī*, 1:457; English tr. 1:636.

89 The beginning of Raḍiyya's reign is usually dated to 19 November 1236 as well, though Juzjānī does not specifically note it as such. But 'Isāmī dates her accession to 1237, which would accord better with Juzjānī's calculation of the length of her reign as three years, six months and six days. See Habibullah, 'Sulṭanah Rāziah', 759 n. 43.

90 Juzjānī, *Ṭabaqāt-i Nāṣirī*, 1:457; English tr. 1:639, 641.

91 Ibid., 1:459; English tr. 1:639.

92 Peter Jackson, 'Sulṭān Raḍiyya bint Iltutmish', in Hambly, *Women in the Medieval Islamic World*, 188.

93 Juzjānī, *Ṭabaqāt-i Nāṣirī*, 1:460; English tr. 1:642-3.

94 Ibid., 1:460; English tr. 1:643.

95 I follow here Jackson's rendering of the name rather than the more common 'Altunia'.

96 Juzjānī, *Ṭabaqāt-i Nāṣirī*, 1:461; English tr. 1:645.

97 Ibid., 1:462; English tr. 1:647.

98 Jackson, 'Sulṭān Raḍiyya', 183.

99 Ibid., 184.

100 Juzjānī, *Ṭabaqāt-i Nāṣirī*, 1:457; English tr. 1:637.

101 Jackson, 'Sulṭān Raḍiyya', 189.

102 Ibid., 189-90.

103 Szuppe, 'Status, Knowledge, and Politics', 141; Keddie, *Women in the Middle East*, 48–50.

104 Habibullah, 'Sulṭanah Rāziah', 752.

105 Ibid., 752.

106 Ibid., 753–4.

107 See poem mentioned in Chapter 2.

108 This view resembles those held in Western societies; see Valerie R. Hotchkiss, *Clothes Make the Man: Female Cross Dressing in Medieval Europe* (New York: Garland, 1996), 17.

109 For a fascinating contemporary example, see Dan Bilefsky, 'Albanian Custom Fades: Woman as Family Man', *The New York Times*, 25 June 2008, https://www.nytimes.com/2008/06/25/world/europe/25virgins.html

110 Habibullah, 'Sulṭanah Rāziah', 765–6.

111 Amīr Khusraw, *Duval Rānī Khiżr Khān*, ed. Mawlānā Rashīd Aḥmad Sālim Anṣārī and Khāliq Aḥmad Niẓāmī (Delhi: Idāra -yi Adabiyāt-i Dellī, 1988), 49:3-6.

112 Jackson, 'Sulṭān Raḍiyya', 187, 195 n. 40; H. Nelson Wright, *The Coinage and Metrology of the Sultans of Delhi* (Delhi, 1936), 40.

113 Interestingly, some contemporary historians feminize her title by calling her 'sultana' or 'queen'.

114 Niẓām al-Dīn Aḥmad, *Ṭabaqāt-i Akbarī*, trans. Brajendranath De, 3 vols. (Calcutta: The Asiatic Society, 1973), 1:75.

115 Contemporary scholar Selim Kuru, for example, writes of the frequency of honourable women being introduced as 'man-like' in medieval Turkic literature. See 'Representations: Poetry and Prose, Premodern: Turkish', in Joseph, *EWIC*, 2:497.

116 Lisa Balabanlilar, 'The Begims at the Mystic Feast: Turco-Mongol Tradition in the Mughal Harem', *Journal of Asian Studies* 69, no. 1 (2010): 125.

117 For more on this, see Hotchkiss, *Clothes Make the Man*, 128; Susan Schibanoff, 'True Lies: Transvestism and Idolatry in the Trial of Joan of Arc', in *Fresh Verdicts on Joan of Arc*, ed. Bonnie Wheeler and Charles T. Wood (New York: Garland, 1996), 42–53.

118 Schibanoff, 'True Lies', 31–3.

119 See Deuteronomy 22:5.

120 Sulayman ibn al-Ash'ath Abū Dāwud, *Sunan Abī Dāwūd: kitāb al-libās, bāb fī libās al-nisā'*, ed. Muhammad Muḥyī al-Dīn 'Abd al-Ḥamīd (N.p.: Dār al-Iḥyā' al-Sunna al-Nabawiyya, [197–], 60; see also Al-Qāḍī al-Nu'mān, *Da'ā'im*, 2:144.

121 'Abd al-Malik 'Isāmī, *Futūḥ al-salāṭīn*, ed. and trans. Agha Mahdi Musain as *Futūhu's Salātīn or Shāh Nāmah-i Hind of 'Iṣāmī* (London: Asia Publishing House, 1977, 3 vols), 2:253.

122 Peter Jackson, *The Delhi Sultanate: A Political and Military History* (Cambridge: Cambridge University Press, 1999), 47.

123 Habibullah, 'Sulṭanah Rāziah', 764–8; Jackson, 'Sulṭān Raḍiyya', 185–8.

124 Jackson, 'Sulṭān Raḍiyya', 189.

125 Fīrūz Shāh ruled for less than seven months before he was executed. Bahrām Shāh's reign lasted just over two years; he was 'overthrown when many of his commanders mutinied and stormed Delhi'. See ibid., 47.

126 The 'favour' that she showed Jamāl al-Dīn Yāqūt, no matter how it has been interpreted by later historians, hardly appears in a damning light in Juzjānī's account. The same word for favour or preference, *qurbat*, is used with regard to those servants of the state who had access to Sultan Iltutmish. See Juzjānī, *Ṭabaqāt-i Nāṣirī*, 1:458; English tr. 1: 638.

127 Juzjānī, *Ṭabaqāt-i Nāṣirī*, 1:457; English tr. 1:637–8.

128 Not to be confused with the earlier offspring of Iltutmish of the same name.

129 Indeed, Jackson observes that Juzjānī, writing soon before Balaban's accession, seems 'to have felt inhibited from revealing circumstances which cast his benefactor in a poor light'. See *Delhi Sultanate*, 48. The situation is complicated by the fact that Balaban received an important promotion from Raḍiyya.

130 Amīr Khusraw, *Duval Rānī*, 49:7–8.

131 'Isāmī, *Futūḥ al-salāṭīn*, 2:253–4.

132 Ibid., 2:254.

133 Ibid., 2:255.

134 Ibid., 2:259.

135 Ibid., 2:261.

136 Ibid., 2:263.

137 Ibn Baṭṭūta, *Riḥlat ibn Baṭṭūta*, trans. Mahdi Husain as *The Reḥla of Ibn Baṭṭūta (India, Maldive Islands and Ceylon)* (Baroda: Oriental Institute, 1976), 34. Later historians have spun Raḍiyya's favour towards Jamāl al-Dīn Yāqūt into a full-fledged romance. Edward Thomas (d. 1886) writes, in prose suited to any Harlequin-style bodice-ripper, 'It was not that a virgin Queen was forbidden to love – she might have indulged herself in a submissive Prince Consort, or reveled almost unchecked in the dark recesses of the Palace Harem – but wayward fancy pointed in a wrong direction, and led her to prefer a person employed about her Court, an Abyssinian moreover, the favours extended to whom the Túrkí nobles resented with one accord'. See *Chronicles of the Patháṅ Kings of Delhi* (London: Trübner and Co., 1871), 106. A poster advertising the 1983 film *Razia Sultan*, starring Hema Malini, shows the sultan in close embrace with a man whose skin is significantly darker than hers; her eyes are closed in apparent ecstasy. In case audiences miss the point, the word 'eros' appears in upper-case letters at the poster's top left.

138 Ibn Baṭṭūta, *Riḥlat*, 34–5.

139 John Anson, 'The Female Transvestite in Early Monasticism: The Origin and Development of a Motif', *Viator* 5 (1974): 11.

140 Schibanoff, 'True Lies', 128.

141 Ibid., 54.

142 Hotchkiss, *Clothes Make the Man*, 9.

143 See the historian Iskandar Munshī, who says she was 'betrothed to Badī' al-Zamān Mīrzā b. Bahrām Mīrzā, but the marriage was never solemnized'. *Tārīkh*, 1:135; English tr., 1:218.

144 Babayan, 'Aqā'id al-Nisā', 352.

145 Ibid.

146 Szuppe, 'Status, Knowledge, and Politics', 156.

147 Babayan, 'Aqā'īd al-Nisā', 352–3.

148 Iskandar Munshī, *Tārīkh*, 1:119; English tr., 1:198; Muhammad Afūshta-yi Natanzī, *Naqāwat al-Āthār fī dikhr al-akhyār*, ed. Iḥsān Ishrāqī (Tehran: Bungāh-i Tarjama va Nashr-i Kitāb, 1971), 70; quoted in Shohreh Gholsorkhi, 'Pari Khan Khanum: A Masterful Safavid Princess', *Iranian Studies* 28, nos. 3/4 (1995): 146.

149 Natanzī, *Naqāwat*, 70; quoted in Gholsorkhi, 'Pari Khan Khanum', 147.

150 Iskandar Munshī, *Tārīkh*, 1:135; English tr., 1:218.

151 See Babayan, 'Aqā'īd al-Nisā', 377 n. 16.

152 Iskandar Munshī, *Tārīkh*, 1:119; English tr., 1:197.

153 Ibid., 1:119; English tr., 1:197-8.

154 Ibid., 1:192–3; English tr., 1:284.

155 Ibid., 1:192; English tr., 1:283–4.

156 Ibid., 1:192, 195; English tr., 1:284, 288–9.

157 Ibid., 1:197; English tr., 1:291.

158 Ibid., 1:197; English tr., 1:291.

159 Muhammad Yūsuf Vālah Iṣfahānī, *Khuld-i barīn*, ed. Mīr Hāshim Muḥaddiṯ (Tehran: Mawqūfāt-i Duktur Maḥmūd Afshār Yazdī, 1993), 520.

160 Iskandar Munshī, *Tārīkh*, 1:197; English tr., 1:292.

161 Ibid., 1:201; English tr., 1:297. For more on Husaynqulī, see ibid., 1:140; English tr., 1:224–5.

162 Ibid., 1:201; English tr., 1:298.

163 Ibid., 1:201; English tr., 1:298.

164 Ibid., 1:201; English tr., 1:298.

165 Ibid., 1:201–2; English tr., 1:298.

166 Ibid., 1:201; English tr., 1:298. As the same author writes, Ismā'īl was 'not possessed of normal feelings of affection toward his family', having had several relatives murdered or blinded. Ibid., 1:208; English tr., 1:309.

167 Ibid., 1:203; English tr., 1:301.

168 Ibid., 1:219; English tr., 1:327.

169 Ibid., 1:219; English tr., 1:327. See also Gholsorkhi, 'Pari Khan Khanum', 152–3, for other chroniclers imputing his death to Parī Khān Khānum.

170 Iskandar Munshī, *Tārīkh*, 1:220; English tr., 1:328.

171 Natanzī, *Naqāwat*, 62; quoted in Gholsorkhi, 'Pari Khan Khanum', 153.

172 Iskandar Munshī, *Tārīkh*, 1:220; English tr., 1:329.

173 Ibid., 1:223; English tr., 1:333.

174 Ibid., 1:223–4; English tr., 1:334. See also Manučehr Pārsādust, 'Pari̲kān K̲ānom', in *EIr*.

175 Iskandar Munshī, *Tārīkh*, 1:223; English tr., 1:333. The historian calls her 'the architect and organizer of the affairs of state; no decision was taken without her approval, and Sultan Muhammad Shah deferred to her constantly'. See ibid., 1:224; English tr., 1:334–5.

176 Ibid., 1:225; English tr., 1:336.

177 Ibid., 1:225–6; English tr., 1:336–7.

178 Ibid., 1:226; English tr., 1:337–8.

179 Ibid., 1:226; English tr., 1:338. For a description of her activities, see ibid., 1:235–52; English tr., 1:353–73.

180 Szuppe, 'Status, Knowledge, and Politics', 155.

181 Iskandar Munshī, *Tārīkh*, 1:248; English tr., 1:368.

182 Szuppe, 'Status, Knowledge, and Politics', 160.

183 Iskandar Munshī, *Tārīkh*, 1:249–50; English tr., 1:370.

184 Ibid., 1:250–1; English tr., 1:371.

185 See Szuppe, 'Status, Knowledge, and Politics', 161.

186 See ibid., 159-60.

187 Iskandar Munshī, *Tārīkh*, 1:249–50; English tr., 1:370.

188 Babayan, 'Aqā'īd al-Nisā', 351. As Rizvi notes, Iskandar Munshī also spoke rather misogynistically about women at times, crediting 'the failure of the prince to his listening to the advice of feebleminded and intellectually limited women … however when he refers to the women of the Safavid household directly, it is with the utmost respect'. See 'Gendered Patronage', 148 n. 26.

189 Iskandar Munshī, *Tārīkh*, 1:135; English tr., 1:219.

190 Although, to be sure, he would have refrained from passing harsh judgment on the mother of his patron, Shāh 'Abbās.

191 Iskandar Munshī, *Tārīkh*, 1:238, 248; English tr., 1:356, 368.

192 Natanzī, *Naqāwat*, 72; quoted in Babayan, 'Aqā'īd al-Nisā', 356.

193 Babayan, 'Aqā'īd al-Nisā', 353.

194 Ibid., 353.

195 Maryam Sabbaghi, 'The Court Poet and the Lady Patron: Muḥtasham Kāshānī's Illustration of Illustration of Parī Khān Khānum' (paper presented at the Annual Meeting of the Middle East Studies Association, Washington, DC, November 2014), 12-13. Much of my discussion here is inspired by Sabbaghi's work, with some significant departures.

196 Gholsorkhi, 'Pari Khan Khanum', 147.

197 Sabbaghi, 'Court Poet', 13.

198 See Gholsorkhi, 'Pari Khan Khanum', 147; Iskandar Munshī, *Tārīkh*, 1:274.

199 See Sabbaghi, 'Court Poet', 12–17.

200 Muḥtasham, *Dīvān*, 300, 326.

201 Ibid., 323.

202 Ibid., 323.

203 Ibid., 300, 327.

204 Sabbaghi, 'Court Poet', 12.

205 Muḥtasham, *Dīvān*, 300, 325.

206 Ibid., 323–4; 327.

207 Muḥtasham, *Dīvān*, 325.

208 See Sabbaghi, 'Court Poet', 14–17.

209 Muḥtasham, *Dīvān*, 322; see also Sabbaghi, 'Court Poet', 14; with modifications.

210 Muḥtasham, *Dīvān*, 326.

211 Sabbaghi, 'Court Poet', 12; slightly altered.

212 See ibid., 18, where she suggests that because Parī Khān Khānum was celibate, she became 'unclassified in gender'. Compare also to Ahmed, who notes that wearing modest dress freed women to mix with men in contemporary Egypt; see *Women and Gender in Islam*, 224.

213 See Sabbaghi, 'Court Poet', 15.

214 See Babayan, 'Aqā'īd al-Nisā', 354–8.

Epilogue

1 Emma Graham Harrison, 'Afghan Clerics' Guidelines "A Green Light for Talibanisation"', *The Guardian*, 5 March 2012. See https://www.theguardian.com/world/2012/mar/05/afghanistan-women

2 Ibid.

3 See for example, UNHCR, 'Background Note'.

4 See Joseph, 'History and Its Histories', 14; UNHCR, 'Background Note'; Hoodfar, 'Divorce and Custody', 2:105; Musawah, *Women's Stories, Women's Lives: Male Authority in Muslim Contexts* (Kuala Lumpur?: Musawah, 2016), 57.

5 Joseph, 'History and Its Histories', 14; UNHCR, 'Background Note'.

6 UNHCR, 'Background Note'.

7 Moors, 'Debating Islamic Family Law: Legal Texts and Social Practices', in *A Social History of Women and Gender in the Modern Middle East*, ed. Margaret L. Meriwether and Judith E. Tucker (Boulder: Westview Press, 1999), 153.

8 Tucker, *Themes in Islamic Law*, 164. For other inheritance reforms, including in Indonesia, see Tucker, *Themes in Islamic Law*, 169–70, and Aharon Layish, 'Mīrāth: In Modern Islamic Countries', *EI*[2].

9 See Heba Kanso, 'Is Women's Inheritance Next on Reformist Tunisia's Rights Agenda?', *Reuters*, 25 January 2018; available at https://www.reuters.com/article/us-tunisia-women-rights/is-womens-inheritance-next-on-reformist-tunisias-rights-agenda-idUSKBN1FE2UC; Amel al-Hilali, 'Tunisian Women Fighting for Equal Inheritance Rights', *Al-Monitor*, 13 March 2018; available at https://www.al-monitor.com/pulse/originals/2018/03/tunisian-women-rally-demand-equal-inheritance-rights.html; and Ursula Lindsey, 'Can Muslim Feminism Find a Third Way?', *The New York Times*, 11 April 2018; available at https://www.nytimes.com/2018/04/11/opinion/islam-feminism-third-way.html

10 Benazir Bhutto, *Daughter of Destiny: An Autobiography* (New York: Simon and Schuster, 1989), 47.

11 Katherine Butler, 'Lipstick Revolution: Iran's Women Are Taking on the Mullahs', *The Independent*, 26 February 2009; available at http://www.independent.co.uk/news/world/middle-east/lipstick-revolution-irans-women-are-taking-on-the-mullahs-1632257.html

12 Seema Chishti, 'We Believe We Are on the Right Track and Victory Will Be Ours', *The Indian Express*, 12 June 2009; available at http://archive.indianexpress.com/news/we-believe-we-are-on-the-right-track-and-victory-will-be-ours/475164/2

13 Massoume Price, 'Meeting Faezeh', *The Iranian*, 5 October 2000, https://www.iranian.com/Features/2000/October/Faezeh/index.html

14 Edith Szanto, 'Speaking in the Name of Zaynab: Female Shi'i Religious Authority in Syria', in Künkler and Stewart, *Female Religious Authority in Shi'i Islam.*

15 Keiko Sakurai, 'Making Qom a Centre of Shi'i Scholarship: Al-Mustafa International University', in *Shaping Global Islamic Discourses: The Role of al-Azhar, al-Madinah and al-Mustafa*, ed. Masooda Bano and Keiko Sakurai (Edinburgh: Edinburgh University Press, 2015), 60. See also Sakurai, 'Women's Empowerment and Iranian-style Seminaries in Iran and Pakistan', in *The Moral Economy of the Madrasa: Islam and Education Today*, ed. Sakurai and Fariba Adelkhah (Abdingdon: Routledge, 2011).

16 Pierce, 'Remembering Fāṭimah', 359.

17 Ibid., 359–60.

18 Sharī'atī, '*Fatima Fatima Ast*', 144–6; 181.

19 Pierce, 'Remembering Fāṭimah', 360.

20 Lawson, 'Authority of the Feminine', 138.

21 Pierce, 'Remembering Fāṭimah', 356; also, Kashani-Sabet, 'Who is Fatima?', 2–3; 18, 20.

22 See, for example, Afsaneh Najmabadi, 'Power, Morality, and the New Muslim Womanhood', in *The Politics of Social Transformation in Afghanistan, Iran, and Pakistan*, ed. Myron Weiner and Ali Banuazizi (Syracuse: Syracuse University Press, 1994), 374-6; Ziba Mir-Hosseini, *Islam and Gender: The Religious Debate in Contemporary Iran* (Princeton: Princeton University Press, 1999), 54-8; Soufi, 'Image', 204.

23 Najmabadi, 'Power, Morality, and the New Muslim Womanhood', 366.

24 See Shaikh, *Sufi Narratives*, 22–3; Ziba Mir-Hosseini, 'Beyond "Islam" vs. "Feminism"', *IDS Bulletin* 42, no. 1 (2011): 67–77; Ahmed-Ghosh, 'Dilemmas of Islamic and Secular Feminists and Feminisms'.

25 See Ahmed, *Women and Gender*, 128–9; Abu-Lughod, *Do Muslim Women Need Saving?*, 30–4.

Bibliography

Primary sources

'Abdī Beg Shīrāzī 'Navīdī'. *Takmilāt al-akhbār*. Edited by 'Abd al-Husayn Navā'ī. Tehran: Nay, 1990.

Abū al-Faḍl. *Ā'īn-i Akbarī*. Translated by Heinrich Blochmann and Henry Sullivan Jarrett. Calcutta: The Asiatic Society, 1993.

Abū al-Faḍl. *Akbarnāma*. Translated by Henry Beveridge as *The Akbarnama of Abu'l Fazl*. Calcutta: The Asiatic Society, 1907; reprinted 2000, 3 vols.

Abū Dāwūd, Sulayman ibn al-Ash'ath. *Sunan Abī Dāwūd*. Edited by Muhammad Muḥyī al-Dīn 'Abd al-Ḥamīd. N.p.: Dār Iḥyā' al-Sunna al-Nabawiyya, [197–].

Abū Tammām, Ḥabīb ibn Aws al-Tā'ī. *Dīwān al-Ḥamāsa*. 2 vols. Cairo: al-Maktaba al-Azhariyya, 1927.

Aeschylus. *Oresteia*. Edited and translated by Alan H. Sommerstein. Cambridge: Harvard University Press, 2008.

Amīr Khusraw. *Duval Rānī Khiżr Khān*. Edited by Mawlānā Rashīd Aḥmad Sālim Anṣārī and Khāliq Aḥmad Niẓāmī. Delhi: Idāra-yi Adabiyāt-i Dillī, 1988.

Amīr Khusraw. *Hasht bihisht*. Edited by Ja'far Iftikhār. Moscow: Idāra-yi Intishārāt-i Dānish, Shu'ba-yi Adabiyāt-i Khāvar, 1982.

Amīr Khusraw. *Matla' al-anwār*. Edited by Ṭāhir Aḥmad Ughlī Muharramūf. Moscow: Idāra-yi Intishārāt-i Dānish, Shu'ba-yi Adabiyāt-i Khāvar, 1975.

Amīr Khusraw. *Nihāyat al-kamāl*. Edited by Yāsīn 'Alī Niẓāmī. Delhi: Maṭba'-i Qayṣarīyah, 1913/4.

Aristotle. *Generation of Animals*. Translated by A.L. Peck. Cambridge: Harvard University Press, 1942.

'Aṭṭār, Farīd al-Dīn. *Manṭiq al-ṭayr*. Edited by Muhammad Riża Shafi'ī Kadkanī. 3rd ed. Tehran: Intishārāt-i Sukhan, 2006. Translated by Afkhan Darbandi and Dick Davis as *The Conference of the Birds*. London: Penguin, 1984.

Aṭṭār, Farīd al-Dīn. *Tazkirāt al-'Awliyā'*. Translated by A.J. Arberry as *Muslim Saints and Mystics*. London: Arkana, 1966.

'Ayyāshī, Abū al-Naḍr Muhammad ibn Mas'ūd al-. *Kitāb al-tafsīr*. Edited by Hāshim al-Rasūlī al-Maḥallātī. 2 vols. Qum: Chāpkhāna-yi 'Ilmiyya, 1961.

Bābur, Emperor of Hindustan. *Bāburnāma*. Translated by Wheeler M. Thackston as *The Baburnama: Memoirs of Babur, Prince and Emperor*. New York: The Modern Library, 2002.

Balādhurī, Aḥmad ibn Yaḥyā al-. *Ansāb al-ashrāf*. Vol. 1. Edited by Muhammad Ḥamīd Allah. Cairo: Dār al-Maʿārif, 1987.

Balādhurī, Aḥmad ibn Yaḥyā al-. *Kitāb futūḥ al-buldān*. Translated by Philip Khûri Ḥitti as *The Origins of the Islamic State*. New York: Columbia University, 1916, 2 vols.

Bukhārī, Muhammad ibn Ismāʿīl al-. *Al-Adab al-mufrad*. Cited by chapter, subchapter system.

Bukhārī, Muhammad ibn Ismāʿīl al-. *Ṣahīḥ al-Bukhārī*. Cited by chapter, subchapter system.

Darīr, Muṣṭafā. *Siyer-i Nebī*. Turkish MS 419, Chester Beatty Library, Dublin.

Firdawsī, Abū al-Qāsim. *Shāhnāma*. Edited by Evgeniĭ Ėduardovich et al. 9 vols. Moscow: Idāra-yi Intishārāt-i Adabiyāt-i Khāvar, 1960–1971.

Ḥaddād, Ṭāhir al-. *Imraʾatunā fi al-Sharīʿah wa al-Mujtamaʿ*. Translated by Ronak Husni and Daniel L. Newman as *Muslim Women in Law and Society*. Abingdon: Routledge, 2007.

Ḥallāj, Manṣūr al-. *Dīwān*. Edited by Kāmil Muṣṭafā al-Shaybī. Cologne: Manshūrāt al-Jamāl, 2007. Translated by Herbert W. Mason as *Al-Hallaj*. Richmond, Surrey: Curzon Press, 1995.

Ibn ʿAbd al-Wahhāb, Husayn. *ʿUyūn al-muʿjizāt*. Najaf: Al-Maṭbaʿa al-Ḥaydariyya, 1950.

Ibn Abī al-Ḥadīd. *Sharḥ nahj al-balāgha*. 21 vols. 2nd ed. Beirut: Muʾassasat al-Aʿlamī lil-Maṭbūʿāt.

Ibn Abī Ṭāhir Ṭayfūr, Abū al-Faḍl. *Balāghāt al-nisāʾ*. Edited by Barakāt Yūsuf Habbūd. Beirut: Al-Maktaba al-ʿAṣrīya, 2000.

Ibn Bābawayh, Abū Jaʿfar. *Amālī al-ṣadūq*. Najaf: Al-Maṭbaʿa al-Ḥaydariyya, 1970.

Ibn Bābawayh, Abū Jaʿfar. *ʿIlal al-sharāʾiʿ*. Najaf: Al-Maṭbaʿa al-Ḥaydariyya, 1963.

Ibn Bābawayh, Abū Jaʿfar. *Maʿānī al-akhbār*. Edited by ʿAli Akbar al-Ghaffārī. Tehran: Maktabat al-Ṣadūq, 1959.

Ibn Bābawayh, Abū Jaʿfar. *Risālat al-iʿtiqādāt*. Translated by Asaf A.A. Fyzee as *A Shiʿite Creed*. London: Oxford University Press, 1942.

Ibn Bābawayh, Abū Jaʿfar. *ʿUyūn akhbār al-Riḍā*. Qum: Manshūrāt Dhawī al-Qurbā, 2006 or 2007.

Ibn Baṭṭūta. *Riḥlat ibn Baṭṭūta*. Translated by Mahdi Husain as *The Reḥla of Ibn Baṭṭūṭa (India, Maldive Islands and Ceylon)*. Baroda: Oriental Institute, 1976.

Ibn Ḥanbal, Aḥmad. *Al-Musnad*. Cairo: Dār al-Maʿārif, 1956–7.

Ibn Ḥanbal, Aḥmad. *Kitāb faḍāʾil al-ṣaḥāba*. Edited by Waṣī Allah ibn Muhammad ʿAbbās. Beirut: Muʾassasat al-Risāla, 1983.

Ibn Isḥāq, Muhammad. *Sīrat rasūl Allah*. Translated by A. Guillaume as *The Life of Muhammad*. Oxford: Oxford University Press, 1955.

Ibn Kathīr, Ismāʿīl ibn ʿUmar. *Tafsīr al-Qurʾan al-ʿaẓīm*. 9 vols. Beirut: Dār al-Kutub al-ʿIlmiyya, 1998.

Ibn Qayyim al-Jawziyya. *Al-Tibyan fī aqsām al-Qurʾan*. Edited by Muhammad Ḥāmid al-Fiqqī. Cairo: Maṭbaʿat Ḥijāzī, 1933.

Ibn Saʿd, Abū ʿAbd Allah Muhammad. *Kitāb al-ṭabaqāt al-kabīr*. Vol. 1. Translated by S. Moinul Haq and H.K. Ghazanfar. Karachi: Pakistan Historical Society, 1967.

Ibn Saʿd, Abū ʿAbd Allah Muhammad. *Kitāb al-ṭabaqāt al-kabīr*. Vol. 2. Translated by S. Moinul Haq and H.K. Ghazanfar. Karachi: Pakistan Historical Society, 1972.

Ibn Saʿd, Abū ʿAbd Allah Muhammad. *Kitāb al-ṭabaqāt al-kabīr*. Vol. 3. Translated by Aisha Bewley as *The Companions of Badr*. London: Ta-Ha, 2013.

Ibn Saʿd, Abū ʿAbd Allah Muhammad. *Kitāb al-ṭabaqāt al-kabīr*. Vol. 7. Translated by Aisha Bewley as *The Men of Madina*. London: Ta-Ha, 1997.

Ibn Saʿd, Abū ʿAbd Allah Muhammad. *Kitāb al-ṭabaqāt al-kabīr*. Vol. 8. Translated by Aisha Bewley as *The Women of Madina*. London: Ta-Ha, 1997.

Ibn Shahrāshūb, Muhammad ibn ʿAli. *Manāqib āl Abī Ṭālib*. Najaf: Al-Maṭbaʿa al-Ḥaydariyya, 1956.

Ibn Ṭāwūs, ʿAli. *Iqbāl al-aʿmāl*. Beirut: Muʾassasat al-Tārīkh al-ʿArabī, 2004.

Ibn Ẓāfir, Jamāl al-Dīn. *Akhbār al-duwal al-munqaṭiʿa*. Edited by A. Ferré. Cairo: IFAO, 1972.

ʿIṣāmī, ʿAbd al-Malik. *Futūḥ al-salāṭīn*. Edited and translated by Agha Mahdi Husain as *Futūhu's Salātīn or Shāh Nāmah-i Hind of ʿIṣāmī*. London: Asia Publishing House, 1977, 3 vols.

Iṣfahānī, Muhammad Yūsuf Vālah. *Khuld-i barīn*. Edited by Mīr Hāshim Muḥaddis. Tehran: Mawqūfāt-i Duktur Maḥmūd Afshār Yazdī, 1993.

Iskandar Munshī. *Tārīkh-i ʿālamārā-yi ʿAbbāsī*. Edited by Īraj Afshār. 2 vols. 2nd ed. Tehran: Amīr Kabīr, 1971. Translated by Robert M. Savory as *History of Shah ʿAbbas the Great*. Boulder: Westview Press, 1978, 2 vols.

Jāḥiẓ, Abū ʿUthmān al-. *Kitāb al-ḥayawān*. Edited by ʿAbd al-Salām Hārūn. 8 vols. Beirut: Dār al-Jīl, 1996.

Jawharī, Abū Bakr Aḥmad al-. *Al-Saqīfa wa fadak*. Edited by Muhammad Hādī al-Amīnī. Beirut: Sharīkat al-kutub, 1993.

Juzjānī, Minhāj-i Sirāj-i. *Ṭabaqāt-i Nāṣirī*. Edited by ʿAbd al-Ḥay Ḥabībī. 2 vols. Tehran: Dunyā-yi Kitāb, 1984. Translated by Henry George Raverty as *Tabaḳāt-i-Nāṣirī: A General History of the Muhammadan Dynasties of Asia*. Calcutta: The Asiatic Society, 1881, 2 vols.

Kalbī, Hishām ibn al-. *Kitāb al-aṣnām*. Translated by Nabih Amin Faris as *The Book of Idols*. Princeton: Princeton University Press, 1952.

Kalīm, Abū Ṭālib. *Divān*. Edited by Partaw Bayżāʾī. Tehran: Kitābfurūshī-yi Khayyām, 1957.

Kulaynī, Muhammad ibn Ya'qūb al-. *Al-Kāfī*. Edited by 'Alī Akbar al-Ghaffārī. 8 vols. Tehran: Dār al-Kutub al-Islāmiyya, 1957–61. Translated by Muhammad Sarwar. New York: The Islamic Seminary, 2015, 8 vols.

Majlisī, Muhammad Bāqir al-. *Biḥār al-anwār*. 110 vols. Tehran: Maṭba'at al-Islāmiyya, 1956–1972.

Maqrīzī, Taqī al-Dīn. *Itti'āẓ al-hunafā' bi-akhbār al-a'imma al-fātimiyyīn al-khulafā'*. Edited by Jamāl al-Dīn al-Shayyāl and Muhammad Ḥilmī. 3 vols. Cairo: Lajnat Iḥyā' al-Turāth al-Islāmī, 1967–73.

Muḥtasham, 'Ali ibn Aḥmad. *Dīvān-i Muḥtasham Kāshānī*. Edited by Akbar Bihdārvand. Tehran: Nigāh, 2000.

Mufīd, Muhammad ibn Muhammad al-Nu'mān al-. *Al-Irshād*. Edited by al-Sayyid Kāẓim al-Mīyāmawī. Tehran: Dār al-Kutub, 1958.

Mufīd, Muhammad ibn Muhammad al-Nu'mān al-. *Kitāb al-amālī*. Translated by Mulla Asgharali M.M. Jaffer as *Al Amaali: The Dictations of Sheikh al-Mufid*. Stanmore: World Federation of Khoja Shia Ithna-Asheri Muslim Communities, 1998.

Musabbiḥī, Muhammad ibn 'Ubayd Allah, al-. *Akhbār Miṣr*. Vol. 1. Edited by Ayman Fu'ād Sayyid and Thierry Bianquis. Cairo: Institut Français D'Archéologie Orientale, 1978.

Muslim ibn al-Ḥajjāj, *Ṣahīḥ Muslim*. Cited by chapter, subchapter system.

Nabhānī, Yusūf ibn Ismā'īl al-. *Al-Sharaf al-mu'abbad li-āl Muhammad*. Cairo: Muṣṭafā al-Bābī al-Ḥalabī, 1961.

Natanzī, Muhammad Afūshta-yi. *Naqāwat al-āthār fī dhikr al-akhyār*. Edited by Iḥsān Ishrāqī. Tehran: Bungāh-i Tarjama va Nashr-i Kitāb, 1971.

Nīsābūrī, Muhammad ibn al-Fattāl al-. *Rawḍat al-wā'iẓīn*. Edited by Muhammad Khurāsānī. Najaf: Al-Maṭba'a al-Ḥaydariyya, 1966.

Niẓām al-Dīn Aḥmad. *Ṭabaqāt-i Akbarī*. Translated by Brajendranath De. 3 vols. Calcutta: The Asiatic Society, 1973.

Niẓām al-Mulk. *Siyāsat-nāma*. Translated by Hubert Darke as *The Book of Government or Rules for Kings*. New Haven: Yale University Press, 1960.

Niẓāmī Ganjavī. *Haft paykar*. Edited by Bihrūz Sarvatīyān. Tehran: Intishārāt-i Ṭūs, 1998. Translated by Julie Scott Meisami as *The Haft Paykar: A Medieval Persian Romance*. Oxford: Oxford University Press, 1995.

Pliny. *Naturalis Historia*. Translated by John Bostock and H.T. Riley as *The Natural History of Pliny*. London: George Bell and Sons, 1890.

Qāḍī al-Nu'mān, al-. *Da'ā'im al-Islām*. Translated by Asaf A.A. Fyzee as *The Pillars of Islam*. Oxford: Oxford University Press, 2004, 2 vols.

Qāḍī al-Nu'mān, al-. *Sharḥ al-akhbār fi faḍā'il al-a'imma al-aṭhār*. Edited by M.H. al-Jalālī. Qum: Mu'assasat al-Nashr al-Islāmī, 1988–92.

Qalānisī, Ḥamza ibn Asad ibn al-. *Tārīkh Dimashq*. Edited by S. Zakār. Damascus: Dār Hassān, 1983.

Qurṭubī, Muhammad ibn Aḥmad. *Al-Jāmiʿ al-aḥkām al-Qurʾan*. Edited by ʿAbd Allah ibn ʿAbd al-Muḥsin al-Turkī and Muhammad Riḍwān ʿIrqsūsī. 24 vols. Beirut: Muʾassasat al-Risāla, 2006.

Rāzī, Fakhr al-Dīn al-. *Al-Tafsīr al-kabīr*. 32 vols. Beirut: Dār Iḥyāʾ al-Turāth al-ʿArabī, [198–?].

Saʿdī, Abū Muhammad Muṣliḥ al-Dīn ibn ʿAbd Allah Shīrāzī. *Būstān*. Edited by Ghulām Husayn Yūsufī. Tehran: Khvārazmī Publications, 2008.

Ṣadr, Muhammad Bāqir, al-. *Fadak fī al-tārīkh*. Beirut: Dār al-Taʿāruf al-Maṭbuʿāt, 1990. Translated by Abdullah al-Shāhīn as *Fadak in History*. Qum: Anṣāriyān, 2002, http://www.shiavault.com/books/fadak-in-history/.

Ṣaffār al-Qummī, Muḥammad ibn al-Ḥasan al-. *Baṣāʾir al-darajāt*. Edited by Muḥsin Kūchabāghī. 2nd ed. Qum: Maktabat Āyat Allah al-ʿUẓmá al-Marʿashī al-Najafī, 1983.

The Secret History of the Mongols: The Life and Times of Chinggis Khan. Translated and edited by Urgunge Onon. Richmond, Surrey: Curzon Press, 2001.

Sharīf al-Rāḍī, al-. *Nahj al-Balāgha*. Translated by Sayed Ali Reza as *Nahjul Balagha = Peak of Eloquence: Sermons, Letters, and Sayings of Imam Ali ibn Abu Talib*. Elmhurst, NY: Tahrike Tarsile Quran, 1996.

Suhaylī, Abū al-Qāsim, al-. *Al-Rawḍ al-unuf fī sharḥ al-sīrat al-nabawiyya li- Ibn Hishām*. 7 vols. Cairo: Dār al-Kutub al-Ḥadītha, 1967–70.

Suyūṭī, Jalāl al-Dīn ʿAbd al-Raḥmān al-. *Al-Khaṣāʾiṣ al-kubrā*. Edited by Muhammad Khalīl Harrās. 3 vols. Cairo: Dār al-Kutub al-Ḥadītha, 1967. See also http://islamport.com/w/ser/Web/3331/66.htm.

Ṭabarī, Abū Jaʿfar Muḥammad ibn Jarīr al-. *Tafsīr al-Ṭabarī: Jāmiʿ al-bayān ʿan taʾwīl āy al-Qurʾan*. Edited by Maḥmūd Muhammad Shākir and Aḥmad Muhammad Shākir. 16 vols. Cairo: Dār al-Maʿārif, 1955–.

Ṭabarī, Abū Jaʿfar Muḥammad ibn Jarīr al-. *Tārīkh al-rusul wa al-mulūk*. Vol. 9. Translated by Ismail K. Poonawala as *The History of al-Tabari: The Last Years of the Prophet*. Albany: State University of New York Press, 1990.

Ṭabarī, Abū Jaʿfar Muḥammad ibn Jarīr al-. *Tārīkh al-rusul wa al-mulūk*. Vol. 28. Translated by Jane Dammen McAuliffe as *The History of al-Tabari: ʿAbbasid Authority Affirmed*. Albany: State University of New York Press, 1995.

Ṭabarī al-Shīʿī, Muhammad ibn Jarīr ibn Rustam al-. *Dalāʾil al-imāma*. Najaf: Al-Maṭbaʿa al-Haydariyya, 1949.

Ṭabāṭabāʾī, Muhammad Husayn al-. *Al-Mīzān fī tafsīr al-Qurʾan*. Vol. 8. Translated by Sayyid Saeed Akhtar Rizvi as *Al-Mīzān: An Exegesis of the Holy Qurʾan*. Tehran: World Organization for Islamic Services, 2014.

Tirmidhī, Abū ʿĪsā Muhammad al-. *Sunan al-Tirmidhī*. Edited by ʿIzzat ʿAbīd al-Daʿās. Homs: Maktabat Dār al-Daʿwa, 1967.

Ya'qūbī, Aḥmad al-. *Al-Tārīkh* [Historiae]. Edited by M. Th. Houtsma. 2 vols. Leiden: Brill, 1969.

Yāqūt al-Hamawī. *Mu'jam al-buldān*. Beirut: Dār Ṣādir, 1984.

Secondary sources

Abdel Haleem, M.A.S. *The Qur'an*. Oxford: Oxford University Press, 2010.

Abou El Fadl, Khaled. *Speaking in God's Name: Islamic Law, Authority and Women*. Oxford: Oneworld Publications, 2001.

Abu-Lughod, Lila. *Do Muslim Women Need Saving?* Cambridge: Harvard University Press, 2013.

Aceves, Joseph B. *Identity, Survival, and Change: Exploring Social/Cultural Anthropology*. Morristown, NJ: General Learning Press, 1974.

Aghaie, Kamran Scot. 'The Gender Dynamics of Moharram Symbols and Rituals in the Latter Years of Qajar Rule'. In Aghaie, *Women of Karbala*, 45–63.

Aghaie, Kamran Scot, ed. *The Women of Karbala: Ritual Performance and Symbolic Discourses in Modern Shi'i Islam*. Austin: University of Texas Press, 2005.

Ahmed-Ghosh, Huma. 'Dilemmas of Islamic and Secular Feminists and Feminisms'. *Journal of International Women's Studies* 9, no. 3 (2008): 99–116.

Ahmed, Leila. 'Women and the Advent of Islam'. *Signs* 11, no. 4 (1986): 665–691.

Ahmed, Leila. *Women and Gender in Islam: Historical Roots of a Modern Debate*. New Haven: Yale University Press, 1992.

Algar, Hamid. 'Āl-e 'Abā'. In Yarshater, *EIr*. Article originally published 15 December 1984. Updated 29 July 2011, http://www.iranicaonline.org/articles/al-e-aba-the-family-of-the-cloak-i.

Ali, Abdullah Yusuf. *The Holy Qur'an: Text, Translation and Commentary*. Elmhurst, NY: Tahrike Tarsile Qur'an, 1987.

Ali, Kecia. *Marriage and Slavery in Early Islam*. Cambridge: Harvard University Press, 2010.

Ali, Kecia. *Sexual Ethics and Islam: Feminist Reflections on Qur'an, Hadith, and Jurisprudence*. Oxford: Oneworld Publications, 2006.

Allan, James W. *The Art and Architecture of Twelver Shi'ism: Iraq, Iran and The Indian Sub-continent*. London: Azimuth editions, 2012.

Amir-Moezzi, Mohammad Ali. *Le Guide Divin Dans Le Shi'isme Originel*. Translated by David Streight as *The Divine Guide in Early Shi'ism: The Sources of Esotericism in Islam*. Albany: State University of New York Press, 1994.

Amir-Moezzi, Mohammad Ali. 'Šahrbānu'. In Yarshater, *EIr*. Article published 20 July 2005, http://www.iranicaonline.org/articles/sahrbanu.

Anees, Munawar Ahmad. *Islam and Biological Futures: Ethics, Gender, and Technology*. London: Mansell, 1989.

Anson, John. 'The Female Tranvestite in Early Monasticism: The Origin and Development of a Motif'. *Viator* 5 (1974): 1–32.

Arbabzadah, Nushin. 'Women and Religious Patronage in the Timurid Empire'. In *Afghanistan's Islam*, edited by Nile Green, 56–70. Oakland: University of California Press, 2017.

Arendonk, Cornelis van. 'Sharīf'. In *EI²*.

Asher, Catherine B. *Architecture of Mughal India*. Cambridge: Cambridge University Press, 1992.

Ayoub, Mahmoud. *Redemptive Suffering in Islām: A Study of the Devotional Aspects of 'Āshūrā' in Twelver Shī'ism*. The Hague: Mouton, 1978.

Babayan, Kathryn. 'The "Aqā'id al-Nisā": A Glimpse at Safavid Women in Local Isfahani Culture.' In Hambly, *Women in the Medieval Islamic World*, 349–81.

Badran, Margot. *Feminism Beyond East and West: New Gender Talk and Practice in Global Islam*. New Delhi: Global Media Publications, 2007.

Baer, Gabriel. 'Women and Waqf: An Analysis of the Istanbul *Tahrîr* of 1546'. *Asian and African Studies* 17 (1983): 9–27.

Baker, Alison. *Voices of Resistance: Oral Histories of Moroccan Women*. Albany: State University of New York Press, 1998.

Balabanlilar, Lisa. 'The Begims at the Mystic Feast: Turco-Mongol Tradition in the Mughal Harem'. *Journal of Asian Studies* 69, no. 1 (2010): 123–47.

Bano, Masooda and Hilary Kalmbach, eds. *Women, Leadership, and Mosques: Changes in Contemporary Islamic Authority*. Leiden: Brill, 2012.

Barlas, Asma. *'Believing Women' in Islam: Unreading Patriarchal Interpretations of the Qur'an*. Austin: University of Texas Press, 2002.

Bauer, Karen. *Gender Hierarchy in the Qur'ān: Medieval Interpretations, Modern Responses*. Cambridge: Cambridge University Press, 2015.

Bauer, Karen. 'Spiritual Hierarchy and Gender Hierarchy in Fāṭimid Ismā'īlī Interpretations of the Qur'an'. *Journal of Qur'anic Studies* 14, no. 2 (2012): 29–46.

Beauvoir, Simone de. *Le Deuxième Sexe*. Translated by Constance Borde and Sheila Malovany-Chevallier as *The Second Sex*. New York: Knopf, 2010.

Bhutto, Benazir. *Daughter of Destiny: An Autobiography*. New York: Simon and Schuster, 1989.

Blake, Stephen P. 'Contributors to the Urban Landscape: Women Builders in Ṣafavid Isfahan and Mughal Shahjahanabad'. In Hambly, *Women in the Medieval Islamic World*, 407–28.

Bokhari, Afshan. 'Imperial Transgressions and Spiritual Investitures: A Begam's "Ascension" in Seventeenth Century Mughal India'. *Journal of Persianate Studies* 4, no. 1 (2011): 86–108.

Bosworth, Clifford Edmund. *The New Islamic Dynasties: A Chronological and Genealogical Manual*. New York: Columbia University Press, 1996.

Brown, Jonathan A.C. *Muhammad: A Very Short Introduction*. Oxford: Oxford University Press, 2011.

Buhl, Frantz. 'Hind bint 'Utba'. In *EI*².

Buhl, Frantz. 'Muḥammad b. 'Abd Allāh'. In *EI*².

Burton, John. 'Those Are the High-Flying Cranes'. *Journal of Semitic Studies* 15, no. 2 (1970): 246–65.

Calmard, Jean. 'Fāṭema'. In Yarshater, *EIr*. Article published 15 December 1999. Last updated 24 January 2012, http://www.iranicaonline.org/articles/fatema.

Canby, Sheila R. *Shah 'Abbas: The Remaking of Iran*. London: British Museum Press, 2009.

Chaudhry, Ayesha S. 'Islamic Legal Studies: A Critical Historiography'. In *The Oxford Handbook of Islamic Law*, edited by Anver M. Emon and Rumee Ahmed, 5–43. Oxford: Oxford University Press, 2018.

Cheikh, Nadia Maria el-. *Women, Islam, and Abbasid Identity*. Cambridge: Harvard University Press, 2015.

Chelkowski, Peter J. 'Iconography of the Women of Karbala: Tiles, Murals, Stamps, and Posters'. In Aghaie, *Women of Karbala*, 119–39.

Choksy, Jamsheed K. *Evil, Good, and Gender: Facets of the Feminine in Zoroastrian Religious History*. New York: Peter Lang, 2002.

Clancy-Smith, Julia. 'The Shaykh and His Daughter: Coping in Colonial Algeria'. In *Struggle and Survival in the Modern Middle East*, edited by Edmund Burke III and David N. Yaghoubian, 119–36. Berkeley: University of California Press, 2006.

Clohessy, Christopher Paul. *Fatima, Daughter of Muhammad*. Piscataway, NJ: Gorgias Press, 2013.

Collier, Jane Fishburne and Sylvia Junko Yanagisako, eds. *Gender and Kinship: Essays Toward a Unified Analysis*. Stanford: Stanford University Press, 1987.

Collier, Jane Fishburne and Sylvia Junko Yanagisako. 'Introduction'. In Collier and Yanagisako, *Gender and Kinship*, 1–13.

Combs-Schilling, M.E. *Sacred Performances: Islam, Sexuality, and Sacrifice*. New York: Columbia University Press, 1989.

Connor, Carolyn L. *Women of Byzantium*. New Haven: Yale University Press, 2004.

Corbin, Henri. *Terre Céleste et Corps de Résurrection: De l'Iran Mazdéen à l'Iran Shīʿite*. Translated by Nancy Pearson as *Spiritual Body and Celestial Earth: From Mazdean Iran to Shīʿite Iran*. Princeton: Princeton University Press, 1977.

Cortese, Delia and Simonetta Calderini. *Women and the Fatimids in the World of Islam*. Edinburgh: Edinburgh University Press, 2006.

Coulson, Noel J. *A History of Islamic Law*. Edinburgh: Edinburgh University Press, 1964.

Coulson, Noel J. *Succession in the Muslim Family*. Cambridge: Cambridge University Press, 1971.

Daftary, Farhad. 'Ṣayyida Ḥurra: The Ismāʿīlī Ṣulayḥid Queen of Yemen'. In Hambly, *Women in the Medieval Islamic World*, 117–30.

Dakake, Maria. 'Ḥojjat'. In Yarshater, *EIr*. Article published 15 December 2004. Last updated 23 March 2012, http://www.iranicaonline.org/articles/hojjat.

Dale, Stephen F. 'Empires and Emporia: Palace, Mosque, Market, and Tomb in Istanbul, Isfahan, Agra, and Delhi'. *Journal of the Economic and Social History of the Orient* 53 (2010): 212–29.

Daryaee, Touraj. *Sasanian Persia: The Rise and Fall of an Empire*. London: I.B. Tauris, 2009.

Deeb, Lara Z. 'From Mourning to Activism: Sayyedeh Zaynab, Lebanese Shiʿi Women, and the Transformation of Ashura'. In Aghaie, *Women of Karbala*, 241–66.

Delaney, Carol. 'The Meaning of Paternity and the Virgin Birth Debate'. *Man* 21, no. 3 (1986): 494–513.

Doostkhah, Jalil. 'Homāy Čehrzād'. In Yarshater, *EIr*. Article published 15 December 2004. Last updated 23 March 2012, http://www.iranicaonline.org/articles/homay-cehrzad.

Elias, Jamal. 'Female and Feminine in Islamic Mysticism'. *The Muslim World* 77 (1988): 209–24.

Elfira, Mina. 'Kinship, Descent Systems: East Asia, Southeast Asia, Australia, and the Pacific'. In Joseph, *EWIC*, 2: 331–4.

Eller, Cynthia. *The Myth of Matriarchal Prehistory: Why an Invented Past Won't Give Women A Future*. Boston: Beacon Press, 2000.

Emrani, Haleh. 'Like Father, Like Daughter: Late Sasanian Imperial Ideology and the Rise of Bōrān to Power,' *e-Sasanika* 5 (2009): 1–16, https://www.sasanika.org/wp-content/uploads/e-sasanika5-Emrani.pdf.

Encyclopaedia of Islam, 2nd ed. CD-ROM, version 1.1. (*EI*²)

Ernst, Carl. *How to Read the Qur'an: A New Guide, with Select Translations*. Chapel Hill: University of North Carolina Press, 2011.

Ernst, Carl. *Sufism: An Introduction to the Mystical Tradition of Islam*. Boston: Shambhala, 2011.

Esack, Farid. *The Qur'an: A User's Guide*. Oxford: Oneworld Publications, 2005.

Fadlallah, M.H. *The Infallible Fatimah: A Role Model for Men and Women*. Beirut: Dar al-Malak, 2002.

Fancy, Nahyan. 'Generation in Medieval Islamic Medicine'. In *Reproduction: From Antiquity to the Present*, edited by Nick Hopwood, Rebecca Flemming, and Lauren Kassell. Cambridge: Cambridge University Press, forthcoming.

Farrin, Raymond. *Structure and Qur'anic Interpretation: A Study of Symmetry and Coherence in Islam's Holy Text*. Ashland, OR: White Cloud Press, 2014.

Fayazi, Hamed. 'Rashid al-Din's Interpretation of Surat al-Kawthar'. *The Muslim World* 102 (2012): 284–307.

Feder, Rachel Kantz. 'Fatima's Revolutionary Image in *Fadak fi al-Ta'rikh* (1955): The Inception of Muhammad al-Sadr's Activism'. *British Journal of Middle Eastern Studies* 41, no. 1 (2014): 79–96.

Ferdows, Adele. 'The Status and Rights of Women in Ithna 'Ashari Shi'i Islam'. In *Women and the Family in Iran*, edited by Asghar Fathi, 13–36. Leiden: Brill, 1985.

Foltz, Richard. *Religions of Iran: From Prehistory to the Present*. London: Oneworld, 2013.

Friedl, Erika Loeffler. 'Inheritance: Contemporary Practice: Iran and Afghanistan'. In Joseph, *EWIC*, 2: 302–3.

Frye, Richard N. 'Women in Pre-Islamic Central Asia: The Khātūn of Bukhara. In Hambly, *Women in the Medieval Islamic World*, 55–68.

Gabbay, Alyssa. *Islamic Tolerance: Amīr Khusraw and Pluralism*. Abingdon: Routledge, 2010.

Gabbay, Alyssa. 'Rebels, Virtuous Adorers and Successors: The Agentic Daughters of the Shahnama'. In *Shahnama Studies III: The Reception of Firdausi's Shāhnāma*, edited by Gabrielle van den Berg and Charles Melville, 293–313. Leiden: Brill, 2018.

Gabbay, Alyssa, and Julia Clancy-Smith, eds. Special issue on 'Fathers and Daughters in Islam: Spiritual and Inheritance and Succession Politics', *The Journal of Persianate Studies* 4, no. 1 (2011).

Gadelrab, Sherry Sayed. 'Discourses on Sex Differences in Medieval Scholarly Islamic Thought'. *History of Medicine and Allied Sciences* 66, no. 1 (2011): 40–81.

Gholsorkhi, Shohreh. 'Pari Khan Khanum: A Masterful Safavid Princess'. *Iranian Studies* 28, nos. 3/4 (1995): 143–56.

Gleave, Robert. '"She Should Not Raise Her Voice When Amongst Men": Imāmī Arguments against (and for) Women Judges'. In Künkler and Stewart, *Female Religious Authority in Shi'i Islam*, forthcoming.

Goldziher, Ignác, Cornelis van Arendonk, and Arthur Stanley Tritton. 'Ahl al-Bayt'. In *EI*[2].

Gorgi, Monir. 'The Sermon of Fatima Zahra (AS)'. *Farzaneh: Journal of Women's Studies and Research in Iran and Muslim Countries* 3, no. 8 (1997), http://www.islamwomen.org/pages/view/viewDoc2.aspx?gel=26&sel=80221&langid=2.

Gorgi, Monir and Massoumeh Ebtekar. 'The Life and Status of Fatima Zahra: A Woman's Image of Excellence'. *Farzaneh: Journal of Women's Studies and Research in Iran and Muslim Countries* 3, no. 8 (1997): 1–10, https://tinyurl.com/y8vuohdo.

Gristwood, Sarah. *Game of Queens: The Women Who Made Sixteenth-Century Europe*. New York: Basic Books, 2016.

Guy, Michelle Lee. 'Sexualities: Transvestism: Overview'. In Joseph, *EWIC*, 3: 418–20.

Habibullah, A.B.M. 'Sulṭanah Rāziah', *The Indian Historical Quarterly* 16, no. 4 (1940): 750–72.

Haitami, Meriam el-. 'Restructuring Female Religious Authority: State-Sponsored Women Religious Guides (*Murshidat*) and Scholars (*'Alimat*) in Contemporary Morocco', *Mediterranean Studies* 20, no. 2 (2012): 227–40.

Hambly, Gavin, ed. *Women in the Medieval Islamic World: Power, Patronage, and Piety*. New York: St. Martin's Press, 1998.

Hennigan, Peter C. *The Birth of a Legal Institution: The Formation of the Waqf in Third-Century A.H. Ḥanafī Legal Discourse*. Leiden: Brill, 2004.

Hermansen, Marcia. 'Fatimeh as a Role Model in the Works of Ali Shari'ati'. In *Women and Revolution in Iran*, edited by Guity Nashat, 87–96. Boulder: Westview Press, 1983.

Herrin, Judith. 'The Imperial Feminine in Byzantium'. *Past & Present* 169 (2000): 3–35.

Hinds, Martin. 'Mu'āwiya I'. In *EI*².

Hodgson, Marshall G.S. *The Venture of Islam: Conscience and History in a World Civilization*. 3 vols. Chicago: University of Chicago Press, 1974.

Holum, Kenneth G. *Theodosian Empresses: Women and Imperial Dominion in Late Antiquity*. Berkeley: University of California Press, 1982.

Hoodfar, Homa. 'Divorce and Custody: Contemporary Practices: Iran and Afghanistan'. In Joseph, *EWIC*, 2: 105–6.

Horovitz, Josef and Louis Gardet. 'Kawthar'. In *EI*².

Hotchkiss, Valerie R. *Clothes Make the Man: Female Cross Dressing in Medieval Europe*. New York: Garland, 1996.

Hyder, Syed Akbar. 'Sayyedeh Zaynab: The Conqueror of Damascus and Beyond'. In Aghaie, *Women of Karbala*, 161–81.

Imber, Colin. 'The Ottoman Dynastic Myth'. *Turcica* 19 (1987): 7–27.

Isom-Verhaaren, Christine. 'Süleyman and Mihrimah: The Favorite's Daughter'. *Journal of Persianate Studies* 4, no. 1 (2011): 64–85.

Jackson, Peter. *The Delhi Sultanate: A Political and Military History*. Cambridge: Cambridge University Press, 1999.

Jackson, Peter. 'Sulṭān Raḍiyya bint Iltutmish'. In Hambly, *Women in the Medieval Islamic World*, 181–97.

Jamil, Tariq al-. 'Ibn Taymiyya and Ibn al-Mutahhar al-Hilli: Shi'i Polemics and the Struggle for Religious Authority in Medieval Islam'. In *Ibn Taymiyya and His Times*, edited by Yossef Rapoport and Shahab Ahmed, 229–46. Oxford: Oxford University Press, 2010.

Jay, Nancy. *Throughout Your Generations Forever: Sacrifice, Religion, and Paternity*. Chicago: University of Chicago Press, 1992.

Joseph, Suad. 'History and Its Histories: Story-Making and the Present'. *Review of Middle East Studies* 46, no. 2 (2012): 6–22.

Joseph, Suad, ed. *Encyclopaedia of Women and Islamic Cultures* (*EWIC*). 5 vols. Leiden: Brill, 2003–2007.

Kashani-Sabet, Firoozeh. 'Who Is Fatima? Gender, Culture, and Representation in Islam'. *Journal of Middle East Women's Studies* 1, no. 2 (2005): 1–24.

Kearns, Cleo McNelly. *The Virgin Mary, Monotheism, and Sacrifice*. Cambridge: Cambridge University Press, 2008.

Kechichian, Joseph A. *Succession in Saudi Arabia*. New York: Palgrave, 2001.

Keddie, Nikki R. *Women in the Middle East: Past and Present*. Princeton: Princeton University Press, 2007.

Keddie, Nikki R. and Beth Baron. *Women in Middle Eastern History: Shifting Boundaries in Sex and Gender*. New Haven: Yale University Press, 1992.

Khaleghi Motlagh, Djalal. *Frauen im Schahname*. Translated by Brigitte Neuenschwander as *Women in the Shāhnāmeh: Their History and Social Status within the Framework of Ancient and Medieval Sources*. Costa Mesa: Mazda, 2012.

King, Diane E. 'Kinship and State: Arab States'. In Joseph, *EWIC*, 2: 347–9.

Klemm, Verena. 'Image Formation of an Islamic Legend: Fāṭima, The Daughter of the Prophet Muḥammad'. In *Ideas, Images, and Methods of Portrayal: Insights into Classical Arabic Literature and Islam*, edited by Sebastian Günther, 181–208. Leiden: Brill, 2005.

Kohlberg, Etan. 'Kolayni'. In Yarshater, *EIr*. Article published 20 July 2004, http://www.iranicaonline.org/articles/kolayni.

Kohlberg, Etan. 'The Term Muḥaddath in Twelver Shīʿism'. In *Belief and Law in Imāmī Shīʿism*. Hampshire: Variorum, 1991.

Kozlowski, Gregory C. 'Imperial Authority, Benefactions and Endowments (*Awqāf*) in Mughal India'. *Journal of the Economic and Social History of the Orient* 38, no. 3 (1995): 355–70.

Kozlowski, Gregory C. 'Muslim Women and the Control of Property in North India'. *The Indian Economic and Social History Review* 24, no. 2 (1987): 163–81.

Kueny, Kathryn. *Conceiving Identities: Maternity in Medieval Muslim Discourse and Practice*. Albany: State University of New York Press, 2013.

Künkler, Mirjam. 'The Life of Two *Mujtahidahs*: Female Religious Authority in 20th Century Iran'. In Bano and Kalmbach, *Women, Leadership, and Mosques*, 127–60.

Künkler, Mirjam and Devin Stewart, eds. *Female Religious Authority in Shiʿi Islam: Past and Present*. Edinburgh: Edinburgh University Press, forthcoming.

Kuran, Timur. 'The Provision of Public Goods under Islamic Law: Origins, Impact, and Limitations of the Waqf System'. *Law & Society Review* 35, no. 4 (2001): 841–98.

Kuru, Selim. 'Representations: Poetry and Prose, Premodern: Turkish'. In Joseph, *EWIC*, 5: 493–8.

Laiou, Angeliki. *Gender, Society and Economic Life in Byzantium*. Aldershot, Hampshire: Variorum, 1992.

Laiou, Angeliki. *Women, Family, and Society in Byzantium*. Farnham, Surrey: Ashgate, 2011.

Lal, Ruby. *Domesticity and Power in the Early Mughal World*. Cambridge: Cambridge University Press, 2005.

Lammens, Henri. *Fatima et les Filles de Mahomet*. Rome: Sumptibus Pontifcii Instituti Biblici, 1912.

Lawson, Todd. 'The Authority of the Feminine and Fatima's Place in an Early Work by the Bab'. *Journal of Baha'i Studies* 1 (2007): 137–70.

Layish, Aharon. 'Mīrāth: In Modern Islamic Countries'. In *EI*[2].

Lukito, Ranto. 'Law: Customary: Indonesia'. In Joseph, *EWIC*, 2: 419–21.

Madelung, Wilferd. 'Abd-Al-Ḥamīd b. Abu'l-Ḥadīd'. In Yarshater, *EI*[r]. Article published 15 December 1982. Last updated 14 July 2011, http://www.iranicaonline.org/articles/abd-al-hamid-b-abul-hadid.

Madelung, Wilferd. Introduction to *The Study of Shi'i Islam: History, Theology and Law*, 3–16. Edited by Farhad Daftary and Gordofarid Miskinzoda. London: I.B. Tauris, 2014.

Madelung, Wilferd. 'Shi'i Attitudes toward Women as Reflected in Fiqh'. In *Society and the Sexes in Medieval Islam*, edited by Afaf Lutfi al-Sayyid-Marsot, 69–79. Malibu: Undena Publications 1979.

Madelung, Wilferd. *The Succession to Muhammad: A Study of the Early Caliphate*. Cambridge: Cambridge University Press, 1997.

Mahendrarajah, Shivan. 'The Shrine of Shaykh Aḥmad-i Jām: Notes on a Revised Chronology and a Waqfiyya'. *Iran* 50 (2012): 145–8.

Mahmood, Saba. 'Feminist Theory, Embodiment, and the Docile Agent: Some Reflections on the Egyptian Islamic Revival'. *Cultural Anthropology* 16, no. 2 (May 2001): 202–36.

Mahmood, Saba. *Politics of Piety: The Islamic Revival and the Feminist Subject*. Princeton: Princeton University Press, 2004.

Malandra, William W. 'Zoroastrianism: Historical Review up to the Arab Conquest'. In Yarshater, *EI*[r]. Article published 20 July 2005, http://www.iranicaonline.org/articles/zoroastrianism-i-historical-review.

Manz, Beatrice Forbes. 'Gowhar-Sād Āḡā'. In Yarshater, *EI*[r]. Article published 15 December 2002; updated 17 February 2012, http://www.iranicaonline.org/articles/gowhar-sad-aga.

McAuliffe, Jane Dammen. 'Chosen of All Women: Mary and Fatima in Qur'anic Exegesis'. *Islamochristiana* 7 (1981): 19–28.

McAuliffe, Jane Dammen, ed. *Encyclopaedia of the Qur'an (EQ)*. Leiden: Brill, 2005. CD-ROM.

Meeker, Michael. 'The Black Sea Turks: A Study of Honor, Descent and Marriage'. PhD diss., University of Chicago, 1970.

Meisami. Julie Scott. 'Fitnah or Azadah? Nizami's Ethical Poetic'. *Edebiyāt* 1, no. 2 (1989): 41–75.

Meriwether, Margaret L. *The Kin Who Count: Family and Society in Ottoman Aleppo, 1770–1840*. Austin: University of Texas Press, 1999.

Meriwether, Margaret L. 'Women and *Waqf* Revisited: The Case of Aleppo, 1770–1840'. In *Women in the Ottoman Empire: Middle Eastern Women in the Early Modern Era*, edited by Madeline C. Zilfi, 128–52. Leiden: Brill, 1997.

Meriwether, Margaret L. and Judith E. Tucker, eds. *A Social History of Women and Gender in the Modern Middle East*. Boulder: Westview Press, 1999.

Mernissi, Fatima. *Beyond the Veil: Male-Female Dynamics in Muslim Society*. Cambridge, MA: Schenkman Publishing, 1975.

Mernissi, Fatima. *Le Harem Politique*. Translated by Mary Jo Lakeland as *The Veil and the Male Elite: A Feminist Interpretation of* Women's *Rights in Islam*. New York: Basic Books, 1991.

Mernissi, Fatima. *Sultanés Oubliées: Femmes Chefs d'État en Islam*. Translated by Mary Jo Lakeland as *The Forgotten Queens of Islam*. Minneapolis: University of Minnesota Press, 1993.

Mīlānī, Fāḍl al-Husaynī al-. *Fatima al-Zahra': Umm Abīhā*. Najaf: Maktabat al-Ṣādiq, 1968.

Mir-Hosseini, Ziba. 'Beyond "Islam" vs. "Feminism"'. *IDS Bulletin* 42, no. 1 (2011): 67–77.

Mir-Hosseini, Ziba. *Islam and Gender: The Religious Debate in Contemporary Iran*. Princeton: Princeton University Press, 1999.

Mir-Hosseini, Ziba, Mulki al-Sharmani, and Jana Rumminger, eds. *Men in Charge? Rethinking Authority in Muslim Legal Tradition*. London: Oneworld Publications, 2015.

Mirza, Mohammad Wahid. *Life and Works of Amir Khusrau*. Lahore: Panjab University Press, 1962.

Mohammadi, Adeel. 'The Ambiguity of Maternal Filiation (*nasab*) in Early and Medieval Islam'. *The Graduate Journal of Harvard Divinity School* 11 (Spring 2016), http://projects.iq.harvard.edu/files/hdsjournal/files/journal.final_.content.2016.pdf.

Moin, A. Azfar. *The Millenial Sovereign: Sacred Kingship and Sainthood in Islam*. New York: Columbia University Press, 2012.

Momen, Moojan. *An Introduction to Shi'i Islam: The History and Doctrines of Twelver Shi'ism*. New Haven: Yale University Press, 1985.

Momen, Moojan. 'Women: In Shi'ism'. In Yarshater, *EIr*. Article published 11 February 2011. Last updated 4 December 2012, http://www.iranicaonline.org/articles/women-shiism.

Moors, Annelies. 'Debating Islamic Family Law: Legal Texts and Social Practices'. In Meriwether, *A Social History*, 141–75.

Moors, Annelies. 'Inheritance: Contemporary Practice: Arab States'. In Joseph, *EWIC*, 2: 299–302.

Moosa, Ebrahim. '"The Child Belongs to the Bed": Illegitimacy and Islamic Law'. In *Questionable Issue: Illegitimacy in South Africa*, edited by Sandra Burman and Eleanor Preston-White, 171–84. Cape Town: Oxford University Press, 1992.

Mudarrisī Ṭabāṭabā'ī, Husayn. *Turbat-i pākān*. 2 vols. Qum: Chāpkhāna-yi Mihr, 1976.

Mukherjee, Siddhartha. *The Gene: An Intimate History*. New York: Scribner, 2016.

Musallam, Basim. 'Avicenna: Medicine and Biology'. In Yarshater, *EIr*. Article published 15 December 1987. Last updated 18 August 2011, http://www.iranicaonline.org/articles/avicenna-x.

Musallam, Basim. *Sex and Society in Islam: Birth Control before the Nineteenth Century*. Cambridge: Cambridge University Press, 1983.

Musawah. *Women's Stories, Women's Lives: Male Authority in Muslim Contexts*. Kuala Lumpur?: Musawah, 2016, http://www.musawah.org/women%E2%80%99s-stories-women%E2%80%99s-lives-male-authority-muslim-contexts-0.

Nadwi, Mohammad Akram. *Al-Muḥaddithāt; The Women Scholars in Islam*. 2nd ed. Oxford: Interface Publications, 2014.

Najmabadi, Afsaneh. 'Power, Morality, and the New Muslim Womanhood'. In *The Politics of Social Transformation in Afghanistan, Iran, and Pakistan*, edited by Myron Weiner and Ali Banuazizi, 366–89. Syracuse: Syracuse University Press, 1994.

Najmabadi, Afsaneh. *Women with Mustaches and Men without Beards: Gender and Sexual Anxieties of Iranian Modernity*. Berkeley: University of California Press, 2005.

Nasr, Seyyed Hossein. 'Shi'ism and Sufism'. In *Shi'ism: Doctrines, Thought and Spirituality*, edited by Seyyed Hossein Nasr, Hamid Dabashi, and Seyyed Vali Reza Nasr, 101–8. Albany: State University of New York Press, 1988.

Nasr, Seyyed Hossein, Caner K. Dagli, Maria Massi Dakake, Joseph E.B. Lumbard, and Mohammed Rustom, eds. *The Study Qur'an: A New Translation and Commentary*. New York: HarperCollins, 2015.

Necipoğlu, Gülru. *The Age of Sinan: Architectural Culture in the Ottoman Empire*. Princeton: Princeton University Press, 2005.

Neuwirth, Angelika. 'The House of Abraham and the House of Amram: Genealogy, Patriarchal Authority, and Exegetical Professionalism'. In *The Qur'an in Context:*

Historical and Literary Investigations into the Qur'ānic Milieu, edited by Michael Marx Neuwirth and Nicolai Sinai, 499–531. Leiden: Brill, 2010.

Newman, Andrew J. *The Formative Period of Twelver Shī'ism: Ḥadith as Discourse Between Qum and Baghdad*. Richmond, Surrey: Curzon Press, 2000.

Ordoni, Abū Muhammad. *Fatima the Gracious*. Qum: Anṣāriyān, 1987?, https://www.al-islam.org/fatima-the-gracious-abu-muhammad-ordoni.

Osman, Rawand. *Female Personalities in the Qur'an and Sunna: Examining the Major Sources of Imami Shi'i Islam*. Abingdon: Routledge, 2015.

Pārsādust, Manučehr. 'Pari̱kān Ḵānom'. In Yarshater, *EIr*. Article published 20 July 2009.

Peirce, Leslie. *The Imperial Harem: Women and Sovereignty in the Ottoman Empire*. Oxford: Oxford University Press, 1993.

Perikhanian, Anahit. 'Iranian Society and Law'. In *The Cambridge History of Iran*, edited by Ehsan Yarshater, 627–80. Vol. 3 (2), *The Seleucid, Parthian and Sasanian Periods*. Cambridge: Cambridge University Press, 1983.

Petry, Carl F. 'Class Solidarity versus Gender Gain: Women as Custodians of Property in Later Medieval Egypt'. In Keddie and Baron, *Women in Middle Eastern History*, 122–42.

Petry, Carl F. 'Al-Sakhāwī'. In *EI*[2].

Pfluger-Schindlbeck, Ingrid. 'Kinship, Descent Systems and State: The Caucasus'. In Joseph, *EWIC*, 2: 336–8.

Pick, Lucy K. *Her Father's Daughter: Gender, Power, and Religion in the Early Spanish Kingdoms*. Ithaca: Cornell University Press, 2017.

Pierce, Matthew. 'Remembering Fatimah: New Means of Legitimizing Female Authority in Contemporary Shi'i Discourse'. In Bano and Kalmbach, *Women, Leadership, and Mosques*, 345–62.

Pierce, Matthew. *Twelve Infallible Men*. Cambridge: Harvard University Press, 2016.

Pinault, David. 'Zaynab bint 'Alī and the Place of the Women of the Households of the First Imāms in Shī'ite Devotional Literature'. In Hambly, *Women in the Medieval Islamic World*, 69–98.

Pollack, Daniel, Moshe Bleich, Charles J. Reid, Jr., and Mohammad H. Fadel. 'Classical Religious Perspectives of Adoption Law'. *Notre Dame Law Review* 79, no. 2 (2004): 101–58.

Pourshariati, Parvaneh. *Decline and Fall of the Sasanian Empire: The Sasanian-Parthian Confederacy and the Arab Conquest of Iran*. London: I.B. Tauris, 2008.

Powers, David S. *Studies in Qur'an and Ḥadīth: The Formation of the Islamic Law of Inheritance*. Berkeley: University of California Press, 1986.

Prusak, Bernard P. 'Woman: Seductive Siren and Source of Sin?' In *Religion and Sexism: Images of Women in the Jewish and Christian Traditions*, edited by Rosemary Radford Ruether, 89–116. New York: Simon and Schuster, 1974.

Qāḍī, Wadād al-. 'Biographical Dictionaries: Inner Structure and Cultural Significance'. In *The Book in the Islamic World: The Written Word and Communication in the Middle East*, edited by George N. Atiyeh, 93–122. Albany: State University of New York Press, 1995.

Rizvi, Kishwar. 'Gendered Patronage: Women and Benevolence during the Early Safavid Empire'. In *Women, Patronage, and Self-Representation in Islamic Societies*, edited by D. Fairchild Ruggles, 123–53. Albany: State University of New York Press, 2000.

Robins, Gay. *Women in Ancient Egypt*. Cambridge: Harvard University Press, 1993.

Robinson, Neal. 'Jesus'. In McAuliffe, *EQ*.

Roded, Ruth. *Women in Islamic Biographical Collections: From Ibn Sa'd to Who's Who*. Boulder: Lynne Rienner, 1994.

Roemer, Hans Robert. 'The Türkmen Dynasties'. In *The Cambridge History of Iran*, edited by Peter Jackson and Laurence Lockhart, 147–88. Vol. 6, *The Timurid and Safavid Periods*. Cambridge: Cambridge University Press, 1986.

Rose, Jenny. 'Three Queens, Two Wives, and a Goddess: Roles and Images of Women in Sasanian Iran'. In Hambly, *Women in the Medieval Islamic World*, 29–54.

Rubin, Uri. '"Al-Walad li-l-Firāsh" on the Islamic Campaign against "Zinā"'. *Studia Islamica* 78 (1993): 5–26.

Rubin, Uri. 'Nūr Muḥammadī'. In *EI*².

Rubin, Uri. 'Pre-existence and Light: Aspects of the Concept of Nūr Muḥammad'. *Israel Oriental Studies* 5 (1975): 62–119.

Ruffle, Karen. 'May Fatimah Gather Our Tears: The Mystical and Intercessory Powers of Fatimah al-Zahra in Indo-Persian, Shi'i Devotional Literature and Performance'. *Comparative Studies of South Asia, Africa and the Middle East* 30, no. 3 (2010): 386–97.

Ruffle, Karen. 'May You Learn from Their Model: The Exemplary Father-Daughter Relationship of Mohammad and Fatima in South Asian Shi 'ism'. *Journal of Persianate Studies* 4, no. 1 (2011): 12–29.

Sabbaghi, Maryam. 'The Court Poet and the Lady Patron: Muḥtasham Kāshānī's Illustration of Parī Khān Khānum'. Paper presented at the Annual Meeting of the Middle East Studies Association, Washington, DC, November 2014.

Sakurai, Keiko. 'Making Qom a Centre of Shi'i Scholarship: Al-Mustafa International University'. In *Shaping Global Islamic Discourses: The Role of al-Azhar, al-Madinah and al-Mustafa*, edited by Masooda Bano and Keiko Sakurai, 41–72. Edinburgh: Edinburgh University Press, 2015.

Sakurai, Keiko. 'Women's Empowerment and Iranian-style Seminaries in Iran and Pakistan'. In *The Moral Economy of the Madrasa: Islam and Education Today*, edited by Keiko Sakurai and Fariba Adelkhah, 32–58. Abingdon: Routledge, 2011.

Satrapi, Marjane. *Persepolis 2: The Story of a Return*. Translated by Anjali Singh. New York: Pantheon Press, 2004.

Schacht, Joseph. 'Mīrāth: In Pre-Modern Times'. In *EI²*.

Schibanoff, Susan. 'True Lies: Transvestism and Idolatry in the Trial of Joan of Arc'. In *Fresh Verdicts on Joan of Arc*, edited by Bonnie Wheeler and Charles T. Wood, 42–53. New York: Garland, 1996.

Schilcher, Linda Schatkowski. 'The Lore and Reality of Middle Eastern Patriarchy'. *Die Welt des Islams*, new series 28, no. 1 (1988): 496–512.

Schimmel, Annemarie. *Meine Seele ist eine Frau: Das Weibliche im Islam*. Translated by Susan H. Ray as *My Soul is a Woman: The Feminine in Islam*. New York: Continuum, 1997.

Schmucker, Werner. 'Mubāhala'. In *EI²*.

Schwarz, Florian. 'An Endowment Deed of 1547 (953 h.) for a Kubravi Khanaqah in Samarqand'. In *Die Grenzen Der Welt: Arabica et Iranica ad honorem Heinz Gaube*, edited by Lorenz Korn, Eva Orthmann and Florian Schwarz, 189–209. Weisbaden: Reichert Verlage, 2008.

Shaikh, Sa'diyya. 'In Search of *al-Insān*: Sufism, Islamic Law, and Gender'. *Journal of the American Academy of Religion* 77, no. 4 (2009): 781–822.

Shaikh, Sa'diyya. *Sufi Narratives of Intimacy: Ibn 'Arabī, Gender, and Sexuality*. Chapel Hill: University of North Carolina Press, 2012.

Sharī'atī, 'Ali. '*Fatima Fatima* Ast' (Fatima is Fatima). In *Shariati on Shariati and the Muslim Woman*, edited and translated by Laleh Bakhtiari, 75–213. USA: ABC International Group, 1996.

Sharon, Moshe. *Black Banners from the East*. Jerusalem: Magnes Press, 1983.

Sharon, Moshe. 'The Development of the Debate Around the Legitimacy of Authority in Early Islam'. *Jerusalem Studies in Arabic and Islam* 5 (1984): 121–41.

Shatzmiller, Maya. *Her Day in Court: Women's Property Rights in Islamic Law and Society*. Cambridge: Harvard University Press, 2007.

Shirazi, Faegheh. 'The Daughters of Karbala: Images of Women in Popular Shi'i Culture in Iran'. In Aghaie, *Women of Karbala*, 93–118.

Shively, Kim. 'Kinship and State: The Ottoman Empire'. In Joseph, *EWIC*, 2: 349–51.

Sinai, Nicolai. 'An Interpretation of Sūrat al-Najm (Q. 53)'. *Journal of Qur'anic Studies* 13, no. 2 (2011): 1–28.

Soucek, Priscilla P. 'Tīmūrid Women: A Cultural Perspective'. In Hambly, *Women in the Medieval Islamic World*, 199–226.

Soufi, Denise L. 'The Image of Fatima in Classical Muslim Thought'. PhD diss., Princeton University, 1997.

Spellberg, Denise A. *Politics, Gender, and the Islamic Past: The Legacy of 'A'isha bint Abi Bakr*. New York: Columbia University Press, 1994.

Spellberg, Denise A. 'The Politics of Praise: Depictions of Khadija, Fatima and 'A'isha in Ninth-Century Muslim Sources'. *Literature East & West* 26 (1990): 130–48.
Steigerwald, Diana. 'Twelver Shi'i Ta'wīl'. In *The Blackwell Companion to the Qur'an*, edited by Andrew Rippin, 373–85. Malden, MA: Blackwell, 2006.
Stetkyvich, Suzanne Pinckney. *The Mute Immortals Speak: Pre-Islamic Poetry and the Poetics of Ritual*. Ithaca: Cornell University Press, 1993.
Stowasser, Barbara Freyer. 'Mary'. In McAuliffe, *EQ*.
Stowasser, Barbara Freyer. *Women in the Qur'an, Traditions, and Interpretation*. New York: Oxford University Press, 1994.
Strathern, Marilyn. 'Producing Difference: Connections and Disconnections in Two New Guinea Highland Kinship Systems'. In Collier and Yanagisako, *Gender and Kinship*, 271–300.
Subtelny, Maria. *Timurids in Transition: Turko-Persian Politics and Acculturation in Medieval Iran*. Leiden: Brill, 2007.
Szanto, Edith. 'Speaking in the Name of Zaynab: Female Shi'i Religious Authority in Syria'. In Künkler and Stewart, *Female Religious Authority in Shi'i Islam*, forthcoming.
Szuppe, Maria. 'Status, Knowledge, and Politics: Women in Sixteenth-Century Safavid Iran'. In *Women in Iran from the Rise of Islam to 1800*, edited by Guity Nashat and Lois Beck, 140–69. Urbana: University of Illinois Press, 2003.
Takim, Liyakat N. *The Heirs of the Prophet: Charisma and Religious Authority in Shi'ite Islam*. Albany: State University of New York Press, 2006.
Takim, Liyakat N. 'Law: The Four Sunnī Schools of Law'. In Joseph, *EWIC*, 2: 440–5.
Takim, Liyakat N. 'Law: Other Schools of Family Law'. In Joseph, *EWIC*, 2: 446–9.
Thomas, Edward. *The Chronicles of the Pathán Kings of Delhi*. London: Trübner and Co., 1871.
Thurlkill, Mary F. *Chosen Among Women: Mary and Fatima in Medieval Christianity and Shi'ite Islam*. Notre Dame: University of Notre Dame Press, 2007.
Tillion, Germaine. *Le Harem et Les Cousins*, Translated by Quintin Hoare as *The Republic of Cousins: Women's Oppression in Mediterranean Society*. London: Al Saqi Books, 1983.
Toorawa, Shawkat M. *Ibn Abi Tahir Tayfur and Arabic Writerly Culture: A Ninth-Century Bookman in Baghdad*. Abingdon: RoutledgeCurzon, 2005.
Tritton, Arthur Stanley. 'Ahl al-Kisā''. In *EI*².
Tucker, Judith E. 'Pensée 2: We've Come a Long Way, Baby – But We've Got a Long Way to Go'. *International Journal of Middle East Studies* 40, no. 1 (2008): 19–21.
Tucker, Judith E. *Themes in Islamic Law: Women, Family, and Gender in Islamic Law*. Cambridge: Cambridge University Press, 2008.
Tucker, Judith E. *Ties That Bound: Women and Family in Eighteenth- and Nineteenth-Century Nablus*. In Keddie and Baron, *Women in Middle Eastern History*, 233–53.

Tucker, Judith E. *Women in Nineteenth-Century Egypt*. Cambridge: Cambridge University Press, 1985.

Üçok, Bahriye. *Female Sovereigns in Islamic States*. Edited and translated by Milena Rampoldi. Berlin: epubli GmbH, 2014.

'Uṭāridī, 'Azīz Allah. *Tārīkh-i Āstān-i Quds-i Rażavī*. 2 vols. Tehran: Sāzmān-i Chāp va Intishārāt-i Vizārat-i Farhang va Irshād-i Islāmī, 1992.

Veccia Vaglieri, Laura. 'Fadak'. In *EI*².

Veccia Vaglieri, Laura. 'Fāṭima'. In *EI*².

Wadud, Amina. *Qur'an and Woman: Rereading the Sacred Text from a Woman's Perspective*. Oxford: Oxford University Press, 1999.

Walker, Paul E. 'The Fatimid Caliph al-'Aziz and His Daughter Sitt al-Mulk: A Case of Delayed but Eventual Succession to Rule by a Woman'. *Journal of Persianate Studies* 4, no. 1 (2011): 30–44.

Watt, W. Montgomery. *Muhammad at Medina*. Oxford: Oxford University Press, 1956.

Werner, Christoph. 'Ein Vaqf für meine Töchter: Ḥātūn Bēgum und die Qarā Quyūnlū Stiftungen zur 'Blauen Moschee' in Tabriz'. *Der Islam* 80: 94–109.

Whyte, Martin King. *The Status of Women in Preindustrial Societies*. Princeton: Princeton University Press, 1978.

Wright, H. Nelson. *The Coinage and Metrology of the Sultans of Delhi: Incorporating a Catalogue of the Coins in the Author's Cabinet Now in the Delhi Museum*. Delhi, 1936.

Yanagisako, Sylvia Junko and Jane Fishburne Collier. 'Toward a Unified Analysis of Gender and Kinship'. In Collier and Yanagisako, *Gender and Kinship*, 14–50.

Yarshater, Ehsan, ed. *Encyclopaedia Iranica* (*EIr*) New York: Columbia University Center for Iranian Studies, 1996–, http://www.iranicaonline.org/.

Yarshater, Ehsan. 'The Persian Presence in the Islamic World'. In *The Persian Presence in the Islamic World*, edited by Richard G. Hovannisian and Georges Sabagh, 4–125. Cambridge: Cambridge University Press, 1998.

Zahraa, Mahdi and Normi A. Malek. 'The Concept of Custody in Islamic Law'. *Arab Law Quarterly* 13, no. 2 (1998): 155–77.

Index

'Abbās I (Shah) 49, 64, 179
'Abbās ibn 'Abd al-Muṭṭālib, al- 24, 36, 55, 80, 89–91
'Abbāsid Empire 24, 36, 38, 47, 55, 57–8, 91–2, 95–6, 156, 163
'Abd Allah ibn 'Abd al-Muṭṭālib 31, 41, 55
'Abd al-Muṭṭālib 55
Abraham (Ibrāhīm) 27–8, 32–3, 37–9, 44, 46, 130
Abū al-Faḍl 65–6
Abū Bakr (Caliph) 9, 11, 52, 130, 151
  and Fadak 12, 79–80, 89–96, 123, 131–2, 137
Abū Bakra 126
Abū Ṭālib 55–6
Adam 27–8, 31, 41, 44, 46, 97, 130, 136, 139
Afaq Begum 109
Afghanistan 184
agency, female 147, 164
  and chastity 8, 46, 138–9
  expanded views of 7–8, 18, 25
  and Fatima al-Zahra (*see under* Fatima al-Zahra)
  and inheritance 80, 103–19
  and Virgin Mary (*see under* Virgin Mary)
agnates 82, 86–7, 96, 100, 103, 118, 186, *see also* *'aṣaba*
ahl al-bayt 26, 28–9, 47, 134, 136–7, 153, 157, 162, 196 n.65
ahl al-farā'id 86
ahl al-kisā', *see* cloak, hadith of the
'Ā'isha bint Abū Bakr 12, 22, 25–6, 52, 63, 89, 111, 126–8, 139, 150–1
Akbar (Emperor) 65–6, 114
Ālanquwā 65–6, 107
Aleppo 116–18
'Ali al-Riḍā (eighth imam) 108, 112
'Ali ibn Abū Ṭālib (first imam)
  ahl al-bayt, member of 26–8
  and *ashrāf* 74
  attempt to take a second wife 11, 25
  conception and birth 55–6
  conflict with Abū Bakr 11–12, 138
  conflict with 'Ā'isha 126–7
  and Fadak 89–91
  and Fatima bint Asad 34, 54–5
  and Ibn al-Ḥanafiyya 24, 51
  and inheritance 99–100, 103
  and marriage of Husayn 56–9
  marriage to Fatima al-Zahra 11
  and Muhammadan light 31–2
  and the Safavid Empire 64
  in *Siyer-i Nebī* 123–4
  and succession 9–10, 79–80, 92, 130, 134, 140–1
  and Sufism 73
  and the Timurid Empire 64
  and Umm Kulthum 52
  on women 127
  and Zaynab 153–5
Āmina 31, 41, 55, 57
Amīr Khusraw 66–73, 74, 75, 168–9, 171
'Ammār ibn Yāsir, *see* Ibn Sumayya
Anāhitā 29, 40, 58
Arabia, contemporary (Saudi Arabia) 6, 50, 185
Arabia, pre- and early Islamic 41–2, 82–5, 141, 150–1
architectural patronage, female 102, 104–14, 118–19
Aristotle 18–20, 22, 23, 66, 70–2
Arwa bint Aḥmad al-Sulayhiyya 155, 157–8, 160–3
'aṣaba 36, 79, 80, 82–7, 91–2, 97, 99–100, 115, *see also* agnates
asceticism 146–9, 152, 183
Asmā' bint Abū Bakr 52
'Aṭṭār, Farīd al-Dīn 72
Avicenna, *see* Ibn Sīnā, Abū 'Ali al-Husayn
'Ayyāshī, Abū al-Naḍr Muhammad ibn Mas'ūd al- 99–100
Āzarm Dukht (Queen) 143, 145, 164

Bābur (Emperor) 64, 169
Balāghāt al-nisā' 92–4
Banū Hāshim 36, 41, 54, 57, 92
Bāqir, al-, *see* Muhammad al-Bāqir
Battle of the Camel 126–7, 229 n.137
Beauvoir, Simone de 81
Bhutto, Benazir 186
Biḥār al-anwār 37, 54, 133–4
bilateral descent
  and ambiguity 50, 61, 66, 75
  and biographical dictionaries 49, 50–4
  in contemporary societies 184–8
  defined 2
  and Fatima al-Zahra (*see under* Fatima al-Zahra)
  and generation 18, 22–3
  in historical chronicles 49, 61–6
  and inheritance 2, 6, 7, 11, 23, 80–1, 87–8, 103–19, 134
  in legal texts 49, 73–4
  and maternal ascription 24, 36, 51–3
  in poetry of Amīr Khusraw 49, 66–72
  pre-Islamic precedents for 7, 39–42, 98, 141–51
  and the Qur'an 2, 6, 13, 18, 25–30, 32–3, 35, 37–9, 42–7, 48 (*see also under* Fatima al-Zahra; inheritance; succession)
  ramifications of 2–3, 6
  and Saudi Arabia 50
  in Shi'i and Sunni hadith collections 25–9, 30–3, 37–9, 41, 125–6, 150–1
  in Shi'i hadith collections 54–61, 79–80, 87, 92, 95, 131–4, 135–9, 153–5
  and succession 119, 153–84
  and Sufism 73
  and Virgin Mary (*see under* Virgin Mary)
Bilqīs 111, 161, 181–3
Bint al-Huda 187
biographical dictionaries 6, 13, 24, 49, 50–4, 103
Blue Mosque 102, 106
Bukhārī, Muhammad ibn Ismā'īl al- 25
Byzantine Empire 40, 48, 62, 98, 141, 146–50, 156, 160

Central Asia 62, 64, 98, 103, 105–9, 114–16, 118, 164, 167
charismatic leadership patterns 3, 116, 119, 143, 146, 148, 152, 168, 180, 187
chastity, female
  and agency (*see* agency, female)
  and the Byzantine Empire 146–50
  challenged 155, 159, 171–3, 178
  as condition for *mutawallis* 115
  and Fatima al-Zahra (*see under* Fatima al-Zahra)
  and mothers of the imams 54, 60–1
  and Niẓām al-Mulk 127
  in poetry of Amīr Khusraw 67–9, 71
  and the Prophet's origins 41
  and rulers 65, 111, 113, 148–50, 159, 174–5, 177, 180–3
  and the Safavid Empire 64, 113, 127–8, 174–5, 176–7, 180–3
  and sovereignty 14, 155, 164, 182–4
  and Virgin Mary (*see under* Virgin Mary)
  and Zaynab 154–5
Chinggiz Khān 64, 106–7
Christianity 33, 40, 146, 149, 170
Christians 27–8, 40, 43, 45, 159–60, 183
cloak 73, *see also* Hadith of the Cloak
cross-dressing 143–4, 166, 168–74, 228 n.130, *see also* gender, transcending
custody 2, 4, 5–6, 17, 18, 22–3, 50, 185, 194 n.34

daughters, *see* bilateral descent; generation; inheritance; matrilineality; succession
David (Dāwūd) 93, 132
Day of Judgement 29–31, 52, 61, 79, 128–9, 138, 183
Delhi Sultanate 6, 67, 72, 164–74
Downton Abbey 4

Egypt 156–60, 185
Elizabeth I (Queen) 230 nn.161, 172
endowment deeds, *see waqfiyyāt*
endowments, *see* waqfs

Fadak 11–13, 79–81, 89–92, 94, 95–6, 100–1, 131, 133, 137–8
farr 143 (*see also* charismatic leadership patterns)

Fatima al-Ma'ṣūma 112–13
Fatima al-Zahra (Fatima bint Muhammad)
- and agency 12, 25, 48, 138–9
- and *ahl al-bayt* 26–8
- and al-Kawthar (*see* Kawthar, al-)
- and bilateral descent 2, 6, 8, 13, 18, 24–40, 47–8, 59, 68, 71, 128, 132
- biographical details of 10–12
- and chastity 8, 64, 111, 113, 128, 138–40, 149, 152, 154, 155, 180–4
- and Day of Judgement (*see* Day of Judgement)
- death of 12, 90, 137–8
- as Fāṭir 34, 200 n.121
- gender, transcending 14, 34, 139, 140
- gnostic knowledge of 124, 132, 134–6
- as *ḥujja* 134, 156
- and infallibility 26, 129, 130, 134
- and inheritance 11, 13, 37, 79–81, 89–98, 100–1, 102–3, 128, 131–2
- interpretation of the Qur'an 93–4, 131–2
- invoked by later dynasties 63, 64, 110–11, 113, 155–7, 161–2, 175, 180–3
- and khutba (*see* khutba, Fatima al-Zahra's)
- as martyr 137–8
- miracles attending birth of 136
- as *muḥaddatha* 135, 226 n.72
- and Muhammadan light (*see* Muhammadan light)
- *muṣḥaf* of 135–6, 152
- in poetry of Amīr Khusraw 68–73
- purified of menstruation 32, 36, 41, 126, 139, 152
- and redemption 30, 129, 136, 139
- as role model 128, 130–4, 136, 187–8
- in *Siyer-i Nebī* 123–4
- and succession 13–14, 123–5, 128–41, 151–2, 153
- and Sufism 73
- as *umm abīhā* (*see umm abīhā*)
- and Virgin Mary 25, 33, 37–9, 40–1, 47–8, 139, 199 n.110
- and weeping (*see* weeping)
- and Zoroastrian goddesses 40

Fatima bint Asad 34, 54–6
Fatima bint Hasan 55, 59–60
- 'The Fatima Syndrome' 51–2

Fatimid Empire 6, 89, 103, 134, 155–64, 177
feminism 7–8, 188, 190 n.7
Firdawsī, Abū al-Qāsim 144–6

Gabriel 31–2, 135, 152
Galen 18–19
Gawhar-Shād Begum 108–9
gender, transcending 3, 143–4, 149–50, 152, 162, 164, 166, 168–70, 184, *see also* cross-dressing
- and Fatima al-Zahra (*see under* Fatima al-Zahra)

generation, contemporary views of 21, 194 n.34
generation, pre-modern views of 13, 17–24, 41–2, 68–72
'Gunpowder' empires 62, 109–14

Hādī, al- (tenth imam) 97
Hadith of the Cloak 25, 26–8, 36, 48, 73, 196 n.65
Ḥākim, al- (Caliph) 157–60, 162–4, 177
Ḥallāj, Manṣūr al- 73
Ḥamīda Bānū Begum (Maryam-makānī) 65, 114
Hārūn al-Rashīd (Caliph) 38
Hasan ibn 'Ali (second imam)
- and bilateral descent 61
- and Fadak 91
- in genealogy of the imams 55, 59–60
- and Hasanids 57–8
- and inheritance 97, 103
- and leadership of umma 9–10, 39, 89
- and 'Light Verse' 31–2
- member of the Prophet's lineage 6, 17, 26–8, 33, 36–9, 47

Hasht Bihisht 69–71
Hind bint 'Utba 53, 151
Hippocrates 18–19
ḥujja 134, 156, 162–3
Humayda 55, 60
Husayn ibn 'Ali (third imam)
- and Fadak 91
- in genealogy of the imams 55
- as Ibn Fatima 36
- and inheritance 97, 103
- and leadership of umma 9–10, 39, 89

and 'Light Verse' 31–2
marriage to Shahrbānū 56–8, 59
martyrdom 24, 136–8
member of the Prophet's lineage 6, 17, 26–9, 33, 36–9, 47

Ibn Abī Ṭāhir Ṭayfūr, Abū al-Faḍl 92–4
Ibn al-Ḥanafiyya, Muhammad 24, 51
Ibn Bābawayh, Abū Ja'far (al-Shaykh al-Ṣadūq) 25, 31, 47, 94–6, 132–3, 137
Ibn Baṭṭūta 173–4
Ibn Kathīr, Ismā'īl ibn 'Umar 27, 29, 35, 196, 215 n.105
Ibn Qayyim al-Jawziyya 22–3
Ibn Rushd, Abū al-Walīd Muhammad 19
Ibn Sa'd, Abū 'Abd Allah Muhammad 51–3
Ibn Shahrāshūb, Muhammad ibn 'Ali 28, 33
Ibn Sīnā, Abū 'Ali al-Husayn (Avicenna) 19–20
Ibn Sumayya ('Ammār ibn Yāsir) 51
'Ilal al-sharā'i' 94, 132–3
Iltutmish (Sultan) 164–7, 169, 171
imams (Shi'i) 9, 26
and bilateral descent 33, 49, 54–61
and inheritance 88–9, 96, 99
and Muhammadan light 30–2
in Shi'i hadith collections 9–10, 54–61, 132
status of vis-à-vis Fatima al-Zahra 123, 125, 128–30, 132, 134, 135–6, 139, 141, 152
'Imrān 33, 42–5, 65
India 64, 66–73, 113–14, 134, 144, 164–74, 175, 180
Indonesia 185
inferiority, female (perceptions of)
and Christianity 146
in contemporary societies 185
and the Delhi Sultanate 168, 172–3
and generation 5, 17, 19, 70
and intelligence 127–8
and menstruation 139
and the Safavid Empire 178–9
and Zoroastrianism 141–2
inheritance, female
and bilateral descent (*see under* bilateral descent)
in the Byzantine Empire 98
in contemporary law 18, 185–6
and land 81–2, 85, 88–9, 211 n.20
and patrilineality (*see under* patrilineality)
in pre- and early Islamic Arabia 82–5
in pre-Islamic Central Asia 98
and the Qur'an 79, 82–7, 93–7, 99–100, 131–2
in Sassanian Iran 98, 142
in Sunni and Shi'i law 13, 81, 85–6, 87–9, 96–8, 99–101, 132
Iran, contemporary
and brain drain 5
and custody laws 17–8
and female succession 186–7
and Fatima al-Zahra 12, 129, 131, 133, 140, 187
and nationality laws 1, 5, 14
and Shi'ism 9
and Zaynab bint 'Ali 155
Iran, pre-modern (Islamic) 39–40, 58, *see also* Safavid Empire; Timurid Empire
Iran, pre-modern (pre-Islamic) 29, 40, 56–9, 102, 105–6, 141–2, 143, 164, 168, 180, *see also* Sassanian Empire; Zoroastrianism
'Isā ibn Maryam, *see* Jesus
Iskandar Beg Munshī 49, 175–9
Ismā'īl I (Shah) 112–13
Ismā'īl II (Shah) 176–7, 179
Ismā'īl ibn Ja'far 156
Isma'ilis 10, 55, 89, 103, 134, 156, 160–2

Ja'far al-Ṣādiq (sixth imam) 30, 32–3, 60, 79, 87–8, 97–100, 135–6, 156
Jahānārā Begum 114
jāhiliyya, *see* Arabia, pre-Islamic
Jamāl al-Dīn Yāqut 166–7, 170, 172–3, 236 n.126, 237 n.137
Jesus ('Isā) 13, 18, 25, 33, 37–9, 41, 43, 45–8, 69–70, 97
early speech 136
and Emperor Akbar 65
part of a chain of ancestors 130
prophesying of the Paraclete 27–8
Jewish scripture 43, 45–6
Jews 43, 80, 159–60
Juzjānī, Minhāj-i Sirāj-i 164–7, 170–1

Ka'ba 56, 110, 111, 151
Kāfī, al- 32, 54–61, 131
Karbala 24, 137, 153
Kawthar, al- 25, 29, 40
Kāẓim, al-, *see* Mūsā al-Kāẓim
Khadīja 55
and bilateral descent 36, 51
death of 10
as idealized female 111, 128, 162
and inheritance 84
pregnancy of with Fatima al-Zahra 32, 55–6, 61, 138
Khānzāda Begum 106–7
Khātūn Jān Begum 102, 106
Khayr al-Nisā' Begum (Mahd-i 'Ulya') 49, 64, 178–9
Khomeini, Zahra Mostafavi 186
khutba, Fatima al-Zahra's 79–80, 92–4, 96, 131–4
Kulaynī, Muhammad ibn Ya'qūb al- 32, 54–61, 95, 97–9, 131, 135

land, *see under* inheritance, female
leadership, female, *see* succession
'Light Verse', 32, 199 n.106

Mādayān ī Hazār Dādestān 98, 142
Mahdī, al-, *see* Muhammad al-Mahdī
Mahdī, al- (Caliph) 95
Mahd-i 'Ulya', *see* Khayr al-Nisā' Begum
Majlisī, Muhammad Bāqir al- 37–9, 54, 59, 133, 182
Ma'mūn, al- (Caliph) 91
Manṣūr, al- (Caliph) 36–7, 57, 91, 201 n.137
Mary, mother of Jesus, *see* Virgin Mary
Maryam bint 'Imrān, *see* Virgin Mary
Maryam-makānī, *see* Ḥamīda Bānū Begum
Maṭla' al-anwār 67–70
matrilineality, *see also* bilateral descent
in biographical dictionaries 53
and inheritance (*see under* bilateral descent)
and Jesus 33
in the Mughal Empire 64–5
in the Ottoman Empire 62–3
in pre-Islamic Arabia 41, 84–5
and the Qur'an 42
in the Safavid Empire 63–4
in Shi'i discourse 47, 56, 61
menstrual blood 19–21, 66–72
Mihrümah Sultan 110–12
Mirzakhani, Maryam 1, 5
Morocco 185–6
Moses (Mūsā) 27–8, 130
mothers, *see also* bilateral descent; generation; matrilineality
daughters as *see umm abīhā*
in hadith 34
of imams 54–61, 156
in the Qur'an 34–5, 42–7
of rulers 49, 63–6, 107, 165
Mu'āwiya (Caliph) 53, 134
Mubāhala 26–8, 39
Mufīd, al-, *see* Shaykh al-Mufīd, al-
Mughal Empire 62, 64–6, 78, 107, 113–14, 169
muḥaddatha, *see under* Fatima al-Zahra
Muhammad (Prophet)
and *ahl al-bayt* 26–7, 47
and 'Ā'isha 139, 151
ancestry and birth family 41
and bilateral descent 36, 54, 62, 71, 74
in biographical dictionaries 51–3
birth of 136
closeness to Fatima al-Zahra 11, 25–6, 33, 68, 70, 125–6, 137, 141
closeness to Fatima bint Asad 54–6
closeness to Husayn ibn 'Ali 28–9
on cross-dressing 170
and Day of Judgement 52, 61, 138
death of 11, 12, 80, 92, 138
and Fadak 80, 90–1, 93, 95–6, 131
and Fatima al-Zahra's marriage to 'Ali 11
on female rule 126–7, 145–6
on generation 22
in hadith collections 9–10
and inheritance 83–6, 94, 98, 99
lack of surviving sons 29–30
and marriage of Shahrbānū 59
on menstruation 139
on mothers 34
and Muhammadan light 30–2
and Satanic Verses 42
in *Siyer-i Nebī* 123–4

succession to 6, 8–10, 24–5, 28, 33–4, 37–9, 47–8, 56, 126, 132
on women as equals to men 72
Muhammadan light (*nūr Muhammadī*) 25, 27, 30–4, 41, 48, 56, 57, 61, 136
Muhammad al-Bāqir (fifth imam) 38, 55–7, 59–60, 88, 99
Muhammad al-Mahdī (twelfth imam) 34, 36
Muhammad ibn ʿAbd Allah, *see* al-Nafs al-Zakiyya
Muḥtasham Kāshānī 180–3
Mūsā, *see* Moses
Mūsā al-Kāẓim (seventh imam) 38, 55, 60, 87, 95, 112, 156
muṣḥaf of Fatima, *see under* Fatima al-Zahra
mutawalli (trustee) 102, 104–5, 107–9, 111, 115, 117–19

Nafs al-Zakiyya, al- (Muhammad ibn ʿAbd Allah) 36, 57, 91, 201 n.137
nasab 23–4, 61, 74, *see also* bilateral descent
nationality laws 1, 2, 5, 6, 18, 50, 185
Nihāyat al-Kamāl 71
Niẓām al-Mulk 127–8, 179
nūr Muhammadī, *see* Muhammadan light

Osman (founder of Ottoman Empire) 62–3
Ottoman Empire 7, 62–5, 110–12, 114, 116–18, 123, 178

Pakistan 186–7
Parī Khān Khānum 174–83
passion play, *see taziyih*
patrilineality
and biographical dictionaries 53
and generation 4–5, 18–22
and inheritance 4, 81–5, 87, 98, 117–18
and laws 1–3, 5–6
and the Ottoman Empire 63
and the Qur'an 43–4
and Saudi Arabia 50
and succession 4, 183
Persia, *see* Iran
Pride and Prejudice 4
Prophet Muhammad, *see* Muhammad (Prophet)
Pulcheria 148–50, 183
Pūrān Dukht (Queen) 143–6, 164, 229 n.137

Qāḍī al-Nuʿmān, al- 89, 96–7, 100, 103, 134, 156
Qārā Quyūnlū 102, 106
Qizilbāsh 175–6, 178–9
Qur'an
and bilateral descent (*see under* bilateral descent)
and Fatima al-Zahra (*see under* Fatima al-Zahra)
and inheritance (*see under* inheritance)
and patrilineality (*see under* patrilineality)
and succession (*see under* succession)
Qurṭubī, Muhammad ibn Aḥmad 99

Rābiʿa 111, 182–3
Raḍiyya bint Iltutmish (Sultan) 72, 164–74
Rafsanjani, Fāʿiza Hāshimi 186–7
Rashīd al-Dīn Faḍl Allah, Abū al-Khayr 21
Rāzī, Fakhr al-Dīn al- 27, 29, 35, 82
religious authority, female, *see* succession
Riḍā, al-, *see* ʿAli al-Riḍā

Ṣadr, Muhammad Bāqir al- (Ayatollah) 96, 130, 134
Safavid Empire 49, 50, 62–5, 112–14, 127, 133–4, 174–83
Saffāḥ, al- (Caliph) 91
Ṣaffār al-Qummī, Muḥammad ibn al-Ḥasan al- 56–7, 135
Sajjād, al-, *see* Zayn al-ʿĀbidīn
Sakhāwī, Shams al-Dīn al- 53–4
Sarakhsī, Muhammad ibn Aḥmad al- 74
Sassanian Empire 40, 48, 56, 58–9, 69, 98, 126–7, 142–6, 149, 164, 181
Satanic Verses 42
Saudi Arabia, *see* Arabia, contemporary
semen 19–20, 22, 56, 66, 68–9, 70–1, 195 n.38
Shah ʿAbbās I, *see* ʿAbbās I
Shah Ismaʿil I, *see* Ismaʿil I
Shah Ismaʿil II, *see* Ismaʿil II
Shāhnāma 59, 144, 168, 228 n.123
Shahrbānū 55–9
Shāh Rukh (Sultan) 108

Shāhzāda Sulṭanum 112, 175, 177
Sharīʿati, ʿAli 129–30, 187
sharīf/ashrāf 74, 117, 206 n.37
Shaykh al-Mufīd, al- 61, 153–4
Shaykh al-Ṣadūq, al-, *see* Ibn Bābawayh, Abū Jaʿfar
Sitt al-Mulk 155, 157–60, 162–4
Solomon (Sulayman) 93, 132, 161
succession, female
  and bilateral descent (*see under* bilateral descent)
  in the Byzantine Empire 146–50
  in contemporary Iran 186–7
  in contemporary Pakistan 186–7
  in contemporary Syria 187
  in the Delhi Sultanate 72, 164–74
  discouraged 125–8
  and Fatima al-Zahra (*see under* Fatima al-Zahra)
  in the Fatimid Empire 155–64
  in pre-Islamic and early Islamic Arabia 150–1
  in pre-Islamic Iran 141–6
  and the Qur'an 131–2
  in the Safavid Empire 64, 174–83
  in Shiʿi discourse 37
  in Sufi orders 114–16, 155
  and Zaynab bint ʿAli 153–5
Sufis
  attitudes toward women 72–3, 75
  in biographical dictionaries 50, 54
  and poetry of Amīr Khusraw 66–72
  and the Safavid Empire 63, 175, 182
  and succession 114–16, 155
  and waqfs 104, 108–9, 114–16
Sulayman, *see* Solomon
Süleyman I (Sultan) 110

Ṭabarī, Abū Jaʿfar Muḥammad ibn Jarīr al- 27, 35, 82, 84, 86, 89–90, 136, 146
Ṭāḥirih 187
Tājlū Khānum 112–13, 175
taziyih 57, 96, 128
Timur (Amir) 64, 66, 106–7
Timurid Empire 64, 66, 106–9
trustee, *see* *mutawalli*
trusts, *see* waqfs
Tunisia 185–6
Turko-Mongol societies 7, 62, 105–6, 109, 167, 175, 180

Twelfth Imam, *see* Muhammad al-Mahdī
Twelver Shiʿism 10, 34, 49, 55, 87–8, 156, 175

ūlū al-arḥām 99–100
ʿUmar ibn al-Khaṭṭāb 11, 52, 55–6, 59, 90, 93, 95–6, 137, 138
umm abīhā 33, 35, 40, 48, 68
umm al-kitāb 35, 43–7
Umm Ayman 90–1, 197 n.77
Umm Kulthum bint ʿAli 11, 52, 55
ʿUthmān ibn ʿAffān 99–100

Virgin Mary (Maryam bint ʿImrān) 40–1, 56, 75, 156, 162, 175
  and agency 146–7
  and Ālanquwā 65
  and bilateral descent 13, 18, 25, 33, 37–9, 42–8, 69–70
  and the Byzantine Empire 146–50, 156, 183
  as embodiment of chastity 8, 41, 42, 46, 65, 139, 180–3
  and Fatima al-Zahra (*see under* Fatima al-Zahra)
  as idealized female 8, 72, 128
  and inheritance 97

walad/awlād 97, 105, 107, 108, 216 n.114
walaya 26, 57
waqfiyyāt 6, 13, 102–19
waqfs 85, 86, 89, 102–19
weeping 128, 130, 136–7
wombs
  and generation 20, 23, 68, 70, 195
  as protective, purified vessels 31–2, 42
  in the Qur'an 42–6, 100
  in waqfs 108

Yaʿqūbī, Aḥmad al- 91
Yāqūt al-Hamawī 90
Yazdigird III (Shāhanshāh) 56
Yemen 160–2

Zayd ibn al-Ḥāritha 39
Zaynab bint ʿAli 11, 53, 153–5
Zayn al-ʿĀbidīn (fourth imam) 49, 56–9, 136, 153–4
Zoroastrianism 7, 40, 42, 58, 141–2, 146